Wages for Hou

Wages for Housework

A History of an International Feminist Movement, 1972–77

Louise Toupin

Translated by Käthe Roth

PLUTO PRESS

UBCPress · Vancouver · Toronto

© Pluto Press and UBC Press, 2018

Originally published as *Le salaire au travail ménager: Chronique d'une lutte féministe internationale (1972–1977)* © Les Éditions du remue-ménage, Montréal, Canada, 2014

First English-language edition (world, less North America) published by:
Pluto Press
345 Archway Road, London N6 5AA
www.plutobooks.com

First English-language edition (North America) published by:
UBC Press
The University of British Columbia
2029 West Mall
Vancouver, BC V6T 1Z2
www.ubcpress.ca

Canada Council   Conseil des arts
for the Arts   du Canada

We acknowledge the financial support of the Government of Canada through the National Translation Program for Book Publishing, an initiative of the Roadmap for Canada's Official Languages 2013–2018: Education, Immigration, Communities, for our translation activities.

Every effort has been made to identify, credit appropriately, and obtain publication rights from copyright holders of the material reproduced in this book. Notice of any errors or omissions in this regard will be gratefully received and correction made in subsequent editions.

British Library Cataloguing in Publication Data
A catalogue record for this book is available from the British Library

ISBN 978 0 7453 3868 2   Hardback
ISBN 978 0 7453 3867 5   Paperback
ISBN 978 1 7868 0381 8   PDF eBook
ISBN 978 1 7868 0383 2   Kindle eBook
ISBN 978 1 7868 0382 5   EPUB eBook

This book is printed on paper suitable for recycling and made from fully managed and sustained forest sources. Logging, pulping and manufacturing processes are expected to conform to the environmental standards of the country of origin.

Typeset by Stanford DTP Services, Northampton, England

Printed in the United Kingdom

*To the memory of my mother and my aunts,
housewives for whom a salary would no doubt
have enabled them to imagine their life differently.*

Contents

Illustrations

Introduction
A Political and Personal History

"Our place in any history of the women's movement, or of anti-capitalist struggle in general, is already assured. Any article written in the past couple of years about the women's movement has had to deal with Wages for Housework, even where that treatment has been critical ... We represent an attempt to build a new women's movement, organized internationally, around a perspective that has revolutionary implications for the entire anti-capitalist struggle. What we do with this perspective – how we develop it and how we organize around it – should now be our principle concern."
– Montreal Power of Women Collective, April 1975[1]

"You should title your book 'The *Desaparecidos* of the Feminist Movement.'"
– Mariarosa Dalla Costa, 1994[2]

This book is about a subject that has fallen off the radar screen of contemporary feminism, a movement born at the very beginning of second-wave Western feminism. It was called Wages for Housework – or, depending on the country, *salaire au travail ménager, salario al lavoro domestico,* or Lohn für Hausarbeit. In this book, I shed light on this movement, through its writings and its struggles, from its origin in 1972, when the International Feminist Collective (IFC) was formed, to its apogee in 1977, after which certain components of the IFC continued their activities under other names.

The ideas and action strategies of this current of feminism, expressed in a pioneering essay by Mariarosa Dalla Costa, "Women and the Subversion of Community," covered much more than the group of material tasks commonly listed under the label "housework" or "domestic work," and were deployed well beyond the objective of obtaining a salary for such work.[3] I am talking about multi-faceted, invisible, and unrecognized labour, indispensable and wealth-producing, the vast majority of which was performed by women within families and in the community. Until then considered from the angle of being "free" – an act supposedly born of the love and generosity inherent to women – this activity was now seen by certain neo-feminist theoreticians as real work and, what is more, work that was being exploited. The Wages for Housework movement specifically identified this work as being the hidden face of the wage world, its unpaid flip side, created with the rise of industrial society and capitalism, and as defining the place of women in social organization and the gendered division of labour. This feminist current raised the issue of social reproduction and women's place within it.

Having housework recognized as real – and, moreover, exploited – work constituted one of the most important theoretical concerns for early thinkers of second-wave feminism. The question gave rise to a proliferation of analyses and debates on all sides. However, the idea of basing women's struggle on the specific question of housework and campaigning to demand pay for that work fell to Wages for Housework groups.[4]

Surprisingly, despite the turmoil raised by this debate, both in the academic world and among militant feminists in the 1970s and early 1980s, barely a trace of the issue can be found today. And it is even more difficult to dig up evidence of the current that initiated it. It is almost completely ignored in university curricula, and few historiographic accounts mention its existence. Its contribution to the critique and the deconstruction of the concept of labour is no longer mentioned at all in assessments or reviews of documentation of the topic. It has reached the point that the very theme of domestic work draws almost no interest from scholars.[5]

A TRANSNATIONAL MOVEMENT WITH A UNIQUE ALCHEMY ...

This current of thought, which was also an activist movement, was intended to be transnational – a first for second-wave feminism. Starting in 1972, it included groups active in Italy, England, the United States, English-speaking Canada, Switzerland, and Germany. Some called it the "embryo of a Women's Internationale."[6]

The network also included a wide variety of activists – something unusual at the time. The spectrum of thought was broad enough to accommodate not only white heterosexual women but also lesbians, racialized women, women on social assistance, and workers of all sorts (waitresses [as they were then known], nurses, hospital employees, and even prostitutes [as they were then known]); some were able to form their own groups, on their own premises, within the network, and to develop very original and striking analyses from their respective stances. In some countries, men's study groups were even developed in this perspective. These groups, of different sizes, were active on various fronts in their own countries: invisible aspects of family work and salaried women's work, but also abortion, medical practices, sterilization, childbirth conditions, women's health, sexuality, social assistance, family allowances, housing conditions, education, family violence, prostitution/sex work, and more.

In each of these struggles, activists developed connections with women's invisible and free labour. The struggles around housework and family work were extended into other aspects of social reproduction, which also became fields of application for the idea of wages for housework. "We saw the fragmented life of women as a totality for the first time," said one of the activists I interviewed. Unpaid housework constituted a prism through which the multiple facets of women's lack of power over their lives in society as a whole could be seen, understood, and reassembled. The vast majority of women were not paid for all the work they did, and were permanently available to serve their family: this was the "lowest common denominator" of all women in capitalist societies, although it was experienced quite differently depending on the class, ethnicity, and race to which the person in that position belonged. Their work was that of production and reproduction of labour power, according to the definition formulated by the Wages for Housework current at the time.

... AND HOTLY DEBATED STRATEGIES

Although many women and women's groups agreed with much of the analysis formulated by Wages for Housework theoreticians, few of them were prepared to undertake a campaign to demand such wages. In fact, this demand provoked heated debate in the women's movement everywhere it was discussed; one might say, without exaggerating, that the issue affected all of militant feminism in the 1970s in North-America and Europe to some degree.

The women's movement as a whole, however, rejected the Wages for Housework strategy. It was seen as a step backward in the demand for women's equality rather than one of its essential conditions, as was claimed by the current's instigators and activists. The women's movement saw it as a renunciation of the objective of socialization of domestic work (daycare centres, community services, and so on). In the labour field, the movement preferred to invest its efforts in women's access to the labour market, improvements to working conditions, the obtaining of parental leave, and the creation of community services to facilitate access to paid labour. The negotiation of demands concerning housework and family work was left to private arrangements between partners, or "task sharing." In short, the domain of social reproduction was not the strategic choice of the women's movement; then as today, a strategy of "family-job reconciliation" was preferred.

Given how domestic work and family work have evolved today, we can look back and ask, Was this what we could call a "winning strategy"? And what are the tangible results of this strategy today? Without wanting, for anything in the world, to denigrate the enormous efforts that the women's movement devoted for several decades to establishing various measures and getting them enshrined in public policies, some of which were considered models of the genre in North America, a quick summary exposes trends that are worthy of examination.[7]

The objections to the Wages for Housework demand:

- The effect of salarization would be to chain or, in some cases, return women to the home and tie them more firmly to their domestic responsibilities. Women's liberation would thus be rolled back.
- The salarization of housework would disrupt any possibility of sharing tasks within the couple and would sanction the practice of home education.
- The smaller size of families (two or three children) makes the demand obsolete.
- Because it is paying for housework, the state would no longer feel obliged to institute community services. Because they receive wages, women would likely have to assume care for patients, people with handicaps, and the elderly. Day centres for the elderly and people with handicaps might close. Thus, the effect might be damaging to women's social demands.
- Once salaried, housework would be controlled in terms of number of hours, quality of work, and so on. Who would exercise this control? The spouse? The state? And under what terms?
- Paid housework would reinforce gendered division of roles, keeping women in their traditional role of wife and mother.
- A salary would isolate women from the community.
- A salary would legitimize their oppression.
- A salary would have no effect on poverty.
- Salarization of housework would probably not lead to this work being seen as valuable, if one considers that salaries have not led to the valuing of a number of jobs performed by women (such as housecleaner, waitress, and laundry worker).
- In the current context of decentralization of workplaces, many people now work at home. How will the distinction be made between paid housework and paid social work?
- A salary for housework would discriminate against those who work outside the home and do housework outside of paid work hours. So, those who "work a double day" would be penalized.
- Paid housework would take away any chance for women to have their right to social work clearly recognized.
- Such a salary would encourage women to stay away from the labour market and would be detrimental to improving their situation in society.

This list of objections to paid housework comes, word for word (our translation), from documents issued by three Quebec trade union federations: Fédération des travailleurs du Québec (FTQ), *Travailleuses et syndiquées, Rapport du Comité FTQ sur la situation de la femme*, FTQ 13th Congress, December 3–7, 1973; Confédération des syndicats nationaux, *La lutte des femmes, combat de tous les travailleurs*, 1976; and Centrale de l'enseignement du Québec, *Le droit au travail social pour toutes les femmes*, 27th General Congress, June 26–30, 1980. Also from the women's status "Livre noir" of the Conseil du statut de la femme, *Pour les Québécoises: égalité et indépendance*, Éditeur officiel du Québec, 1978.

"FAMILY-JOB RECONCILIATION": A WINNING STRATEGY?

Today, in Western countries, young working mothers seem to be exhausted by the "double day," as they are constantly running between the daycare centre and the workplace – it not being a given that the spouse (when there is one) will share the chores. Recent figures attest to this: "In spite of significant progress with regards to sharing domestic responsibilities, women remain the primary caregivers for children, spending an average of 50 hours per week in this role, according to data from the 2010 General Social Survey. This amount is more than twice the burden that men assume."[8] And then there's the fact that salaried mothers always earn less than salaried women without children, with "maternity benefits compensat[ing] for about half of this loss."[9]

Stress, burnout, psychological distress, piling on of tasks, and work-based competition seem to be the lot of many women who have children; at the same time, the standards for the "good mother" are always rising. In-depth interviews with young feminist mothers show that they are not sheltered from the trend: they are still "the ones mainly responsible for the work of social reproduction: care for children and dependent family members, domestic work, and family organization." These young feminists deplore also the fact that "the work of social reproduction is not recognized or valued," and they note "inequalities in the sharing of tasks and in parental roles, while social gender roles do not change as quickly as one would believe."[10] They conclude, "Today, work-family reconciliation is not a success." In this context, they "believe it necessary to relaunch a debate in the women's movement over the question of social reproduction."[11]

Even today, women are still mainly responsible for the work of social reproduction. In Quebec, websites have been created to enable young mothers to discuss among themselves the highs and lows of housework and family care, and blogs written by "unworthy mothers" are very successful.[12] And when money is available, it is most often being used to hire other women, usually poor ones, to perform certain domestic tasks and family care. Some of them come from very far away to perform this work. In Canada, the number of caregivers coming from abroad reached a "record level" in 2014.[13]

SOMETHING NEW: A RELATIONSHIP OF DIRECT EXPLOITATION BETWEEN WOMEN

Thus, today reproductive work has taken on unequalled amplitude worldwide. Women from the other side of the planet, forsaking their own families and leaving them in the care of other women in their community, are called upon to "fly to the rescue" of wealthier Western women, for whom they perform domestic work and family care at prices defying any competition. There is talk of a "crisis of reproduction."[14] This phenomenon is also labelled "globalization of maternal love," "love and gold," and "care drain."[15] We are even seeing the appearance of something new in the history of capitalism, the "dualization of women's work," which should draw the attention of feminists the world over:

> Simultaneous with the casualization and poverty of a growing number of women ... we are therefore seeing an increase in the economic, cultural, and social capital of a sizable proportion of working women. For the first time in the history of capitalism, we are seeing a stratum of women whose direct (not mediated, as before, by men: father, husband, lover, and so on) interests are squarely opposed to the interests of those affected by the generalization of part-time work, by very poorly paid and socially unrecognized service jobs, and more generally by insecurity.[16]

Some Wages for Housework theoreticians conceived of the recourse to female labour from poor countries as "a colonial solution to the 'housework problem,'" as part of the new gendered and international division of labour.[17] Was this the outcome (undesired, of course) or one of the "perverse effects" of the "job-family reconciliation" strategy and "task sharing"?

The importance to feminism today of the issue of reproductive work on the global scale could, in itself, be sufficient reason to reread the analysis formulated by the Wages for Housework current. It offers an opportunity to (re)discover rich intellectual and activist resources that could serve as tools for understanding the issue of social reproduction and how it is evolving, as well as the key role played in it, still and always, by the majority of women on the planet.

Since these texts were written (forty years ago!), the analytical approaches, the vocabulary used, and the context within which women live have changed a great deal, but the revolt against the injustice caused by the growing burden that reproductive work represents for women, to which is now added the organization of care of dependents in the family, has not changed.[18] Some young feminists even believe that it is necessary to "relaunch a debate in the women's movement on the question of social reproduction." A (very) few scholars are also returning to this question: "Our governmental programs must be re-examined, but so must the premise of the women's movement that a woman is fulfilled through work."[19] This book may contribute by providing the debate with a historical background and interesting resources. I must admit, though, that there were other, more personal reasons for me to reread these texts and write this book.

AT THE BEGINNING, GREAT FRUSTRATION

Although I was old enough, in the mid-1970s, to join a Wages for Housework collective, I never did so for one simple reason: there were no such collectives in francophone feminist Quebec, even though anglophones in other Canadian provinces – and even, for a time, anglophone feminists in Montreal – had organized them. There were none, and there could not be any, because the vast majority in the francophone women's movement in Quebec didn't want them.

So I was not part of this feminist "internationale," despite the fact that most women within the group that I was then a member of, Les Éditions du remue-ménage, were in favour of demanding wages for housework. In fact, the primary intention of the founders of this feminist publishing house was to translate and publish texts from the Wages for Housework current. The first book published by Remue-ménage, in 1976, *Môman travaille pas, a trop d'ouvrage,* was a play written and performed by the collective Le Théâtre des cuisines that raised the question of housework and its recognition.[20] The play toured throughout Quebec and made an enormous contribution to the discussion, often heated and difficult, on the Wages for Housework perspective.[21]

The affinities of the first Remue-ménage team with this struggle spurred some of us to attend one of the international conferences of the network of Wages for Housework groups, the International Feminist Collective, in Toronto in October 1975. We were there as observers and sympathizers, as we were not, as such, a Wages for Housework group. Nevertheless, we were able to give a presentation in French on the situation and the particular history of francophone women in Quebec.

Having missed the boat on this feminist "internationale," even though I had anticipated its political and philosophical significance, has always been a great frustration for me. Indeed, for a long time I lived with the feeling of having missed out on something very important in the feminist struggle, something essential in the comprehension of the place of women in society, in both the North and the South, and how it could be "subverted."[22]

AN INTERSECTIONAL PERSPECTIVE BEFORE ITS TIME

For me, *The Power of Women and the Subversion of the Community,* by Mariarosa Dalla Costa and Selma James, as well as *Sex, Race and Class, Wages against Housework,* and several other essays, published in translation in *Le foyer de l'insurrection,* were great intellectual discoveries, of a nature to stimulate activism.[23] In these texts, the patriarchy, as it had been conceived by early radical feminists, finally no longer appeared as an eternal, timeless, ahistorical system – on the contrary. Without claiming to explain the "origin" of the patriarchy, these analyses attributed it a specific historical embodiment. Housework, as practised, was seen as a historical form of reproductive work, inherent to capitalist society. It was no longer analyzed as a retrograde appendix to waged work, but represented the gendered division of work established by capitalism. Capitalism had relaunched and reorganized the patriarchy on this basis. In other words, in the capitalist wage society, the patriarchy was embodied in the free housework assigned to women as a group.

At the time, the analyses of the Wages for Housework current seemed to me to be the patriarchy-capitalism articulation par excellence – that is, a happy linkage between a (non-orthodox) Marxist analysis of production and a feminist analysis of reproduction at the international scale. What was called, at the time, an anti-patriarchal and anti-capitalist perspective would be stated today, in sociological terms, as an articulation between gender relations and class relations. The sex, race, and class triad triggered what we now call an "intersectional" analysis, the precursor to a cross-sectional analysis of dominations. The analysis of oppressions and their interdependence – the solidarity among women, despite their differences, that we sought so eagerly at the time – was proposed in the Wages for Housework strategy.

Thus, in the early 1970s, this perspective offered utterly new analyses and a global comprehension of the various components of the oppressive situation experienced by most women. It provided a common thread, which linked a number of otherwise incomprehensible aspects of the situation: women were not paid for all the work they did, even as they formed the backbone of the reproduction of societies.

This focus on work produced, on the subject of (heterosexual) love, analyses that were innovative – and, in the view of many, revolutionary – notably with regard to lesbianism and sex work. For instance, the Wages for Housework perspective shed entirely new light on the work of prostitutes, who were beginning to organize and demand their rights, leading us to feel solidarity with their struggle and even to the creation of surprising "unnatural" – and highly symbolic – alliances with Wages for Housework groups. The same perspective also returned dignity to women on social assistance. From within the Wages for Housework movement, African American women produced texts that were at the origin of Black feminism.[24] And this is not to mention that the Wages for Housework perspective prefigured today's issues of the realities of care work, pay equity, recognition of acquired knowledge and skills, and recognition of women's invisible work in agriculture and in small companies belonging to their husbands. And finally, there is paragraph 120 of the report of the UN's Nairobi Conference on Women in 1985 advocating recognition of the contribution (paid and unpaid) of women in all sectors of development and its inclusion in countries' national accounts.[25] This perspective allowed us to move beyond the differences among women by making it possible for them to forge alliances without being subjected to a single standard.

On a more personal level, this idea represented, for many of us, what an activist from the Collectif L'Insoumise called a "way to 'avenge' the fate of our mothers, to return dignity to the labour of past, present, and future generations of mothers and grandmothers."[26] Yes, the Wages for Housework perspective also represented this.

All of this is a roundabout way of saying that my feminism was influenced primarily by this incomparable perspective, and I have always had the deep conviction that there is value in having today's generations of women and feminists learn about this wealth of thought, as it was formulated in the time of the IFC, and as certain of its main theoreticians have deployed and updated it since, in the context of global economic reorganization.

A BOOK WITH A LONG JOURNEY

All history books have their own history: that of the context in which they are written. So here is the history of this book. Although it simmered in my mind for a long time, this research first took shape in the context of a post-doctoral project, funded by the Social Sciences and Humanities Research Council from 1994 to 1996. The project took me to the European University Institute (EUI) in Florence, Italy, in the fall of 1994. That year, one of the EUI research centres, the European Forum, was studying the question of work time from a gendered perspective. The invisible reproductive work done by women was at the heart of this issue.

This research project on the history of the International Feminist Collective for Wages for Housework, presented to the EUI authorities, enabled me to study the European portion of the network. Northern Italy being a sort of cradle of the Wages for Housework strategy, the EUI was an ideal starting point from which to expand my research into Italy, Germany, and Switzerland (and into England, as I had hoped from the start). The intellectual, academic, and material support offered by the EUI and the research activities of its European Forum (workshops, seminars, conferences) were to serve as important assets to the project.

While in Italy, I was able to meet Mariarosa Dalla Costa, Leopoldina Fortunati, and Giovanna Franca Dalla Costa, of the Italian Wages for Housework groups, and Gisela Bock of the German group. In Geneva, I met Viviane Luisier, Alda De Giorgi, and Suzanne Lerch of the Collectif L'Insoumise, the Wages for Housework group there. I had an opportunity to consult their personal archives, to which all gave me free access, as well as the archives of documentation centres in Italy, particularly in Milan and Bologna. In Paris, I met Marie-Christine Gaffory, an "orphan" Wages for Housework activist (as there was no group in France[27]). Despite several attempts, I was not able to meet Selma James.[28]

When I returned to North America, I met Silvia Federici, of the New York Wages for Housework group and the main initiator of other American groups, in Brooklyn. At the time, I couldn't find Judy Ramirez, a pivotal figure of the Toronto group. I was, however, able to consult the Canadian Women's

Movement Archives, conserved at the University of Ottawa, where an activist from the Toronto Wages for Housework Committee (Francie Wyland, who has my undying gratitude) had deposited the group's archives. These archives have been very valuable to me, because they contain a good number of documents from other groups in the international network.

However, due to the unprecedented nature of this research, the dispersed and multilingual nature of the pertinent documentation, and the distance problems inherent to an international investigation, the two years covered by the post-doctoral grant did not enable me to complete my study. As a lecturer and independent researcher, I was able to return to work on the subject only occasionally, which explains the long delay that occurred between the beginning of this history project and its completion. In the end, a teaching fellowship from the Université du Québec à Montréal in 2012 and 2013 enabled me to devote myself full time to finalizing my research and writing this book.

That said, other factors were also at play. In particular, Federici was pushing me to complete and publish my research. Throughout the years, we had maintained occasional email contact, promising to see each other again to complete an interview on her intellectual journey, which could not be finalized at the time. A conference in Montreal in March 2012, to which she had been invited, provided us with an opportunity to meet. She convinced me that it was urgent for me to make widely accessible as possible all the material I had in my possession before I ... let's say ... went to heaven.

In the end, I realized that this research was, in a way and from many angles, my encounter with my own intellectual and activist history – a sort of full circle from youth to wisdom. It also expressed, above all, my desire to provide today's young people with historical feminist intellectual tools that address the question of gendered division of labour and social reproduction and its new forms at the time of neo-liberal capitalist globalization. And finally, deep within me is an ardent desire to rescue from oblivion, through this book, the rich intellectual heritage of the Wages for Housework perspective, to be certain that it will now take its proper place in the history of thought and of the feminist movement. This book is an attempt to take a step in this direction, which others may continue.

WHY 1972 TO 1977?

The Wages for Housework network of groups has been through various phases. The first was a period of establishment and organization between 1972 and 1977, under the name International Feminist Collective. Then there was a period of reorganization, which began around 1977 or 1978, during which certain groups withdrew, new ones arrived, and some older groups continued their activities. The name International Feminist Collective, however, was no longer used after this time, even though certain components of the collective remained active under other names.[29]

Thus, the IFC's lifespan in itself defined the study period. This was the phase during which the network's foundations were established and debates took place on its components, on the definition of the network's bases, on the organization of the Wages for Housework campaign, and on the theoretical perspective underpinning the campaign. It was also when international conferences were held. For each national collective, it was an intense period of production and publication of journals, brochures, and tracts of all types accompanying a variety of demonstrations. In a word, it was a period of generalized effervescence, which left behind a large amount of documentation.

It was also the period before major dissent arose and certain groups withdrew from the initial network. It appeared to me almost impossible to deal with these events in a way that is significant for feminist history. Even after twenty-five years, activists had trouble talking about it, and they did not want to discuss it in a casual way.[30] Leaving it to others to reconstruct this part of the network's history seemed to be the wisest decision under the circumstances.

The period of the IFC, from 1972 to 1977, is also the one that the activists interviewed had the most pleasure remembering. For many, it was an exceptional time in their life. Some even spoke, retrospectively, in terms of "paradise lost." It was the period of great feminist mobilizations during which, as Federici observed, "We felt that we were part of a great historic transformation." This "first phase of the new feminism," as historian Gisela Bock (the figurehead of the Berlin Wages for Housework group) called it in an interview, corresponds, in the memories of activist founders of various national collectives whom I interviewed, a time when women, together, felt that they were in a position of power. "We lived as a community, we mobilized easily, we were flying high, and we thought we had the power to change life, right away," said one of the activists from the Collectif L'Insoumise in Geneva. This observation was corroborated by another activist from the group, who told me about "the immense power of the women at that time who, united, were able to make power retreat." "We felt dangerous," she continued. "We felt that together, united around a cause, we had power." Yes, she remembered, "we certainly had some power in Geneva."

The end of this period also coincides, historically, with the end of an era in second-wave feminism. The next period, which, at least in Europe, began in 1978 or 1979 – depending on the country – saw no more great feminist mobilizations. These years sounded the knell for this historical phase, the demise of which was punctuated, especially in a number of European countries, by repressive laws (mainly in Italy, but also in West Germany and even Switzerland).

Most activist groups then went through a period of crisis, during which various components of the feminist movement were forced to redefine themselves, reorient themselves, or, in some cases, stop being active. For example, speaking of the evolution of the feminist movement in Geneva during these years, an Insoumise member said, "We left more and more space for the creation of services. Little by little, we lost the Women's Liberation Movement dimension and, little by little, no one availed herself of [it] anymore."[31] The period of the International Feminist Collective, from 1972 to 1977, overlaps with this first phase of the new feminism.

MORE PRECISELY ...

To complete this research, I drew on various sources: publications by national collectives (books, journals, brochures, press releases, tracts, and press clippings); IFC publications; personal archives – those of activists I met, my own, and those of my friends, notably Nicole Lacelle; the Canadian Women's Movement Archives conserved at the University of Ottawa; various documentation centres in Italy; and information provided by some of the figureheads of the national Wages for Housework collectives whom I encountered and talked to along the way.[32]

Because this is almost virgin territory, we must see this work on the IFC and the vision that it promoted as a historical sketch, with the interpretation biases inherent to the genre. This is especially true because I took the closest look at what interested me the most in the movement and what seemed to me relevant to retain with regard to feminist concerns today, notably the movement's theoretical production and some of its struggles.

Thus, in this book I modestly reconstruct fragments of this network's history. I dwell upon the popularization of the current of thought that it induced and how it was embodied in certain struggles. The first chapter is therefore devoted to placing in context the publication, in the early 1970s, of the book-manifesto *The Power of Women and the Subversion of the Community*. What was the theoretical and activist environment into which this Wages for Housework perspective was inserted? What did it bring that was new to feminist theorization and activism at the beginning of what was later called second-wave feminism?

In the second chapter I look at the popularization of works that were the basis for Wages for Housework thought, written between 1972 and 1977 – the period of the IFC. The third chapter gives a general portrait of the IFC as a network of groups and as an international forum: how it was formed and how it functioned.

In Chapters 4 and 5, I look at how the Wages for Housework perspective was embodied in action, in some of the mobilizations organized or supported by groups in the network. I will perform this analysis through the various documents issued for these mobilizations. In Chapter 6, I present examples of struggles undertaken by and political perspectives of two groups on the periphery of the network: Lohn für Hausarbeit in Berlin and the Collectif L'Insoumise in Geneva.

In the conclusion, I attempt to sketch out the background for the evolution of social reproduction in the domestic and private sphere. The afterword, devoted to two interviews with figureheads of the Wages for Housework perspective, Mariarosa Dalla Costa and Silvia Federici, will address this same question in the broader context of neo-liberal globalization and give an overview of their intellectual trajectory since 1977.

Finally, I believe that it is possible to read the chapters of this book independently of each other. To read about the intellectual atmosphere of the early second-wave feminism, see Chapter 1; for Wages for Housework theory and current of thought, see Chapter 2; for fragments of history of an embryonic feminist "internationale," see Chapter 3; and for examples of mobilizations and struggles of Wages for Housework groups in six countries (Italy, England, the United States, Canada, West Germany, and Switzerland), see Chapters 4, 5, and 6. Readers who are more interested in the evolution of the perspective of Wages for Housework and reproductive work to the present should see the final part (Conclusion and Afterword). Reading all the chapters in order is, of course, not forbidden!

Part 1

The International Feminist Collective: Historical Overview and Political Perspective

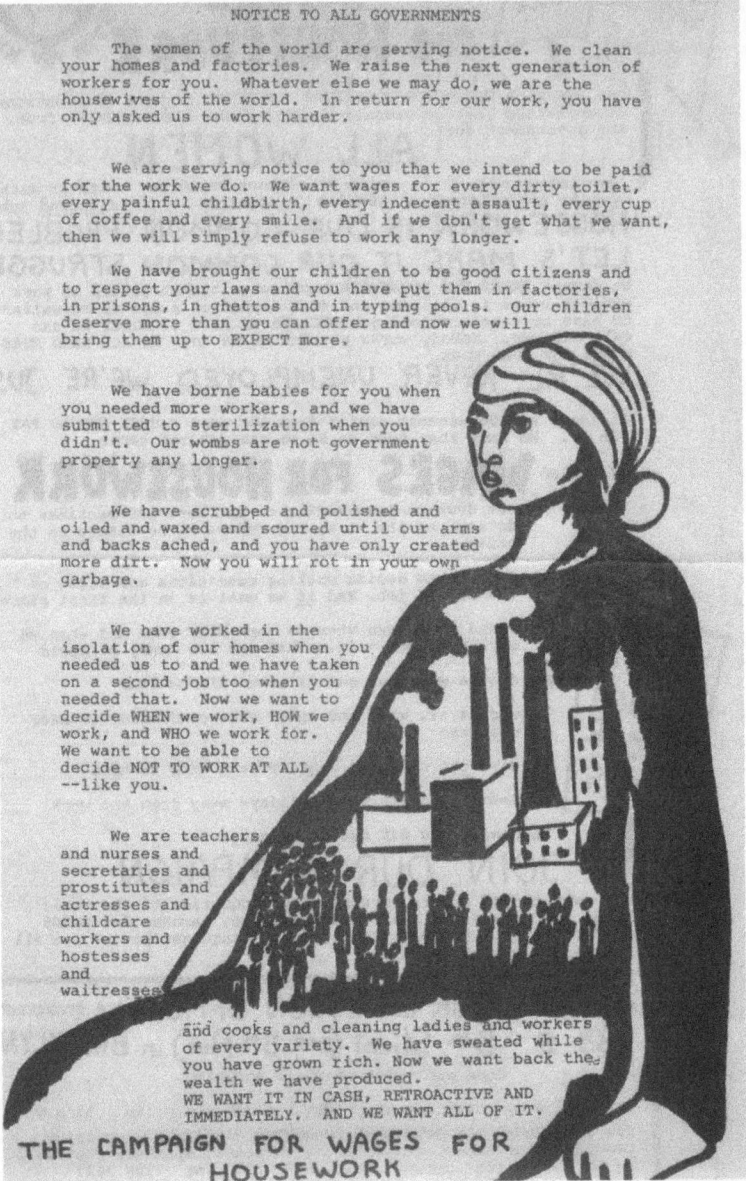

NOTICE TO ALL GOVERNMENTS

The women of the world are serving notice. We clean your homes and factories. We raise the next generation of workers for you. Whatever else we may do, we are the housewives of the world. In return for our work, you have only asked us to work harder.

We are serving notice to you that we intend to be paid for the work we do. We want wages for every dirty toilet, every painful childbirth, every indecent assault, every cup of coffee and every smile. And if we don't get what we want, then we will simply refuse to work any longer.

We have brought our children to be good citizens and to respect your laws and you have put them in factories, in prisons, in ghettos and in typing pools. Our children deserve more than you can offer and now we will bring them up to EXPECT more.

We have borne babies for you when you needed more workers, and we have submitted to sterilization when you didn't. Our wombs are not government property any longer.

We have scrubbed and polished and oiled and waxed and scoured until our arms and backs ached, and you have only created more dirt. Now you will rot in your own garbage.

We have worked in the isolation of our homes when you needed us to and we have taken on a second job too when you needed that. Now we want to decide WHEN we work, HOW we work, and WHO we work for. We want to be able to decide NOT TO WORK AT ALL --like you.

We are teachers and nurses and secretaries and prostitutes and actresses and childcare workers and hostesses and waitresses

and cooks and cleaning ladies and workers of every variety. We have sweated while you have grown rich. Now we want back the wealth we have produced. WE WANT IT IN CASH, RETROACTIVE AND IMMEDIATELY. AND WE WANT ALL OF IT.

THE CAMPAIGN FOR WAGES FOR HOUSEWORK

Figure 1.1 "Notice to All Governments." Tract distributed during many demonstrations organized by Wages for Housework. Drawing: Jacquie Ursula Caldwell. Text: Judy Quinlan, Toronto Wages for Housework Committee.

1

1972: Wages for Housework in the Universe of Feminism

How can we give a fair accounting, so many years later, of this current of feminist thought and the movement that underpinned it? How can we explain the thought and actions of this movement meaningfully and comprehensibly, when the political and cultural context and the intellectual climate during which it took place were so utterly different from today's? How can it resonate in the present? How can we extrapolate from it to offer, as I propose in this book, relevant tools for addressing the gendered division of labour and for critiquing dominant systems and the different social relations that they bring about?

We simply have to remember how removed and old-fashioned Simone de Beauvoir's essay *Le deuxième sexe*, published in 1949 (translated as *The Second Sex*), and especially its second volume, *L'expérience vécue* (translated as *Lived Experience*), seemed from our realities at the turn of the 1970s. Born in the postwar years, we were eagerly seeking theoretical bases for our new feminism. *Le deuxième sexe* had been published twenty years before, which seemed to put it in an impossibly distant past. And yet, the current of thought and the movement that I discuss here took place not twenty years but double that, forty years, ago. To young people today, that probably seems like the Middle Ages.

Therefore, it is necessary to provide a context – the social, intellectual, and activist horizons of feminism, and the daily life of women, forty years ago – in order to understand the world in which a book such as *The Power of Women and the Subversion of the Community* appeared in 1972. This context also clarifies the contributions that the book made to the neo-feminist landscape of ideas and action that was surging onto the political scene at the time.[1]

A GLANCE AT THE DAILY LIFE OF WOMEN IN THE EARLY 1970S

In most Western countries where what is commonly called neo-feminism or second-wave feminism appeared, the legal equality of women was far from a settled matter. In Quebec, for example, women could not serve on juries, and civil marriage and divorce had just been legalized, as had homosexuality "between consenting adults."[2] Access to abortions was in the process of being liberalized:

at first very restricted, it also depended on the goodwill of physicians.[3] Advertising of contraceptive methods was illegal. Access to the Pill was chancy, as one had to find a physician who was willing to prescribe it.

Pay equity was an illusion: in general, women earned half what men did. If they complained, they were likely to be fired. Rape was a criminal offence, unless it was rape of a wife. However, unlike for every other criminal offence, the rape victim was presumed guilty and had to prove her innocence in court. Similarly, any woman suspected of "prostitution" had to explain her presence in a public place whenever asked by the police. In 1970s, the Canadian Criminal Code still treated prostitution as a "crime of status": it penalized women for who they were and not for what they did.[4] Meanwhile, Indigenous women living on reserves were in an aggravated discriminatory situation: they lost their status and their rights if they married a non-Indigenous man.[5]

In the early 1970s, financially accessible daycare centres were non-existent for all intents and purposes. The female labour force participation rate formed between one-quarter and one-third of the total female population, depending on the country (rising toward 40 percent in some European countries and North America).[6] This meant that the proportion of women whose occupation was full-time housekeeper was around two-thirds, ranging from 60 percent in Quebec to 72 percent in Italy. Half of the wives of immigrants to Canada worked outside the home.[7]

The unionization rate of women wage earners was very low, and they worked mainly in female "job ghettos" (in jobs related to their tasks in the home). In practice, the career of women wage earners followed this path: when the first child came, they left the job market; they rejoined it when the children were grown. In both situations, women's workday was assessed as follows: "The housewife in the labour force and the housewife with two or more children are likely to work over 11 hours a day. An 11-hour work day on a regular basis would not be countenanced in industry."[8]

Meanwhile, the situation of married women in the home left much to be desired in 1970. Again using the example of Quebec, the province was heir to the Napoleonic Code and French civil law, which considered women to be "incapable," like minors and the "feebleminded." Marital and paternal power prevailed in all circumstances, and women and children were subjected to it. In 1964, the Act Respecting the Legal Capacity of Married Women (tabled by the first woman elected to the Legislative Assembly of Quebec, Claire Kirkland-Casgrain) partially remedied the situation, although the statute was far from being fully integrated into society at the end of the 1960s.

Governments were little inclined to change things before the arrival of neo-feminism. In Canada, the Royal Commission on the Status of Women, created in the late 1960s under pressure from women's groups and mandated to recommend to the federal government measures to put women on the path to equality, said little about the situation of women in the home. Aside from one major recommendation that "housewives should be entitled to pensions in their own right under the Canada Pension Plan or the Quebec Pension Plan" and a few minor recommendations, the commission threw up its hands: "With few rare exceptions, the woman who stays at home depends on her husband for money ... Unfortunately, we have no over-all solution for the financial dependency of housewives."[9]

It was not until the resurgence of neo-feminism, in 1971–72, that the first large-scale study on the situation of houseworkers was published by a collective of feminist activists, some of whom came from the defunct Front de libération des femmes du Québec (1969–71).[10] This first attempt at a general compilation of data on the situation of women working full time in the home was used, in the years that followed, as a training and intervention tool by numerous activists in the feminist, community, and union movements, and also by political parties.

When Mariarosa Dalla Costa and Selma James came to Montreal in the spring of 1973 to discuss the ideas expressed in their book, *The Power of Women and the Subversion of the Community*, many women recognized themselves in the discourse expressed by the authors, according to which "all women are houseworkers." The question was already in the air. Opposition political parties on both the left and the right were weighing the idea of paying "the housewife" (and not the *housework* itself, regardless of the person performing it). The National Council of Welfare, an independent agency charged with advising the Canadian government on welfare, recommended such wages in its 1972 report.[11] Similarly, in 1973, some authors, such as Marcelle Dolment and Marcel Barthe, suggested the creation of a "new class of workers" called "home educators."[12] They proposed that this aspect of housework be paid: a full-time wage for parents of children aged zero to six years, and a half-time wage for parents of children six to thirteen years; the parent who decided to stay at home for this period of the children's life would receive the salary. Among women's associations, AFEAS (Association féminine d'éducation et d'action sociale), the membership of which was mainly women at home, had been demanding an "allowance for the mother at home in recognition of the work of educating small children" since 1968.[13]

The perspective expressed by Dalla Costa and James in *The Power of Women and the Subversion of the Community* was different. Like so many other neo-feminist demands, it was anchored in a critique of society. "The neo-feminists' new contribution, however, was to include these demands in an analysis of society that completely challenged the traditional role of women within the family and aimed to fight against the profound causes of the specific oppression of which women were victims" ... in capitalist society, I would add, to be faithful to the spirit of the times.[14] Neo-feminism, in effect, was born in the wake of the New Left.

Figure 1.2   Graffiti: "Toutes les femmes sont d'abord ménagères" (All women are houseworkers first). Photo: Raymonde Lamothe.

NEO-FEMINISM: IN THE CIRCLE OF INFLUENCE OF THE NEW LEFT

A shared social and intellectual climate brought autonomous groups of women together as neo-feminism was being born.[15] This early era was that of the publication of *The Power of Women*. Some neo-feminist authors sought to identify the currents of feminist ideas emerging at the time. In general, there were three major trends, united under the banner of the autonomous struggle of women: a reformist (or liberal) trend, a "New Left" trend (bringing together "revolutionary feminists" or "politicos" or unorthodox socialists and Marxists), and a cultural or "women's lib" trend, which would be called radical and also included leftist feminists.[16] For the purpose of this book, I limit myself to the intellectual sphere of the last two trends, as they are more pertinent to my subject. Because at first they were not clearly delineated, these trends require a few clarifications.

The New Left

The New Left, a banner under which many activists were gathered at the inception of neo-feminism, was essentially an eclectic movement in terms of ideology, and very differentiated by country and by tradition of thought on social transformation. In the United States, New Left feminist activists drew on the ideals borne by the anti-racist struggles of the civil rights movement and were much less marked and influenced by the tradition of socialist and Marxist thought than were the activists in France, Italy, and Great Britain. In Quebec, a "colonial-colonized" society, a good number of the francophone New Left activists who were to form the ranks of neo-feminism had drawn their intellectual sources from thinkers of the decolonization and national independence movements of the time (Frantz Fanon, Albert Memmi, and Aimé Césaire, whose ideas were conveyed during the 1960s, notably, by the socialist and independentist magazine *Parti pris*).[17]

In the late 1960s, Western countries were seeing unprecedented social unrest as workers, students, African Americans, gays and lesbians, Indigenous people, and other groups rose up. Underlying these groups' mobilizations was, to some degree – depending on the different cultural, racial, or identity-related issues – an anti-authoritarian struggle, a desire for social change or a reversal of the balance of capitalism. Life had to change, and a world had to be created in which the hierarchies that produced injustices and exploitation were uprooted

Figure 1.3   The first issue of the journal *Québécoises Deboutte!* (No Women's Liberation without Quebec Liberation, No Quebec Liberation without Women's Liberation!). Illustration: Francine Jean.

and destroyed. The women's liberation movement emerged from this context of struggle.

For those who formed it, the new women's movement was truly a liberation movement, in solidarity with anti-colonialist and anti-imperialist national liberation movements of the time (those of African Americans, Latino Americans, Indigenous peoples, Africans, and Vietnamese) and the women in those movements. The autonomous struggle of women also had its place in this political landscape. To legitimize this new form of political intervention and action, these activists sought an explanation for the subordinate position of women in society – a position that a good number of them were experiencing personally within the very New Left groups in which they were involved. This was the age-old difficulty that women had in making a place for themselves and making themselves heard in these spaces of mixed-sex progressivism. This is probably as true today as it was then, but no doubt it was even more difficult then, when women's membership in and commitment to these groups were still fresh.[18]

Men in the New Left were not taking into account the discourses and denunciations of female activists, were refusing to take seriously the question of women as essential and not "secondary" within their theories of reference (whether they were anti-colonialist, socialist, or Marxist), and were accusing women activists of dividing the working class. All of this, added to the humiliation of being relegated to tasks of serving male activists, was to provoke the most militant feminists to resign and depart. In fact, this was how they had to begin to conceive of "their" revolution: to make women's struggle a political issue and an autonomous political struggle, something that was denied to them from within the New Left groups.[19] It is why some chose to leave the progressive mixed-sex groups to join the emerging feminist movement or, in certain cases, to create it out of whole cloth.

Women's Lib

But alongside these women, and often *with* them, were activists who would be called "radicals" – in the original sense of the word – who intended to go to the root of the exploitation of women. A number of them came from the New Left movement of the 1960s, the "counterculture" or "sexual liberation" or hippie movement, the movement for homosexual rights, and the effervescent student movement. They, too, were seeking explanations for the alienation of women, but, unlike the feminists within the socialist trend of the New Left, they were looking outside of the existing explanatory systems. The systems of thought formulated by and for men had to be swept away. New language, new concepts, and new knowledge would have to be invented to explain the domination of women through the ages. The values of the old world had to

Tu vois le féminisme recouvre pour moi quelque chose de plus concret, par exemple la lutte des classes, la résistance, l'antifascisme.

Figure 1.4 "You see, for me feminism is part of something more concrete, like class struggle, the resistance, anti-fascism." Illustration: Giuliana M. (Reproduced in Louise Vandelac, ed., *L'Italie au féminisme* [Paris: Tierce, 1978], 231.)

be subverted, and ways of life, customs, culture, and systems of representation had to be completely rethought. Some women revisited Freud in this regard, or Wilhelm Reich, or Herbert Marcuse.

The patriarchy, the historical power of men over women, was found to be the source of the explanation and the root of the oppression of women. In 1969, Kate Millett, in *Sexual Politics*, proclaimed that in all known societies, the unequal relationship between men and women in favour of the class of men constituted the basis for all other relations of domination, whether economic or political. The system that underlay this primary relationship of inequality was called patriarchy. It was expressed first and foremost within the family, in sexuality and reproduction. The relationship of inequality was political, as it consisted of a relationship of power. The "personal" became "political." This meant that what had been considered "private" problems (relationships between men and women, sexuality, and others) were in fact a collective issue, which, once denounced, became visible and, by this fact, political.

At the inception of neo-feminism, the question was how the oppression of women was linked to capitalism – and, thus, how an analysis of the patriarchy could be articulated with this economic system. Although radical feminists abandoned this research as the 1970s progressed, for socialist feminists, an explanation for the patriarchy could never be totally severed from that for capitalism.[20]

Of course, this description of the evolution of the radical and socialist-Marxist currents and their respective nebulas, which have undergone many refinements, is too short and cursory. This evolution has been studied in depth and in breadth elsewhere for at least three decades, and it is not my objective in this book to present more detail on the subject. I have restrained myself, for the purpose of my subject, to authors writing at the turn of the 1970s who tried to identify the trends in nascent neo-feminism, as they appeared to activists at the time.

I am at risk of falling into the same shortcuts in describing how the question of housework arose within these neo-feminist trends. I will, however, provide references for those who would like to refine their reflection on the subject.

IN SEARCH OF THE "SPECIFIC" OPPRESSION OF WOMEN

At the turn of the 1970s, very few books dealt with the question of women as a political issue. Feminist studies as a scholarly discipline within universities either did not exist or was in the very early stages, and in just a few countries.[21] As a first step, certain explanatory theories for the situation of women had to be reread and sexist biases revealed. Many turned to the theories of Sigmund Freud and Friedrich Engels, either to contest their foundations or to situate themselves within these revisited traditions. Others chose to situate themselves outside of all traditions.

At the time, neo-feminist activists, all trends combined, were eager to find a single source of oppression *shared* by all women. The more it was discussed, the more the thin documentation available was mined, the more the oppression seemed to be generalized and to go back to the dawn of time. The interest in women's history and the search for "origins" also started in the early 1970s. No history of past feminist struggles – that is, those of the first wave – had been passed down.[22]

From the start, neo-feminists were focused on identifying the specific oppression" (the "main enemy") of women and advancing collective strategies to eradicate it. They were searching for a system to make society intelligible, a new way to understand the world. To do this, they first had to figure out where the oppression of women was situated, on what foundations and which power structures it was based. To legitimize the autonomous struggle of women, neo-feminists had to find the oppressive structure specific to them.

This quest for origins led some activist researchers, engaged in a critique of Engels, to seek out an "original matriarchy" that may have existed before the patriarchy. Others chose to understand the causes of the subordinate situation of women in society by orienting their research more toward defining male domination. Some authors identified sexist culture and chauvinistic representations and macho ideology as factors in this domination, and others characterized it as a stranglehold by the class of men over the bodies of women, notably with regard to maternity and sexuality. Other feminist scholars decided to explore the economic exploitation of women by studying the economy and the forms of sexual division of labour in industrial society.

HOUSEWORK: FROM LABOUR "OF LOVE" TO "EXPLOITED" LABOUR

Among this last group of researchers, invisible work done in the home by women was quickly identified and highlighted by a large segment of new activist-theoreticians. Above all, the oppression of women was to be found in the home – where it was, fittingly, invisible.

Up to then, housework, domestic work, or care work (as it was to be called later) was not considered true work, at the same level as other jobs. It was referred to as a labour of love. The family was supposed to be a place of consumption and of satisfaction of personal needs. With the advent of capitalism and a wage society, however, it gradually lost the pre-industrial productive role that it had had as an economic unit. In the new industrial context, it was seen as outside of production, a private zone, a haven of repose, a place to rebuild physical and mental strength and to deal with the personal, the private, and consump-

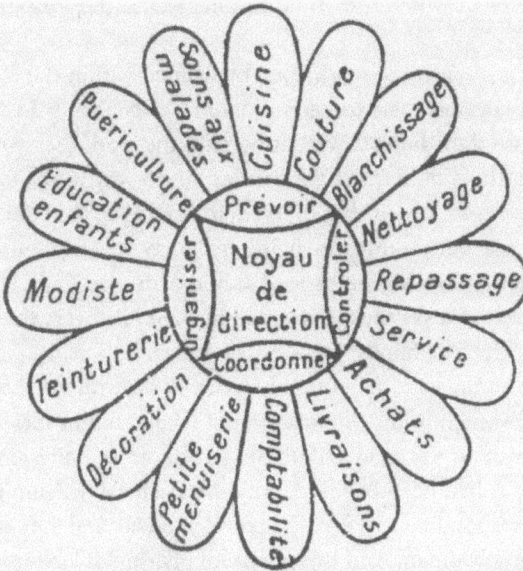

Figure 1.5   "La ménagère est une cellule complète coordonnée" (The cellular components of domestic work) (excerpted from Paulette Bernège, De la méthode ménagère [Paris: Édition Dunod, 1928]).

tion. The women at the heart of this representation thus could not be true workers. Their activities were conceived as *natural*, arising from self-sacrifice and resulting from their biological faculty of giving life, which explained why these tasks were provided for free. The *real* work was done outside the home, in the world of waged production. To enfranchise and liberate themselves, women simply had to emerge from the home to work "outside," invading the labour market. This was the proposed road to emancipation, a true launch pad for equality.

This was more or less what reformist women's associations were proposing, as were theoreticians of the situation of women in the traditional socialist movement. In the view of Engels and Bebel, for example, the struggle for women's emancipation was a struggle of the working class (the only revolutionary class), and therefore took place on the wage-labour front, shoulder to shoulder with male comrades.[23] Housework and domestic work, in this context, were considered "backward" forms of work, relics of a pre-capitalist world, which would be socialized as the dictatorship of the proletariat took over in a communist world. In the meantime, the labour market was the solution offered to women.

The advent of neo-feminism on the political scene was to challenge, and shake the belief in, the myth of liberation and equality through waged work. Between 1968 and 1972, in the United States, Western Europe (as it was known at the time), Canada, and Quebec simultaneously, neo-feminist activists published analyses in which they tried to understand the reasons for women's dependency in society.

Looking at the quantity of work done by women within the home, feminist theoreticians discovered that women's economic dependency in families came about not because they didn't work but because the work they were doing was unpaid. These authors then made the connection to why women's wages in the labour market were so low. They observed, for example, that the jobs filled by women (nurses, teachers, waitresses, hairdressers, cooks, maids, and so on) were "extensions" of tasks that they performed at home for free. Thus, women's wages were low because the tasks they performed in their jobs were those performed free of charge within the family.

Finally, these feminists realized that housework determined the position and the situation of women in the organization of labour and in society as a whole. They then understood the gendered division of labour as a division that was not complementary, as had been believed, but a hierarchical division between men and women, corresponding to a division between power and non-power, exerted to the detriment of women. And this gendered division of labour had roots that were not "natural" but historical – and thus social.

From the early writings, which put the focus on the home and the amount of work that women did in the family sphere, neo-feminists discovered that women, with or without a paid job, experienced a "specific oppression" in the family – that they performed there, absolutely for free, both material mainte- nance work and "immaterial" (emotional) work for their loved ones, and often for the extended family.[24] But what are the reasons and the foundations for this labour being free – a situation that some called exploitation or extortion, pure and simple?

Many of the authors writing in the early 1970s turned to Marxism to answer this question. Indeed, most neo-feminists used a Marxist lens, in both their writings and their actions, to situate themselves within this tradition of thought, to contest and revisit it, or to distinguish themselves from it. Why?

MARXISM: AN UNAVOIDABLE THEORY OF REFERENCE FOR NEO-FEMINISM

In this effervescent era marked by ideals of emancipation and justice, young feminists were concerned with understanding and explaining the ongoing social crisis and finding strategies for acting to change the dominant social and economic system. They felt that it was time to return to Marx, as at the time, Marxism embodied ideas about social change and global transformation of society. It was *the* explanatory theory for oppression and exploitation, although not those of women specifically. Marxism, revisited and updated, seemed at first glance to offer the best tools for thinking about this oppression and conducting the feminist analysis.

This was even truer because Engels, Marx's alter ego, was one of the rare thinkers to have written a revolutionary essay on the family in which the fate of women within the family was analyzed in historical and social terms.[25] This book, dating from the late nineteenth century, was still very popular in leftist circles in the early 1970s. Engels argued that historical factors explained the situation of women in families. In his view, imprisonment of women within the family, and the resulting subordinate status, had not always existed; this phenomenon was due to the appearance of private property, "the great historical defeat of the female sex"; and the status of women was thus linked to the evolution of private property and the institution of the family.

According to this narrative, it was with the arrival of capitalism that women were removed from social production and placed under the control and grasp of husbands, within the private sphere of the family. The origin of the oppression of women, according to Engels, was this gendered division of labour, which was created with the appearance of private property: to men went social production and waged work; to women went domestic and childcare work, unpaid, outside of social production. So, in Engels's view, the oppression of women in the family was not natural at all. The problem was economic; its solution also had to be economic, and could occur only within a socialist society.

Another factor that might explain the attraction of Marxism among neo-feminist activists was the prominent position accorded to eminent female thinkers, notably Rosa Luxemburg, Clara Zetkin, and Alexandra Kollontai, within the international socialist movement.[26] Whereas Luxemburg, among other things, clashed with Lenin over his theories on imperialism, Zetkin and Kollontai wrote several works on the situation of women at the turn of the twentieth century.[27] Kollontai's analyses of the relationships between the sexes and the "new woman," censored by Communist Party authorities for almost fifty years, became accessible in translation during the 1970s.

In addition, although there was an attraction to Marxism, there was also the need to be differentiated from one of its deplorable tangents, represented by small extreme-left groups that espoused a dogmatic ideological line with regard to the question of women and wanted to control the new autonomous feminist groups. These extreme-left groups fiercely contested and fought the advent of feminism and the autonomous struggle of women because they felt that social struggle was their own field of action. In their view, feminism was nothing but an "individualist-bourgeois" movement that went against the interests of the working class and would only divide it.[28] Neo-feminism and autonomous women's groups had to be either defeated or contained. The hostility shown by the extreme-left groups toward nascent neo-feminism was more vehement than all other forms of opposition then sweeping through the movement.[29] To defend their right to autonomous struggle against this opposition, activist feminists turned to Marxist analytic tools. The relationship of neo-feminism with the left was, to say the least, difficult.

These groups' opposition to the autonomous struggle of women was manifested in Quebec and various parts of Europe. The writings by a number of early neo-feminist authors who made efforts to distinguish themselves from leftist orthodoxy to present autonomous feminism thought and defend the validity of women's autonomous struggle nevertheless bore a trace of the "cold war" with feminism waged by these small groups.

SEVERAL PRECURSOR TEXTS ON HOUSEWORK

To provide a better understanding of the early neo-feminist theoretical and activist perspective on housework, I present an overview of three pivotal texts, written in 1969, 1970, and 1971, that had a marked influence on what was written about housework later in the 1970s. All three used the intellectual tools of Marxism to conceptualize this work, up to then invisible.

Chronologically (even though the texts were published almost simultaneously), there is first the pioneering essay by Margaret Benston, a chemist and assistant professor at Simon Fraser University in British Columbia, "The Political Economy of Women's Liberation."[30] Next is the essay by Christine

Delphy (who, for this occasion, used the pseudonym Christine Dupont), an early feminist activist and researcher at the Centre national de la recherche scientifique in France, "L'ennemi principal," and finally the essay by Mariarosa Dalla Costa, an activist feminist teaching at the University of Padua in Italy, "Donne e sovversione sociale."[31] These essays, written by feminists "separated by thousands of miles and having no contact with each other," are considered to have lit the way for a legion of other writings on housework and domestic work that would appear during the 1970s.[32]

Margaret Benston: Domestic Labour Defines All Women (1969)

Margaret Benston was known as one of the first neo-feminists to highlight the faults in the common beliefs and theories about unpaid and economically unvalued domestic labour. According to the widespread Marxist interpretation, housework has a use value and not an exchange value. From this point of view, goods produced and services rendered in the family have no economic value as such, only immediate use value; only goods and services that can be exchanged or sold on the market are part of economic production. Therefore, the energy deployed to produce goods and services dispensed in the family cannot be considered "real" work, as it is outside the market sphere.

Partially endorsing this cleavage, Benston establishes the following important distinction: even though women, through their housework and domestic labour, produce goods and services with a use value and not an exchange value, these tasks, added to that of raising children, are essential to the economy and to capitalism. It is "socially necessary production" and thus far from being "marginal," as the Marxist vulgate would have it. No, Benston says, "it is just not wage labor and so it is not counted."

The fact that women, despite all the differences among them, are assigned to this work en masse constitutes them as a *group* with a *specific* relationship with production. Benston asserts, "In arguing that the roots of the secondary status of women are in fact economic it can be shown that women as a group do indeed have a definite relation to the means of production and that this is different from that of men."[33] In her view, domestic work is "the work which is reserved for women, and it is in this fact that we can find the basis for a definition of women" as "that group of people which is responsible for the production of simple use-value in those activities associated with the home and family." And she adds, "The material basis for the inferior status of women is to be found in just this definition of women ... whether or not they are married, single, or the heads of households."[34] Her conclusion is clear: "There *is* a material basis for women's status; we are not merely discriminated against, we are exploited."[35]

It is Benston's opinion that the solution is not in the integration of women into the labour market as it exists, for "as long as work in the home remains a matter of private production and is the responsibility of women, they will

THE LEGACY OF MARGARET BENSTON

Figure 1.6 Cover of an issue of *Canadian Women Studies/Les Cahiers de la femme* (13, 2 [Winter 1993]) in tribute to Margaret Benston: "Women in Science and Technology: The Legacy of Margaret Benston."

simply carry a double work-load."[36] She nevertheless puts all her hope, as do most classic Marxists, in the socialization of domestic work and equal access to the labour market.

Benston revisited the Marxist analysis of the situation of women in the home and developed the basis for a materialist theory of the oppression and exploitation of women and of "reproduction." Up to then, analyses and explanations had considered reproduction only from the angle of maternity or biology; Benston situated it in the more general context of domestic work and the relationships that link domestic work to the economic system.

She was criticized for not going further. For example, she did not question the production categories of use value and exchange value in themselves. Although she saw domestic work as "labour necessary" to capitalism, it was "still left ... floating in a historical limbo somewhere quite outside of the capitalist economy," according to some of her critics.[37] She was also criticized for not having formulated a specific analysis of the relations between men and women. This is what Christine Delphy, among others, was to do.

Christine Delphy: Domestic Services – A Mode of Production (1970)

In her essay intended to be "the basis for a materialist analysis of the oppression of women," published the following year, in 1970, Christine Delphy (using the pseudonym Christine Dupont) implicitly endorses one of Benston's conclusions to the effect that the family is "the site of an economic exploitation: that of women" and that women perform socially necessary productive work there.[38] The economic importance of this production, she reminds us, has long been attested to in many ethnological studies.

However, Delphy inverts Benston's reasoning regarding the cleavage, dear to Marxists, between use value and exchange value. In Delphy's view, the fact that women's work within the family is free is not related to the nature of this work; it is free because it is performed inside the family and within the institution of marriage. Indeed, as soon as goods and services supplied by women are produced outside the family framework, they become convertible into cash;

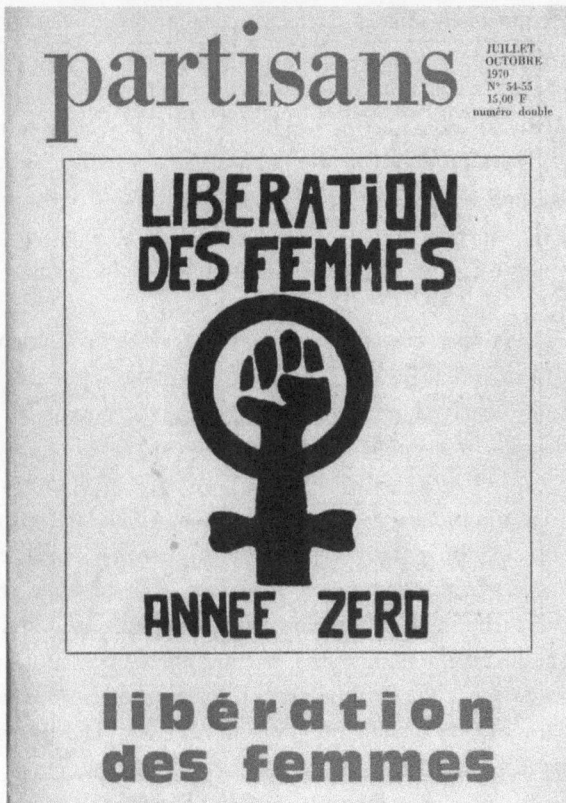

Figure 1.7   Partisans 54–55 (July–October 1970), in which the first version of Christine Delphy's "L'ennemi principal" was published (under the pseudonym Christine Dupont).

"thus women's production always has an exchange value (can be exchanged by them) except within the framework of the family."[39]

In addition, women's work (the value of the energy spent, of their labour power) supplied in the matrimonial-familial framework remains free even if their production is commercialized. Delphy uses the examples of women's work in agriculture, crafts, and small business, performed in the context of family production. In these cases, she notes, the woman "thus does not dispose of her own labor power," as it is appropriated by the husband.[40] It is "a relationship of slavery." This "appropriation and exploitation of their labor in marriage constitutes the oppression common to all women," and it constitutes them as a class. By participating in capitalist production, they also enter other relations of production.[41] Waged work outside the house, however, does not exempt a woman from her family obligations, and this double labour clearly demonstrates "the legal appropriation of her labour power." Indeed, the unpaid performance of domestic work cannot therefore be justified by the argument that it is supplied in exchange for the wife's upkeep. Delphy's class analysis is thus sketched out as follows:

The existence of two modes of production in our society is established: (1) most goods are produced in the industrial mode; (2) domestic services, child rearing, and a certain number of goods are produced in the family mode. The first mode of production gives rise to capitalist exploitation. The second gives rise to familial, or more precisely, patriarchal exploitation.[42]

In Delphy's analysis, the patriarchy is "theoretically independent of capitalism." And so, "only this understanding will make it possible to account for the historically observed independence of these two systems."[43]

Delphy concludes by noting that it has not been possible to study, within the framework of her article, the relations between exploitation of women's productive labour and of their reproductive labour, which are "both cause and means of the other great material oppression of women – sexual exploitation ... the second aspect of the oppression of women." She observes that "understanding how and why these two exploitations are conditioned and reinforced by each other, and have the same framework and the same institutional means, the family, must be one of the first theoretical objectives of the movement." This is one of Mariarosa Dalla Costa's intentions in her essay "Donne e sovversione sociale," written in 1971.

It is important to underline the importance of Delphy's essay in the feminist theorization of women's work. This text would have, at least in the francophone feminist academic world, considerable impact and influence.[44] It was to establish the bases for radical materialist feminism.

Delphy's feminism is *radical* because she makes unpaid domestic work the basis of a distinct mode of production that is different from the capitalist mode of production: the patriarchal mode of production. The "main enemy" is thus not capitalism but the patriarchy, which creates men and women as distinct gender classes: the class of men and the class of women. It is men, as a class – and not capitalists – who are the main beneficiaries of domestic work. The feminist struggle must therefore be directed against the patriarchy.

It is *materialist* because Delphy uses, to theorize this domestic work, the conceptual forms of Marxism (class relations, production relations, mode of production), but gives them a different content. She discovers in the free domestic work that women perform for their families – the material basis of economic exploitation of all women whatever their class – specific relations of production that parallel relations of capitalist production: the patriarchy, the gender-relations system. The particular form of exploitation of women is not capitalist but patriarchal. Capitalism and patriarchy constitute two separate systems. With this theorization, Delphy traces the foundation of the French version of radical materialist feminism.[45]

There was some criticism of Delphy's theorization of domestic work, conceived as a mode of production "theoretically independent of capitalism."[46] Among other things, her critics felt that her definition of domestic work as "apart from or outside of the capitalist space" induced "the idea that the world of capitalist production could be defined excluding the gendered dimensions of production relations."[47] In addition, she did not articulate how the patriarchal system, embodied in the mode of domestic production, affected seemingly unrelated areas, such as how it fit with the capitalist mode of production.[48] According to this critique, "What we call 'domestic work' ... is a particular historical form of reproductive labour, a form inseparable from wage society."[49]

Furthermore, the gendered division of labour, according to these critics, was not specific to the domain of the family; rather, it appeared as "one of the elements composing the capitalist division of labour." It was then "possible to develop, within the same movement, an analysis of capitalism and of the double dimensions of class and gender in social relations that shows the capitalist form of the family."[50]

This, among other things, was what Mariarosa Dalla Costa was interested in when she wrote "Donne e sovversione sociale," in which a Marxian analysis of production was articulated with a feminist analysis of reproduction.

Mariarosa Dalla Costa: Wages for Housework as a Lever of Power for All Women (1971)

Whereas Delphy conceived of free domestic work as a mode of production intrinsic to the patriarchy, Mariarosa Dalla Costa presented it as a mode of production and reproduction linked to capitalism.[51] What did she bring that was new to the intellectual and activist landscape of early neo-feminism, and why did the book in which her essay was published raise such controversy throughout the 1970s?[52]

The novelty of the analysis

Dalla Costa and Selma James defined themselves as Marxist feminists, but they nevertheless seriously revisited and subjected to a feminist critique the postulates of Marxist theory concerning women's place in society. The context was a Marxian horizon of analysis – that is, an analysis that adopts a redefined

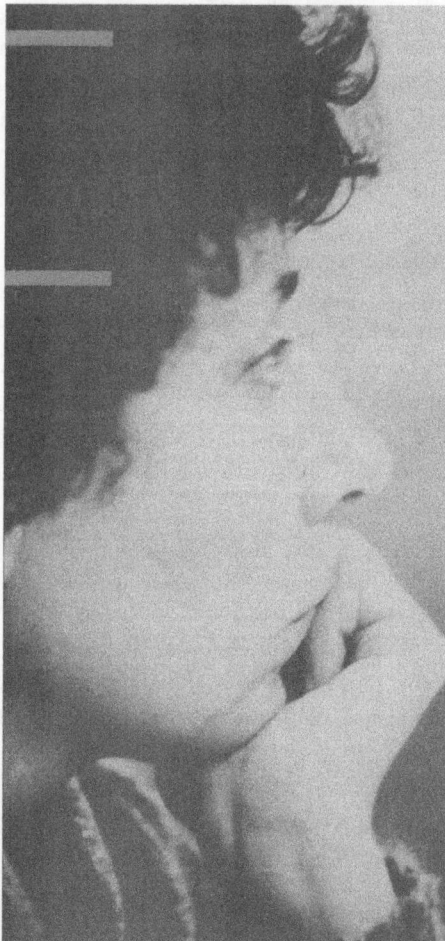

Figure 1.8   Mariarosa Dalla Costa. Photograph by Fausta Daldini published in the magazine of the Centrale de l'enseignement du Québec, *Mouvements* (Spring 1985): 23.

class perspective. Dalla Costa's essay offered a theoretical explanation of the exploitation of women in modern society, paired with a political proposal for change and action. Below is an overview.

"The oppression of women, after all, did not begin with capitalism. What began with capitalism was the more intense exploitation of women *as* women and the possibility at last of their liberation" (21). In effect, "capitalism has created the modern family and the housewife's role in it, by destroying the types of family group or community which previously existed. This process is by no means complete" (19–20). The result is that today "all women are housewives and even those who work outside the home continue to be housewives. That is, on a world level, it is precisely what is particular to domestic work, not only measured as number of hours and nature of work, but as quality of life and quality of relationships which it generates, that determines a women's place wherever she is and to whichever class she belongs" (19).

These three quotations, drawn from the first pages of Dalla Costa's essay, situate housework in a specific historical context (the advent of capitalism), while specifying that the oppression of women (the patriarchy) pre-existed capitalism, rather than resulting from it. Dalla Costa is thus describing the historical roots of the "role of the housekeeper" as reserved for all women – a role that now defines and determines their place in the social organization.

How did capital create the modern nuclear family and the role of women within it? Briefly, by displacing the centre of production from the family unit, where it had been situated in pre-capitalist society, to the factory. Those who worked at the plant received a wage; the others did not. This was the advent of wage society. As the family and the community were dismissed as the centre of production, women, children, and the elderly found themselves losing the (relative) power that they had held, for the family depended on their work. Capitalism thus "detached the man from the family and turned him into a *wage laborer*" and "put on [his] shoulders the burden of financial responsibility for women, children, the old and the ill, in a word, all those who do not receive wages" (22, emphasis in original). These unpaid people now saw themselves excluded, put outside the system of production. Women were isolated within the family unit, totally dependent on men and "cut off from direct socialized production" (27). The myth of female incapacity is founded on this basis.

The resulting family type, the nuclear family, subordinates the woman to the man, cutting her off from any possibility for autonomy, and notably of "expression of her sexual, psychological and emotional autonomy" (29). Her sexuality is oriented toward and transformed into a "function for reproducing labor power" (29). The "female role" is built on this "complete diminution of woman." The man, now the head of the family and a waged worker, also becomes "the specific instrument of this specific exploitation which is the exploitation of women."

Figure 1.9   Swiss edition of *The Power of Women and the Subversion of Community* (1973).

One of the novelties of Dalla Costa's analysis resides in her deconstruction of the idea that women's labour in families does not produce true value but has only use value, because it is unwaged and situated "outside of organized social production." In Dalla Costa's view, housework is "productive." It is a "source of social productivity ... firstly within the family" (31). For instance, "the enormous quantity of social services which capitalist organization transforms into privatized activity, putting them on the backs of housewives ... are social services inasmuch as they serve the reproduction of labor power."

She thus explains the process of reproduction of labour power:

And capital, precisely by instituting its family structure, has "liberated" the man from these functions so that he is completely "free" for *direct* exploitation; so that he is free to "earn" enough for a woman to reproduce him as labor power. It has made men wage slaves, then, to the degree that it has succeeded in allocating these services to women in the family, and by the same process controlled the flow of women onto the labor market. (31–32, emphasis in original)

Women are producers of free social services in the family, but also "a safety valve for social tensions" (40) and, above all, producers of the most valuable good: human beings themselves. These are examples of women's social productivity within families. They produce and reproduce labour power.

The family is thus not simply a site of consumption; it is also a centre of social production and a site of production and reproduction of labour power. And this labour is produced completely for free and in utter dependency. It is a place of exploitation of women. The family is thus the hidden source of capital accumulation, even the "very pillar of the capitalist organization of work" (33), and its foundation. Unpaid housework is described in this context as "a masked form of productive labor" (34), the hidden face of wage society. And because housework is not salaried, "the figure of the boss is concealed behind that of the husband" (33).

For, until now, what has never been highlighted

is that precisely through the wage has the exploitation of the non-wage laborer been organized. This exploitation has been even more effective because the lack of a wage hid it. That is, the wage commanded a larger amount of labor than appeared in factory bargaining. *Where women are concerned, their labor appears to be a personal service outside of capital.* (26, emphasis in original)

In other words, housework is not situated outside of economic production. It is simply non-salaried and paid through the husband's salary. This means that the boss benefits from the labour power of two people for the price of one.

The family is described as the "other factory," the "social factory," in which labour power is produced and reproduced, representing an economic value, a surplus value for capital. Therefore, women's labour in families contributes to the accumulation of capital and constitutes the pillar on which it rests. Women are the backbone of this social factory. This specific form of exploitation – housework – "demands a corresponding, specific form of struggle, namely the women's struggle, *within the family*" (33, emphasis in original).

Strategic involvement

Another novelty in Dalla Costa's essay resides in the political conclusion that she draws from the form of exploitation that is free housework: if the family is a centre of production, essential to capitalism and to life, it may also be a centre of subversion – especially if women refuse to work there. If they reject the role of houseworker and the "'femininity' imposed upon" them (35–36), if they refuse to work and join other women "to struggle against all situations which presume that women will stay at home" (39), it "undermines the very pillar supporting the capitalist organization of work, namely the family" (46). They may "destroy ... the role of housewife" (46).

"To abandon the home is already a form of struggle, since the social services we perform there would then cease to be carried out in those conditions" (39). And "we must refuse housework as women's work, as work imposed upon us, which we never invented, which has never been paid for, in which they have forced us to cope with absurd hours, 12 and 13 a day, in order to force us to stay at home" (39).

For a woman, struggling to recover her individuality, "the integrity of her basic physical functions, starting with the sexual one which was the first to be robbed" (46), demanding abortion rights, opposing contraceptive experiments performed on the bodies of poor third world women, linking all of these struggles to the struggles against "motherhood conceived as the responsibility of women exclusively" (47), and housework conceived as female work, "is to struggle against the division and organization of labor" (47):

> Let us sum up. The role of housewife ... must be destroyed ... Up to now, the myth of female incapacity ... has been broken by only one action: the woman getting her own wage ...
>
> *The advent of the women's movement is a rejection of this alternative* ... the rejection by millions of women of women's traditional place, [the rejection of] the myth of liberation through work. For we have worked enough.
>
> Every time they have "let us in" to some traditionally male enclave, it was to find for us a new level of exploitation ... Women must completely discover their own possibilities. (47–48, emphasis in original)

Refusing housework, rejecting the role of houseworker, making this refusal and this rejection a lever and a strategy for women's power was, to paraphrase Maria Mies, to reintroduce women into history as subjects – and, what is more, as revolutionary subjects.[53] Women became active historical subjects, with subversive power. They could change their situation, and therefore the system on which this situation rested. This interpretation of women's possible resistances and of the power of unpaid workers to subvert the social and economic system was unprecedented in the feminist movement. Theory became action.

Before looking at the strategy for struggle proposed by Dalla Costa, let us pause for a moment to underline some of the differences between her essay and those by Benston and Delphy.

In Dalla Costa's view, unlike Benston's, housework does not have solely a use value simply because it is executed outside the labour market. It is truly "productive": it produces and reproduces labour power. The strategy proposed therefore is not to emerge from the house and enter the waged labour market, which would only add more labour (another exploitation) to that which women already bear. "The specific form of exploitation represented by domestic work demands a corresponding, specific form of struggle, namely the women's struggle, *within the family*" (33, emphasis in original).

The main difference between Dalla Costa's essay and Delphy's lies particularly in the analysis of the foundations of the unpaid nature of housework. Why are housework and the services rendered by women inside families free?

In Delphy's view, they are free because they are executed within the family and within the context of marriage; women's labour is thus appropriated by the beneficiaries of this extortion, the class of men, giving rise to patriarchal exploitation. In Dalla Costa's view, women's labour within families is free because of the capitalist form of the family. This labour has the function of producing, reproducing, and maintaining the labour power of wage earners (men and women) and their families. It constitutes the hidden source of accumulation of capital, the very pillar on which it rests, and a site of exploitation for women. The links between exploitation of women and economic functions of the sexual division of labour in the family in a capitalist regime are analyzed within this framework.

In Delphy's view, free domestic labour is conceived as a mode of production within the patriarchy, whereas for Dalla Costa it is like a centre of production and reproduction within capitalism. These positions define Delphy as one of the founders of radical materialist feminism (the French version) and Dalla Costa as a "Marxist" feminist – the quotation marks indicating a revisited Marxism, combining Marxism and feminism.[54]

The Wages for Housework strategy

In Dalla Costa's view, "clearly, the specific form of exploitation represented by domestic work demands a corresponding, specific form of struggle, namely the women's struggle, *within the family*" (33, emphasis in original). Wages for Housework is thus advanced as a political strategy.

It is to be noted, in a historical perspective, that the Wages for Housework strategy was not included in Dalla Costa's 1971 Italian-language text, but it would be the following year in the Italian and English editions and in subsequent editions in other languages.[55] The spirit of the demand is expressed thus:

> The demand for a wage for housework is only a basis, a perspective, from which to start, whose merit is essentially to link immediately female oppression, subordination and isolation to their material foundation: female exploitation. At this moment this is perhaps the major function of the demand of wages for housework.

This gives at once an indication for struggle, a direction in organizational terms in which oppression and exploitation, situation of caste and class, find themselves insolubly linked.

The practical, continuous translation of this perspective is the task the movement is facing in Italy and elsewhere. (53n16)[56]

This demand would be further developed in subsequent texts in the Wages for Housework current, which I explore in greater depth in coming chapters.

Dalla Costa and James's book triggered heated debates among feminist theoreticians and activists throughout the decade. Among activists, the debate bore particularly on the legitimacy of the wage-for-housework demands.[57] Among theoreticians, it also triggered what was called the domestic labour debate – a debate mainly among English-speaking Marxist theoreticians. The level of Marxist exegesis reached such a degree of sophistication that no activist would participate in it, and so the debate was thereby left to Marxist academics, whose concern was more, according to certain critics, to "save Marx" than to promote women's liberation.[58]

The domestic labour debate was extinguished in the mid-1980s, even though the debate itself lasted a few years longer in the women's movement. In Quebec, for example, the government's advisory council on the "status of women," the Conseil du statut de la femme, undertook a broad-based study on the issues,

i haven't had time to Read it yet...

Christine Roche

Figure 1.10   Caricature of the domestic labour debate by Christine Roche, *Feminist Review* 6 (1980): 51.

which led to the publication of *Du travail et de l'amour: Les dessous de la production domestique* (Labour and love: The underside of domestic production), edited by sociologist Louise Vandelac, in 1985. The study rejected the Wages for Housework strategy, and one might say that this document marked, in effect, the end of the discussion in Quebec, after a decade of debates.[59]

FEMINIST FOREBEARS OF WAGES FOR HOUSEWORK

The demand for wages or compensation for work done by women in families is not a novelty specific to the feminist second wave. It forms an important linkage between the first and second waves of feminism.

Indeed, although formulation of the political perspective on wages for housework can be traced to the book-manifesto *The Power of Women and the Subversion of Community*, the idea had been advanced well before, as Wages for Housework groups and the International Feminist Collective (IFC) recognize in their publications.[60] In this regard we can refer to the struggles of the welfare rights movement, led mainly by welfare mothers (most of them African American) in the 1960s in the United States and the "unsupported mothers" in England who formed claimants' unions in order to claim compensation from the state for work they were performing at home. These women refused to look for spouses, or to live with spouses for the sole reason that they had children. They also refused state "charity"; in fact, they were demanding a salary from the state because they were working.[61] In 1977, Gisela Bock and Barbara Duden,

Figure 1.11   Demonstration by welfare mothers, 1968. *Safire* 1, 1 (Fall 1977): 1.

Figure 1.12   Dolores Hayden, *The Grand Domestic Revolution*
(Cambridge, MA: MIT Press, 1982).

of the German Wages for Housework group Lohn für Hausarbeit, published
a pioneering essay, the last part of which deals with the historical feminist
tradition of demanding wages for domestic and childcare work – a tradition
that went back to the early nineteenth century among utopian socialists, such as
in Fourierist communities.[62]

In her essay *The Grand Domestic Revolution,* Dolores Hayden highlights a
feminist current that she calls material feminism, which, from the end of the
American Civil War to the beginning of the Depression – for three generations
– effected a radical critique of women's unpaid domestic work and childcare
activities.[63] These feminists also proposed and practised solutions that were just
as radical, including a wage for the unpaid work that women were performing
at home, from their earliest campaigns in 1868.[64] Bock reinforced the analysis
of this "maternalist" current from 1890 to the 1930s, which made the theme

of maternity as a "social function" its main axis for demands.[65] Bock quoted no fewer than thirty feminists and groups that demanded effective recognition of childcare activity, in one form or another, in Europe and the United States during this period.[66]

Continuity among Twentieth-Century Feminist Waves

The battle for family allowances constitutes an example of continuity between the two feminist waves, which is rarely highlighted in the historiography of second-wave feminism. The campaign conducted by Eleanor Rathbone in England between 1924 and 1945 for implementation of a public family-allowance plan for mothers is worth mentioning. She opened the door to mobilizations by Wages for Housework groups in England and Canada, which would take the torch twenty-seven years later to maintain and expand those allowances.

Rathbone (1872–1946), an Irish social worker, came up with the formula for public family allowances for mothers, which were instituted in England and Canada immediately after the Second World War. She had formulated the theory behind this demand in a treatise titled *The Disinherited Family*, published in 1924.[67] In her view, these allowances represented pay for services rendered by women to the family. She actively and relentlessly militated in favour of their adoption by the British Parliament during the interwar period, although credit was given, in history books, to Lord Beveridge, the architect of the British welfare state.

A leading figure of British feminism, Rathbone, with *The Disinherited Family*, penned a true economic theory in which family allowances were seen as an alternative solution to a family wage based on men's wages. This wage system of the breadwinner, the man as provider, was, she felt, the cornerstone of female dependency in the family and in society. It was the central aspect of women's dependency, as nothing in the law expressly guaranteed that men had to provide food and board for their family.

In Rathbone's view, women should be able to choose the work that they judged the most appropriate for themselves, either inside or outside the home. If they chose to work in the home, they should be paid for that. Family allowances, paid every month by the state to all mothers without exception, and scaled according to the number of children, would represent compensation for their services to the family. Rathbone saw these allowances as a means of establishing the financial independence of married women and mothers.[68] However, they were not to limit the extension of community services.

Rathbone published her book in 1924, formed a pressure group (the Family Endowment Society), and was elected as an independent member of the British Parliament in 1929, putting her in a better position to promote allowances. It was only fifteen years later, in 1945, that a bill on universal family allowances

Figure 1.13 Eleanor Rathbone (1872–1946). Photograph
reproduced in Eleanor Rathbone, *The Disinherited Family*
(Bristol: Falling Wall Press, 1986), 121.

was finally voted on. This formula was exported to Canada and Quebec at the
same time.

Rathbone's struggle was long and difficult up to the very end. The initial
bill that was tabled planned for allowances to be paid to fathers rather than
mothers. Rathbone had to throw all of her weight into the cause (this was one
year before her death): she threatened Parliament that she would organize an
unprecedented women's demonstration if the bill was not changed so that the
allowances were paid directly to mothers.

Finally, the bill was amended in favour of mothers, but because the subject
was so contentious, members of Parliament were released from voting by party
line and the bill was passed by a free vote. And it was this system of universal
family allowances, paid to mothers by mail in their name, that was, as I have
said, exported to Canada at the same time.[69]

Twenty-seven years later, in 1972, as neo-feminism was booming, the British Conservative government was planning to abolish universal family allowances, replacing them with a tax credit for dependent children. Up to then independent of wages, family allowances would now be linked to the husband's salary when he represented the only family income. The response to the government's proposal was a gigantic demonstration by women. And it was in the wake of this 1973 demonstration that Power of Women, the English Wages for Housework collective, was formed; it became a pillar of the IFC, which had been formed in June 1972 in Padua.[70]

A Snag for Feminists

To close, an interesting fact: the mobilization concerning family allowances in Rathbone's time and those organized by Wages for Housework groups almost thirty years later highlighted, in these two eras of struggle, a similar type of opposition and of polarization within the feminist movement.

In the struggle to obtain family allowances in England in the interwar period, a type of opposition was undertaken similar to that used during the demands for wages for housework in the 1970s: both sets of demands were seen by the egalitarian fringe of the women's movement as contrary to the demand for equality.[71] Paying women for their domestic and childcare work, it was maintained, would only perpetuate their status of dependence in the family by likening them to children. The egalitarians preferred to demand equal wages, greater commitment by men to fatherhood, and sharing and socialization of domestic tasks, as in the Soviet Union.[72] These past oppositions were taken up almost word for word some thirty years later, during the 1970s, to object to the Wages for Housework strategy, and again in the late 1990s to oppose all forms of financial support given to a parent remaining at home.[73] This was truly a snag for feminists, to which I return in the conclusion.

But in the 1970s, what were people really objecting to? What was the political perspective of Wages for Housework? It was neither more nor less than a new school of feminist thought.

2
A Wage as a Lever of Power: The Political Perspective

Women work for nothing the world over.[1]

The demand for a wage [for housework] is the political claim par excellence, because it responds to our need for social power.[2]

In the 1970s, the idea of Wages for Housework that most people had in mind can be summarized as follows: it was simply a question of money, an essentially material, reformist demand; in addition, it would have the effect of chaining women to the home. In the women's movement – both then and now – this demand has generally been considered reactionary. It was felt – and it is still felt – that it contravenes the objective of women's social equality, as their economic liberation will be obtained through waged work, outside the home.

Essentially, this has been the lasting impression of the Wages for Housework theory and the manifesto-book in which it was first expressed, *The Power of Women and the Subversion of the Community*. In the following chapters, I intend to show that Wages for Housework was not a simple demand but a global perspective. When it is reduced to a monetary demand, the entire political analysis with which it was associated, as well as its subversive capacity, is too easily bypassed. In fact, given the intellectual tools of the era and the embryonic state of feminist research, the authors of *The Power of Women* proposed a global analysis of the gendered division of reproductive labour, constructed as "female," and a strategy to deconstruct and subvert it.[3] "This demand is not a partial and reformist request. It challenges all capitalist organization of labour and the entire traditional family structure," Mariarosa Dalla Costa and Selma James had declared in 1973 in the feminist journal *Québécoises Deboutte!*[4] "Our struggle aimed to undermine capitalism and not to fit within it," said Silvia Federici.[5] She problematized as follows the question of the Wages for Housework demand in relation to its political perspective:

Many times, the difficulties and ambiguities which women express in discussing wages for housework stem from the reduction of wages for housework to a thing, a lump of money, instead of viewing it as a political perspective. The difference between these two standpoints is enormous. To view wages for housework as a thing rather than a perspective is to detach the end result of our struggle from the struggle itself and to miss its significance in demystifying and subverting the role to which women have been confined in capitalist society.

Federici explained the dialectical link that exists between a demand and the struggle to achieve the goal as follows:

When we view wages for housework in this reductive way, we start asking ourselves: what difference could some more money make to our lives? ... [and then ask], so what? on the false premise that we could ever get that money without at the same time revolutionising – in the process of struggling for it – all our family and social relations. But if we take wages for housework as a political perspective, we can see that struggling for it is going to produce a revolution in our lives and in our social power as women.[6]

In reality, a wage is much more than money. It must be understood, in political terms, as a power relationship that structures society. To illustrate the close linkage between the Wages for Housework demand and a political perspective, I discuss the embodiment of this perspective in struggles undertaken by certain Wage for Housework groups at the time that the International Feminist Collective (IFC) was active – that is, between 1972 and 1977. This is the subject of the last three chapters.

Before plunging into the action, I sketch out in broad terms the horizon of thought that stimulated both these struggles and the general political perspective of the Wages for Housework demand as expressed by several theoreticians and in different movement documents. In other words, this chapter summarizes a theoretical corpus that constitutes a completely original contribution to the history of feminist thought.

I analyze this system of thought through several of its dimensions: a wage as lever of power under all circumstances (M. Dalla Costa), a wage to denaturalize the labour of women (Federici), heterosexuality as a component of the definition of housework (Wages Due Lesbians), African American women's specific relationship with housework (Wilmette Brown), the school and its connections to housework (Maria Pia Turri), the disciplinary function of domestic violence (Giovanna Franca Dalla Costa), and the connection between the wageless of the planet and reproductive labour (Selma James). At the centre of this perspective of thought are women – their autonomy of organization and of action making them active historical subjects, with subversive power. To give a context, I briefly describe the horizon of thought within which this perspective was situated.

A RENEWED VERSION OF MARXISM

As I mentioned at the end of Chapter 1, the Wages for Housework political analysis is situated at the confluence of an unorthodox and renewed vision of Marxism that adopts some concepts from the Italian workerist current, on the one hand, and the struggles of the anti-colonialist, feminist, student, and civil rights movements, on the other hand.[7] To opponents who accused them of "borrowing categories from the Marxist world," Wages for Housework activists would respond that Marx had devised analytic tools that, to date, were unmatched with regard to comprehension of the position and functions occupied by everyone in capitalist society.[8] And they proposed to use these tools to reject the place that Marxism reserved for women in families.

Classic Marxists saw the nuclear family as a site of consumption and of transmission of values, and not as a centre of production as such, and house-workers simply as a reserve of labour for the needs of capitalism. This was to be contested by the Wages for Housework theoreticians, who saw the family as the institutionalization of women's wageless labour – of their dependence on men – and, consequently, the institutionalization of a power hierarchy.[9] So, let us take a quick look at this renewed vision of Marxism inaugurated by Wages for Housework theoreticians.

In the Beginning Was the House, the Social Factory

Wages for Housework theoreticians saw, aside from the factory – the site of paid work – another, hidden "factory," composed of the family and its community. This was where labour power was produced and reproduced. It was "the other half of capitalist organization, the other area of hidden capitalist exploitation, *the other, hidden, source of surplus labor.*"[10] Indeed, the capitalist economic system was deployed well beyond the classic sphere of production (waged work) to encompass the sphere of reproduction of capital itself – the sphere of reproduction of labour power (unwaged work):

> Employed or not, we spend 24 hours a day working for capital in the social factory. Waged laborers spend their remaining hours "after work" reproducing themselves to return to work. Eating, sleeping, drinking, movies, fucking are all essential work which we do in order to be prepared for the next day's labor ... Women play an essential role in the social factory.[11]

Capitalism was actually a "social factory," in which each moment of women's lives became integrated with the entire production cycle. M. Dalla Costa and the other Wages for Housework theoreticians were the main artisans of the extension of this notion to the home and to women's domestic and reproductive work.[12]

> Traditionally, production has been assumed to take place in the factory. In reality, production takes place at every moment in every worker's life. Once we discovered our work in the home and the community reproduces labor power, then we began to see that the whole society is an assembly line that runs from the factory to the community and back again. Capital is created by the collective laborer: we who are shut inside the factory and we who are shut outside the factory – and therefore shut out of wages.[13]

Women's work in families was the fulcrum of this social factory – composed of the family, the neighbourhood, the community, and the social fabric – that enabled the "economic factory" to operate. This labour thus contributed to the accumulation of profit and formed the pillar upon which the capitalist system rested, and it was the capitalist system that profited the most from its unpaid nature. This free – unwaged – labour by women was extorted labour.

In the view of Wages for Housework theoreticians, the reproductive work done by women had never been considered as such and seen for what it is, as it was camouflaged under the cover of love and under the pretext that family was a site not of capital production but of consumption. These theoreticians revealed that this classic Marxist vision of the family gave a poor accounting of the consumption dispensed in families because it ignored the fact that "this consumption presupposes work done," and that "this work is housework ... done by women." Yet, "this work has never been accounted for, precisely because it is unwaged."[14]

Absence of Wages as Basis of Oppression, Waged Men as Oppressors

The unwaged nature of reproductive labour thus helped render this essential part of the productive cycle invisible. This provoked M. Dalla Costa to write, "What has been neither clear nor assumed by the organizations of the working class movement is that precisely through the wage has the exploitation of the non-wage laborer been organized. This exploitation has been even more effective because the lack of a wage hid it. That is, the wage commanded a larger amount of labor than appeared in factory bargaining. *Where women are concerned, their labor appears to be a personal service outside of capital.*"[15]

The Wages for Housework demand thus revealed the relationship between women and the capitalist system. Their work was that of reproduction – that is, procreation and maintenance, material and emotional – of labour power. Such work was part of the productive cycle of capitalism. It was a source of surplus value, though it was not paid for. Women's reproductive work was the

Figure 2.1   Cover of the main anthology of French-language essays by the Wages for Housework movement (1977).

"other pole of capitalist accumulation." In demanding a wage, women were thus claiming the wealth created by their free work, which was extorted from them.

Another twist to Marxism, as conceived up to then: to change their situation, women did not have to join the working class in waged workplaces and fight side by side with comrades. They could change their situation by fighting autonomously, starting with their own work. They could fight from their own relationship with production, on their own territory, whether it was the home, the neighbourhood, or the community – integral parts of the social factory of reproduction. Waged men, in this context, occupied a position of oppressors of women.

Because capitalist society was a wage society, capitalism governed everyone via wages. The relative power of each stratum within a social class was determined by the position that each occupied in the wage hierarchy: man or woman, "black" or "white," young or old. This meant that to the wage hierarchy corresponded a hierarchy of genders, "races," and ages.

Because the houseworker was unwaged, she was subjected to this wage relationship: the man, as wage earner and breadwinner, had the power to command and discipline her work in the home, and she was in a position of dependence and service, since she depended on his wages. To extricate themselves from oppression, women had to organize not with the oppressors but autonomously, with other women, on their own field of oppression: housework.

This led Wages for Housework theoreticians to advance a new definition of class, which was to be at the heart of the founding manifesto of the IFC in 1972: "This new definition is based on the subordination of the wageless worker

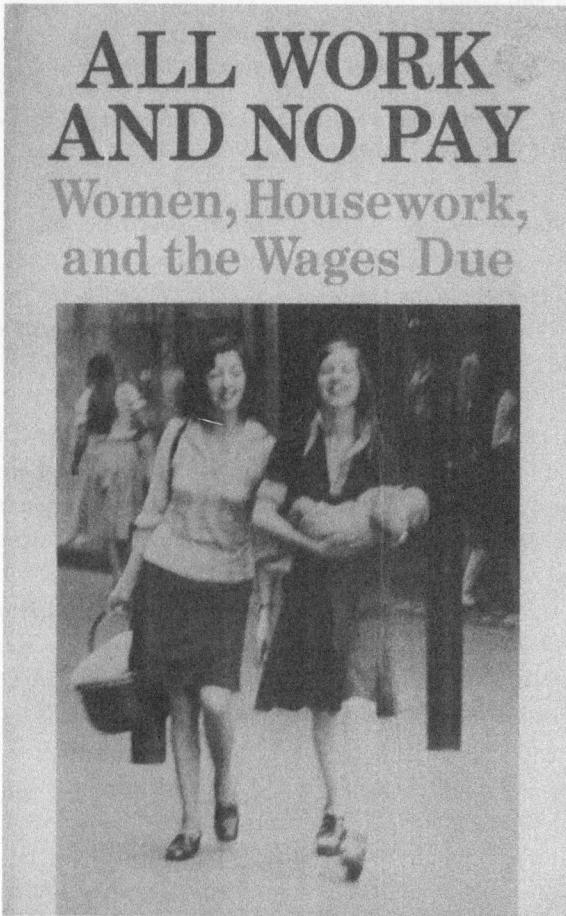

ALL WORK AND NO PAY
Women, Housework, and the Wages Due

Figure 2.2 Cover page of the main anthology of English-language essays in the Wages for Housework movement (London: Power of Women Collective; Bristol: Falling Wall Press, 1975).

to the waged worker behind which is hidden the productivity, i.e. the exploitation of the labour of women in the home and the cause of their more intense exploitation out of it."[16] In this new perspective, all categories of non-wage earners were part of the working class, which was no longer formed, as in classic Marxism, solely of "productive" waged workers. All "wageless of the world," including colonized peoples, peasant populations in the South, unemployed people, prisoners, and those working in slavery conditions, were part of the capitalist production cycle and could subvert its accumulation process.[17] This opened a space for autonomous struggle for each of these categories of people. It also reintroduced houseworkers as historical actors in social change, with a capacity for subversion. They had to organize autonomously to develop their own autonomy and power.

The Subversive Role of the Wages for Housework Demand

In the preface to the Italian edition of *The Power of Women and the Subversion of Community*, M. Dalla Costa wrote,

> When the aforementioned "Marxists" claimed that the capitalist family did not produce for capital, and was not part of social production, they repudiated as a consequence the potential social power of women ... If the production that we perform is vital to capitalism, *refusing to produce*, refusing *to work*, is a fundamental lever of social power.[18]

This is where the subversive role of the Wages for Housework demand intervened as a lever of power available to assist women in different circumstances in their struggle against their economic exploitation. If free reproductive labour was essential to the cycle of production of capital, then demanding a wage was to defy and block this process. It meant attacking the capitalist wage system and upsetting traditional measurements of wages and work. It meant attacking the hierarchical organization of work between waged and non-waged people, between the work of production of goods (done mostly by men) and the work of production and reproduction of labour power (done essentially by women). It meant attacking the hierarchical division between men and women, the division between power and non-power, inherent to the wage relationship. And finally, it meant attacking the system of dominance relations between gender and the class system. It meant politicizing the issue of housework.

Demanding a wage for housework was thus a strategy based on the historical position of women in the organization of work, truly "counterplanning from the kitchen."[19] This demand constituted a lever of power in many regards, according to M. Dalla Costa: for "negotiating the conditions for housework," for improving working conditions outside the home in the job market, for socializing housework on women's own terms, for negotiating the conditions "of procreation and of our overall health" and sexuality. In a word, to demand wages for housework constituted a lever of power to open negotiations on the *conditions of reproduction*. I revisit these points after describing the new definition of the category "women" on which the Wages for Housework perspective and strategy were founded, a definition from which it would be possible to negotiate "our living conditions in their totality."

A DEFINITION OF WOMEN THROUGH THE WORK THEY SHARE

Up to then, women "didn't count."[20] They were conceived ideologically and considered in fact to be appendages to someone else: "mother of," "wife of," "daughter of," "fiancée of," or "unattached." The foundation upon which these different roles were constructed went unperceived, and as a result, the basis for these divisions was not understood.

Wages for Housework activist-theoreticians identified the common foundation for these different roles: housework. For each of these roles was based on the variable quantity and quality of housework that women had to execute at home, with all that this work involved. The "highest-productivity" housework fell to wives and mothers. Sisters, daughters, and fiancées were "in apprenticeship," and they were initiated to this work as they waited to become wives and mothers. This was a *cycle of housework* that required certain roles during the apprenticeship period (daughters, sisters, fiancées, and so on) and others during the high-productivity period (wives and mothers).

Therefore, a stratification was created between those women with high housework productivity and those who refused to engage in the cycle of housework. One thinks here of the wife who refuses to bear children; of the woman who, although she has children, does not want to become a wife; of the woman who does not wish to become either wife or mother; and so on. These women offered fairly low housework productivity. In short, this division among women was constructed on the basis of the different levels of housework productivity imposed upon them. It had never been questioned and therefore contributed to codifying the hierarchy among women.

In addition, as wives, mothers, daughters, and sisters, women were generally defined in terms of social class: either as proletarian, if the man's wage was a proletarian one, or as bourgeois, if his income was at that level. No one took note, however, that in none of these cases did women earn their own money for the work that they did. This, above all, was what determined their lack of power. They were thus defined generally (including by classic Marxists) according to their husband's class, and according to the power hierarchy among men within the classes. Wages for Housework theoreticians would define them differently.

"Workers of the House"

Whereas other feminist currents at the time defined the foundation of women's oppression as being their biology (Shulamith Firestone), or the sexism of patriarchal culture, or their sexual domination (Kate Millett), Wages for Housework theoreticians defined the category of women and their exploitation in capitalist society specifically on the basis of the work that they all performed:

> If we, on the contrary, define women precisely on the basis of *their* work, we must assume that all the women who on a mass scale do housework, [and see their] labor power consumed in the process of producing and reproducing labor power, are *workers;* they are the *workers of the house.* They are workers without a wage of their own, but they are workers. The fact that on a mass scale women are unwaged workers has determined such a radical lack of power in working class women as to determine a lack of power even among bourgeois women. In fact, the wife of a powerful man, for example, certainly enjoys a reflected power through her husband, but she is not powerful on her own. The wife of a man who has a low level of power has little power because of the level of power of her husband, but to his low power she adds her own lack of power. (2, emphasis in original)

The stratifications built among women further reduced their capacity to establish a common field for struggle. These divisions were based on "aesthetic" assessments (beautiful/ugly) and moral judgments (saint/prostitute). It is important to emphasize as well that high housework productivity has always received a positive moral judgment (she who works "like an animal" is a saint), whereas rejection of or rebellion against housework has always been judged very negatively (she who refuses to do her work is not a good woman).

Other constructed stratifications included that between a woman who "didn't work" (the houseworker) and one who "worked" (the woman who had another job – this one paid – outside the home). Among the latter there was another division: between those who had a "clean job" (employees, workers, secretaries, and so on) and those who had a "dirty job" (prostitutes"). This last stratification concealed the fact that both categories of women were houseworkers and that "prostitution is nothing but socialized housework."[21]

> [Leftist groups have] always approached women starting from the divisions of power capital has created among us, taking them as "natural" and therefore "inevitable" ... By ignoring the "housewife" as "too weak," "non-organizable" or "too backward" or even "non-existent as a worker," these political forces deprived women of any possibility for a mass organization. All women, in fact, as we well know, are fundamentally "housewives," that is, "workers in the

Figure 2.3   Potere femminile e sovversione sociale
(The power of women and the subversion of
community), Padua, March 1972.

home," for housework is the first and only front where we all are and which
determines all aspects of our life. (3)

As the theoreticians said, "But nobody ever started from this," and that is why
no one was able to "see" housework as the determining factor in the organization of women's lives as a whole or the interdependence of all aspects of their
situation. As a consequence,

nobody ever tried to build an organizational continuity between the women
who work in the home and the women who also work outside the home ...
they had never even tried to make an organizational connection between the
women who work in the big factory and the women who work in the small
factory, the women who work in the countryside and the women who work
in the city ...
We, the women of the [Veneto Wages for Housework] Committee had
started precisely in the opposite way, by assuming that the power divisions
capital has created must be destroyed ... We, as women, can achieve this growth

of power only if we organize ourselves starting from that battlefront in which we all are, that is housework. Only in this way will it be possible, always and in every place, to bargain around the entire work we do: housework first of all and, in addition to it, also the secondary jobs, and thus bargain around the entire wage, the entire work-time, and the entire conditions of our life, in one word, our social power which is based on them. (3)

The Interdependence of All Aspects of Women's "Condition"

How could "workers in the home" move into action? To start with, by ending the isolation of women's struggles: isolation within the four walls of the house, isolation of waged workers in relation to houseworkers, isolation of daycare activists from one neighbourhood to another. Also, isolation of the patient in the doctor's office, who was unaware that the other patients languishing in the doctor's waiting room would receive the same cavalier treatment as she was receiving. Isolation of these women from other women in hospitals – all of them unaware that their individual revolt could be combined with that of the others.

From that point on, the central point of interdependence of all aspects of women's situation *as women* had to be highlighted: "Housework not only claims all of us, but it is the work which determines all other aspects of our life"; "Every moment of our lives is work for capital, to reproduce labour power." For example, making oneself beautiful to go to work – capitalism profited from this. "Our perspective is that everything, as long as it is commanded to us, must be paid for to us" (6).

> Our struggle for wages for housework does not end with a certain wage level, but with the destruction of their command over us to make us work ... Only if our time is not commanded by others, only if our space is not confined by other, will we be able to develop our full capacities: the capacity to understand, to invent, to act and to build completely different social relations. (6)

The Wages for Housework demand in fact offered women a new perspective from which to act, and "the power to see with new eyes her life" (5).

A WAGE AS LEVER OF POWER

In *Le operaie della casa*, published in 1975, M. Dalla Costa analyzed the limitations of the strategies used by the women's movement, and then concretely clarified and detailed the subversive significance of the Wages for Housework demand.[22]

The Losing Strategies of the Women's Movement

In general, three items had been on the women's movement's agenda for action since the beginning: work outside the home and its attendant forms of discrimination, the socialization of services, and overall conditions for procreation and sexuality. Although the women's movement was almost unanimous in recognizing and denouncing housework as the first link in the chain of women's exploitation, it "leapt from denouncing the unpaid nature of housework to the struggle on the front of outside work, and the struggle in favour of daycare" (22). Indeed, the solutions advanced by the women's movement up to then to break the chain of exploitation focused on the "alternative" of work outside the home. And to those who were already working outside the home and were unsatisfied, the women's movement offered a fight to obtain public services such as daycare. In M. Dalla Costa's view, neither of these struggles was a winning strategy for women, as they "do not respond to women's interests and do not succeed in improving their overall quality of life" (20).

In addition, these calls to action were seen as separate and independent from each other. There seemed to be no understanding that housework was the "common root of these areas of struggle." The result was that it was impossible to "organize a collective power relationship that could link all of these areas and, through this connection, create a new lever of power that could result in a real possibility of victory" (20).

The women's movement did build levers of power, notably through its fight against discrimination in the waged workplace and for obtaining high-quality public services that would enable women to have more free time and greater possibilities for social life. But these were partial and weak victories: by simply denouncing housework without going further, as did many factions of the feminist movement, the movement was implicitly accepting that this work would be done for free.

> Taking wagelessness as a starting point means ... holding the key to understanding all other aspects [of oppression] ... On the other hand, taking one of the many aspects of housework as a starting point and ignoring its wagelessness means not recognizing fundamentally that it is work ... Yet, we have never started the fight against wagelessness, against the lack of compensation for housework, even though the organization of work outside the home has also imposed an increasingly intense pace of work within the home. As a consequence, we have seen the results of our struggles continually vanish. (29)

Housework, M. Dalla Costa reminds us, was the primary work of women all over the world, and it determined the living conditions and quality of life for each one of them. "The fight must therefore open from this front, from the housework that we unanimously denounce as being our first area of exploitation and oppression ... Up to today, housework has been free. Starting today, let's start the fight for it to be waged" (23).

Let us look at how this demand was fashioned into a more concrete lever of power. The perspective of *Le operaie della casa* was inspired, as we will see, by a union strategy that was adapted to the field of social reproduction and reproductive work. It involved *negotiating the conditions for social reproduction*, starting to "be able to 'contract' like individuals, and as individuals, for our entire sphere of individual freedom" (39). Wages played a central role in a wage society: "Under capitalism, having money of our own is the only guarantee of being able to situate ourselves as individuals, to be able to fight freely on our own behalf" (28).[23]

A Lever of Power to Negotiate Conditions for Housework

Demanding a wage meant, first, demystifying the belief that housework is not real work. It meant women discovering themselves as workers. From this position, they could, for example, fight to define the scope of this work: determine the length of the workday and the services to be offered, and lighten and shorten the workday. Unacceptable working conditions would no longer seem so normal. "We have the right, like all workers, to fight against such working conditions" (34).

Negotiating a wage also gave a woman greater power to escape a husband's abuse. If a woman had a wage, it would be more difficult to require from her "unlimited and unconditional servitude. We have the right to sit down, smoke a cigarette, take time for ourselves, go to the movies or on vacation" (35). And if there was a case of contestation or dispute, her wage would give her the opportunity to oppose it and, if necessary, the means to leave.

A Lever of Power to Improve Working Conditions Outside the Home

A wage for housework would also give women a lever of power to improve working conditions outside the home.[24] "The fundamental market for female labour power is the family; her work contract is marriage," wrote M. Dalla Costa. "The job market for labour power outside the family is closely tied to the cycle or marriage and the conditions of housework." Indeed, the type of work generally offered to women in the waged labour market was based on the experience and knowledge gained through housework. These jobs essentially reproduced the roles that women played in the home (waitress, hairdresser, telephone operator, daycare worker, and so on). This was why they were so poorly paid. Why would bosses pay more for tasks that were performed free of charge at home?[25]

The more women put a price on all the tasks involved in housework and what came with it (smiling, being sweet, consoling, performing all sorts of small

Figure 2.4 Document listing the activities marking
the first public demonstration in favour of Wages
for Housework in Italy (Mestre, March 8–10, 1974),
organized by the Comitato Triveneto per il salario al
lavoro domestico (Committee of the Three Venices for
Wages for Domestic Work).

favours, being at the beck and call of those around her, and so on), and the higher
this price was, "the more strength we will have to negotiate the cost of our work
outside with the bosses" (36). In fact, the feminist movement uncovered and
denounced hidden tasks such as smiling. "Who thought of smiling as a job?
And yet, it has to be said: smiling is a job" (37). It was one of the requirements
of many jobs filled by women.

> Did they want to force us to smile, to degrade us in this way? Well. These
> forced smiles have to be paid for. The more expensive we make them, the less
> we will be forced to do them. Until one day when, in the kitchen and in the
> department store and in the office, we will smile only when we want to! (37)
>
> ...

If women had a wage in return for work done in the home, no boss would be able to offer employees lower wages and worse working conditions than those of housework.

That means that in fighting to acquire a wage for housework, we are engaging in a struggle that has immediate repercussions on work outside ... In fighting on the terrain of housework, we are changing the conditions for marriage and those of the female labour market and, as a consequence, the conditions of the market for the male workforce. (38–39)

It also meant that the struggle for wages for housework opened up to new levels of power beyond the home. The Wages for Housework theoreticians and activists were thus not "against work outside" in the sense that they were "for work in the home":

We are against both because of what they represent for women up to the present, and we want to have a lever of power to determine new conditions for both types of work, conditions that reflect our interest in a less tiresome and more social life. The fight for wages for housework is a fight that opens to a level of power on housework itself and, as a consequence, on work outside. (39)

A Lever of Power to Socialize Housework on Women's Own Terms

Instead of demanding a wage for housework, why not demand socialization of housework? This was the objection often raised within the feminist movement to those demanding a wage for housework. But the Wages for Housework demand was founded on the fact that total socialization of housework would clearly be impossible, as housework was not simply a set of material tasks to be executed, but also "production of nonmaterial things, such as affection and comfort."

As for housework services that were already socialized, their scarcity and poor quality reflected the weak position of women: having never had a housework contract as such, "we have had no bargaining power to determine the quality and quantity of these services, which should have transformed certain housework services into socialized structures" (42). This was the case, for example, for care of the elderly and childcare, traditionally dispensed free of charge by women in the home. The state therefore had good reason not to develop such services, or to raise their quality. The result, M. Dalla Costa notes, was that in Italy the Church controlled things, and this was made possible "precisely because of our weakness ... The delay in service provision was made on our backs" (43):

If we want to be the ones to dictate the conditions of any particular service (when we want, where, how, and so on), we must build the power to be able to dictate them. And this power is built by putting a price tag on the work that we want to partially transform into service, and thus by beginning immediately to fight for wages for housework. At that time, we will be able to determine not only the quantity but also the quality of services that we are interested in having. (44)

The demand for a wage was a "necessary transition" toward undertaking, for example, a struggle around the question of rent – "not only to fight against increases, but even to require that housing be free" (49) and of high quality. Other demands that M. Dalla Costa mentioned included that housing be situated in areas far from sources of pollution and close to services and green spaces.

The struggle to obtain a wage for housework also entailed a snowball effect, opening the prospect for new political struggle for all other strata of unwaged workers, thus constituting a lever of power for unwaged workers in general – as well as for those who depended on the free and invisible work of women and benefited from their services, such as the elderly, the young, the sick, and people with handicaps. The process of women's struggle for their autonomy as social individuals "catalyzes the same desire and process of struggle among those who depend on the labour of women ... Putting the issue of our power on the agenda means also putting on that agenda those from each exploited and oppressed stratum that depends on us" (44, 47).

The fight for wages for housework put new wind in the movement's sails, and provided a new autonomous space, to all of these categories of powerless people.

A Lever of Power to Negotiate the Conditions for Procreation, Women's Overall Health, and Sexuality

The conditions for women's procreation and general health were also determined by women's lack of money and power. In this sphere, the Wages for Housework struggle would "also change the conditions under which we give birth, the quality of contraception, and the conditions of our overall health." In this regard, too, a wage would act as a lever of power:

- To impose our needs on medical research, in order to have contraceptives that are safe and harmless to our health; so that our diseases – for example, vaginitis ... will be properly treated; so that our conditions for childbirth will be improved: childbirth will occur without pain or danger to us or our children.

- To force the state to supply complete and comprehensible sexual information to everyone.
- To force the state to supply us with free medical assistance that we control. We want our own sickness fund, like other workers.
- To have all the children we want with the guarantee that we can bring them up comfortably.
- To have legal and free abortions now, but also to eliminate abortions as violence and risk implicit to our condition as women. (51)

The struggle to obtain wages from the state for housework helped break dependence on men and to free a capacity for struggle in other areas, including sexuality. Indeed, this process of struggle was also "destined to uncover a new field for the very manifestation of sexuality" (53). We shall return to this.

A WAGE TO "DENATURALIZE" HOUSEWORK[26]

Wages for Housework had a very specific meaning: to achieve financial autonomy, to escape the state of "powerlessness"; and to have the capacity to reduce the duration and extent of reproductive work, have the power to reject it, if applicable, and be in a position to manage its socialization. It was not about "institutionalizing the role of houseworker," as the opponents of the strategy believed, but, on the contrary, about destroying this role as an integral facet of the "nature" of women. The stake in Wages for Housework was, in a way, about breaking the biological definition of woman as capitalism had crystallized it by imprisoning them in the role of houseworker. "For the fact that housework is unwaged has given this socially imposed condition a natural appearance ('femininity') that affects us all wherever we go."[27]

A Wage to Separate "Nature" and Work

It was about this important aspect of the Wages for Housework perspective, among others, that Silvia Federici, co-founder of the New York Wages for Housework Committee, wrote in *Wages against Housework* in 1975, the year that the IFC was most active:

> Housework had to be transformed into a natural attribute rather than be recognised as a social contract because from the beginning of capital's scheme for women this work was destined to be unwaged. Capital had to convince us that it is a natural, unavoidable and even fulfilling activity to make us accept our unwaged work ... This fraud that goes under the name of love and marriage affects all of us, even if we are not married, because *once housework was totally naturalised and sexualised,* once it became a feminine attribute, all of us as females are characterised by it. (2, 4; emphasis in original)

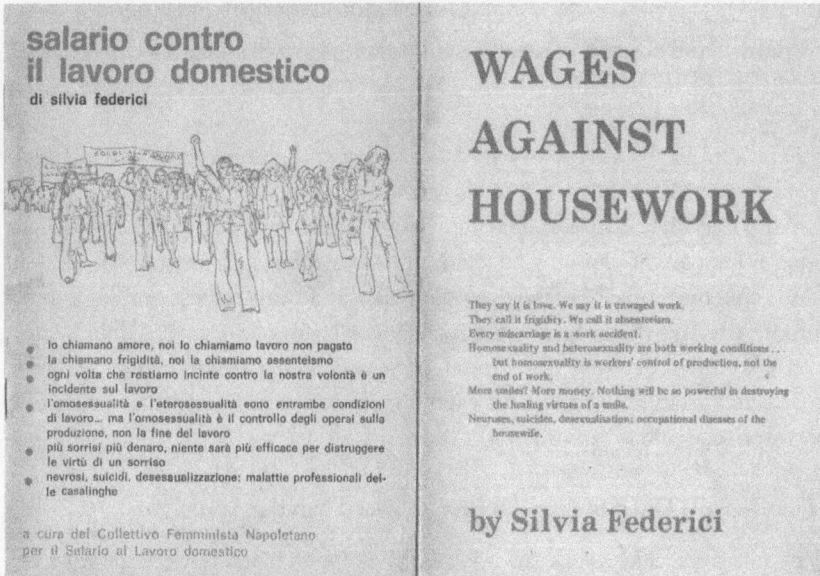

salario contro
il lavoro domestico
di silvia federici

- lo chiamano amore, noi lo chiamiamo lavoro non pagato
- la chiamano frigidità, noi la chiamiamo assenteismo
- ogni volta che restiamo incinte contro la nostra volontà è un incidente sul lavoro
- l'omosessualità e l'eterosessualità sono entrambe condizioni di lavoro... ma l'omosessualità è il controllo degli operai sulla produzione, non la fine del lavoro
- più sorrisi più denaro, niente sarà più efficace per distruggere le virtù di un sorriso
- nevrosi, suicidi, desessualizzazione: malattie professionali delle casalinghe

a cura del Collettivo Femminista Napoletano
per il Salario al Lavoro domestico

WAGES
AGAINST
HOUSEWORK

They say it is love. We say it is unwaged work.
They call it frigidity. We call it absenteeism.
Every miscarriage is a work accident.
Homosexuality and heterosexuality are both working conditions...
but homosexuality is workers' control of production, not the end of work.
More smiles? More money. Nothing will be so powerful in destroying the healing virtues of a smile.
Neuroses, suicides, desexualization: occupational diseases of the housewife.

by Silvia Federici

Figure 2.5 Cover pages of the Italian and English editions of *Wages against Housework* by Silvia Federici.

Federici explains that, as it is "natural" for women to execute certain tasks, it is expected that all women will execute them, even those who have the means to get out of doing them. All women live under this law of "nature." "Even if we do not serve a specific man, we are all placed in a servant relation with regard to the male world as a whole" (4).

This analysis enables Federici to apprehend the eminently subversive implications of a Wages for Housework perspective: "*It is the demand by which our nature ends and our struggle begins because just to want wages for housework means to refuse that work as the expression of our nature,* and therefore to refuse precisely the female role that capital has invented for us" (4, emphasis in original).

Earning a wage established a separation between the person and the work that she was doing: she was then a party to a social contract. "But exploited as you might be, *you are not that work*" (2, emphasis in original). Therefore, "to ask for wages for housework will by itself undermine the expectations society has of us." It is to fight "unambiguously and directly against our social role" (5). And that "does not mean to say that if we are paid we will continue to do it. It means precisely the opposite." It means "the first step towards refusing to do it, because the demand for a wage makes our work visible, which is the most indispensable condition to begin to struggle against it, both in its immediate aspect as housework and its more insidious character as femininity" (5).

The role of a wage was therefore crucial, not only to make the work of reproduction visible but also to make "our femaleness as labour" – women's role

– visible. It was for women to refuse to accept their work as biological destiny. In contrast, the absence of a wage sunk them into invisibility. The message of the demand was clear:

> *From now on they have to pay us because as females we do not guarantee anything any longer.* We want to call work what is work so that eventually we might rediscover what is love and create what will be our sexuality which we have never known ... From now on we want money for each moment of it, so that we can refuse some of it and eventually all of it. In this respect nothing can be more effective than to show that our female virtues have a calculable money value, until today only for capital, increased in the measure that we were defeated; from now on against capital *for us* in the measure we organise our power. (6, emphasis in original)[28]

"The Overalls Did Not Give Us More Power Than the Apron"

Why not trade housework for a job on the labour market? Because working outside the home did nothing to change the role of women: "The second job not only increases our exploitation, but simply reproduces our role in different forms" (6). Indeed, jobs for women were generally "feminine" jobs: waitressing, teaching, secretarial, nursing – that is, extensions of housework and reproductive work, "all functions for which we are well trained in the home" (6).

> Wages for housework will be much more educational than trying to prove that we can work as well as them, that we can do the same jobs. We leave this worthwhile effort to the "career woman" ... And we don't have to prove that we can "break the blue collar barrier." A lot of us broke that barrier a long time ago and have discovered that the overalls did not give us more power than the apron; if possible even less, because now we had to wear both and had less time and energy to struggle against them. (8)

In Federici's view, "We will never achieve any real change unless we attack our female role at its roots [, that is,] if we do not first establish that our work is work. Unless we struggle against the totality of it we will never achieve victories with respect to any of its moments" (6).

HETEROSEXUALITY: A COMPONENT OF HOUSEWORK

Another important dimension of the theoretical Wages for Housework perspective involved analysis of heterosexuality as a component of the definition of housework:

They say it is love. We say it is unwaged work.

They call it frigidity. We call it absenteeism.

Every miscarriage is a work accident.

Homosexuality and heterosexuality are both working conditions ...
    but homosexuality is workers' control of production, not the end of work.

More smiles? More money. Nothing will be so powerful in destroying
    the healing virtues of a smile.

Neuroses, suicides, desexualisation: occupational diseases of the housewife. (1)

Analyzing sexuality through the prism of housework was a shocking idea
at the time. Conceiving heterosexual intercourse in this way, as a clause in the
contract for married women's work that was their marriage contract – and
compliance with this clause as a condition for their material maintenance – was
an even more shocking idea.[29] Yet, the establishment of connections between
the economic dependence of women at home on men and their lack of power
over their sexuality was coherent with the Wages for Housework perspective.

"We are the only ones whose sexuality and emotions have been so profoundly
stifled and deviated in 'service,'" M. Dalla Costa wrote. For many women, she
felt, "it is sexuality that is the breaking point for their oppression and exploitation, and thus the primary field for their rebellion."[30] "Female infidelity," one of
the manifestations of this rebellion, was, however, historically exercised to their
risk and peril and – for many of them – at a high price.

Sexuality was in effect stifled and channelled into being an instrument of
production and reproduction of human beings and their labour power, and into
the provision of sexual services to men. Sexual services were thus, in this context,
considered to be work, a component of housework, and the first condition for
provision of these services was heterosexuality.

According to Federici, "The subordination of our sexuality to reproduction
of labor power has meant that heterosexuality ... has been imposed on us as
the only acceptable sexual behavior."[31] Sexuality was therefore a site of power
relations between men and women. Lesbianism was socially unacceptable, as
it was a form of sex that was both "non-productive" and "non-procreative":
"Lesbianism is condemned as a form of deviancy because it is a direct attack
on the work-sexual discipline imposed on women in capitalist society."[32] As
M. Dalla Costa wrote in "Women and the Subversion of Community," "In this
sense, the gay movement is the most massive attempt to disengage sexuality and
power."[33] This aspect of the theoretical production of the Wages for Housework
current was explored, within the IFC, by Wages Due Lesbians groups.[34]

In 1975, lesbians active within Wages for Housework groups decided to
organize in autonomous groups, adopting the same Wages for Housework
strategy. They took the name Wages Due Lesbians.[35] The first Wages Due
Lesbians group, the one in Toronto, "came out" during the IFC conference in

Montreal in February 1975, with the launch of a text called "Fucking is Work."[36] I give an overview here of some of the documents produced by Wages Due Lesbians to highlight the originality of their analyses and their contribution to the multi-dimensional Wages for Housework perspective.[37]

Heterosexuality Is Not in Our Genes

The theoreticians of the Wages for Housework perspective conceived of the family as a production centre that extorted the work of women. Wages Due Lesbians pushed the analysis of the family further by substantiating the point that the production centre that was the family, and that extorted the work of women, was heterosexual.

Heterosexuality was a component of housework and therefore was "part of the definition of our housework."[38] Heterosexuality "is a morality that says that all women 'naturally' serve men sexually (and in other ways – emotionally, physically etc.). We know that many women are lesbians, many women are 'frigid,' many women are celibate, so we know that heterosexuality is not in our genes." Rather, heterosexuality was "in our training for the work that we must do. We create and service the workers of the world (including ourselves). The existence of lesbianism ... exposes sexual servicing as WORK."[39]

> The existence of lesbianism helps define the sexual needs of women. It is the expression of all women's need to control our own sexuality, just as demanding community controlled daycare is an expression of our need to be free from the responsibility of training new workers. It is not in itself a solution to our sexual needs. It is not in itself a victory. But it is a struggle against capital's institutionalisation of our sexuality nevertheless.[40]

Lesbianism was a refusal to serve men sexually and emotionally, the authors continued, and it therefore consisted of a struggle against this work. Taking care of oneself and another woman – the lesbian relationship – constituted "a form of workers' control." All women struggled in one way or another against housework, and lesbianism was one of these ways, notably as it pointed out "the work involved in heterosexuality."[41]

By becoming visible, lesbians made it clear that they were fighting against the institutionalization of women's sexuality. Lesbianism was in fact often used by society as a threat to keep women on the "right path" – as in the accusation that a lesbian was "not a true woman." Instead of being paralyzed by this threat, lesbians could use it, according to Wages Due Lesbians, by affirming the possibility of such a sexual choice. Even in her individual relations with a man, a woman could always, as needed, leave open the possibility of lesbianism. It was a sort of lever of power for women, and it was why it was important for lesbians to be visible in the Wages for Housework movement. The strength that we have gained as lesbians in the movement, proclaimed Wages Due Lesbians, is something that we must share with all women.

"Why Lesbians Want Wages for Housework"

Many people thought that single women, and particularly lesbians, were free from housework.[42] This was not true, as all women were obliged to perform housework: it was an imposed role. Often, said Wages Due Lesbians, we do not like to identify ourselves as houseworkers and it is often completely understandable, considering how little power houseworkers have, whereas we want power. It is a mistake, however, to think that we can escape this work, as long as capitalism exists:

> People sometimes say that single women don't do housework (especially lesbians). ALL women do housework. That's our role. That is what we are all expected to do ... When we work outside the home, much of the work we do is unpaid housework. We have all been taught the skills of licking ass, making coffee, being feminine, keeping quiet, etc. But this work is not included in our job description. This training is not included in our pay packet ... And when we have finished our job, we don't go home to a wife. We have to cook our own supper, do our own laundry, clean up, pay the bills, etc. We maintain ourselves as workers, and this too is unpaid work. As is our occasionally being raped; whether we are lesbian or straight, we are assumed to be heterosexual, even though we have tried to refuse the work of fucking.[43]

In this view, lesbianism was "the organized form women's struggle against fucking-as-work has taken."[44]

Figure 2.6   Poster by Black Women for Wages for Housework and the New York Wages for Housework Committee. (CWMA, box 624.12)

Wages Due Lesbians organized autonomously within Wages for Housework groups because their members doubted that heterosexuals would struggle for and defend the interests of lesbians. They believed, however, that it was important to struggle within the Wages for Housework movement not only to have their own voices heard but also because women, both lesbian and hetero-sexual, were socially identified as houseworkers. They considered it imperative to self-organize to end their exploitation as women, and this struggle was conveyed through the Wages for Housework demand.

Wages Due Lesbians thus demonstrated that the lesbian movement was not uniquely a movement concerning "lifestyle" and different sexual choices, but also a movement against the work extorted from women by the capitalist orga-nization of labour, and against divisions among women. Wages Due Lesbians wanted the movement to draw "greater strength from these contradictions," without "denying the respective autonomy of women whose immediate interests do not coincide."[45]

Exposing the unnatural character of heterosexuality, analyzing (hetero)sexual relations as work done free of charge in the context of marriage and extorted from women in this relationship, represented, in 1975, a truly revolutionary theoretical innovation. Lesbianism had never before been analyzed through this prism. Situating the struggle of lesbians in a horizon of Marxist thought, within the Wages for Housework perspective, was also a completely unprecedented phenomenon, even within lesbian currents of thought at the time.[46]

The Wages for Housework perspective was obviously broad enough to allow for women of many identities and in multiple situations to rub shoulders, mobilize, and form coalitions. It was also broad and inclusive enough to allow another category of women, racialized women, to make their unique voices heard and the interest of their struggle felt. This was the case for African American women.

THE DISTINCTIVE RELATIONSHIP BETWEEN AFRICAN AMERICAN WOMEN AND HOUSEWORK

The inclusive potential of the Wages for Housework perspective was high-lighted in an essay, *The Autonomy of Black Lesbian Women*, by Wilmette Brown of Black Women for Wages for Housework. This group was formed, as we will see in the next chapter, following the Welfare Conference organized by the New York Wages for Housework Committee in April 1976. Brown's essay was later among the seminal texts inaugurating Black feminist criticism as an academic discipline in the United States.[47]

The purpose of the Wages Due Lesbians conference in Toronto, at which Brown's essay was first presented, was to clarify various aspects of the meaning of lesbian autonomy. In her presentation, Brown discussed what autonomy meant for African American, racialized, and lesbian women. She felt that this autonomy had to be exercised on three levels: with regard to African American men, with regard to white women, and with regard to black heterosexual women.[48] In her view, the situation and struggles of black women exposed the meaning of racism and sexism.

Multi-dimensionality of the Struggle for Autonomy

Because of racism, black men had less access to wages than did white men. The scarcity of money and absence of wages in the African American community meant more work for black women, as it forced them to accept any job available. However, even if black men had much less power than white men – less access to education, training, and decent wages – the "power of the masculine wage" nevertheless ruled also in the African American community. In short, black men had power over black women.

In fact, the Black Liberation movement of the 1960s did not mean liberation for African American women, as the organizations of this movement were founded on "the ideology of Black male sexual superiority" (3). A number of women left these organizations at the end of the decade, and this often meant that the organizations crumbled, for they were "built on the backs of Black women, who were doing the housework ... We were the backbones of these organizations" (4). Now, black women had to organize independently from black men – and from white women as well.

White women had privileged access to the wages of white men. They enjoyed what one might call "protection of the wage" (even if this protection was quite relative depending on class). Historically, black women did not have such access, notably because of the fact that during slavery times it was difficult for them to aspire to marriage, and thus to the protection brought by a wage.

In the United States, a division of labour emerged from slavery that defined white women as "ladies": the "white woman" object had the characteristics of beauty, femininity, an object of love placed on the pedestal. For black women, there were no such criteria for femininity and beauty. The counterparts of "ladies" were "mammies": white women's servants, but also prostitutes seeking access to men's wages, and illegitimate mothers. Given this division of labour between white and black women, and given the power – relative, of course – of white women over black women, the latter had to organize autonomously:

We organize on the basis of the particular conditions of our lives as Black women, and the particular nature of our struggle which is a constant battle against scarcity, against indignity, and against self-hatred. And we organize autonomously to struggle for wages for housework from the vantage point of our particular situation to do away with our work as Black people and to do away with our work as women. (5)

Finally, Brown spoke about black lesbians' need for autonomy from black heterosexual women, and of the extra challenge represented by the fact of defining oneself as lesbian in the African American community. Both the slavery past of the United States and capitalism had constructed black people as having great sexual potential, according to Brown. The black man was thus defined sexually. Among black women, this definition was conveyed by the representation of the black woman as a prostitute. In this context,

> [for] the Black lesbian, who is refusing the sexual work of relating to men, and who is refusing the working conditions of femininity that go along with servicing men sexually, it means that the Black woman lesbian is a superfreak. Because not only is she a freak in relation to other women – because she is refusing that heterosexual work, she is a freak from Blackness as well. Because Blackness under capital is defined sexually. And Black people themselves, Black men themselves, during the '60s took up that same definition of Black people as sexual because it was a way of reinforcing their own male power – which is heterosexuality. So that the Black lesbian must organize autonomously of Black heterosexual women because we are the freaks; and unless we state our needs first, our needs will not be articulated and they will not be struggles for – the satisfaction of those needs will not be struggles for ...
>
> Because we have to be visible. And the only way that we can be visible is to be autonomous. Because all Black women are not heterosexual ... The only way for us to connect with other Black lesbians is to be visible ... So that we organize to be visible ... to put forward our own interests, to put forward our own particular vantage point of struggle. (6)

The Challenge of the Multiple Identities of African American Women

Being black and lesbian thus represented a major challenge, according to Brown: "It's a challenge both to our sexual identity, the sexual identity of women: it's a challenge also to our racial identity". (7). Woman, black, and lesbian: these were the multiple identities of many African American women.[49]

And this was how the challenge was met, in Brown's words:

> The perspective of wages for housework makes it possible for Black lesbian women to organize autonomously with the possibility of getting something by organizing. By getting money, which is the power to struggle to be lesbian and which is the power for many Black women who are trapped in marriages now – because of dependency on the male wage – to come out as lesbian ... The wages for housework perspective ... also made it possible for Black lesbian women like myself to be able really for the first time to connect with Black heterosexual women ... The wages for housework perspective has made

possible ... for us to go beneath that appearance of difference to the fact that all Black women are struggling against housework and for money to survive. It makes it possible for us to see that Black women with ten children who are on welfare struggling ... for money directly from the state are making the same struggle I am making, which is for money against dependency on the power of men. And that perspective – that wages for housework perspective – then, has made it possible for me for the first time in my life to be able to connect with other Black women in whatever situation, because we are all struggling against housework, against heterosexual discipline, heterosexual work discipline, and for money – to be independent. (7–8)

To become visible, black lesbians had to create autonomous organizations. It was urgent to create solidarity with other black lesbians so that they could emerge from isolation – come out of the closet. The Wages for Housework perspective made this solidarity with all black women, and all other women, possible: "Because the wages of all women are lower than the wages of all men[,] [a]ll women are subordinate to all men" (9). According to Brown, women's autonomy, which was necessary, could not be allowed to have the effect of dividing women's power; rather, it had to increase its range, which was made possible by the Wages for Housework strategy.[50]

HOUSEWORK: BEFORE, WITHIN, AND AROUND THE SCHOOL

Among its many dimensions, Wages for Housework thought also involved original reflections and feminist strategies regarding the school. In 1972, M. Dalla Costa had raised "a number of considerations concerning the relationship which ties women to the entire organisation of work inside and outside the home; that is, the relationship which, from our viewpoint, ties the community to school and to the factory." M. Dalla Costa felt that women's movements, in their struggles, first had to discover all the places where the amount of effort put into domestic labour was invisibly incorporated, in order to apprehend the full extent of unwaged reproductive work.[51] Another theoretician of the Wages for Housework current, Maria Pia Turri, a member of the Wages for Housework group in Padua, reflected more deeply on the school in this regard.[52]

In Turri's view, women had a very specific relationship with work linked to the school. This specificity concerned those who worked there, those who taught and did not teach there, those who studied there, and houseworkers, "who, as mothers, sisters, and grandmothers, devote parts of their work day to it" (173). In a word, women worked "inside, outside, and around the school." How, she wondered, could "the interests shared by all of these women [be reconstructed] ... in order to formulate a feminist strategy" of the school on this basis?

Figure 2.7   Cover of the anthology of essays on the
Italian feminist movement edited by Louise Vandelac,
L'Italie au féminisme (Paris: Tierce, 1978).

Up to then, no one, including those on the left, had perceived the complexity
of the exploitation of women inherent to the school, because no one had ever
based the explanation on housework done in the home. In Turri's view, there
was "an interdependence between domestic work and school work," and both
involved "a large share of free work"; "whether they are students, teachers,
guardians, or in other roles, women in the school are above all houseworkers"
(175).

Analyzing the specificity of work within the school system from our point
of view as women, the resemblances (and, we might say, the "homogeneity")
between this work and that in the home seemed extremely significant to
us. *In both cases, it is work of reproduction performed essentially by women and
including a good number of volunteer tasks* ... In fact, teaching, like the work of
reproduction of the other, directly exploits the great specialization of women,
a specialization that they acquire through a long apprenticeship that begins
at birth. (176, emphasis in original)

Indeed, as little girls played, they learned housework. The work of women was revealed to be an ongoing cycle, "which begins in childhood and continues without a break for their entire life." Women taught mainly in elementary school – teaching "that involves a number of unpaid functions that have their counterpart in housework: emotional and psychological tasks, 'having patience,' 'treating students affectionately,' consoling them, encouraging them when necessary, and so on" (176–77). Those who didn't teach, such as janitors, were relegated to "women's work"; secretaries, for example, were constantly asked to perform domestic tasks. There was a specificity of women's working conditions at school that referred to reproductive work in the home.

Then, at home, mothers had to become improvised teachers in order to complement the children's schoolwork and see to their leisure time, which "intensifies the pace of housework" (177–78). School also dictates the pace of the mother's workday. Indeed, for lack of adequate transportation, mothers had to drive their children to school and pick them up, as well as make and serve meals, according to the school schedule of each child.

So, Turri summarizes, "behind the pupil who arrives at school, clean, clothes washed and ironed and stomach full, there is a woman who has already performed a considerable amount of work. And yet, this unpaid work is never acknowledged." Thus, it could be said that housework took place "before, around, and within the school":

> Indeed, even if we see school as one of the most important sites of reproduc-tion of labour power, the central site of this reproduction remains the home. *It is in effect the housework done in the home that ensures reproduction of labour power, and this work then supports what continues at school.* (174, emphasis in original)

In Turri's view, the centrality of housework to the school offered all sorts of new perspectives for struggle, by making it possible to "open up the shared interests of women ... by breaking the fundamental division between waged and unwaged women," or by engaging in a fight to gradually destroy the roles that keep them divided, both within the family and within the school (176). Thus, "by making the school a site of organization and struggle with other women, women refuse to allow this public institution to continue to model and maintain the female role based on unwaged work" (178).

To make this thought a reality, the national coordination committee for the Wages for Housework campaign in Italy organized a first feminist congress on the school, held in Florence in November 1976, which brought together women from several Italian cities. Turri noted,

The organization of the congress represented the work accomplished by Wages for Housework groups to interpret, connect, and make known the struggles that develop at school, from our point of view as women, and using the entire heritage of information, observations, experiences, and contradictions that we experience with regard to school, whether we are students, janitors, mothers, teachers, or play another role. (179)

The congress was intended to raise debate over the school, and to bring together women working in different and dispersed sites, in order to allow a pooling of experiences and making it possible to "begin to think of collective actions." Proposals for struggle emerged from this feminist congress on the school, which had oriented these actions.[53]

THE DISCIPLINARY FUNCTION OF DOMESTIC VIOLENCE

Among the many components of the school of political thought elaborated by different Wages for Housework theoreticians was an in-depth reflection on domestic violence against women. Analyzed through the prism of housework, this reflection inspired struggles against violence, including demonstrations during trials involving abortion or rape. "It is by fighting against domestic working conditions that we may develop struggles that attack the very foundations of organized violence against women," wrote activists inspired by this analytic perspective.[54]

Giovanna Franca Dalla Costa targeted this aspect of Wages for Housework thought in her theoretical essay *Un lavoro d'amore*.[55] Once the family had been defined, in *The Power of Women and the Subversion of the Community*, as a site of production and reproduction of labour power, and housework as an action of producing and reproducing this labour power, G.F. Dalla Costa felt that there was a need in the movement to define the conditions for housework.

What were the specific aspects of this labour? The feminist movement of the time had already denounced violence in male-female relations and exposed its various forms. In G.F. Dalla Costa's view, the movement had to go further by "defin[ing] the specificity of this violence in an attempt to identify the causes and the mechanisms which provoke it and examine its most significant forms" (33). She sought the explanation for this violence in the nature of women's relationship with housework.

Certain groups in the women's movement considered women in the home to be slaves, working in the framework of marriage and the family in a slavery relationship. Even our mothers often exclaimed, G.F. Dalla Costa recalled, "I live the life of a slave!" or "He treats me as if I were a slave!" or "One works like a slave here!" (34). From this concept of woman-slaves, she concluded that although there were numerous similarities with slavery situations (undefined,

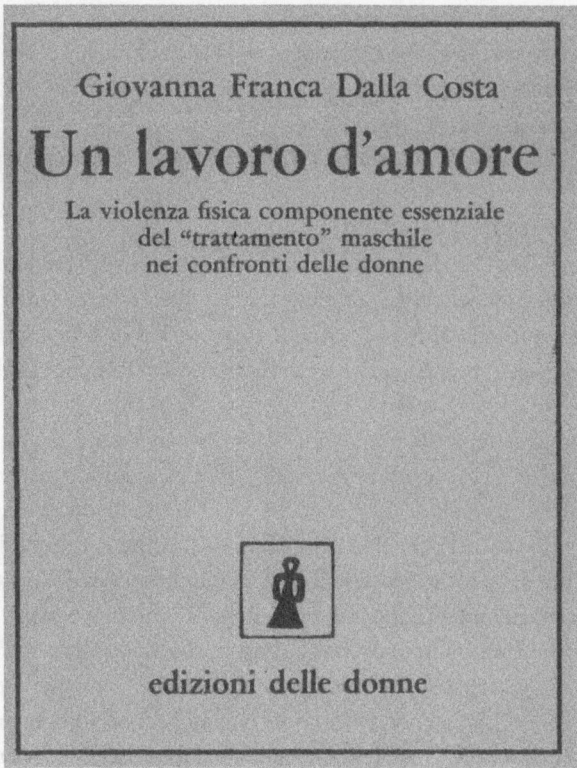

Figure 2.8   Cover of the Italian edition of *Un lavoro d'amore*
(The work of love) by Giovanna Franca Dalla Costa.

unlimited work time and types of tasks, absence of monetary compensation, lifetime sale of her labour power in the marriage, and so on), the woman in the home, according to G.F. Dalla Costa, should be classified as a worker – more precisely, a worker in discretionary, unwaged service to the family: "To describe her condition a new term is required. She is ... a houseworker" (44).

Domestic Violence Covered by "Immunity of Love"

Among the specific aspects of this work, first was its ideological justification: it was a labour of love. The relationship with the work flowed from love: just as love was not measured, so a labour of love could not be measured.[56] And since love had no price, women's labour power was thus without measure and without price. Therefore, houseworkers received in exchange no wage that might ensure them a measure of independence.

The fact that the houseworker's relationship with work was a "labour of love" for a man and for the entire family forced her – a first element of coercion – to love the boss, the husband, the primary beneficiary of her work, as she depended on his salary. Consequently, "it falls to him to be the direct discipliner of the women's work." And the instrument of this disciplinary control over the conditions of housework and reproductive work, the means of coercion, resided in physical violence, or the threat of such (53).

Having the power to command such services (since the woman depended on his salary),

> he is authorized to exercise a continual pressure that we can certainly describe as psychological violence. Every time ... that the "love contract" is transgressed, he is authorized to use physical violence, because "he loves his wife" and therefore has the right to demand that the wife "love him back." (54)

Housework and reproductive work thus incorporated, in this context, coercion – control of the work and of the conditions for its performance, as well as the threat of violence. But, specifies G.F. Dalla Costa, unlike all other masters in all other forms of exploitation relationship, the master of the house – in the role of foreman – was "covered by the immunity of love." This authorized him to use physical violence against his spouse. If this "love pact" broke, the husband's position as discipliner was revealed, and "he turns from 'love' to physical violence ... he assumes the function of judge ... of the perfection or imperfection of the housework ... Yet after having judged and determined the sanction ... it is he who will apply it, acting as a policeman after having carried out his role of judge" (55).

Foreman, judge, and cop: in every country, this was how common sense defined the functions assumed by husbands toward their wives, wrote G.F. Dalla Costa. Several proverbs attested to it (for example, "Beat your wife three times a day: even if you don't know why, she will"). And these three functions gave capitalist social organization the assurance that these tasks would be accomplished.

G.F. Dalla Costa also examined what distinguished the different situations and forms of violence to which wives might be subjected, among them sexual violence. The wife's sexual availability being inherent to the marriage contract, the exercise of coercion following a refusal to engage in sex was not considered violence or rape. The woman's economic dependency left this type of violence unresolved and insoluble.

Impunity of Husbands, Criminalization of "Fugitives from the Family" (Lesbians and Prostitutes)

Another innovative focus of analysis in *Un lavoro d'amore* concerned the state's role in domestic violence. Through its codification of the marriage contract, the state legitimized the power relations within the family based on women's unpaid work – a relationship that included violence. This was how the state ensured the impunity of the assaulter. The husband who was violent toward his wife knew that he would be neither charged nor even bothered by the police; he would not be accused of rape or of incest, as the case may be. The laws criminalizing personal violence did not apply to marital relations. The state approach to violence against women was perfectly laissez-faire, and thus enabled the husband to continually ensure family discipline over women's work. In G.F. Dalla Costa's view, this was changing under pressure from the women's movement.[57]

There were, however, cases when the man's surveillance was insufficient and the state had to exercise its authority directly through its own repressive institutions. G.F. Dalla Costa names two categories that are examples of "deviancy" from the family model: lesbians and prostitutes. These two categories of women challenged the gendered division of labour inherent to the housework contract. They broke the "love pact" and contravened the expected roles of wife and mother: prostitutes because they expected money in exchange for these relations, and lesbians by removing themselves from the obligation to provide these services in the context of a heterosexual exchange. In both cases, criminalization and stigmatization awaited them.

State violence against these groups of women consisted of demonstrating the risk of deviating from the right path of the instituted family – the risk of separating oneself from what was expected of the "good" woman, and the price to pay for deviating and becoming a "bad" woman. The prostitute was the paragon of the bad woman

> because she is the one who, in refusing to perform "for love" that which is the central task of domestic work, thus strikes at the heart of the ideology of love upon which domestic work rests. She denies, therefore, domestic work as a labor of love ... Because of this, she constitutes a menace to the reproduction of the family. She seeks direct payment, outside of family discipline. She controls its times and its forms. (90)

It was not enough simply to socially condemn prostitutes, noted G.F. Dalla Costa. A "generic social condemnation" was instituted to describe the prostitute's life as "terrible." The mass media depicted her in the most miserable terms, emphasizing the price to pay for such a life, in order to discourage all women from taking this path. Direct state violence against prostitutes included criminalization and the threat of taking away their children because of "immoral conduct on the part of the mother."[58]

Lesbians, similarly, were "fugitives" virtually as dangerous as prostitutes to the family and to the labour of love in that they contravened the fundamental rule of reproduction of the family. "The threat that [lesbians represent] is also considerable because it infringes upon the myth of heterosexuality as the only sexuality upon which the family can be based" (93). And, like prostitutes, they might lose their children to the state because of their supposed immorality.

However, in the 1970s, lesbians and sex workers organized to form a movement against the state's criminalization of their activities, thus circumventing the left, which had ignored and discredited this type of struggle. Both movements involved refusal of housework. It was similar for the women's movement, which had now acquired an organizational capacity on the international level to counter physical violence, and especially sexual violence, against women. G.F. Dalla Costa saw these as struggles against housework, because this work and what it implied determined all aspects of women's lives.

As an example of mobilization in this regard, G.F. Dalla Costa cited the International Tribunal on Crimes against Women held in Brussels in 1976, chaired by Simone de Beauvoir. At this platform for denouncing different kinds of violence perpetrated against women around the world, the closing plenary session offered an opportunity to discuss strategies for change. Among the resolutions passed almost unanimously during the plenary session by the two thousand attendees from forty countries was one presented by the IFC demanding "wages for housework for all women to be paid by all governments of the world."[59]

In G.F. Dalla Costa's view, women's struggle against housework as destiny was exploding throughout the women's movement and reconstructing women as a class. Notably, it jumped the barrier between "good" and "bad" women, between "women at home" and "women working outside," between "development" and "underdevelopment" – barriers constructed on the international level by the capitalist system with the collusion of different nation-states. According to G.F. Dalla Costa, the Wages for Housework strategy was the decisive factor in this reconstruction of the category of women, thanks to the autonomous organization of each stratum of the category of "woman" upon which the strategy rested.[60] It was the only strategy, she argued, that left no woman behind. In fact, it was "through this strategy that large sections of the movements of women prostitutes and of lesbian women [were] recomposing themselves" (113).

THE WAGELESS AND REPRODUCTIVE WORK: SEX, RACE, CLASS

The Wages for Housework perspective was inclusive enough to allow multiple identities and situations of women to coexist, mobilize, and coalesce. This was so for lesbians and racialized women from certain major cities. The Wages for Housework perspective, with the central figure of the houseworker and her pivotal work of reproduction that allowed the capitalist wage economy to function, was thus broadened into an analysis of the international division of labour.

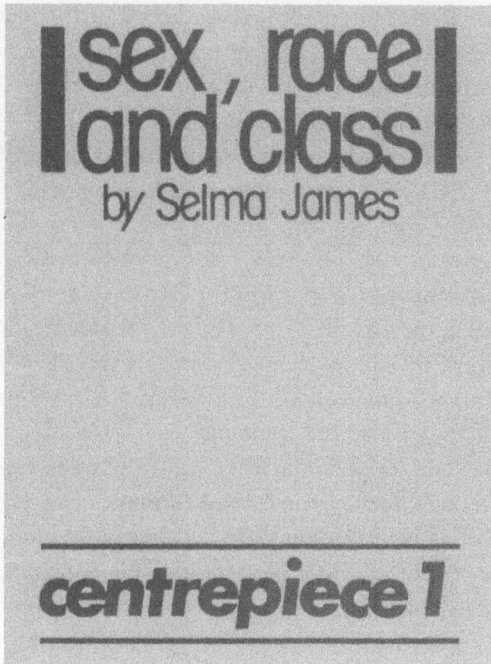

sex, race and' class
by Selma James

centrepiece 1

Figure 2.9   Reprint of *Sex, Race and Class* (London: Housewives in Dialogue, 1986) (original edition, Bristol: Falling Wall Press, 1975).

One of the important contributions of Wages for Housework thought lies, as we have seen, in the discovery that women's free work had a fundamental impact on the accumulation of capital, of profit. If this work was hidden, it is because it was unwaged in a wage society. It was its unpaid nature that made this essential part of the productive cycle of the economy invisible. The reproductive work of women was in reality a source of surplus value and constituted the other pole of capitalist accumulation.

The Hidden Face of the International Division of Labour

This discovery, which was made by Wages for Housework theoreticians and activists, led to another discovery: other activities, and other categories of persons, "*appear* to be outside of the capitalist wage labour relation because the workers themselves are wageless. *In reality*, their activities are facets of capitalist production and its division of labour," both national and international, stated Selma James, long-standing anti-colonial activist and one of the co-founders of the IFC and of the Wages for Housework group in London, Power of Women, in a document that was widely circulated at the time and is still popular today, *Sex, Race and Class*.[61]

Among these categories of people – these "strata of the hierarchy of labor powers" – were the colonized, the peasant populations of the South, students, racialized people, the unemployed, those in prison, and those working under slavery conditions. All of these wageless people on the planet were part of the cycle of global capitalist production and participated in creating its surplus value: "Race, sex, age, nation, each an indispensable element of the international division of labour. *Our feminism bases itself on a hitherto invisible stratum of the hierarchy of labour powers – the housewife – to which there corresponds no wage at all.*"[62] In other words, the hidden source of the surplus value of capitalism on the global scale resided in the exploited labour of all of these categories of wageless people and the work of reproduction of women everywhere on earth. This led German feminist Claudia von Werlhof to say, "Once we have understood housework, we will understand the economy."[63]

In James's view, "The social power relations of the sexes, races, nations and generations are precisely, then, particularized forms of class relations."[64] Being part of the cycle of capitalist production in one way or another, these strata might now subvert the process of accumulation. This opened in each of them, as they were excluded from the traditional Marxist definition of class (reduced to wage earners), a space for autonomous struggle from within the very site of their exploitation.

During the 1960s, "the Black movement was the first section of the class massively to take its autonomy from these [working class] organizations, and to break away from the containment of the struggle only in the factory ... The women's movement was the next major movement" to do so.[65] "Like the Black movement before it, to be organizationally autonomous of capital and its institutions, women and their movement had also to be autonomous of that part of the 'hierarchy of labour powers' which capital used specifically against them. For Blacks, it was whites. For women it was men. For Black women it is both."[66] James thus credited the black movement with having opened the path to other wageless people in the world, enabling them to organize according to their specific interests as exploited people: "Those at the lowest levels of the hierarchy must themselves find the key to their weakness, must themselves find the strategy which will attack that point and shatter it, must themselves find their own modes of struggle."[67]

The reference to the black movement was not intended, James noted, to establish false parallels or to designate "who is the most exploited":

We are seeking to describe that complex interweaving of forces which is the working class; we are seeking to break down the power relations among us on which is based the hierarchical rule of international capital. For no man can represent us as women any more than whites can [represent] the Black experience. Nor do we seek to convince men of our feminism. Ultimately they will be "convinced" by our power. We offer them what we offer to most privileged women: power over their enemies. The price is an end to their privilege over us.[68]

This was thus a "perspective ... founded on the least powerful – the wageless" – that is, on those who were part of the global "factory of reproduction" in both Western metropolises and Southern countries, such as houseworkers, unemployed people, racial minorities, ethnic minorities, and peasants.[69] In James's view, all of these wageless workers found themselves divided not according to the hierarchy of social classes but according to the different levels of power that they held within various sectors of society.

This booklet, written in 1973, presaged the intersectional analyses of today, in which the overlapping of different domination systems that are race, gender, classes, and sexualities are taken into account without putting them in a hierarchy – at least in principle.

The Global Factory of Reproduction

In "Wageless of the World," James illustrates how the man-woman hierarchy, imposed by wages, was international, "where there is a wage," and "each situation of course is unique":[70]

The reproduction of workers for mines, mills or factories is the product of unwaged female labour everywhere ... In some parts of Africa it is often in the extended tribal family where women perform this unwaged labour for capital. In Zambia, the copper mines are magnanimously and increasingly surrounded by company housing of two- and three-room bungalows. The same in industrial Mexico City ... How efficient to have workers used up daily and reproduced on the spot by other workers (of another sex)! ... Again, in Caracas ... oil production is absolutely dependent on female domestic labour.[71]

She specifies that, often, it is not through the man's wage that women's labour is constrained but through "*a patriarchal structure which predates capitalist society*," which "may not yet have undergone *the capitalist reorganisation of the patriarchy*."[72]

However, she adds, on the international scale, it was the wage relationship that dominated different types of work. This was true for peasant work: work on the land, and the labour power that was deployed there to cultivate, maintain, sow, and harvest it, was hidden by that labour's non-salaried nature. Similarly, hidden in peasant communities were the reproduction of labour power and the processing of products of the earth performed by women.

In this regard, James gives the example of Latin American women, "Indians, or of Indian extraction." They lived from subsistence agriculture by performing two types of unpaid labour: on the one hand, they were agricultural workers (*jornaleras*), holders of parcels of land (*minifundistas*) and workers on collective farms (*ejiditarias*); on the other hand, they were houseworkers. Here, the unit of production was thus the family. The work of women in the home, where they processed raw materials into food and clothing, was a fundamental aspect of the production of the family unit.

Even when a woman might draw an income in the form of wages – as a *jornalera*, for example – from the sale of harvests, it was the man who often received this salary. Women and children thus worked for capital through the man's authority. But at least the work of the women and children was not hidden: it was recognized as work, which was not the case for houseworkers in cities that were directly dominated by the wage relationship, their family work not being considered to be true work because it was not paid.

"*To be wageless is not necessarily to be outside of the capitalist wage relation*, every mode of labour which exists today must be re-examined to determine the social relation which it reproduces" wrote James, and so did the specific nature of the resulting exploitation of women (and children).[73] In her view,

> Our experiences as exploited women, urban or rural, Third World or metropolitan, are unique in each case. *Our needs and our desires are international and universal*: to be free, to be free of the labour that has worn us down over centuries, to be free of domination and dependence on men ... It is time to put paid to this work ... We demand Wages for Housework in whatever form – child care which we control, free birth control and abortion which do not sicken, kill or sterilise us, the socialisation of our work on our terms to liberate time for ourselves, and most important, money we can call our own.[74]

These are some of James's notable theoretical contributions to the Wages for Housework perspective during the period of the IFC.

This chapter on Wages for Housework theoretical and political perspectives produced by theoreticians cited and published during the existence of the IFC (1972–77) is intended only to give a general idea of several dimensions of these women's thoughts. Obviously, I have not exhausted the wealth of these theoreticians' thought, especially because I was the one who chose the dimensions, with the aim of highlighting what I consider to be fundamental contributions from this school of thought of early neo-feminism in relation to feminist questions today.[75]

How was this thought embodied in action? This is the subject of Chapters 4, 5, and 6. In Chapter 3, we shall see how the IFC, which conveyed this perspective, was created, and how the "embryonic women's Internationale" functioned.

3
The International Feminist Collective, 1972–77

> When it is a question of "network," it is about the "organizational network"
> that exists from one country to another or, if you prefer, the embryo of a
> women's Internationale for wages for housework. In fact, it involves mainly
> Italian, English, American, and Canadian women. Further, there are "wage
> groups" that expressly refuse to be part of this network.
>
> – Collectif L'Insoumise[1]

The International Feminist Collective (IFC) was fundamentally a network of
groups, established in certain northern hemisphere countries, that identified
with a Wages for Housework political analysis and struggled to advance this
strategy. It was also a body for coordination and encounters, for exchanges of
information on mobilizations underway in the network, for reflections and discussions on situations of the moment, and for concerted actions. The intention
was to start from the Wages for Housework political perspective to engage
in international feminist mobilization and to act together. In a word, it was a
feminist "Internationale" ahead of its time. In this chapter, we will look at these
two aspects of the IFC: a network of groups, on the one hand, and a body for
encounters, exchanges, organization, and coordination on the other hand.

A NETWORK OF GROUPS

In July 1972, some twenty activists met for two days in Padua. The majority
were from Italy, but some came from the new women's liberation movement
that had emerged from the heterodox Marxist current in England, the United
States, and France, fed by the activism of the decolonization, civil rights, student,
and Italian workerist movements.[2] In a manifesto, they laid the foundation for
the future international Wages for Housework network, which was to expand
to different countries in the years that followed. The International Feminist
Collective/Collettivo internazionale femminista/Collectif féministe international was born.

The signatories to the manifesto – and the co-founders of the IFC – were,
for Italy, Mariarosa Dalla Costa of the Movimento di Lotta Femminile (soon

renamed Lotta Femminista); for England, Selma James of the Notting Hill Group of the London Women's Liberation Workshop and long-standing anti-colonial activist; for the United States, Silvia Federici, an Italian who had recently immigrated to the United States and was a member of the Women's Bail Fund in New York; and, for France, Brigitte Galtier, a Parisian "workers' autonomy" activist from the mixed-sex group Matériaux pour l'intervention.

The Founding Manifesto

The founding manifesto, issued in July 1972, was largely inspired by an essay by Mariarosa Dalla Costa, "Donne e sovversione sociale" (translated as "Women and the Subversion of the Community"), which had previously been discussed by Italian activists during a meeting in June 1971.[3] At the time of the founding meeting of the IFC, Dalla Costa's essay had just been published in Italian, accompanied by a text written by Selma James, "Il posto della dona" ("A Woman's Place," originally published in the United States in 1953), under the general title *The Power of Women and the Subversion of the Community*, with an introduction by James.[4]

The manifesto's signatories stated the "necessity for the autonomy of the women's movement," affirmed its revolutionary role, and rejected any subordination of feminism to the class struggle. Identifying themselves as Marxist feminists, they detailed the meaning of this commitment by redefining the term "class." The new definition was based on coexistence, in the economic capitalist system, of waged and unwaged workers, and the subordination of the latter to the former. This subordination, it was specified, hid the exploitation of women's work in the home, which induced, in its turn, greater exploitation outside the home.

This definition opened a new field of struggle to women: no longer only in the classic world of labour – the factory and the office – but also in the home, the neighbourhood, and the community, labelled the "other factory," the "social factory." This field of struggle would form the basis for the autonomy of the women's movement. It was noted that potential links with the left would therefore "always be secondary and subordinate to that autonomy."

The manifesto outlined the goal of the new collective, which was "to maintain and develop our own international contacts, our own publications in translation and our own joint discussions which aim ultimately at joint mass actions transcending national borders." This was the objective that the IFC set for itself when it was created in 1972. And it was from this founding moment that most of the initiatives and mobilizations linked to Wages for Housework, on both side of the Atlantic, arose.

The introductory paragraph of the manifesto, written by the editors of the Power of Women Collective's journal *Power of Women*, which reproduced it in its first issue, specified that it was addressed particularly to women in the left and to other women's groups that might fear that belonging to the women's movement would mean the abandonment of a class perspective. The IFC manifesto intended to reassure them by articulating a perspective that was both feminist and class based. As for the egalitarian perspective that the women's movement had advocated (equal salaries, equal access to education and to the same opportunities as men, daycare centres, the right to abortion and contraception), it was described in this same paragraph as being doomed to stalemate. It reflected the illusory idea that women's liberation resided in work outside the home.

Circumstances under Which the IFC Was Formed

According to my research, at least two of the four signatories to the IFC, Dalla Costa and James, and the groups to which they respectively belonged were already working, in their respective countries, on forming an autonomous women's liberation movement, based on mobilizations around unwaged housework as a form of exploitation common to all women. The salarization of housework was already on their list of demands.

In Italy

A year earlier, in 1971, the Movimento di Lotta Femminile (later Lotta Femminista) had been formed in Padua, inspired by Dalla Costa's "Donne e sovversione sociale." An early version of this essay had been circulating since June of that year. The group had also distributed a document, "Maternità e aborto," intended to "clarify the terms of our participation in the struggle for abortion" that was underway at the time.[5]

The following month, the group circulated a document called *Manifesto programmatico per la lotta della casalinga nel quartiere*.[6] In this manifesto-program for the struggle of houseworkers in communities, the question of wages for housework was clearly posed. These wages were to be paid to both women and men, by the state or the municipality. The idea was for communities to have available laundry services, canteens, free twenty-four-hour childcare centres, and free healthcare centres for chronic patients and the elderly, and these services were to be situated in the vicinity and run by specialized personnel, assisted as needed by family members. Also on the list of demands were surgery centres and free distribution of prescription drugs (including contraceptives).

Because the manifesto-program was aimed at women's struggles in communities, more general measures were advocated, such as a guaranteed wage that was independent of productivity and hours of work, a reduction in hours of work, equal wages, and women's access to all jobs. To these demands were added the elimination of dangerous work and night work and free housing, transportation, and education. So, at the time when the IFC was created, wages for housework had already been raised in the women's movement in Italy and had been under discussion throughout 1971.

One can observe, upon reading the first documents published, that in 1972, Lotta Femminista was present in several Italian cities, including Padua, the first nucleus of Wages for Housework groups, but also in Venice, Ferrara, Trieste, and Modena.[7] Its members made speeches in various forums and fields of struggle, related to the "other factory," the "social factory": the home, the neighbourhood, and the community. Lotta Femminista had already produced important theoretical writings not only on housework but also on questions of education, housing, prostitution, abortion, problems with the left, and other issues. It had also translated into Italian key early neo-feminist texts (on lesbianism, unions, and other subjects). As Mariarosa Dalla Costa said in 1996,

> Lotta Femminista's analysis, as well as the perspective that flowed from it, had the effect of reformulating the struggles differently, taking women's day as a whole into account. This might mean, for example, bringing children to the office or, for secretaries, refusing to do all those additional tasks asked of them because they were women. In addition, our Wages for Housework demand was advanced in conjunction with the demand for a shorter workday for everyone. In our early documents, we demanded a twenty-hour workweek.[8]

The main documents related to the Wages for Housework perspective were published in Italy by Marsilio Editori, within a specific imprint, Salario al lavoro domestico: Strategia internazionale femminista, under the IFC label. In the 1970s, this imprint published documents from both the Italian Wages for Housework movement and the IFC.

In England

James, another signatory to the IFC manifesto, was politically active in England, after having worked for a number of years in anti-racist struggles in the United States and Trinidad.[9] In the context of neo-feminism, the Wages for Housework demand apparently appeared in England for the first time during the British National Women's Liberation Conference, in Manchester, in March 1972. It is said that a text titled *Women, the Unions, and Work, or What Is Not to Be Done,* signed with the initials "S.D.," was selling like hotcakes.[10] The author was Selma James, of the Notting Hill Women's Liberation Workshop Group. In the text, six demands were proposed to the movement, including wages for housework. The demands were:

1. The right to work less (Why should anybody work more than 20 hours a week?) ...
2. A guaranteed income for women and for men working or not working, married or not ... We demand wages for housework. All housekeepers are entitled to wages (men too) ...
3. Control of our bodies [free contraception, free access to no-cost abortions on demand]. We demand the right to have or not to have children ...
4. Equal pay for all ...
5. End to price rises ...
6. Free community controlled nurseries and child care.[11]

This text provoked very lively debate, as it went counter to the left's traditional strategies of action with regard to women. The text argued that, contrary to what the left had always claimed, unions were not the best site for women's struggle, and that women did not have to be waged workers to be part of the working class and initiate their own struggles.

This put the unions, and the role they played in maintaining discrimination and exclusion against women, on trial. Because the unions limited women's fight to waged workplaces, James argued, unions were isolated from the wageless (the unemployed, the elderly, children, and houseworkers) as a whole. The struggle had to be organized, instead, on the side of this other aspect of wages, the unwaged – that is, the struggle of the wageless. An analysis specific to the situation of women had to be deployed. As James wrote, "[This field of struggle] reflected the idea, always strong in the movement, that women's liberation must come from a job outside the home ... Goodbye to all that!"[12]

The Wages for Housework demand in particular raised loud debate, again, at another women's movement conference held in November of the same year in the Acton district of London.[13] Although the demand was ultimately rejected, it received the support of single mothers and women on welfare.[14]

Some analysts presented James's essay as a "corollary" to Dalla Costa's "Women and the Subversion of Community," which had not been yet published in English at the time of the conference.[15] In fact, James quoted extensively from Dalla Costa's essay, indicating that its publication was forthcoming. The two essays were seen as complementary: Dalla Costa painted a general portrait of the situation of women and their role as houseworkers in capitalist society, and set out prospects for action from the home as workplace. James highlighted the fact that women did not have to work outside the home to rebel against their situation and that unions had never held the top prize for "revolutionary consciousness."

The English Wages for Housework group, the Power of Women Collective, was formed the following year, in the wake of discussions generated by James's essay and especially in the context of a massive campaign against cuts in family allowances, led in March 1973 by single mothers and women on welfare. The group publicly demanded wages for housework, not only for mothers but also for the work done every day at home, by whoever it was.[16] This mobilization marked the beginning of the International Wages for Housework Campaign, one of the founding objectives of the IFC. In 1973, the Power of Women Collective became a very active member of the IFC.

The group would then publish its documents with Falling Wall Press in Bristol, thanks to the work of an early activist of the Power of Women Collective, Suzie Fleming, and a partner, Jeremy Mulford.[17] The collective published both its own documents and many of the IFC's. Falling Wall Press became the largest centre for dissemination of the Wages for Housework perspective in the English-speaking world, as Marsilio Editori was for dissemination in Italy.

In the United States

Silvia Federici said of the founding meeting of the IFC, held in Padua in 1972,

> I arrived in the middle of the meeting that would culminate with the formation of the International Feminist Collective. I didn't know anyone except Rosa [Mariarosa Dalla Costa] through her article ["Women and the Subversion of Community"] ... I remember the feverish excitement that I felt, and I left Padua knowing that from that moment on, this would be my fight.[18]

It was when she read Dalla Costa's essay "Women and the Subversion of Community," which had been circulating in the United States since 1971, that she was convinced to join the feminist movement:

> At the last page, I knew that I had found my home, my tribe and my own self, as a woman and a feminist. From that also stemmed my involvement in the Wages for Housework campaign that women like Dalla Costa and Selma James were organizing in Italy and Britain, and my decision to start, in 1972, Wages for Housework groups also in this country [the United States].[19]

Upon her return from Padua, in the summer of 1972, Federici, then a philosophy student, interrupted the writing of her dissertation.[20] She spoke of this new perspective for the feminist movement at every political meeting and women's group gathering that she attended at the time (among others, the Women's Bail Fund). In the fall, she met Nicole Cox, who was to become an active member of the future Wages for Housework group in New York, and they decided to work together.[21]

During the same period (autumn 1972), Federici was corresponding with Italian and English IFC groups, beginning to distribute their documentation, and translating texts between Italian and English. But the impetus for the formation of the first American Wages for Housework group, the New York Wages for Housework Committee, arose in March 1973, on the occasion of the speaking tour undertaken by Dalla Costa and James to more than a dozen cities in the United States and Canada. Federici organized most of the meetings in the United States, with the assistance of her own contacts and those of Dalla Costa and James.

The North American tour of Mariarosa Dalla Costa and Selma James

To finance the tour, Federici raised funds from universities and other organizations likely to be interested in hosting Dalla Costa or James as a speaker. The fee was between $200 and $300 per lecture.[22] Lodging was provided by activists in the cities they visited. Other costs were shared by the activists and the speakers.

This is how Dalla Costa and James first travelled through the United States, with an itinerary that included San Francisco, Boston, and New York. Then they went to Canada, where, with the assistance of contacts in various locations, a team coordinated by Judy Ramirez (who was to be the key person in the future Toronto Wages for Housework Committee) organized a tour to a dozen cities. In the wake of their visit, groups began to be formed to join the network.

On April 29 and 30, 1973, Dalla Costa and James were in Montreal. For their visit, the Centre des femmes organized a meeting with activists from various (francophone) spheres and a public lecture attended by a hundred people.[23] The feminist journal *Québécoises Deboutte!*, published by the Centre des femmes, ran a long interview with the two activists, who described the Wages for Housework perspective. As the French translation of *The Power of Women and the Subversion of Community* was not yet available in Quebec, francophone feminists became aware of the Wages for Housework perspective thanks to this public lecture and the subsequent interview in *Québécoises Deboutte!* The journal's editors were careful to specify, however, that it did not endorse this analysis unconditionally.[24]

Dalla Costa was called back to Italy to cope with an emergency in the abortion struggle. James continued the tour to the west coast of Canada alone and returned to Montreal in early June for the Feminist Symposium, the final stop on the tour.[25]

The Feminist Symposium féministe in Montreal, June 1–3, 1973

"A change is about to come/Au seuil d'un jour nouveau" was the theme for the Feminist Symposium, which opened on Friday, June 1, 1973, at McGill University's Leacock Building, in an eight-hundred-seat amphitheatre that was full to bursting. Selma James was the special guest. The event took place in English, which explains the absence of francophone feminist groups.[26]

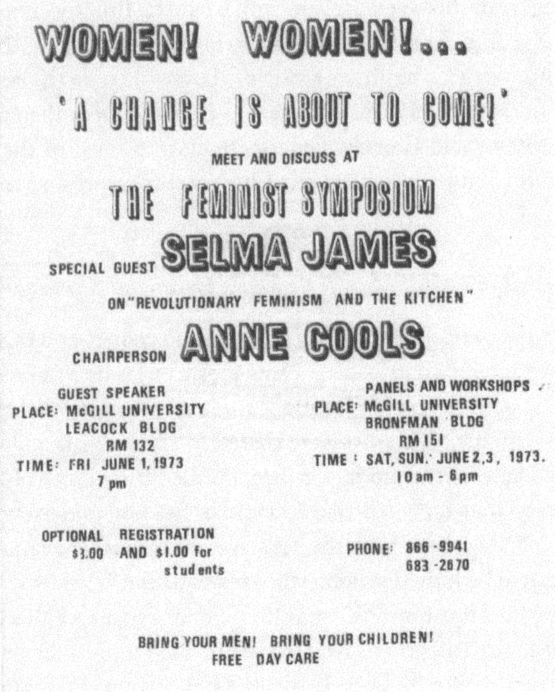

Figure 3.1   Invitation poster for the Feminist Symposium
in Montreal, June 1–3, 1973. (CWMA, box 115)

It is possible to take a closer look at this symposium, as we have archival documents that testify to its organization and, quite unusually, its deliberations. The content of the symposium provides an idea of the anglophone intellectual and activist climate during this neo-feminist period, and an indication of the complexity of relations between anglophone and francophone feminists in Montreal.[27] In addition, the debates at the symposium highlighted not only the originality of the Wages for Housework strategy in relation to mainstream neo-feminist strategies at the time and the objections to the proposition from the start, but also the very novelty of such a conference, which the chair of the organizing committee described as "Montreal's first [anglophone] conference on women."[28]

The symposium organizing committee was formed during a meeting of a small group of Montreal anglophone women at the YWCA Women's Centre in January 1973, on the initiative of Anne Cools. Cools was a student from the West Indies and "one of the strongest voices" of the Montreal Caribbean Conference Committee.[29] Arrested during the Sir George Williams University affair, she was sentenced to six months in prison and fined following her trial for obstruction in April 1971.[30] At the time of the conference, she was appealing this verdict. She had been acquainted with James in England, when James was known as a promoter of an autonomous radical women's movement. Cools felt that this conference-symposium, with James as special guest, was "the most appropriate organisational project for a group of women who wanted to do something autonomously as women."[31]

The organizing committee solicited funding from various organizations. Among the expenses were travel and lodging costs for James, the honorariums for her and the twenty-five planned panellists, advertising, administration, and rental of halls. The total budget was $8,279, a considerable sum at the time, considering the newness of the event, which, on top of it, was feminist in nature. Major banks, trust companies, and other large anglophone corporations came on board.[32]

The symposium's interim report related that the audience was composed of groups of anglophone women from Montreal, Toronto, Windsor, Ottawa, Saint John, New York, Boston, and Washington, DC, "involved in the whole set of women's issues."[33] Many of the participants had come on an individual basis to hear about women's issues. The rapporteur noted the presence of "many grey heads [and] quite a few Blacks."[34] Francophone activists participated neither in the organization of the symposium nor in its running, with the exception of one woman, "but she functioned in English."[35]

We can deduce that the absence of francophone activists – amplified by the fact that Mariarosa Dalla Costa, who spoke French, had had to return to Italy – was among the factors that may explain why the Wages for Housework perspective had difficulty gaining a foothold in Quebec. It was not until the movement's documents were translated into French that the debate truly began there.

Although the organizing committee did not make a great effort to reach out to francophone women in Quebec, it attracted an impressive number of panellists, almost thirty women from various areas of Canada and the United States.[36] The documents consulted mentioned attendance on the order of eight hundred to a thousand. "The miracle of the conference was that such a large and varied group of women accepted the perspective put forward by Selma," wrote the conference rapporteur.[37] The planned program for the weekend was as follows:

Friday evening: opening presentation by Selma James
Saturday: 3 panels
   1 Woman in the First Person – the "I" (4 four panellists)
   (on women's search for identity today)
   2 Medicine – a Social Issue (4 panellists)
   3 The Educational Impasse (5 panellists)
Sunday: 2 panels
   1 The Labour Force (4 panellists)
   2 The Law and Human Rights (4 panellists)

I was particularly interested in the reactions to James's presentation.[38] Wages for housework as an organizational perspective around which to gather all of the disparate demands by women (abortion, childcare, wage parity): in 1973, this was something new in the women's movement! It therefore raised many questions: Where did women who were not houseworkers fit into this proposal? Did it not confirm the role of women as houseworkers? Was this demand achievable? And how? Where would the money come from? The discussion was launched at the opening of the Feminist Symposium. The arguments against wages for housework that were then put forward were representative of the opposition that would emerge throughout the existence of the IFC, and long after.

A first argument was expressed by women with interesting and well-paid jobs, who said that they didn't see themselves as houseworkers. They were distanced from this role and felt that women must be free to work outside the home. There were several responses to this argument. First, these women were forgetting that, for the vast majority of women, working outside the home often meant the assembly line. Was this really liberation? Second, they were forgetting that the majority of waged women were wives, mothers, and sisters, who were houseworkers once they returned home. Third, women's struggle had to be led not from the position of the minority of "liberated" women whose privileges allowed them to live almost "like a man," but from the position of the vast majority of women, who were houseworkers, and whose status as unwaged workers determined the sexist attitudes to which all women were subjected. All women doctors, lawyers, and journalists could testify to the fact that they were all "office wives," even at the highest professional level. The woman's position was always determined by that of the houseworker.

The second argument was that paying women to perform housework would keep them in that role and even help institutionalize it. To this argument, the response was that the role had already been an institution since time immemorial, and no one had ever claimed that workers were institutionalizing their role by demanding better wages. A wage would allow for greater independence and more freedom to leave the home, more freedom to fight for daycare and for "socializing" housework. A wage would give women more power to dictate, on their own terms, the socialization of their work. Wages for Housework was a strategy, a way of thinking that made it possible to change women's situation in all sorts of circumstances.

A third argument deplored the fact that this wage had to come from increased taxes – thus from people's incomes and not from profits. The response was that money from both taxes and profits went back to those who worked.

It was Anne Cools who finally presented the Wages for Housework proposal. The discussion about the proposal lasted three hours. It was, according to the rapporteur, an organized and rigorous debate. Twenty women and three men spoke up. Two or three people were opposed. After three hours of exchanges, all that remained was to fine-tune the resolution so that it would satisfy as many as possible. According to the rapporteur, Marlene Dixon performed this operation, with participation by the audience.[39] There were disagreements over the choice of terms, such as "labour power" (men? labour force?), "houseworkers" (housewives? housework?), "the state" (the government? federal? provincial?). Finally, a formulation was agreed upon and a vote was proposed. After five hours of debate, the resolution that was passed read as follows:

> Whereas the work of production and reproduction of the labour force rests mainly with women;
> Whereas the work of bearing and rearing children (often performed in addition to a job outside the home) is a social function;
> Whereas the work done in the home is unpaid;
> BE IT RESOLVED that the State pay wages to houseworkers.

The resolution was unanimously adopted. Someone writing for the journal *The Other Woman*, which was covering the event, noted, "This resolution was felt by everyone to be a new beginning of a new and positive direction for the movement and perhaps an historical event."[40] And the women's movement's new strategy was launched.

The unanimity recorded in the symposium minutes, however, glossed over some defections and dissent. On June 15, the *Montreal Gazette*, an English-language daily, published an article about complaints by two members who had quit the organizing committee and by panellists: the complaints concerned not Wages for Housework but "the economic and revolutionary ideologies emphasized at that symposium."[41] The coordinators were accused of "using a feminist gathering to advance revolutionary political ideologies." One person lamented that there were not enough solid and energetic spokes-women "involved in more traditional aspects of feminism." Another claimed that the Marxists on the organizing committee were more politicized than the others, knew more feminists, and thus had more influence in the organization of panels. Yet another spoke of "the class divisions within the movement." Given the financial support for the symposium and the type of donors, it is not surprising that such a division appeared.[42]

The post-symposium period and the formation of the network

The IFC has not, to date, been the subject of historical studies as such, at least to my knowledge. The information concerning the formation of its member groups comes from documents that I was able to assemble and consult, and from interviews with some activists from these groups. Since this is a first chronology on the subject, I obviously cannot claim that the portrait that emerges is exhaustive. It intends only to give a general idea of the scope of the IFC as a network of groups, and to give some reference points for future research on the network.

The Italian Wages for Housework groups were the first to form, followed by the English group, as we saw at the beginning of this chapter. In the wake of the North American tour by James and Dalla Costa in the spring of 1973, the New York Wages for Housework Committee formed between March and the fall of that year, upon the initiative of Silvia Federici. Contacts were established with women in every state. In early 1974, Federici was invited to Philadelphia, and a Wages for Housework group was founded there. At about the same time, the Cleveland group was founded.[43] With the New York group, those from Philadelphia and Cleveland constituted the American Wages for Housework contingent at the first IFC conference, which took place in New York in the fall of 1974.

Most of the American groups were formed in 1975 – in Boston, Chicago, New Orleans, and Oberlin, Ohio. On the west coast, on the instigation of Beth Ingber and Sidney Ross (previously from the Cleveland group), groups were formed in Los Angeles and San Francisco (the latter in 1976). The Black Women for Wages for Housework group was born in the wake of a conference

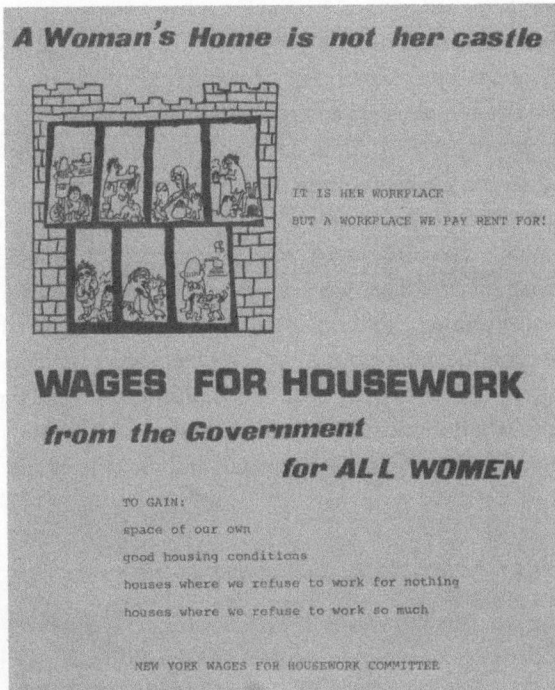

Figure 3.2   Brochure on housing by the New York Wages for Housework Committee, n.d. (Silvia Federici Archives)

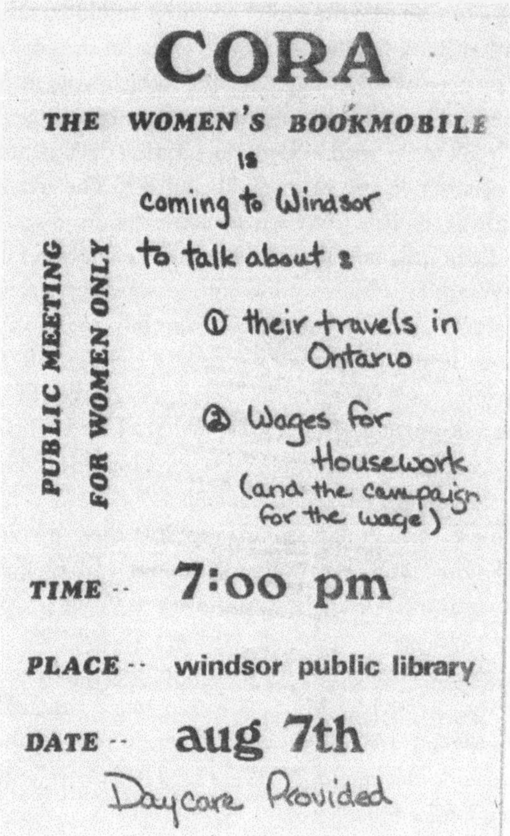

CORA

THE WOMEN'S BOOKMOBILE

is

coming to Windsor

PUBLIC MEETING *FOR WOMEN ONLY*

to talk about :

① their travels in
   Ontario

② Wages for
        Housework
   (and the campaign
    for the wage)

TIME -- **7:00 pm**

PLACE -- windsor public library

DATE -- **aug 7th**

Daycare Provided

Figure 3.3   Advertisement for a meeting organized
by the Women's Liberation Bookmobile (Cora) of the
Toronto Wages for Housework Committee in 1974.
(CWMA, box 625.2)

on welfare cuts, organized in New York in April 1976 by the New York Wages
for Housework Committee, which I discuss below. Wages Due Lesbians also
formed as an autonomous entity within the Philadelphia group during these
years. The most active groups in the United States were, according to Federici,
those in New York and Los Angeles, which became "points of reference" for the
other groups.

In Canada, a first group was formed in Toronto in the spring of 1973. In the
summer of 1974, a second group was formed, also in Toronto.[44] This was the
Toronto Wages for Housework Committee, a group of women who separated
from a mixed-sex group, the New Left Tendency. Judy Ramirez would be its
central figure and main spokesperson until the 1980s.[45]

One of the first initiatives of the new Toronto group was original, to say the
least. To make known the Wages for Housework perspective and extend the

network of groups in Ontario, the group acquired an old bus that became the Women's Liberation Bookmobile, nicknamed Cora (in memory of Cora Hind, a journalist and pioneer of the struggle for the right to vote in Manitoba). On May 1, 1974, the bus, intended to be "a travelling women's centre, bookstore, speakers' bureau" took to the road in Ontario, carrying documents on the Wages for Housework perspective and women's liberation.[46] The activists parked the bus in various towns, engaged women in conversation, discussed wages for housework, and distributed documents. They also gave lectures upon request.[47]

The Toronto Wages for Housework Committee was very active throughout the existence of the IFC, and in the 1980s. From July 1976 to the early 1980s, it published a journal, the *Wages for Housework Campaign Bulletin*. It led and supported many important struggles and acted, within the IFC, as a "point of reference."[48] The autonomous lesbian group Wages Due Lesbians was formed in February 1975 within the Toronto Wages for Housework Committee; this group's original position is analyzed in Chapter 2.[49]

Wages for Housework groups sprang up in other provinces, including Saskatchewan (Regina) and Manitoba (Winnipeg). In Quebec, a group of anglophone women formed the Montreal Power of Women Collective in late 1974.

In Latin America, a Wages for Housework group existed for some time in Mexico City. It was formed by Marta Acevedo, who translated into Spanish *The Power of Women and the Subversion of Community* and other texts of the Wages for Housework movement. A Wages for Housework group also existed in Argentina for a longer time.[50]

In Italy, a directory of the Wages for Housework campaign mentioned groups in the following cities in 1976: Padua, Mestre-Venice, Trieste, Trentino, Varese, Bologna, Ferrara, Modena, Ravenna, Reggio Emilia, Florence, Rome, Naples, and Pescara.[51] The group in Padua also had a music group, the Gruppo musicale del Comitato per il Salario al Lavoro Domestico di Padova; a theatre group, Gruppo Teatrale; a bimonthly journal, *Le operaie della casa;* and a number of titles published with Marsilio Editori.[52]

The Power of Women Collective in England also published its own journal, *Power of Women,* during the period of existence of the IFC. Distinct and autonomous groups came into being within this collective during the same period – among others, Wages Due Lesbians (London) and the English Collective of Prostitutes.[53] Some struggles of the Power of Women Collective are analyzed in Chapters 4 and 5.

During the existence of the IFC, several groups thus were members of the network;[54] however, five people known as "points of reference" clearly emerged from it: Mariarosa Dalla Costa, of the Padua group; Selma James, of the London group; Silvia Federici, of the New York group; Judy Ramirez, of the Toronto group; and Beth Ingber, of the Los Angeles group. What was meant by "points

Figure 3.4   Cover of the journal *Le operaie della casa* 2–3
(September–December 1976), published by the Comitato per il
Salario al Lavoro Domestico di Padova.

of reference"? Federici interprets the expression this way: "It meant people who
had more theoretical and political experience" than the others. They were points
of reference "because of their sense of political understanding."[55] In reality, she
said, the expression meant "leader." (More on this below.)

AN EMBRYONIC WOMEN'S "INTERNATIONALE"

The expression "an embryo of a women's Internationale" to qualify the IFC
comes from the Swiss Wages for Housework group, the Collectif L'Insoumise.[56]
The label "Internationale" may seem a bit overstated, given its historical conno-
tation (internationales of the worker movement, or female or feminist

Figure 3.5   Cover of the journal *Power of Women* 1, 1 (March–April 1974), published by the Power of Women Collective (London).

internationales of the late nineteenth century[57]), and especially because the IFC never attained the scope of a mass movement, as its membership remained relatively small throughout its existence. The label may also seem exaggerated given the outcry raised in the women's movement by its central demand, which was far from unanimously accepted internationally. Finally, there was its short period of existence.

I have nevertheless used this label, as it seems to me to convey well the network's intention and early objectives: to commit, starting from a perspective shared by several groups in different countries, a process of feminist mobilization and to act in concert on the international scene. And this was so even if the women's movement's action strategies with regard to labour pointed in a completely different direction – toward women's access to the waged workplace and correction of the discrimination found there. The IFC threw into question this type of liberation, which consisted of offering women the prospect of working twice as much. In this early neo-feminist context, undertaking feminist mobilization on the international scale with the Wages for Housework perspective was a considerable challenge.

To illustrate what the IFC may have been as an international body and site for acting in concert, I chose to evoke its conception of organizational politics, that is, how it intended to promote the Wages for Housework perspective and demand. I then highlight certain questions that were debated during the IFC's international conferences held between 1974 and 1977, which constituted the key site of this feminist "internationale." But first, a few words about the conditions under which these conferences were held.

The IFC as Epicentre

It must be emphasized from the start that all of the people engaged in the groups fighting for wages for housework between 1972 and 1977 were activists in the true sense of the word – that is, they were full volunteers (their incomes came either from their waged work or from unemployment benefits or welfare allowances). Women's movement activities were not yet receiving funding; only in 1975, decreed International Women's Year by the United Nations, did funding begin to be a possibility.[58] Organizing international activities, such as the IFC conferences, was therefore not an easy task.

So, one of the major challenges was money, and self-funding was the rule of the day. As these were international conferences, the means had to be found to pay the cost of travel for participants, many from overseas, who had to assume part of their own expenses. Some income was drawn from public lectures given by Selma James and Mariarosa Dalla Costa in universities and from contributions solicited during meetings organized by various women's community groups (attendees might be asked to pay $1 to cover part of the guest's travel costs). On some occasions, such as at the IFC International Conference in Toronto, attendees were asked to pay $5 to cover the cost of room rentals. IFC publications were sold at tables set up at these events, and the proceeds also helped with funding.

It was up to the group hosting the international conference to provide the funding for the event. Federici remembered what organization of such a conference meant to these groups: "Holding an international conference in a city where a group from the Wages for Housework network existed was integral to the process of construction and consolidation of that group." There was, in fact, something dialectical in this process, she felt: the group had to have the capacity to organize the conference – enough resources and organizational experience to be able to do it. If this was the case, the conference helped the group become rooted and develop. "There were many lessons in political education to draw from this period," she noted.

As for the means of communication, they were rudimentary – at least according to today's standards. Activists and groups dispersed over two continents communicated essentially by mail or, occasionally, by long-distance phone calls (which were very expensive at the time). Organizing such international activities was thus quite an act of prowess. Federici remembers, "Staying in contact with the international network required a great deal of energy. At that time, we wrote letters very often, two or three times a month, sharing our thoughts, the news on the political situation in the world, our organizational problems, etc."

The work of the IFC, as an epicentre – a nucleus bringing together member groups from different countries – included another important aspect: political training and the circulation of theoretical texts and information through the network. The concern, quite exceptional among these activists, with buttressing and refining their political analysis and gaining a political education is noteworthy. We can only be impressed by the quality and diversity of the text and tools circulated, especially if we consider the limited financial and technical means at their disposal to produce and reproduce them, to translate them, and to distribute them in numerous countries. In this context, to accomplish its goals took activist energy that was either a tour de force or motivated by a powerful inspiration. It is up to you to judge.

The IFC was responsible for various publications, including *Women in Struggle*, a series of three anthologies published in 1975 on different struggles conducted on the international scale and dealing with various aspects of women's lives. In these anthologies were analyses of these struggles, including those of the networks in their respective countries, position statements, and leaflets and other materials. Each anthology was prepared and produced by an IFC group: the first two by the Toronto Wages for Housework Collective, and the third, a special issue on Italy, by the Comitato Triveneto per il Salario al Lavoro Domestico (translated and published by the Toronto and New York Wages for Housework Committees).

Another series of publications, the *Wages for Housework Notebooks*, anthologies of more-theoretical essays, also emanated from various groups in the network. To my knowledge, two seem to have been published in the form of mimeographs in 1975, the first by the Montreal Power of Women Collective and the second by the New York Wages for Housework Committee. These documents were addressed mainly to groups in the network.

In 1975, the *Wages for Housework International Network Newsletter* was added to provide information across the international network about the activities of its member groups and collectives. The first newsletter was probably published in early summer 1975, and another was planned for late September, on the eve of the fourth network conference, which was to be held in Toronto in October 1975.[59]

At first intended as tools for training and information for groups within the IFC network, these publications were to feed the Wages for Housework political perspective and promote the campaign in the countries in which there were member groups. It was suggested that they be read before international conferences, or as post-conference reference texts.

The IFC conferences, on the other hand, pursued different objectives. The first of these was, according to Federici, to discuss organizational politics of the network, the Wages for Housework campaign.

A Campaign to Promote Wages for Housework: The Organizational Perspective

How could as many women as possible be reached, given the specific conditions of housework?[60] This work was different from all other kinds: it comprised nothing less than the production and reproduction of human beings; it was unwaged and thus not seen as work; it was performed in isolation; the workday was unlimited and thus expressly undefined. Women therefore had a limited amount of time to devote to political activities. The conclusion was that a new type of political action to reach and involve houseworkers had to be invented from scratch.

These women were not only isolated from each other but also separated from other women in other situations, creating the illusion that their interests were not the same. For example, younger and older women had neither the same needs nor the same interests. There were also those in the job market who shared (free or waged) housework with others, those who refused to live with a man, sex workers whose sexual services were paid for, and single mothers who demanded money from the state: all of these women performed housework under different circumstances, which could have the effect of hiding what they shared.

Therefore the first step was to consider individual women in particular situations and stress what linked them: they were all houseworkers, even if their level of "productivity" might vary (for example, having or not having children, having one or more children, taking care of sick parents, and so on). How was it possible to mobilize for a struggle on such foundations? The means of action chosen by the IFC was a Wages for Housework promotion, information, and distribution campaign, and construction of a mass movement with the aim of winning such a wage.[61] Why was this choice made?

According to *Notes on Organization*, one of the documents on the organizational perspective was, "our choice is dictated by our political perspective." This perspective involved fighting against unwaged housework as a whole, rather than just some of its conditions. This is one way in which Wages for Housework

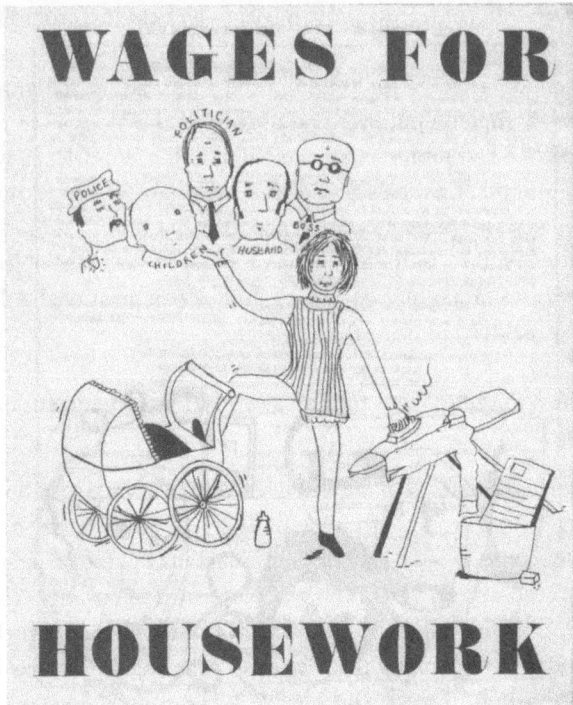

Figure 3.6   Brochure by the Toronto Wages for Housework
Committee, n.d. (Personal archives)

groups in the IFC network distanced their strategies from traditional women's
movement strategies, which generally targeted specific single issues. "We will
not win any partial victory unless we struggle against this work as a whole,"
continued the document. The example often given was that of the fight for
daycare centres: "We will never be able to win day-care centres *on our terms* –
that is, we will not be able to reduce our housework-time – unless taking care of
children is first recognized as work." Therefore, an international campaign was
needed because all women on Earth did housework – some more, some less, but
all of them did it to one degree or another.

The international campaign was thus favoured by the IFC groups for several
reasons: to expose the shared aspect of various situations, to bring houseworkers
out of isolation and invisibility, and to end the divisions that capitalist organization had created among women (waged and unwaged women; married
and unmarried women; "white," "black," and Indigenous women; young and
old women; lesbian and heterosexual women; women in metropolises and in
Southern countries). A campaign also made it possible to link struggles that
were already underway but unconnected to each other. This meant being able
to provide support to these struggles and to highlight the existing link between

wages for housework
campaign bulletin
july 1976 vol. I no. I

Hands Off the Family Allowance

It was a cold and windy day on May 1, but in Toronto and Windsor women from the Wages for Housework Campaign took to the streets to protest the federal freeze in the baby bonus. A series of neighborhood rallies were held in both cities in local supermarkets, playgrounds, and parks. We went to places where women were busy going about their work because, although May 1 is an international workers' holiday, we women keep our noses to the grindstone.

We went with music, banners, speech-

Figure 3.7   First issue of the *Wages for Housework Campaign Bulletin,* published by the Toronto Wages for Housework Committee, July 1976.

a particular struggle and housework. A campaign was also a tool for circulating information on movement experiences that were never heard about otherwise and for teaching each other, giving each other ideas, not repeating errors – in a word, "to realize what is our power."

How could such a campaign be built? How could women who had never met be brought together? A wide variety of means were advocated and used for this purpose throughout the existence of the IFC; even today such means are in the toolbox of many activist projects.

The media

Primary among the media were radio and television, "because that is what women listen to while they are doing the housework," and newspapers – preferably those that women were already reading. Press conferences and media interviews had to be organized.

However, it was most important to have the presence of the movement felt in the community, and on the national and international levels, so that it would become a point of reference for women. To do this would involve several formulas and a variety of tools.

Documentation

There had to be plain-language documentation available to distribute massively and free of charge, in several languages, to explain the goals of the Wages for Housework demand. Publications by IFC groups were used: brochures, pamphlets, leaflets, flyers, and periodical publications such as the London group's *Power of Women*, the Padua group's *Le operaie della casa*, and the Toronto group's *Wages for Housework Campaign Bulletin*.

Public meetings

To build the campaign, public meetings had to be organized in every community, in order to form new groups and attract new members. For this purpose, pamphlets, buttons, posters, videos, songs, films, plays, and other tools had to be created. In addition, public lectures or information sessions had to be held, and arrangements had to be made to participate in forums or panel discussions.

Tools for mobilization

Among the mobilization tools used in struggles by Wages for Housework groups, songs stood out. For instance, the Gruppo musicale del Comitato per il Salario al Lavoro Domestico di Padova (Music Group of the Wages for Housework Committee of Padua) recorded two albums.[62] Boo Watson, of Wages Due Lesbians, affiliated with the Toronto Wages for Housework Committee, performed songs about housework.[63] Such songs played a key role in the different IFC mobilizations, as did photography exhibitions and plays. For example, the Gruppo Teatrale del Comitato per il Salario al Lavoro

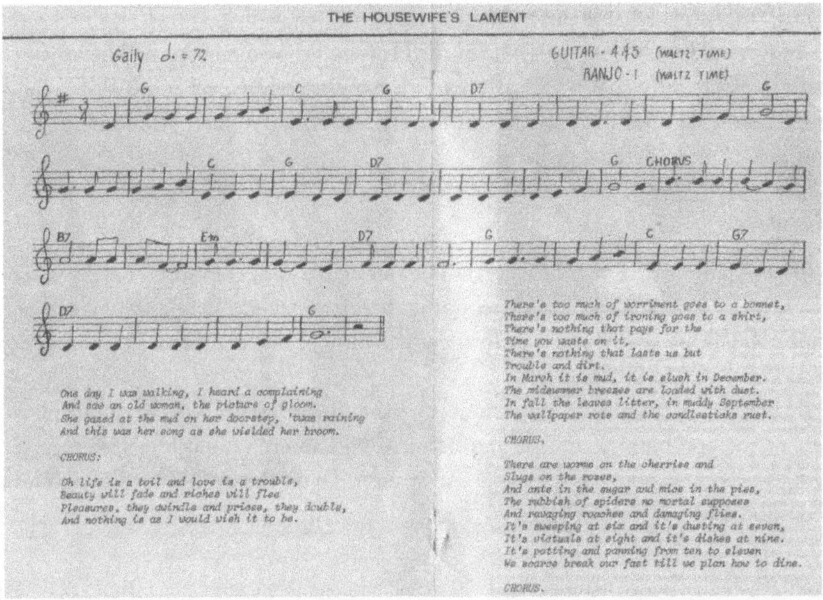

Figure 3.8 "The Housewife's Lament," by Boo Watson (*Women Speak Out: May Day Rally Toronto*, May 1, 1975, 20–21).

Domestico di Padova (Theatre Group of the Wages for Housework Committee in Padua) played an important mobilizing role during major demonstrations in Italy (see *Street events,* below).

In francophone Quebec, although there was no Wages for Housework group as such, a play had a major role in spreading the Wages for Housework perspective everywhere it was presented. This was a play by Le Théâtre des cuisines, *Môman travaille pas, a trop d'ouvrage.*[64]

les ouvrières du trottoir

Nous sommes ici, dehors
A travailler
Nous sommes tellement
Nous sommes la mesure...

Nous sommes tellement à travailler dehors
Nous sommes tellement toute la nuit
A donner sur la rue nos corps pour de l'argent
Nous sommes en fait les «ouvrières du trottoir»

Vendre à rabais, bras, utérus et sourire
C'est la condition, la condamnation de chaque femme
Assurant gratuitement le service général du foyer
Comme dur prix de la respectabilité.

    Chœur   *L'amour, chaque femme l'a cherché*
                              Mais l'amour ils en ont fait un travail
                              Notre corps est pour l'État
                              Machine à enfants et à plaisir

Les patrons cruels nous ont achetées
Les maris et les pères nous ont vendues
Notre corps est anesthésié
Notre cœur rempli de mépris

Hors des rangs contre l'État
Nous aussi, nous avons marché
Contre ceux qui nous veulent
Esclaves et méprisables,
par milliers, nous nous sommes rebellées

Hors des rangs contre l'État
Nous avons aussi lutté pour de l'argent
Cette autonomie nous a coûté
Ame et vie
Bas les mains État et Police !

    Chœur   *L'amour, chaque femme l'a cherché*
                              Mais l'amour ils en ont fait un travail
                              Nous sommes la mesure
                              De ce que signifie
                              Etre femme.

Tiré de Amore e Potere. Canzoniere Femminista mai 77 - Groupe musical
du comité du salaire au travail ménager de Padoue.

Figure 3.9   Lyrics to the song "Le Operaie del Marciapiede" (The Sidewalk Workers) taken from *Amore e Potere. Conzoniere Femminista,* May 1977, by the Music Group of the Wages for Housework Committee in Padua. Translated into French in Louise Vandelac, ed., *L'Italie au féminisme* (Paris: Tierce, 1978), 164.

Women's centres

To have a constant community presence among women, the movement had to open information centres so that women could enter freely, find documentation, meet other women, and have discussions. A concrete example was related to me by Silvia Federici about the New York Wages for Housework Committee:

> We were active at different levels. We saw our work, first of all, as being consciousness raising. We therefore had to publicize our goals, put Wages for Housework on the political map, have a media presence, take part in conferences, speak to women's groups, and be present at street events such as fairs and demonstrations (for instance, International Women's Day, Mother's Day, book fairs, community festivals, and so on).
>
> So, to reach a wider spectrum of women, we had opened, in November 1975, a storefront in a working-class neighbourhood of Brooklyn – where a number of us lived – which became the centre for our meetings and a place where women could come in and chat with us, consult our publications, or ask us for information on issues affecting the situation of women in general. The opening of our storefront, which took a great deal of investment of our time and money to prepare, was widely covered by the media, even the *New York Times!*[65]

Similar centres were created in London by the Power of Women Collective, and in Italy by Wages for Housework groups. In Ontario, the activists who were to form the Toronto Wages for Housework Committee used the Women's Liberation Bookmobile to spread the news, from town to town, of the Wages for Housework demand, and to hand out documents on women's situation.[66]

Street events

The goal of street events was to increase visibility. For example, to publicly launch the Wages for Housework campaign in Italy, the Comitato Triveneto per il Salario al Lavoro Domestico organized three days of activities at the Piazza Ferretto in Mestre, on March 8–10, 1974.[67] On the program were demonstrations, speeches, and conversations with passersby; feminist songs, plays, photo exhibitions, and banners; screenings of feminist films; and distribution of leaflets, brochures, posters, and documentation. A journal, *Bollettino delle donne*, was launched by the Wages for Housework committees of Padua and Venice, and so was the first version of *Le operaie della casa*, by Mariarosa Dalla Costa.[68]

The choice of the form and type of street event was left to each local group. Possibilities included rallies, torch-lit processions, squats in abandoned buildings, occupations, and sit-ins. In fact, the IFC chose a street event as a concerted action to mark the arrival on the public scene of the Wages for Housework

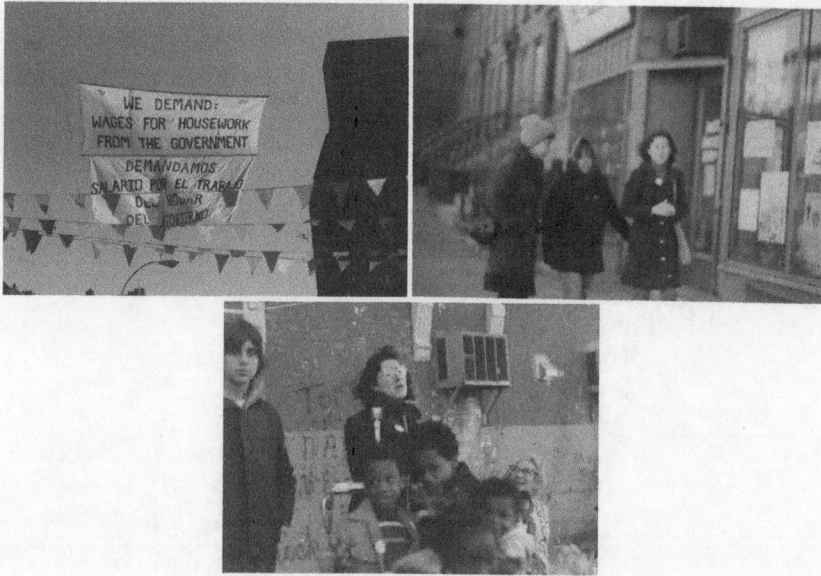

Figure 3.10   Opening of the New York Wages for Housework Committee storefront in Brooklyn, November 1975. The three women on the sidewalk are Mariarosa Dalla Costa, Mary Capps, and Silvia Federici. At the centre in the bottom photograph is Silvia Federici. (Silvia Federici Archives)

struggle.[69] The occasion was May 1, 1975, International Workers' Day. This was the date of the IFC's first international demonstration, held simultaneously in cities where Wages for Housework groups were located.

Why May 1? Because "all over the world women have been saying that society rests on our labour and that we, like all workers, need wages to fight against our exploitation":[70]

> Because we are women, we are all identified with the work of servicing others, looking after their physical and emotional needs, and providing this society with people who can function from one day to the next because we are there to renew and restore them with our labour.[71]

The *Wages for Housework International Network Newsletter* of 1975 gives an idea of the activities that groups in the network organized for the occasion.

The newly created Los Angeles Wages for Housework Committee, with its three members, decided to form a well-identified contingent within a march organized by the Chicano community. The committee's leaflet (in Spanish and English) established links between the struggles of wageless women at home and those of immigrants.[72] "Our May Day leaflet ... has been extremely well received," concluded the *Newsletter* reporter.

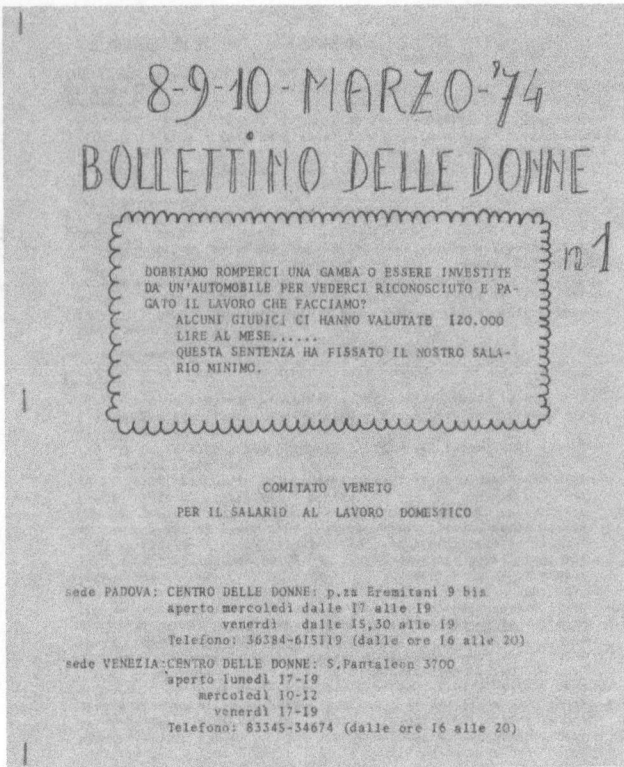

Figure 3.11   First issue of the journal *Bollettino delle donne*
(Comitato Veneto per il Salario al Lavoro Domestico), distributed
March 8–10, 1974, to launch the Wages for Housework campaign
in Mestre, Italy.

The Toronto Wages for Housework Committee (consisting of fifteen
women) organized a gathering in the square in front of City Hall at noon.[73] It
was attended by 250 people, who listened to eight activists from the organizing
committee talk about different situations experienced by women as nurses,
waitresses, factory and office workers, full-time houseworkers, welfare mothers,
and lesbians. It was said that a total of 500 people passed through the square
in front of City Hall during these speeches, which lasted an hour and a half;
five thousand leaflets (in Italian, Spanish, Portuguese, and English – though
apparently not French) were distributed before and during the gathering.

Media coverage was significant, not only before the event but also during
and after, with even the national television news devoting three minutes to
the gathering.[74] It was recorded on video by the committee itself, to use as
a consciousness-raising tool.[75] A brochure, *Women Speak Out: May Day Rally
Toronto*, was published, containing the speeches given that day and reproduc-

tions of the leaflets distributed by the other groups in the network in their respective countries.

In the section of the network newsletter devoted to the activities of the Toronto committee on May 1, 1975, the event's coordinator, Judy Ramirez, wrote that it had had an enormous impact on the visibility of the Toronto group and the Wages for Housework perspective:

> The May Day rally served as an "announcement" that we are on the scene and that we are beginning our organizing to get wages for housework. It has given wages for housework the public visibility it needs in order to begin functioning as a reference point to women in all situations throughout Ontario and Canada.[76]

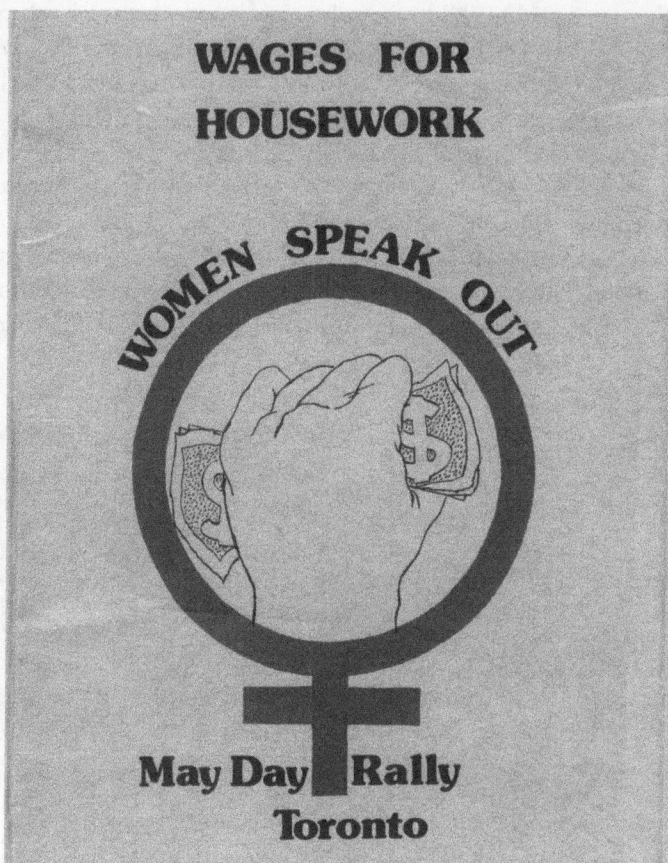

Figure 3.12 Cover page of *Women Speak Out: May Day Rally Toronto*, documenting the May 1, 1975, rally organized by the Toronto Wages for Housework Committee. The brochure contained the speeches made at the event and reproductions of leaflets distributed at the time in similar rallies organized by groups at other locations in the network.

A national Gallup poll, conducted soon after, revealed that 49 percent of the population of Canada was in favour of wages for housework.[77]

In London, the Power of Women Collective organized the first Wages for Housework march in England: the twenty-five women marching, accompanied by a police escort, carried banners, slogans, and leaflets, along with various symbols of women's labour, such as casseroles, brooms, and pots. They were not permitted to distribute leaflets, and the demonstrators were threatened with arrest for obstruction. The march ended with a speech in front of the prime minister's residence.[78]

In Bristol, six activists set up a stand near the city's most popular shopping centre, where Wages for Housework slogans and leaflets from other demonstrations by the groups in the network were on display. The Bristol group's leaflet showed the wages paid to childcare workers and asked what wage was paid to mothers and houseworkers for the same work. Other questions followed: "And after you've done all the housework, what jobs can you get outside the home? Cooking, cleaning, nursing, typing, unskilled factory work."[79] The demonstration was well covered by both local television stations. The local newspaper devoted a long article to the issue of wages for housework, which, according to Suzie Fleming, demonstrated "how much impact a small action can have."[80]

Of course, demonstrations also took place in Italy. Le Comitato Triveneto per il Salario al Lavoro Domestico demonstrated in the Piazza Ferretto in Mestre starting at noon and invited women to engage in a day-long strike from

Figure 3.13   International Day of Struggle for Wages for Housework, May 1, 1975, Mestre (Venice). *In the centre*: Mariarosa Dalla Costa. (Mariarosa Dalla Costa Archives)

housework. On this occasion, the committee launched the first issue of the journal *Le operaie della casa*. Among other things, there were posters, songs, a play by the Gruppo Teatrale, sales of the journal, and distribution of leaflets announcing the demonstration at the end of this May Day.[81]

Different IFC groups organized other street events on International Women's Day and during various mobilizations.[82] To publicize their existence, IFC groups also participated in events such as fairs, community parties, and even an international tribunal. For instance, the IFC participated in the International Tribunal on Crimes against Women, held in Brussels March 3-8, 1976.

International platforms

The International Tribunal on Crimes against Women offered a platform for denunciations of violence committed against all women on the planet, followed by discussions on strategies for change. Simone de Beauvoir opened the tribunal. Some two thousand women from forty countries participated.

The IFC was represented at the tribunal by Wages for Housework groups from Italy (notably the groups from Mestre and Ferrara, the latter to denounce the barbaric childbirth practices in that city's hospital), Canada (letter to the tribunal), and Wages Due Lesbians from the London group. At the closing assembly of the tribunal, during which change strategies were discussed, the IFC presented a resolution in favour of wages for housework, which was passed "almost unanimously" by the participants. It read:

> Wages-for-Housework Groups in Italy, England, Canada, Switzerland, and the United States, decided that unwaged housework is robbery with violence; that this work and wagelessness is a crime from which all other crimes flow; that it brands us for life as the weaker sex and delivers us powerless to employers, government planners and legislators, doctors, the police, prisons, mental institutions, as well as to men for a lifetime of servitude and imprisonment. We demand wages-for-housework for all women from the governments of the world. We will organize internationally to win back the wealth that has been stolen from us in every country, and to put an end to the crimes committed daily against us all.[83]

The presence of a number of IFC groups at such a tribunal could only give international exposure to the Wages for Housework demand.

A campaign to give power to women

According to writings on the organizational perspective, the easiest way to reach out to women was to visit places where housework had already been, in a sense, "socialized." Such places include self-service laundries and supermarkets, unemployment insurance and social welfare offices, and hospitals – places where women had to wait for hours. It was often easier to make connections with them, support them, and eventually undertake actions with them when they had already begun to act themselves, and thus had attained a certain level of power. This was particularly true of women on welfare and of certain categories of women in the workplace who had organized to improve their working conditions.

Whether the chosen site for organization was the community or the waged workplace, the essential thing remained mobilization around wages for housework and reproduction work, the foundation of women's exploitation. The important thing was to mobilize on this basis, whether the women were working at home or in the factory, the office, the hospital, the school, or elsewhere. This was the primary objective and the unifying power of the Wages for Housework campaign.

The campaign was intended to create opportunities for women to show their potential power. Marches and demonstrations were examples of this. Preparing such events, coming into contact with hundreds of people, explaining the Wages for Housework ideas and demands, meeting with the media and preparing to give interviews, designing and distributing documentation – learning how to do these things helped women gain power.

Creating and maintaining contacts with women from all over the world was another important aspect of IFC organizational work. The documents produced by the IFC had to circulate in several languages, and meetings had to be organized to create contacts and mobilize. Conducting an international campaign meant being responsible for women not only from different communities but from other parts of the world. How could strategies and means of action be implemented, what forms of struggle should be advanced? These questions had to be answered depending on each situation.

In order to conduct this kind of campaign, "we need organization," stated the IFC documents on the organizational perspective. This was no "vanguard" party, as were some groups in leftist circles.

We are against the party as a political form because it assumes that the "working class" is homogeneous, that there are no power relations within it and that one organization can express the "general interest" of the class. Such an organization is based on the repression of the interests of the weaker sectors of the working class: women and black people first of all.[84]

So said the documents on the organization. Just as women had to gather in autonomous groups that were separate from male organizations, it was felt that women within the IFC – particularly racialized women and lesbians –

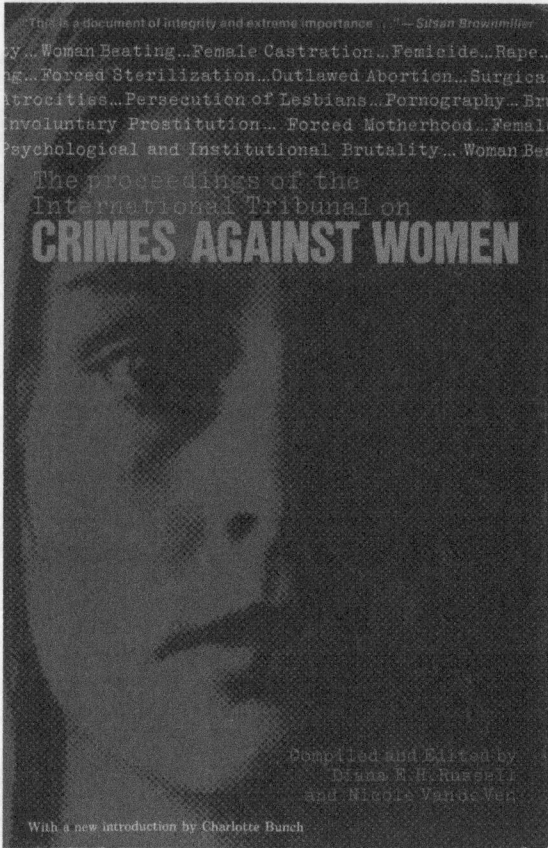

Figure 3.14 Cover of *The Proceedings of the International Tribunal on Crimes against Women.* The tribunal took place in Brussels on March 3–8, 1976.

should be free to create such autonomous entities. Autonomous groups were the only way to guarantee expression of the interests of different categories of women, and the best way to find forms of struggle appropriate to their respective situations.

The choice of a campaign to highlight the shared aspect of diverse situations experienced by women to bring houseworkers out of isolation and invisibility, to end the divisions among women, and to demand a wage for housework required an organization, action priorities, and a network. What role should the network play? How should these priorities be chosen? How could local actions and international organization be accommodated? Different groups in the network did not at first have similar answers to these questions, and it was during the international IFC conferences – key moments in the IFC's life – that debates took place on its organizational vision.

SALARIO POR EL TRABAJO DEL HOGAR

A TODOS LOS GOBIERNOS:

Las mujeres del mundo estamos dando aviso a todos ustedes.
Nosotras limpiamos sus hogares y fabricas. Nosotras levantamos la
proxima generacion de trabajadores para ustedes. Sea lo que sea
lo que hagamos, somos las amas de casa del mundo. En cambio por
nuestro trabajo, nos piden que trabajemos mas fuerte.

Les estamos avisando que es nuestra intencion ser pagadas por
el trabajo que hacemos. Queremos pago por cada servicio sanitario
sucio, por cada parto doloroso, por cada taza de cafe, y por cada
sonrisa. Y si no recibimos lo que queremos, entonces nosotras
simplemente rehusamos seguir trabajando.

Nosotras hemos criado nuestros hijos para que sean buenos
ciudadanos y que respeten sus leyes pero ustedes los han puesto
en fabricas, prisiones, barrios, y grupos de mecanografia. Nuestros
hijos se merecen mas de lo que ustedes pueden ofrecerles y ahora
los levantaremos para que ESPEREN MAS.

Nosotras les hemos criado mas bebes cuando ustedes han necesitado
mas trabajadores y nos hemos sometido a la esterilizacion cuando
no los han necesitado. Nuestras matrices ya no son propiedad del
gobierno.

Les hemos limpiado y brillado y
aceitado, y cerado, hasta que nuestros
brazos y nuestras espaldas nos dolieran,
y ustedes solo han creado mas sucio. Ahora
ustedes se van a pudrir en su propia
basura.

Nosotras hemos trabajado en la soledad
de nuestros hogares cuando asi lo han necesitado, y hemos cojido un segundo trabajo
cuando asi lo han necesitado. Ahora nosotras
queremos decidir CUANDO trabajaremos y para
QUIEN trabajaremos. Nosotras queremos
poder decidir si QUEREMOS TRABAJAR
O NO...tal como ustedes.

Somos secretarias, enfermeras,
maestras, prostitutas, actrices,
nineras, mozas, cocineras, sirvi-
entas y trabajadoras de toda
variedad. Nosotras hemos su-
dado, mientras ustedes se han
hecho ricos. Ahora queremos
recibir la riqueza que hemos
producido.

LO QUEREMOS EN EFECTIVO,
RETROACTIVO, E INMEDI-
ATAMENTE. Y LO
QUEREMOS TODO.

LA CAMPAÑA POR EL
SALARIO POR EL TRABAJO
DEL HOGAR

Figure 3.15 "Salario por el Trabajo del Hogar," Spanish translation
of the leaflet "Notice to All Governments." (Silvia Federici Archives)

Some of the Debates Raised during International Conferences

The international conferences offered excellent opportunities for information
exchanges, presentation of reflections and analyses, discussions surrounding
strategies, and making decisions about common actions.[85] In the documents I
consulted, they were called International Feminist Collective's Meetings until
1977. Here, I concentrate on certain debates and deliberations at one or another
of the five IFC conferences.

Two of these conferences took place in the United States, two others in
Canada, and one in England. The New York conference, organized by the

New York Wages for Housework Committee, took place in October 1974; the one in Montreal, in February 1975, was organized by the Montreal Power of Women Collective; the one in London, in July 1975, by the London Power of Women Collective; the Toronto Wages for Housework Committee organized the Toronto conference, held in October 1975; and the Chicago conference, in April 1977, was organized by the Chicago group, advised and guided by the Toronto Wages for Housework Committee.

Other conferences were called "international." These were meetings organized by autonomous groups within Wages for Housework groups. Below, I discuss one of them, the conference organized in July 1976 by Wages Due Lesbians, linked to the Toronto Wages for Housework Committee.

How to combine an international campaign and the organizational autonomy of participating groups

One of the first great debates that took place during early conferences was about the IFC's chosen means of action – that is, the international campaign – and the organizational coherence to establish within the network to lead this campaign. The participants wondered, What would an international campaign involve on the organizational level? Would it involve a shared strategy? How would local autonomy fit within the context of the network? Did an international campaign necessarily require political coherence? For example, could the Wages for Housework perspective be separated from the demand for a wage? Could a group use the Wages for Housework perspective as a consciousness-raising tool without demanding a wage for housework as such? In short, would an international campaign as an organizational strategy interfere with the local autonomy of groups? What kind of leadership was required for an international campaign? What exactly did organizational autonomy mean for the "autonomous" groups within the IFC? Finally, what relations should be established with Wages for Housework groups that were situated at the periphery of the network?

This was the mid-1970s, remember, and there were very few (if any) reference points in the feminist tradition to which to refer to enlighten discussions on these organizational questions, outside of those designed by the leftist groups of the time, which not only excluded autonomous action by women and feminist perspectives of their world of thought but also proposed centralized action strategies, usually based on a vanguard, which the IFC documents on organization rejected. These documents, as we have seen, expressed the difficulty of "starting from zero" to invent a type of political action based on housework. The IFC had to establish its foundations from practically nothing, which meant going through a period of trial and error, and also of internal turmoils.

The debate on organizational policy apparently surfaced during the first IFC conference, the one in New York in October 1974. It became heated during the next conference, the one in Montreal in February 1975, and was explored in greater depth in the summer of 1975 in an exchange of letters and positions called the Post-Montreal Conference Debate. Discussion centred on the relevance and significance of organizing an international campaign for groups in the network and ended with the eviction of one of the two Toronto groups, and the departure of the Montreal group. Here is what I was able to gather about this debate.

During the first two conferences, in October 1974 and February 1975, two Wages for Housework groups were coexisting in Toronto: Group 1, sometimes called the "Book Group," was a study group formed in the summer of 1973. Group 2, which later became the Toronto Wages for Housework Committee, was formed around the fall of 1974, having separated from a mixed-sex political group.[86] Group 2 produced a document after the New York conference stating its disagreement with Group 1.[87]

According to Group 2, the disagreement was mainly over the question of leadership and the relevance of the international aspect of the Wages for Housework perspective. It interpreted the position of Group 1 as follows: an international network, with common political stances, would run counter to the local autonomy of each collective. Group 1 wanted each collective to be responsible for developing its own wages perspective for its "territory"; in this view, all commitment to an international network would interfere with the local autonomy of its components.[88] These questions arose again in the debates during the second conference of the international network, held in Montreal in February 1975.

Organized by the Montreal Power Women Collective, created only two months before, the Montreal conference opened with misunderstandings on the expectations of participants. The Montreal group advertised widely and organized an event open to all.[89] It had not been made clear that this was an international meeting of specifically Wages for Housework groups and that it was open only to women. To these initial misunderstandings were added different expectations of this second international IFC conference.

For a majority of the groups in the network, the Wages for Housework perspective was already established and the conference was to be about organizing the international campaign. These groups therefore felt that the conference should be more internal in nature, that men were not welcome, and that the legitimacy of Wages for Housework and the campaign were not up for debate. In the view of these groups, it was time for the next step, that of the organization of a campaign as such. It was time to move on to action.

For the newly created Montreal group, and also for Group 1 from Toronto, the conference was intended, rather, to clarify the political perspective of Wages for Housework, and the goal was to discuss that perspective more broadly; it was also to weigh the merits of the wage demand, the pros and cons – hence

INTERNATIONAL CONFERENCE
»WAGES FOR HOUSEWORK«
MONTREAL QUEBEC
FEBRUARY 22-23, 1975

Figure 3.16   Invitation poster for the Montreal conference of the IFC, February 22–23, 1975. (Mariarosa Dalla Costa Archives)

the idea of a public conference.[90] This misunderstanding overlaid and added to the divergences between the two Toronto Wages for Housework groups. These divergences were made public by Group 2 in a statement to the network that circulated before the conference.[91]

These different expectations of the conference and what should or should not be debated were crystallized around the following issues: Was Wages for Housework a tool for consciousness raising, or a material demand? Was it a way of seeing the world so as to understand women's place in it, or a political fight for wages?

The Montreal group spoke of these divergences of views in terms of different "emphasis" or tendencies within a single perspective, whereas others spoke of different political perspectives.[92] In the view of the latter, "It is impossible to be in an organisation that moves in two opposite directions at the same time."[93] The Montreal group (and probably Group 1) was opposed to what it saw as the authoritarian direction that the network was taking, whereas some other groups in the network accused the Montreal group (and Group 1) of being "libertarian."[94]

Beth Ingber, leader of the Los Angeles group, summarized the divergences, which she called "political trends." One trend – that of the network – was based on the international nature of capital and the need to act on the international level, and supported the view that organizational coherence was necessary to gain wages for housework. The other trend saw the Wages for Housework perspective more as a consciousness-raising tool, as something that could be achieved "here and there" with an organization reduced to an agglomeration of local groups, each of which had its local views. This trend subscribed to the formula of international links rather than that of an international strategy. For most groups in the network, however, it would take more than international links to gain a wage for housework.

A total of eighty-five people attended the Montreal conference, most of them from the United States, Canada, Italy, and England. At the end of six hours of hot debate, the groups that wanted to take action held that an international organization could not operate in two different directions. The theoretical perspective of Wages for Housework could not be separated from the campaign to demand such wages. There was therefore a vote on the relevance of keeping Group 1 in the network. Out of sixty-five people who voted, forty-three voted against keeping the group, two voted for, and twenty abstained.

The high abstention rate added to the great frustration of those expelled and the general malaise, and provoked an avalanche of discussions on these subjects during the subsequent months; launched by the Montreal group, the discussions came to be called the Post-Montreal Conference Debate. The groups in the network exchanged views throughout the spring and summer of 1975 about the legitimacy of this expulsion; some of these texts, in favour of the campaign, were considered to reflect the official position of the network and confirmed the direction of the vote taken at the Montreal conference.[95]

Finally, the Montreal group was not invited to the Toronto conference that was to be held in October 1975. It was decided that much clearer criteria for participation would be established for this conference, and discussions on the merits of the claim for wages would be excluded from the agenda. It was time to take the next step: that of organizing and consolidating the Wages for Housework campaign at the international scale.[96]

The question of leadership and the "points of reference"

At the heart of these debates, which might seem Byzantine today, was the thorny question of leadership. What type of leadership did an international campaign require? How could leaders function without renewing the classic hierarchy of power relationships? The documents presenting the IFC's position noted that women were uneasy with addressing this aspect. This was especially true for those who had come from the left, within which they had observed that the exercise of leadership corresponded to the traditional exercise of men's power over women. Leadership in a group was often seen as a hierarchical authority that removed from the activist base all room for action and all autonomy. Many saw it as the equivalent of a vanguard, which caused them to reject all leadership. And then there was the fact that the exercise of power by women in the political sphere was relatively new in the mid-1970s, no "recipe" having been tested ... or transmitted.

The issue of leadership was expressed within the IFC in terms of "points of reference." This expression designated people with more political experience (and therefore a clearer political vision of the struggles) and who were identified in the network as offering guidelines for thought and action. They had been behind the founding of the IFC, and they had a solid past as activists and a capacity for political analysis: Mariarosa Dalla Costa in Italy, Selma James in England, and Silvia Federici in the United States, as well as Judy Ramirez for Canada and, later, Beth Ingber on the west coast of the United States. These five women were recognized, during the existence of the IFC, as points of reference for the organization and action of the International Wages for Housework Campaign in their respective geographic zones. They were also leaders in theoretical development of the perspective, particularly Dalla Costa, James, and Federici.

The documents on the organization were clear on this subject: leadership in itself did not pose a problem; the difficulty lay in defining the type of leadership that should be exercised, on what basis, and to attain what goals.[97] A good test in this regard was to see whether the organization could ensure that other people had the opportunity to take the lead, to rise to take leadership positions, assume responsibilities, and promote action initiatives. "A good test of leadership," wrote Federici, "is the capacity to ensure that other people can grow. Because it is essential for the success of our political campaign that more and more women take leadership positions."[98]

Were these recommendations sufficient to ensure "good" leadership within the IFC? Probably not. The IFC was innovating on the organizational level in relation to this era of the feminist movement; no other feminist grouping had such a broad objective of massive mobilization of women, nor had any others targeted housework in such organizational terms. The IFC thus had to go through a period of experimentation in every respect.

What did organizational autonomy of groups of lesbians and racialized women mean inside the network?

The organizational politics was also the subject of other debates during the IFC's international conferences. For example, what did the organizational autonomy of supposedly autonomous groups within the different Wages for Housework groups, such as Wages Due Lesbians and Black Women for Wages for Housework, mean? The question of autonomy of lesbian groups was on the agenda for at least three of the IFC conferences: those in Montreal in February, London in July, and Toronto in October, 1975.

The Montreal conference was in effect marked by the coming out of lesbians within the network under the name "Wages Due Lesbians." Up to then blended into the Toronto and London groups, they decided to adopt a new organizational form and to compose autonomous groups, but within the network:

> This separation came out of long discussions on our need to organize autonomously within the network but also to work closely with non-lesbian women. We should stress that it is an autonomous organizational form and not a separate or different strategy. Wages for Housework is our perspective and our strategy. Lesbianism is one way in which we make a struggle.[99]

The important manifesto *Fucking Is Work,* presented at the Montreal conference, had previously been hotly discussed and had undergone numerous revisions. It established the theoretical bases for lesbians' participation in the network on their own terms. It was written by the lesbians in the Toronto group, who had come originally from the (nascent) lesbian movement and found in the Wages for Housework movement a collective power conducive to their revealing themselves and their own struggle.

This question was also on the agenda at the IFC conference in London on July 24–26, 1975. A text by Ruth Hall laying out the position of Wages Due Lesbians was read and discussed there. The preamble read:

> It is the result of discussions that took place among the members of the London and Toronto Wages Due Collectives ... It had been preceded by testimonials by three lesbians who spoke of their own experiences and struggles as, respectively, a mother, a black woman, and an office employee in a London office and under even more repressive conditions in Belfast. It was followed by a presentation and a discussion of the meaning of organizational autonomy of lesbians in the Wages for Housework network.[100]

The document thus presented "some of the conclusions that we arrived at as lesbians fighting for wages for housework" – conclusions bearing on "the position and exploitation of lesbians, the position and exploitation of all women, the power relations between women who call themselves lesbians and those who call themselves heterosexual, how these power relations function in capitalism and in the movement. In other words, we want to talk about lesbianism and power."[101]

We know that the question of organizational autonomy of lesbians also arose at the Toronto conference in October 1975. A presentation by the Toronto and London Wages Due groups was planned to discuss the question of "what lesbianism is and is not."[102]

The question of the autonomy of Wages Due Lesbians groups was obviously on the agenda at the international Wages Due Lesbians conference held in Toronto on July 24–25, 1976. The poster announcing the conference presented this meeting as an opportunity to discuss the most crucial issues facing lesbians, the Wages for Housework movement, and the women's movement.

According to the monthly magazine *The Body Politic*, which was covering the conference, eighty women, Canadian, American, and English, "Black and White" lesbians, and heterosexual women participated.[103] Three speakers talked about the significance of lesbian autonomy. These were Ruth Hall, of the Wages Due Lesbians collective of London; Wilmette Brown, from Black Women for Wages for Housework of New York (formed following the Welfare Conference organized by the New York Wages for Housework Collective in April of that year); and Francie Wyland, of the Toronto Wages Due Lesbians collective. In the view of all of these speakers, the Wages for Housework movement had the capacity to unify all women, without their having to put aside their respective differences, because "black" women and lesbians each had their own autonomous organizations within the movement, and each took into account their members' specific needs. In her speech, Brown made an important contribution to what would later be called the intersectional perspective, analyzed in the previous chapter.

Figure 3.17   Left: IFC London Conference, July 24–26, 1975. *Left to right*: Ruth Hall (Wages Due Lesbians – London), Silvia Federici (New York Wages for Housework Committee), Judith Ramirez (Toronto Wages for Housework Committee); *from the back*: Suzie Fleming (Power of Women, London). (Silvia Federici Archives) *Right*: Silvia Federici and Ruth Hall, at the same event. (Silvia Federici Archives)

Figure 3.18 Invitation poster for the International Conference on Lesbianism and the Wages for Housework Campaign, Toronto, July 24–25, 1976. (CWMA, box 625.36) Note the use of the Éditions du remue-ménage logo, designed by Lise Nantel, without mention of the source – a practice common at the time. The logo portrays the countless daily tasks performed by women in the home.

The final declaration of the New York conference

The debates about organizational autonomy held at international conferences discussed up to this point were far from giving an idea of the scope of subjects on the agenda, the presentations given, and the points discussed. Each IFC conference also had the goal of advancing and substantiating the Wages for

Housework political perspective. For example, at the IFC's first international conference, the one in New York in October 1974, a final declaration was written onsite, refining the theoretical perspective on Wages for Housework and explaining further the meaning of the struggle of the wageless:

> Traditionally, production has been assumed to take place in the factory. In reality, production takes place at every moment in every workers [sic] life. Once we discovered our work in the home and the community reproduces labor power, then we began to see that the whole society is an assembly line that runs from the factory to the community and back again. Capital is created by the collective laborer: we who are shut inside the factory and we who are shut outside the factory, and therefore shut out of wages.[104]

If women were wageless in the kitchen, it was because capitalist economic production found it profitable. Women who rejected this situation would subvert the plan made for them by the capitalist system in the international social factory.

This wageless state, the final declaration continued, kept women dependent on men's wages; in this context of dependence, their personal relations, their sexuality, and their emotions would all be transformed into forced labour. Heterosexuality would now become a form of discipline. Women's struggle was against heterosexuality as discipline. Lesbianism, by its very existence, challenged the sexual division of labour and sexuality as power relations. The Wages for Housework struggle, for all women who were wageless or in a proletarian situation, undermined the divisions between homosexuals and heterosexuals, between single women and women with men, between women with children and women without children.

The final statement of the conference asserted,

> To demand wages for housework exposes housework as work and negates it as a function of love. To demand wages for housework, negating it as a labor of love, is already a power.
>
> To demand wages for housework is to find an identity in a struggle for our own needs and to refuse the identity that capitalism imposes on us. To refuse capitalist femininity is already a power.
>
> To demand wages for housework is to demand the socialization of housework on our terms, to liberate our time.
>
> To demand wages for housework is to demand the right to have or not to have children, when and how and with whom we wish ...
>
> To demand wages for housework is to demand to determine the conditions and the wages of work outside the home.

To demand wages for housework is to demand the power to refuse the second job outside the home ...

To win a wage for housework is to begin to destroy all of the power relations within the working class which are based on the division between the waged and the wageless.

To destroy the power relationship within the working class is to destroy capital.

This final position thus specified for the first time, in this new body of the network, precisely what was original about the Wages for Housework perspective: the capacity for the Wages for Housework strategy to link to other demands, up to then claimed separately by various women's movement groups.

The Wages for Housework strategy therefore represented an essential lever of power, a fulcrum for changing numerous aspects of the situation of women – chief among them the hierarchy of power between the waged and the wageless, between men and women. It thus would be powerful enough to undermine capitalist social and economic organization and its foundations, which rested on the division between the waged and the wageless.

Questions submitted to the delegates of the Toronto conference

One hundred delegates were expected at the international conference that took place in Toronto October 17–20, 1975, and, according to the *Toronto Star*, "behind closed doors ... to plot a world-wide campaign that could have housewives paid wages."[105] There was concern with not repeating the problems experienced at the Montreal conference, which had been open to the public. This time, the idea was to concentrate on the objective of the conference: "To refine the general strategy and organize the wage campaign," according to Beth Ingber of the Los Angeles group. It was agreed that the Toronto conference would be internal to the network, and thus open to member groups and limited to women. Female sympathizers would also be admitted, but as observers. A time had to be reserved for them to explain the conjuncture and the situation in their locations.[106]

We gain an idea of the content of the conference from the program offered to participants a month before it took place. The conference opened on Friday, October 17, with a "pre-conference party," which included a registration period, a screening of the video of the May Day rally organized by the Toronto group on the preceding May 1, and songs on the theme of Wages for Housework, written and performed by two members of the Toronto group, Boo Watson and Lissa Donner.[107] A book of songs and music by Watson was distributed.[108]

On Saturday, October 18, the real work of the conference began. On the agenda were a review of the previous conference, international politics, and the economic crisis. The Sunday was devoted to reflections on the organization: the network's structures, international communications, and resources, reports on groups' struggles, development and use of mobilization tools, and the campaign itself.[109] The final day, Monday, was devoted to two themes: sexualities and the third world (including a presentation by Wilmette Brown and Margaret Prescod-Roberts, who was to start the Black Women for Wages for Housework group).[110]

A place was reserved during the last day for guest francophone sympathizers. We presented (in French) the history and situation of francophone women in Quebec, as well as the specifics and difficulties of the Wages for Housework struggle. By making our presentation in French, we also wanted to point out to network members that the French language was one of our "local specificities."

Figure 3.19   Mariarosa Dalla Costa at the IFC Toronto
Conference, October 1975. (Mariarosa Dalla Costa Archives)

When one reads the detailed program, one can't help but be astounded at the scope and content of the themes analyzed during these three days of debate. We can imagine the considerable organizational energy, given the means of the time, that must have gone into making sure it was held.[111] This impressive conference program gives us a good clue to the wealth, extent, and consistency of themes under debate in the embryonic feminist Internationale. This is what Federici remembers:

> The most satisfying conference was the one in Toronto. At that time [1975] we had a broad network. We were convinced that we could reach another level. That is why this conference was important. At the conference, there was a long discussion of international politics, the international economic situation, and the usefulness of the economic crisis. We could progress to

Figure 3.20   A few of the Quebec activists from Les Éditions Remue-ménage invited
to the IFC conference in Toronto, October 17–20, 1975. *Left to right*: Sylvie Dupont
(sitting), Lise Nantel, Louise Toupin, Nicole Lacelle with guitar. Photograph:
Raymonde Lamothe.

this level of discussion because we clearly saw at the time the significance of
Wages for Housework within the feminist movement. We realized that the
Wages for Housework perspective was not a political perspective for women
alone. We were beginning to discover the global issue of the wage, its implications, the links between metropolises and countries of the "periphery," and
all these issues began to be discussed. I remember that it was at the Toronto
conference that we saw the importance and usefulness of having a public
presence in the media. The media had attended our conference.[112]

From this, we can deduce that the conference did not take place entirely "behind
closed doors," and that the media were invited to some activities and covered
the event. In the end, we could only hope that more research and more personal
narratives will uncover more of the extent of debates during the conference.

The end of the IFC

A fifth IFC conference was held in Chicago in mid-April 1977; however, not
in attendance were two of the network's major entities: the Padua group –
the nucleus of the Italian groups – and the New York Wages for Housework
Committee, an absence to which I will return.[113] The existence of the IFC
was drawing to a close. Proof of this is that the name no longer seemed to

be in use starting in 1978. Instead, the International Wages for Housework Campaign took over the cause, with some of the existing groups and some new ones.[114] One of the points on the agenda for the Chicago conference in fact posed the question of the existence of the IFC: "Why the International Feminist Collective?"[115]

Like the preceding conferences, this one, organized by the Chicago and Toronto groups, had planned three days of exchanges and discussion. The first was devoted to a recap and update on the different campaign activities of the past year (struggles for social assistance, family allowances, support for sex workers) and the tools used (petitions, marches, newsletter, and so on).

The second day of exchanges had the theme "Autonomy." The proposed agenda listed presentations and discussions on the role of Wages Due Lesbians in the campaign, the autonomy of black women, and the question about points of reference. On this last topic, discussion was to include leadership in the internal organization, the raison d'être of the IFC, and the relations between groups in the network and the points of reference. Also discussed were publications, Falling Wall Press, and the different art forms (music, theatre, film, video) that should become tools accessible to all groups in the campaign. The third day was devoted to specific issues that should lead to future mobilizations, such as the Equal Rights Amendment, busing, social welfare, and support for sex workers. The final evening was left to meetings devoted specifically to autonomous groups within the network.

The only reports I found on this conference were those in the media, which reported essentially on the network's support for the struggle of sex workers, who were at the time subject to arrests and police harassment in the United States and Canada. Margo St. James, leader and initiator, in 1973, of the first structured sex workers' group, COYOTE, in San Francisco, was one of the guests at the conference. All of the city's media outlets headlined their articles around the "surprising" link between prostitutes and houseworkers.[116]

The question that particularly interests me here is that of the end of the IFC. Why did certain group representatives (including some founding members of the IFC) not participate in this conference, and why did they finally withdraw from the network? Why did the groups that remained decide to change the network's name? Unfortunately, I do not have consistent answers to these questions, only clues gleaned from the documentation I consulted.

It seems that, over time, ideas about the organization of the international campaign, the functioning of groups' autonomy, and the links that were to unite them with the campaign – the conception of the campaign's coordination, in fact – began to diverge among the points of reference – that is, the leaders. At least, that is the interpretation that I can draw from the question posed by the Toronto Wages for Housework Committee in a letter addressed to the network:

"How to proceed with the Campaign when there is disagreement among the points of reference?"[117]

There also seems to have been, as Federici implied in an interview that appears in the afterword to this book, "the tendency to interpret the leadership role rigidly, in too centralized and too hierarchized a way. This would not have been possible if it had been a mass movement in which people autonomously made decisions without waiting for permission from the leadership."

For whatever reason, unfortunately there does not seem to have been, in this embryonic women's Internationale at the dawn of neo-feminism, an adequate problem-solving space or mechanism for when the points of reference, living in four different countries, dispersed on two continents separated by an ocean, found themselves in disagreement. Under these circumstances, the page was being turned on the IFC, this forerunner of the feminist "Internationale." But let's not skip steps. Let us start with a look back at some of the movement's accomplishments. Let us see how this new school of feminist thought, the Wages for Housework perspective, was embodied in action.

Part 2

Mobilizations around Women's Invisible Work

Overview

How was the Wages for Housework perspective embodied in the field of struggle during the period that the International Feminist Collective (IFC) was in existence? Examples of mobilizations are given in the following chapters.

Wages for Housework groups engaged in a vast field of struggle between 1972 and 1977. In the year that the IFC was formed, Mariarosa Dalla Costa outlined its full scope of action. To organize struggles, she wrote, "all places where female domestic labor power is [invisibly] embodied had to be discovered." The expenditure of this hidden energy represented "the cost that capital has made and makes us pay as women" to perform "natural" work.[1]

Dalla Costa gave the example of the school. Even if houseworkers were not present in the school or on the job market, these sites had already embodied the labour of women: students and workers arrived at school, in effect, "fed, cared for, and ironed by their mothers, grandmothers, sisters, and (in the case of richer families) female servants."[2] Reflecting on this phenomenon, activists felt that the field of women's invisible work extended far beyond what was commonly called "housework." Nicole Cox and Silvia Federici, of the New York Wages for Housework Committee, expressed its magnitude this way:

> Housework, in fact, is much more than house cleaning. It is servicing the wage earner physically, emotionally, sexually, getting him ready to work day after day for the wage. It is taking care of our children – the future workers – assisting them from birth through their school years and ensuring that they too perform in the ways expected of them under capitalism.
>
> This means that behind every factory, behind every school, behind every office or mine is the hidden work of millions of women who have consumed their life, their labour power, in producing the labour power that works in that factory, school, office or mine.[3]

This meant, for the various Wages for Housework groups, discovering and identifying the sites, both private and public, in which women's reproductive work was "embodied" – invisibly integrated – and making these sites spaces of action and reflection on the scope of women's unpaid reproductive work. Activists then realized that domestic and reproductive work in fact constituted, in the words of the late Haitian sociologist Mireille Neptune Anglade, a "subsidy, obscure and obscured, that makes it possible for the national economy to function," men being, in this context, "in the objective position of beneficiaries of these subsidies."[4] This idea was expressed by Nicole Cox and Silvia Federici as "Wages for Housework [demand] means first of all that capital will have to pay for the enormous amount of social services which now they are saving on our backs." The most important thing, they added, was the fact that this demand was in itself "the refusal to accept our work as a biological destiny."[5] It consisted of "fighting in all fields against the material roots of our dependence."[6]

Groups in the IFC were involved in two types of struggles: those that were *initiated* by a Wages for Housework group and carried on by that group, and those that were initiated by other types of women's groups and *supported* by Wages for Housework groups. The latter groups saw such support and participation as occasions to establish solidarity with other women and with an aspect of reproductive work that was already the object of mobilization, and also as a key opportunity to highlight the Wages for Housework perspective and demand.

The mobilizations and actions initiated by Wages for Housework groups themselves fell into two categories: those that were led by a local group in the IFC network, and those that shared actions undertaken in concert with other groups in the network. In the latter category, for example, were mobilizations around May 1 events and participation in the International Tribunal on Crimes against Women (discussed in the previous chapter).

Considering the short period under study here, a very wide variety of sites incorporating women's private (home) or public (job market or community) reproductive work became targets for mobilizations by different Wages for Housework groups.[7] Before I present the mobilizations chosen and their political perspective, I will give a few examples of this diversity.

First were the struggles involving the area of physical reproduction as such, as well as the conditions under which it was practised. Obstetrics, gynecology in general, and sites of management of women's health were the targets of several struggles conducted by Wages for Housework groups, notably in Italy. These mobilizations concerned, among other things, conditions for pregnancy and childbirth, abortion, women's health, hospital structures, and violence by doctors.

Other areas of mobilization concerned the conditions for mothering work, such as family allowances, seen as a partial wage in return for women's reproductive work in the home, and welfare benefits, seen as the first historical form of wages for housework. The women most affected by these struggles fell mainly into the categories of welfare mothers, a good many of them racialized women, lesbian mothers who were constantly threatened with losing custody of their children, and immigrants. The intersectionality of oppressions and power relations was at the heart of some of these mobilizations, such as those initiated by groups of racialized welfare women, for whom class oppression cut across racial, gender, and sexual oppressions.[8] The struggles of the Black Women for Wages for Housework groups were of this type.

The waged workplace was the target of actions by a good number of Wages for Housework groups. Public social services facilities, hospitals, factories, restaurants, offices, and sex workers' workplaces were among the sites for "public" reproductive work. The categories of women affected were the employees in these sectors and, in the case of prostitution, "sidewalk workers."[9] Other themes related to domestic and reproductive work – including violence against women, the school, and sexuality – were, as we have seen in Chapter 2, the subjects of analysis, essays, and mobilizations.

The struggles described below were selected from among those that were accompanied by texts explaining the respective mobilization. It seemed to me that this was one way to give an idea of how and in what spirit the Wages for Housework perspective was embodied in action. Among the great diversity of mobilizations, the ones that I have chosen to describe fall into two general categories: struggles concerning women's private reproductive work, in families, and those concerning women's public reproductive work, outside the home. The former are described in Chapter 4; the latter in Chapter 5.

4

Mobilizations around Women's Invisible Work in the Home

The struggles involving women's private reproductive work and the conditions under which it was performed included mobilizations around family allowances, social assistance, and women's health (maternity, abortion), along with lesbian mothers' struggle.

FAMILY ALLOWANCES

In the fight for family allowances, some groups in the International Feminist Collective (IFC) took the torch handed down by first-wave activists. I am thinking notably of Eleanor Rathbone's mobilization to gain a public family-allowance plan in England in between 1927 and 1945.[1] Twenty-seven years later, this new mobilization (as well as the one for increasing social assistance benefits to women on welfare) had the merit of bringing to the public eye the question of unwaged women's economic dependence in the home – and to highlight, by this very fact, these women's lack of power. These struggles constituted a spring-board for the issue of a wage for housework and for launching the campaign in countries such as England in 1973.

It was through a campaign for family allowances, led by associations of mothers on social assistance in March 1973, and supported by women in the English feminist movement, that the Wages for Housework demand first appeared in the public arena, in a massive mobilization. It marked the beginning of the International Wages for Housework Campaign, one of the first objectives of the IFC.

1972–77: The Torch Is Passed in England and then Canada

In 1972, the British Conservative government announced its intention to abolish the universal family allowance instituted in 1945 and replace it with a tax credit for dependent children. Up to then independent of income, family allowances would now be linked to it – in fact, linked to the husband when he represented the only salary in the family.

The response to the government was a huge mobilization by women, with petitions throughout the country, demonstrations with distributions of leaflets, and sit-ins with children in front of the central post office in Trafalgar Square in London, followed by articles and letters in newspapers. These events were heavily covered by the press.

What had begun as a defensive struggle was quickly transformed into a mobilization to increase the allowances and extend them to the first child (at the time, they began with the second child). Another demand was that the allowances remain independent of income, not subject to tax, and not be subtracted from the social assistance allowances.

Finally, in 1974, the English government withdrew its proposal for tax credits, recommitted to universal family allowances, and extended the payment to mothers as of the first child. The family allowances were also increased by 50 percent, although this did not amount to much in real terms, given how small the allowances were in 1972.[2] A new fight to index the allowances to the cost of living would begin in 1976.

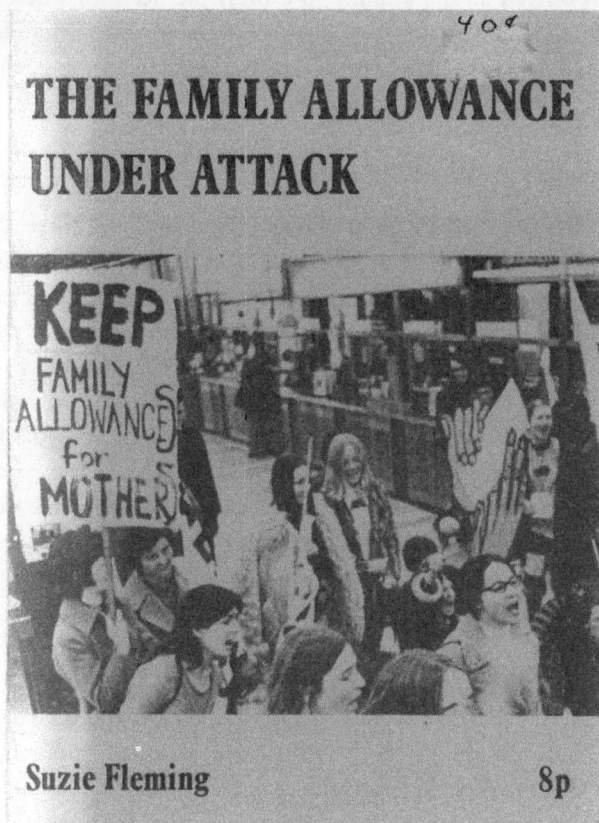

Figure 4.1   Cover page of *The Family Allowance under Attack*, by Suzie Fleming (Bristol: Falling Wall Press and the Power of Women Collective, 1973).

In late 1975, it was the turn of the Canadian government to amend the public family-allowance plan by freezing the planned increase. In January 1976, the Toronto Wages for Housework Committee launched a petition to protest against what was equivalent to real cuts in family allowances and social assistance, and to demand wages for housework.

The petition (in English, French, Italian, Portuguese, and Spanish) was endorsed by the Wages Due Lesbians groups, which, for the first time, expressed publicly in Canada the impacts of the cuts on lesbians. The petition was also endorsed by organizations grouped in the Coalition against Cutbacks. Demonstrations took place in the spring of 1976, then on May Day, to protest against the freeze in allowances. In Toronto, rallies were held in places such as shopping centres and parks, and speeches were made by different categories of women in several languages.[3]

For Wages for Housework groups in England and English Canada, these mobilizations offered an opportunity to express the need for women to have financial independence in a new way, and to promote the Wages for Housework demand and political perspective. To see how this vision was embodied in mobilizations, we can look at certain texts of the time.[4]

Family Allowances: A "Partial" Wage for Housework

The general outcry raised by governments' attempts to cut these allowances surprised many people, as very small amounts of money were in play. It was, however, money that mothers received regularly every week (in England) or every month (in Canada), by mail and to their name. Often, this money saw them through shortfalls in the family budget until the husband's paycheque arrived. For women working in the home full time, it was the only money that did not go through the husband's hands, that they did not have to ask for, that came to them directly, and that they did not have to account for (in theory): "The only money we can call our own ... This is the only money we can rely on."[5] For many women in this situation, the family allowances were, throughout their lives, the only money that was addressed specifically to them until they received their old-age pension at official retirement age.

A new element in the government announcements provoked great anger in England: the proposal that family allowances would be integrated into the spouse's salary. This prospect exposed the question of the financial dependence of women – those working full time in the home, especially mothers of young children and those who could not find a second job outside the home – on men. Such a possibility raised public debate on women's need for money.

The withdrawal of family allowances from women's hands put the wages for housework question squarely on the agenda: "Why don't we ask a lot more than the 90p or 1£ per child? Why don't we ask for a proper income?"[6] "We want

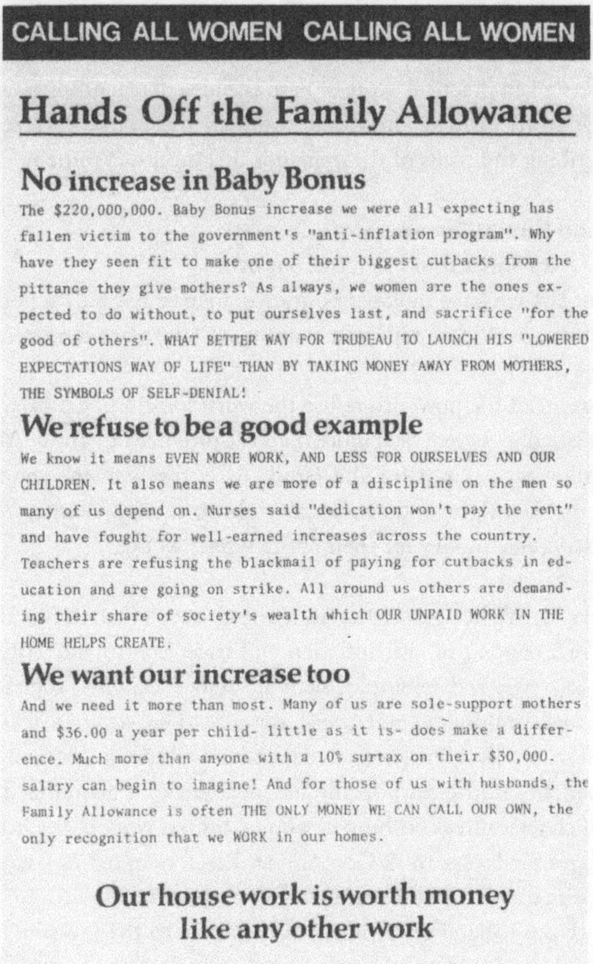

CALLING ALL WOMEN   CALLING ALL WOMEN

Hands Off the Family Allowance

No increase in Baby Bonus

The $220,000,000. Baby Bonus increase we were all expecting has fallen victim to the government's "anti-inflation program". Why have they seen fit to make one of their biggest cutbacks from the pittance they give mothers? As always, we women are the ones expected to do without, to put ourselves last, and sacrifice "for the good of others". WHAT BETTER WAY FOR TRUDEAU TO LAUNCH HIS "LOWERED EXPECTATIONS WAY OF LIFE" THAN BY TAKING MONEY AWAY FROM MOTHERS, THE SYMBOLS OF SELF-DENIAL!

We refuse to be a good example

We know it means EVEN MORE WORK, AND LESS FOR OURSELVES AND OUR CHILDREN. It also means we are more of a discipline on the men so many of us depend on. Nurses said "dedication won't pay the rent" and have fought for well-earned increases across the country. Teachers are refusing the blackmail of paying for cutbacks in education and are going on strike. All around us others are demanding their share of society's wealth which OUR UNPAID WORK IN THE HOME HELPS CREATE.

We want our increase too

And we need it more than most. Many of us are sole-support mothers and $36.00 a year per child- little as it is- does make a difference. Much more than anyone with a 10% surtax on their $30,000. salary can begin to imagine! And for those of us with husbands, the Family Allowance is often THE ONLY MONEY WE CAN CALL OUR OWN, the only recognition that we WORK in our homes.

Our house work is worth money
like any other work

Figure 4.2   "Hands Off the Family Allowance." Campaign of the Toronto Wages for Housework Committee, 1976.

that money from the State, not from the men."[7] Suzie Fleming, an active participant in the family allowances campaign in England, and an early activist in the English neo-feminist movement and the Wages for Housework group, related,

> A lot of women had for the first time articulated [their situation] publicly, and it was really an important moment for us as women. It was also an important moment for the women's movement in Britain, because this was the first campaign that we had been involved in that had spoken to all the women that we met. I had been involved in the women's movement from the beginning, and no other demand that we had ever raised had had that kind of response.[8]

Up to then, feminist demands to break women's financial dependence had been limited to incentives to work outside the house. The family allowances campaign "has given practical expression to the idea of extending payment from the State for work women already do, work in the home."[9] Here are a few slogans describing the focus of the demands by Power of Women:

> We demand Family Allowance
> Because we are entitled to money of our own ...
> Because unless we have money of our own, marriage is only a polite form of prostitution, ... and more rape will continue to take place in marriage than in back alleys ...
> Because we need the power to refuse the worst jobs in industry ...
> We are entitled to a great deal more than the pittance of Family Allowance ... Family Allowance is not for the family. It is the women's money. Family Allowance ... is a right ... the woman's right to money. Women with waged work must receive money for their entire week's work.[10]

In Canada, the fight against the announced freeze in family allowances in 1976 arose in a context of anti-inflation and wage-control austerity measures. The freeze also affected unemployment insurance benefits, social assistance, daycare centres, healthcare, and social services. The struggle was in favour of increases in family allowances, independent of family income and social assistance benefits, and even possibly independent of a guaranteed minimum income, "which guarantees nothing to women for our work in the home."[11] The Toronto Wages for Housework Committee therefore opted in favour of wages for housework provided by the state.

In the end, the Liberal government had to bow to the pressure, and family allowances were indexed to the cost of living in January 1977. This gesture was interpreted by the Wages for Housework Committees as "a victory for all women fighting to have some money of our own."[12]

Wages for Housework groups considered family allowances to be a "partial" wage, "the only universal wage that mothers receive in recognition for some of our work in the home."[13] Its expansion to a full wage for housework was demanded for all women at home, whether they were mothers or not. It was a question of autonomy, to keep women from being dependent on their husbands, and to make it possible for them to refuse to work twice as much by having to take jobs with the lowest wages on the market.

"Coming out with Wages for Housework": Lesbian Support

An unusual fact for this protest was that lesbians, grouped in a caucus called Wages Due Lesbians within the Toronto Wages for Housework Committee,

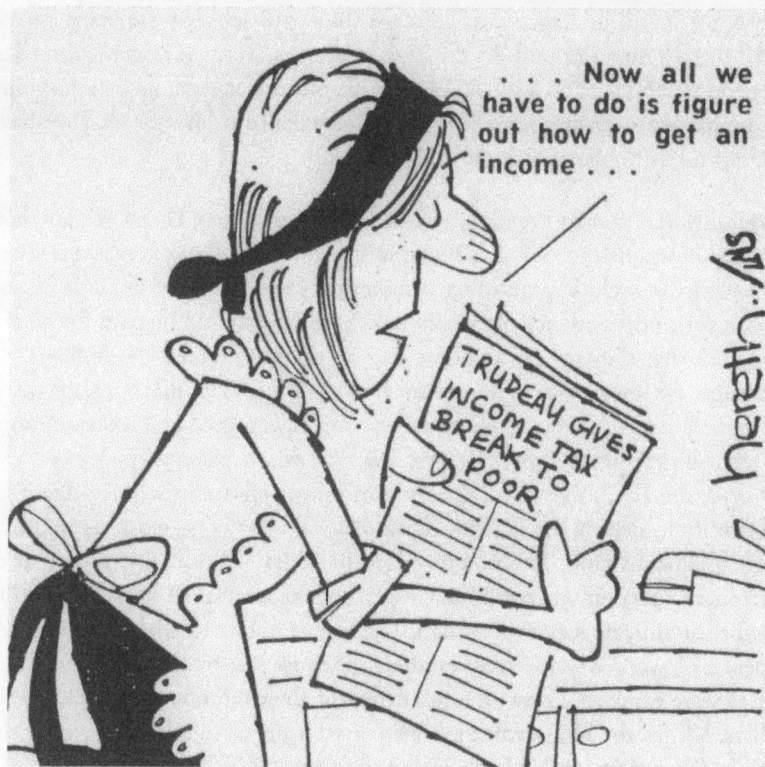

Figure 4.3 Drawing used by the Toronto Wages for Housework Committee during the campaign against increases in family allowances. (CWMA, box 625.9)

publicly supported the mobilization. For the first time, lesbians, refusing to hide their lesbianism any longer, spoke out in public on the effects that government cuts would have on them. "Coming out with Wages for Housework" was the slogan printed on the buttons distributed by Wages Due Lesbians during the mobilization around family allowances in 1976. They supported this protest because, as lesbians, they felt threatened by rising prices, dropping salaries, and the disintegration of certain social services. Threatened in many ways.

For example, many lesbians, not having a man's salary to provide for their basic needs and those of their children, depended on government allowances or income earned in underpaid female job ghettos, often in the healthcare and social services sectors. But these sources of women's jobs were in the crosshairs for government cutbacks. Reductions in family allowances and in welfare and unemployment benefits therefore were attacks on the financial independence of women in relation to men. In addition,

since we have the threat of losing custody of our children constantly hanging over us, it is hard for us to fight against the cutbacks ... For most lesbians, our existence is still underground. Through these cutbacks, we are being forced even further underground. As the crisis continues, women are being forced to depend much more on a man's wages. This means for lesbians that it's going to be harder to fight openly. All the independence from men that we have fought for as lesbian women is under attack![14]

The only solution to the situation, according to Wages Due Lesbians, was economic independence for all women, so that they could make decisions about their own lives, including deciding whether they wanted to be lesbians or not. To have this independence, they concluded, women should be paid for all the housework that they do in the home and on the job market: "As lesbians, we want wages for housework so that we are no longer forced to hide our lesbianism. We're not going to let them take away what we have gained and we want more. Not just a bigger piece of the pie ... we want the whole bakery!"[15]

During the IFC's existence, the issue of family allowances thus offered an opportunity to deploy the demand for a real wage for housework, as well as a specific political vision. The mobilization that followed the announcement of government cuts demonstrated how important the very small sums in question were for certain categories of women. The fragile nature of the financial independence of women – married, mothers, heterosexual or lesbian – and their poverty were exposed, as was the full extent of their reproductive work within families. Wages for Housework groups played a major role in uncovering the multiple dimensions of this issue during the 1970s.

In Quebec, the Coalition des femmes pour les allocations familiales was created in 1985 to oppose a new deindexation measure announced by the federal government. The same struggles as those conducted during the 1970s were seen: issues of poverty and the financial vulnerability of women working in the home. Lucie Bélanger and Ginette Boyer, who studied this mobilization, wrote, "We observed that Quebec women embraced family allowances as a source of economic recognition of their mothering work. Despite the relatively small amounts of money in play, they also considered family allowances to be an important tool for breaking their economic dependence on their spouse."[16]

Universal family allowances were finally abolished at the federal level in Canada in 1992, without protest this time. Various family assistance programs were combined to take their place, including reimbursable and non-reimbursable tax credits for children, all of which were selective assistance programs. Universality was definitively ended.[17]

SOCIAL ASSISTANCE ALLOWANCES: FIRST FORM OF WAGES FOR HOUSEWORK

Whereas Wages for Housework groups saw family allowances as a partial wage for housework, they saw social assistance allowances as an early form of wage for housework (because they were not necessarily linked to the presence of children). Indeed, in countries where these programs existed, the two allowances were considered by these groups to be the only money that women obtained from the state in return for their work in the home, and the only monthly sums that they could count on without having to ask a man or work outside the home in a second job. And, with regard to social assistance allowances, the Toronto Wages for Housework Committee added, "It's that money that has allowed increasing numbers of women to leave marriages that they can't stand, to have kids without getting married at all, to refuse to take on a second shift. And it's that money, and the little bit of freedom it's given us, that is under attack by the government."[18]

While the battle over family allowances was in full swing in Canada, the Ontario government first announced that all increases to family allowances would be deducted from social assistance allowances, and soon after it tabled a bill that strongly "encouraged" women receiving social assistance to accept whatever job was offered to them; if they refused, they would risk losing their allowance. This led to the creation of the Mother-Led Union, a group of single mothers receiving social assistance, and a mobilization against the government's intentions on International Women's Day 1975. The group made a public presentation of its demands. The Toronto Wages for Housework Committee supported the group's initiatives and marched alongside its members.[19]

The New York Wages for Housework Committee was also particularly active with regard to the defence of "welfare women" – to the point that it was, in Federici's view, "the centre of our activities and our campaign." The New York group felt that because social assistance was the first form of a wage for housework, it was a key struggle for the women's movement. Unfortunately, Federici lamented, the American women's movement was more interested in organizing in the workplace.[20]

In New York, a series of welfare cuts were introduced in 1976, and women beneficiaries, in order to avoid extra cuts, were forced to state the name of the father of their children. The New York group reacted by organizing the Welfare Conference on April 24, 1976. Several African American women participated in the conference, providing the impetus for the later formation of the Black Women for Wages for Housework Committee as an autonomous group within the network of Wages for Housework groups.

I will discuss the documents that emerged from these two times of struggle, that of the Mother-Led Union in Canada and the various documents involving the Welfare Conference in New York. In both cases, links were established between the Wages for Housework perspective and social assistance allowances, and a true wage for housework was demanded to replace welfare.

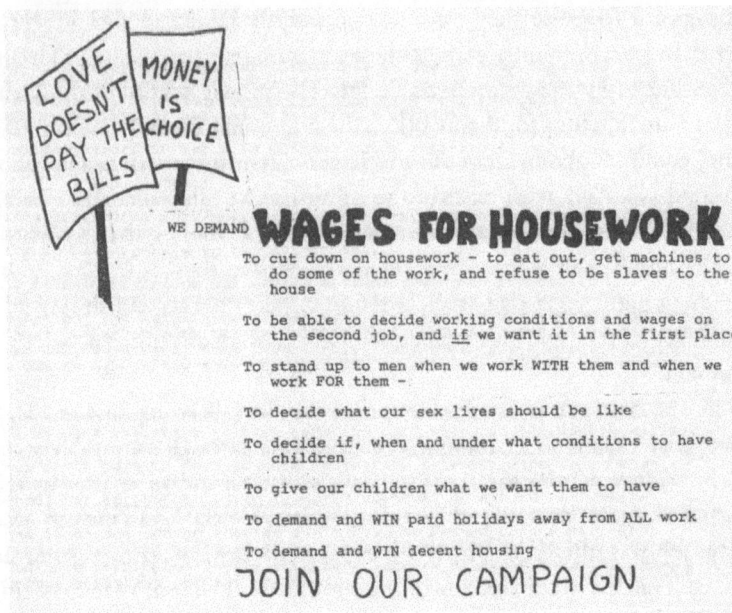

Figure 4.4 "Love Doesn't Pay the Bills," leaflet published by the New York Wages for Housework Committee, 1976. (Silvia Federici Archives)

The Mother-Led Union of Toronto

The Mother-Led Union of Toronto organized its first demonstration, as well as a public presentation of its demands to the Ontario government, for International Women's Day 1975.[21] The Toronto Wages for Housework Committee, Wages Due Lesbians, and a coalition of daycare centres joined the 150 women of the Mother-Led Union and their children to demonstrate in front of the Ontario legislature. The placards brandished and leaflets distributed displayed slogans such as "If women were paid for all they do, there'd be a lot of wages due!" and "Welfare women, single women, married women, same struggle – wages for housework!"

The demonstrators presented three of their demands to the government representatives who met with them:

1. To be paid fairly for raising their children. To this end, they wanted parity with foster parents, who received three times more per child than they were receiving as a total allowance at the time.
2. To be able to work outside the home without being penalized by reductions in welfare allowances.
3. Free daycare centres, managed by the parents and accessible to all women without exception.

The first demand, parity of social assistance allowances with allowances paid to foster parents, highlighted the fact that if the government paid these substitute parents, it proved that it was "*work* to look after kids." In fact, the government paid up to three times more per foster child than the amount allocated for this purpose under social assistance. Yet, caring for one's own children was just as much work as looking for other people's children. If they earned as much as foster parents did, these mothers would no longer be forced to find an extra job at a pittance wage to make ends meet.

The reasons for the total support given by both groups, Wages Due Lesbians and the Toronto Wages for Housework Committee, could not be more obvious. As Frances Gregory put it, "These women were demanding nothing less than Wages for Housework."[22]

The Wages for Housework and Welfare Conference in Brooklyn, and the Formation of Black Women for Wages for Housework

The Wages for Housework groups recognized in the pioneering struggles of the Welfare Rights Movement of the 1960s in the United States the forebear of their own movement.[23] The effect was to give women an unprecedented lever of power: that of refusing to be dependent on a man. It was also to refuse supposed liberation by the addition of a second job outside the house, paid at the bottom of the wage scale, that women were forced to take when they had no other recourse.[24]

The economic crisis of the mid-1970s led to threats of welfare cuts, and an obligation was felt to fight to preserve the gains of the 1960s, and also to fight to give welfare allowances the status of a true wage – a wage for housework for all women. The New York group thus saw this struggle as the first form of wages for housework and considered it to be of utmost importance to the feminist movement.[25]

On April 24, 1976, the New York Wages for Housework Committee, which included African American women among its members, held a welfare conference in New York. In attendance were 150 women from various districts in New York and from the Wages for Housework collectives in Chicago, Philadelphia, Cleveland, Boston, and Los Angeles. They were demanding, in replacement for welfare, a true wage for housework.[26] The invitation leaflet gave a sense of the demands:

Welfare is the first money we women have won directly from the government for the work we do in our homes ... The struggle of welfare mothers has given power to all women because it has opened the way for all of us to demand that housework be paid. And this time, WITH THE POWER OF OUR NUMBERS, WE WILL WIN A WAGE, and not a pittance that can

Wages for Housework & Welfare Conference

NO to Welfare cuts
YES to Wages for Housework from the Government for all Women

Saturday April 24,1976
N.Y. Wages for Housework Committee
288 B Eighth Street Brooklyn, N.Y.
(212) 965·4112 Wed. & Sat.11–4

Figure 4.5 Poster for the Welfare Conference organized by the New York Wages for Housework Committee and held in Brooklyn on April 24, 1976. Drawing: Lise Nantel. (Silvia Federici Archives)

always be taken away from us as if it were a charity ... Come to discuss how to organize to resist the welfare cuts and demand WAGES FOR HOUSEWORK FROM THE GOVERNMENT FOR ALL WOMEN.[27]

Twenty thousand leaflets were distributed in English and Spanish in welfare offices and on the street. Testimonials by various categories of women affected by government cuts were heard: African American women highlighted the special significance of this demand for them, as their presence in the United States was embodied in the specific unpaid work of slavery; lesbians testified to their extremely vulnerable position as mothers due to their sexual orientation, as they were fired more quickly than others from their second job and the courts deemed them "incapable" of being mothers because of their refusal to live with a man.[28] Older women talked about a "cycle of unpaid housework" performed throughout their life, continuing until late in life as grandmothers responsible for their grandchildren.

Several African American women testified to the power relations existing between black and white women, in which the latter were defined as "ladies," whereas the former were defined as "prostitutes." They pointed out that many black women had no job prospects outside the home other than being maids for white women. They also emphasized that they were at the lowest rung of the wage scale in North America and had to struggle against bureaucracy and cuts in the welfare system.

Figure 4.6 Spanish-language poster announcing a day of demonstrations organized by the New York Wages for Housework Committee, June 29, 1976.

There was also discussion of how to resist the cuts and fight for a wage in each particular situation. This enabled participants to see how their own struggle might reinforce the shared struggle for wages for housework for all women.

The Welfare Conference helped consolidate the action of various Wages for Housework groups in the United States, notably those that participated in the conference. The most significant result of the conference was the announcement that the African American participants would be creating an autonomous group within the International Wages for Housework Campaign, Black Women for Wages for Housework.[29]

Vol. 1 No. 1   Fall 1977

SAFIRE

"When woman gets her rights man will be right."
-Sojourner Truth, 1867

WAGES FOR HOUSEWORK

BLACK WOMEN for WAGES for HOUSEWORK (USA)

Sept. 1968 — Welfare mothers demanding more money for winter in Ann Arbor, Michigan.

EVERY MOTHER IS A WORKING MOTHER

1975 was International Women's Year. Under the auspices of the UN at a world conference in Mexico, it was declared as the beginning of the United Nations "Decade for Women". From the start that conference was divided between the feminist proposals from the West—and the demands for economic independence from the women of the Third World, the historic claim of Black people for reparations internationally. It chose as its themes "equality, development, and peace". But the question for Black women was equality—compared to what?; development—for us or against us?; peace—how, when we are still hungry?

During the same year prostitute women in all the cities, ports, and towns of France waged a massive strike against being classed as outlaws and unfit mothers, taxed and jailed, raped and beaten and fined, for demanding money for the work that all women are expected to do for free. When they were attacked by French feminists telling them they should find "decent" work—or at least agree to bring prostitution more under government control, the prostitute women of France answered: "We are women like all women."

1975 was also the year of the women's general strike in Iceland. Coming out of factories, offices, schools, and homes, leaving behind switchboards and typewriters and stoves, the women of Iceland left women's work undone. So on the day of October 24, all Iceland came to a halt.

And it was in 1975, at the annual conference of the International Wages for Housework Campaign in London, that Black Women for Wages for Housework was conceived as the way finally to take back what is ours.

But two decades before, Black women of all ages the world over—from Soweto to New York—had come out of our homes claiming our right to a standard of living equal to the wealth in money and technology that our unpaid work building the world's richest and most developed nations had produced. We took to the streets in marches, boycotts, pickets, sit-ins, freedom rides, rallies, and demonstrations; we took up arms in every possible way demanding food, shelter, clothing, health, education, justice, and peace. With one voice we said it was costing us too much to live among the people we loved in the cities and fields which our own hands had produced. We said ya basta—enough. Uhuru—freedom

continued on p. 2.

Figure 4.7   *Safire*, journal published by Black Women for Wages for Housework.

For these African American women, such mobilizations were in direct continuity with the 1960s struggles for civil and social rights, in which they and their mothers had taken an active role. These struggles, which included the right to welfare benefits, had constituted, as we have seen, the background for the first Wages for Housework movement.[30] The demand for payment of a wage in return for housework was gaining in symbolic resonance with their history as slaves. The figure of the "Black Mammy" personified and embodied both housework and all the other reproductive work (including sexual services) that black women were compelled to perform for masters during slavery times and afterward.[31]

Another unique resonance was that the "homeplace" and the work that women performed for the black community also had a political dimension and a subversive value: the home constituted a safe haven, sheltered from direct racist aggression, a space for construction of solidarities and organization – in a word, a space of resistance in white racist society.[32] Wages for housework could represent in this regard a fair historical reparation.

These women were thus able to substantiate, in the Wages for Housework perspective, an integrated analysis of the different power relations that they were subjected to and of what it meant to be poor, racialized, and a woman, and sometimes also a lesbian and a sex worker.[33] Unfortunately, the Welfare Conference was not able to stop the gradual erosion of welfare in the United States, which had already begun in 1976. Assistance to families with children was almost completely eliminated in 1993, and beneficiaries were increasingly stigmatized.

WOMEN'S HEALTH AND ITS "MANAGEMENT"

During the IFC's existence, Wages for Housework groups also mobilized around the issue of women's health, especially the aspects related to conditions under which reproductive work was performed – that is, conditions for childbirth, abortion, and contraception. They also addressed the "diseases" of housework, understood as the ills derived from the conditions under which it was practised (isolation, depression, oppression).

The neo-feminism that appeared at the turn of the 1970s invested massively in this area in its struggles, even giving rise to an entire women's health movement that denounced, in turn, illegal abortion, the absence of information on contraception, barbaric childbirth conditions, medicalization of the reproductive cycle and of women's mental health, women's loss of control of their bodies, the eradication of midwifery, the abusive power of doctors, and more. In addition to making these denunciations, women instituted innovative alternatives, such as women's health centres, self-health practices, and feminist therapies.

Among many women, awareness of their health situation triggered awareness that, as women, they were second-class citizens. "In relation to development of the feminist consciousness, for many women health constitutes a point of departure for understanding the multiple effects of the 'female condition,' socio-economic and cultural inequality, and the reality of the double task and its repercussions on physical and mental health," wrote Francine Saillant and Françoise Courville.[34]

The Italian feminist movement was no exception.[35] Wages for Housework groups were particularly active in this regard: pro-abortion mobilizations (notably during the trials for abortion starting in 1973), denunciations of obstetrics and gynecology practices, the violence of the doctors practising in these specialties, and management of women's health in general by health institutions. To these struggles were added those of the New York Wages for Housework groups against forced sterilizations, of poor and racialized women in particular.

Let's now look at the particular focus of some of these struggles: those around abortion, forced sterilization, and denunciation of medical practices, and the links that were established between health and housework.[36]

Abortion

The series of events in the campaign for legal, free, medically assisted abortion punctuated the mobilizations of Wages for Housework groups in Italy. June 1973: demonstration in Padua by Lotta Femminista during the trial of a woman who had an abortion. February 1974: demonstration in front of the Trento courthouse when 263 women were charged with having an abortion. January 1975: demonstration in Florence after a police raid on an abortion clinic. April 1976 in Padua: a twenty-seven-year-old woman died following an abortion: the movement occupied the university buildings where gynecology was taught and practised. Other major demonstrations followed in Rome, Padua, Bologna, Trento, Milan, and Turin. At the demonstrations in Florence, Trento, and Padua, the slogans on abortion and wages for housework became intertwined.[37]

On May 1, 1976, the Wages for Housework campaign reached Naples, in southern Italy, where a national demonstration for abortion and wages for housework took place. Three thousand women marched in the street; the demonstration ended with a torchlight procession accompanied by a song, which went: *"Tremate! Tremate! Le streghe son tornate, et non per essere bruciate ma per essere pagate!"*[38] (Tremble, tremble. The witches are returning. Not to be burned, but to be paid!) – because "the struggle for wages for housework and the struggle for legal and free abortion have always been the same struggle" for the Wages for Housework activists in Italy.[39]

Figure 4.8 Vogliamo decidere noi (It's up to us to decide),
brochure published by Lotta Femminista, March 1974.
(Mariarosa Dalla Costa Archives)

The spirit in which abortion and wages for housework were linked was on display at the demonstrations held by Wages for Housework groups:

Either it's a child for the state, or it's an abortion and that's a crime.
They defend the fetus to exploit the child.
Making love is housework, and doing so under these conditions, without safety provisions (laws, contraceptives that are safe and not harmful), is also very risky. Each year, in Italy, there are three million abortions! Under these conditions, getting pregnant against our will is a work-related accident.

And with all the passion of the times, they claimed damages:

We demand compensation from the state for all the times we got pregnant against our will, in addition to money for damages and interest for each abortion that we were forced to suffer! ...

A wage for housework so that we can decide for ourselves if we want to have a child, when and how we want![40]

In all the demonstrations, "from slogans to brief street speeches," Wages for Housework groups related the question of abortion to that of work. Because heterosexuality was an integral part of reproductive work, an undesired pregnancy was considered a (house)work-related accident, and birth control (contraceptives, abortions) was seen as control of the pace and conditions of work. The English group Power of Women explained the meaning of the struggles for abortion in the Wages for Housework perspective:

Wages for Housework is not only an analysis of all of women's work beginning with our work in the home. It also makes political struggle against "women's work" in and out of the home an imperative. The right to abortion is an integral part of the power to determine the size of our family and therefore the power to control the quantity of our work. The abortion struggle is part of the *total struggle against "our" work* which is the only road to greater power for women, since it unites women on the basis of our common exploitation.[41]

The Wages for Housework groups went further than did other feminist groups in this struggle, in particular by demanding compensation from the state in cases of undesired pregnancy and abortion.

Figure 4.9 "The Witches Are Returning." *Conquistiamo il potere di star bene* (literally, Let us conquer the power of carrying ourselves well), manual on women's reproductive health by the Collettivo per il salario contre il lavoro domestico-S.Dona', Padua, February 1977.

Forced Sterilizations

Some of the Wages for Housework groups became engaged in the other side of the struggle for abortion: forced sterilizations. From the start, these groups were aware that at the very moment that some women were demanding the right to abortion, other women, most of them poor and racialized, were struggling against forced sterilization. A battle targeting abortion alone, outside of a broader perspective for struggle, and outside of an analysis of the different levels of power among women, was judged racist. The first issue of the journal published by the English Wages for Housework collective, *Power of Women,* clearly stated, "We also rejected the racism of equating birth control with control of our bodies when population control is being used everywhere to deny Third World women especially the right to *have* children."[42]

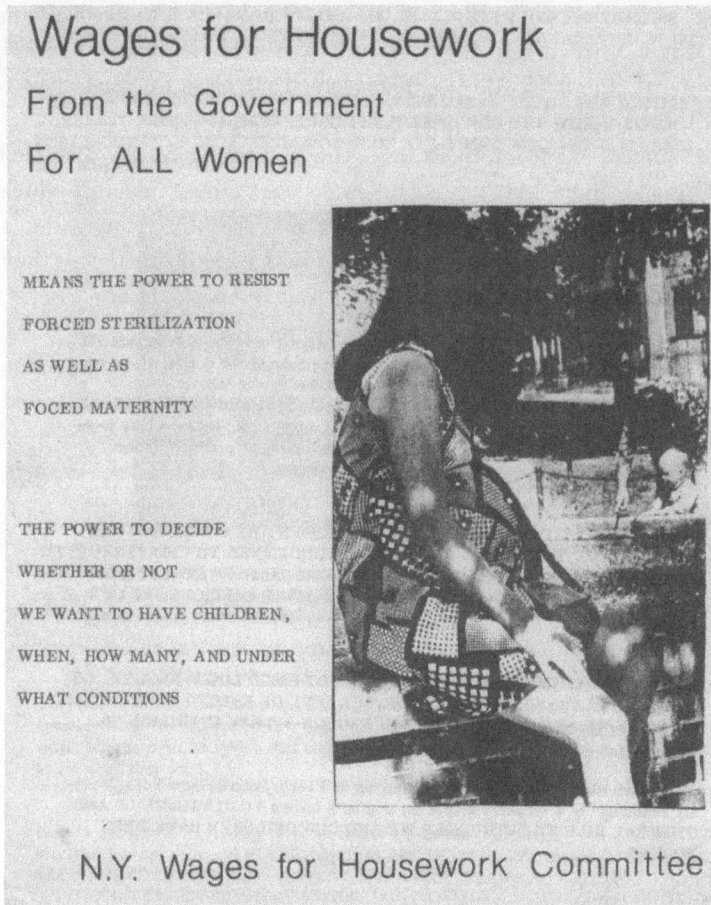

Figure 4.10   Brochure published by the New York Wages for Housework Committee on forced sterilizations, 1976.

Early Lotta Femminista documents situated these related issues – abortion and forced sterilization – as two sides of a single "general policy of control of women's reproductive function and, through it, of the labour power market."[43] The ban on abortion was considered a policy of forced reproduction to profit the social and economic organization of capitalism and its labour needs, whereas forced sterilizations were considered to arise from eugenics.

Puerto Rican women, who "had been used as test subjects in experiments with the birth-control pill before it was introduced into the American market" since the 1930s, were cited as an example.[44] These experiments resulted in the sterilization of many women – estimated to be 35 percent of the subjects in 1975.[45]

Poor welfare women, particularly racialized and immigrant women in the United States, received the support of the New York Wages for Housework group. The group denounced the situation in which the reality of "family planning" was a state policy calling for the use of public funds to sterilize women. One brochure distributed by the New York Wages for Housework Committee in 1976 stated, "In the USA it is welfare women and black women in particular who are the main target of the government sterilization policy."

Some women, many of them very young, were sterilized for "medical reasons," the brochure text continued. Others were forced, under the threat of seeing their welfare allowance cut, to "give their consent" to sterilization after childbirth or an abortion. Still others were told that sterilization was "the only effective contraceptive method" and that it was reversible. In any case, stated the New York Wages for Housework Committee, sterilization could under no circumstances constitute a choice, as long as women did not have the money to bring up the children they wanted: "The struggle against sterilization and for control over our bodies begins by having money of our own, money we don't have to work *harder* to get ... Wages for Housework from the government for all women ... means the possibility of having children without paying for them with our lives." Women could then be in a position to choose whether or not to have children.

A wage for housework would also mean having the power to reduce the amount of housework and have more free time, to demand daycare centres and vacations, and to have the power to refuse a second job. It would also mean the power to require free medical care, including childbirth and contraception, that did not destroy women's bodies and sexuality. The Wages for Housework perspective would thus give women the means to regain power over their bodies, their sexuality, and their lives.

Denunciation of Medical Practices

Touching the core of the issue of women's autonomy and control of their bodies, the struggle for decriminalization of abortion in Italy, home to the Vatican, was difficult. It caused shock waves in Italian society, both north and south, both right and left – including the "revolutionary left" – shaking the foundations of family and medical institutions and man-woman relations. The struggle for legal and free abortion was symptomatic of women's alienation from their bodies, their sexuality, and their reproductive health.

This struggle was accompanied by another struggle: one against the power of doctors and barbaric childbirth practices in hospitals. It also encouraged the creation of a counter-model: the institution of autonomous alternative health practices, such as self-managed health centres for women, called *consultori*, and self-managed abortions. Women were taught how to conduct self-exams, how to use a speculum, how to detect the most common diseases, and how to treat them. They were also taught how to insert diaphragms and other contraceptive devices. The first self-managed feminist *consultorio* in Italy was formed in Padua by the Comitato per il salario al lavoro domestico. In this facility, activists and physicians worked cooperatively without being paid and without charging patients.

The *consultori*, initially conceived as dispensaries of services for women, quickly became places where other struggles were organized, notably against medical structures managing women's health:

> It goes without saying that the struggle over health, understood in a broader sense, presupposes, both inside and outside hospitals and different health institutions, a feminist organization that makes possible the link between the women who go there to give birth or have an abortion and those who work there as nurses, midwives, telephone operators, and cleaning women. In recent years, these women have in fact been more and more mobilized in direct contact with outside feminist groups.[46]

Significant alliances that developed among female patients, hospital workers (nurses, midwives), and activists from feminist groups during different mobilizations made it possible to support women accused of having had an abortion and nurses on trial, and to denounce birthing doctors and childbirth conditions. One typical example was the mobilization organized by the Ferrara Wages for Housework group at the town's hospital. The group publicly denounced the barbaric obstetrics practices in force in this hospital and the doctors who used these practices. The doctors replied by accusing the group of defamation, and the case went to court. The group organized feminist assemblies within the hospital, occupying a wing of the hospital with the support of the hospital's female doctors. These are some of the events that punctuated the struggle, which was in the news from 1972 until the end of the decade.[47]

The Ferrara group went so far as to testify about the situation at the hospital at the International Tribunal on Crimes against Women in Brussels in March

*a cura del Gruppo Femminista per il
Salario al Lavoro Domestico di Ferrara*

DIETRO LA NORMALITÀ
DEL PARTO

lotta all'ospedale di Ferrara

Marsilio Editori

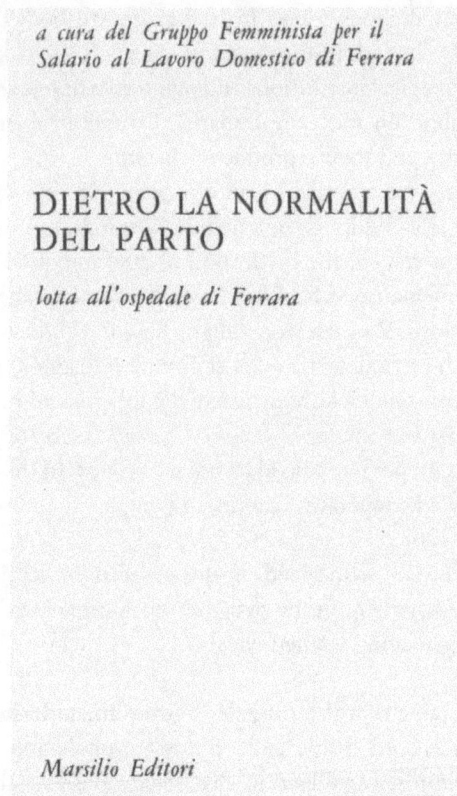

Figure 4.11   Cover page of the book *Dietro la normalità del parto* (Behind the
normalcy of childbirth) (Venice: Marsilio, 1978), a collection of testimonials
and documents related to the struggle by the Gruppo Femminista per il
salario al lavoro domestico di Ferrara at the hospital in Ferrara.

1976.[48] During its testimony, the group identified the reasons for this violence
against women at hospitals during childbirth, linking it to women's lack of power
in the home. The treatment of women at the hospital was only a reflection of
what they were forced to accept every day at home.

In the home, all our physical, emotional, intellectual and sexual energy is
exploited in the service of the family. We are expected, then, to keep quiet and
be subservient in the hospital too ... We have realized that the sacrifice we're
constantly asked to make on behalf of others does not help anyone; rather it
destroys our lives and the lives of our children. Housework is the basis of our
slavery. It is this campaign of wages-for-housework which looks to the real
cause – the vulnerability of having no money – and gives strength to all the
fights wherever they may be – in the factory, in the hospital, in the home, in
the street.[49]

Because it was made by a Wages for Housework group, this mobilization gave exceptional publicity to the perspective and its underlying strategy.

STRUGGLES OF LESBIAN MOTHERS

During the IFC's existence (and also afterward), the autonomous Wages Due Lesbians groups were active within the Wages for Housework movement both theoretically, as we have seen in Chapter 2, and as activists. These groups were able to link lesbianism and Wages for Housework, and they had the opportunity to do so through support at various mobilizations, such as those in favour of family allowances and against government welfare cuts, as mentioned above; during May 1 demonstrations; and by organizing an international conference.[50] Also, as we shall see in the next chapter, they supported the struggles of female waged workers and sex workers, as well as the new groups that the sex workers had just founded.

Wages Due Lesbians, especially the Toronto group, was also very active in organizing and mobilizing lesbian mothers threatened with losing custody of their children because of poverty or discrimination. A wage for housework was demanded so that they could avoid losing custody and therefore being forced to depend on a man:

> One of the most violent punishments lesbian women face for stepping out of line is the loss of the custody of our children. Like prostitutes, welfare women, immigrants, disabled women, prisoners and mental patients – we have our children taken away every day. Almost anyone who comes along can label us "unfit." And that risk more and more faces *any* woman who refuses to raise her children in a nuclear family situation.

This was said by Francie Wyland, an active participant in Wages Due Lesbians, an autonomous group within the Toronto Wages for Housework Committee and the IFC, at the Los Angeles Gay Pride Rally on July 26, 1977.[51] In 1976, she produced a booklet that was republished numerous times, *Motherhood, Lesbianism, and Child Custody: The Case for Wages for Housework.*[52]

Wages Due Lesbians was very present in the media and at different platforms to denounce this situation and to raise funds to defend a lesbian mother in a court case over custody of her children. The group quickly became a clearinghouse for advice and legal references on the matter, as well as for moral support for lesbians in similar situations. In 1978, it founded the Lesbian Mothers' Defence Fund (LMDF), which existed for nine years, and a newsletter, *Grapevine.*[53] A historian of the lesbian movement in Canada, Becki L. Ross, wrote, "Set up to give pre-legal advice and information on custody battles in Canada and the United States, as well as referrals to lawyers, financial assistance, and peer counselling, LMDF provided countless women with support over the course of its remarkable nine-year existence. It announced its official closure in 1987."[54]

Women's housework and reproductive work extended well beyond the house and the context of the family. It overflowed into society as a whole. How was the Wages for Housework perspective embodied in action in the area of women's invisible work practised outside the home?

Figure 4.12   Cover page of Motherhood, Lesbianism and Child Custody: The Case for Wages for Housework, by Francie Wyland (Toronto: Wages Due Lesbians, 1976).

5

Mobilizations around Women's Invisible Work outside the Home

The field of women's reproductive work reached beyond the private sphere of the family and extended, as we have seen, to the public sphere – to both the job market and the community sector. In these areas, too, women's housework and reproductive work were invisibly incorporated in many ways.

This being the case, the groups of the International Feminist Collective (IFC) wanted not only to draw back the curtain on the vast range of women's invisible and unpaid reproductive work outside the home, but also, above all, to highlight one major characteristic of women's paid jobs: the fact that they were extensions of the reproductive work that women performed in the home (as domestics, daycare workers, caregivers, waitresses, laundresses, hairdressers, secretaries, teachers, psychologists, and so on). Thus, it was a question of the *public* aspect of reproductive work.

Highlighting this characteristic of women's jobs was very popular in the second-wave women's movement and was reflected in its discourses and mobilizations. The "pay equity" operation, which was to be initiated in the labour world in the 1980s, would be directly related to making this point. It was accompanied, more rarely, by a reflection on the flip side of the coin: the unwaged aspect of private work by women.[1] The exceptions to this rule were the IFC groups, which turned these sites of work into opportunities for action and reflection on this subject, and thus politicized the issue.

MOBILIZATIONS IN WAGED WORKPLACES

The sites of action chosen to illustrate the phenomenon here involve the following sectors: hospital services, social services, women's shelters, factories, restaurants, and sex work. The categories of women concerned were employees in these sectors, sometimes customers, and, in the case of prostitution, sex workers. The Wages for Housework groups were differentiated within the feminist movement by their support for nascent groups of sex workers and their demands. Indeed, prostitution was a subject of reflection and analysis in the network because sexual services were considered to be part of women's public reproductive work. Solidarity with these workers and their demands was thus established naturally, so to speak, as we shall see.

The Struggle at the Maimonides Community Mental Health Centre in Brooklyn

Struggles in waged workplaces were sometimes initiated by members of Wages for Housework groups who earned their living in those establishments. This was the case for the struggle conducted in 1975 against the sexist organization of work at the Maimonides Community Mental Health Center in Brooklyn.[2]

In the mid-1970s, one of the activists from the New York Wages for Housework Committee, Jane Hirschmann, was working in this small, progressive psychiatric hospital as a social worker. She gradually realized that, as a professional social worker, she was "really working in another, bigger kitchen": "Women's primary jobs – nurses, stewardesses, secretaries, teachers – are extensions of housework."[3]

A reorganization of tasks within her team was to give Hirschmann the opportunity to put the Wages for Housework perspective to the test within this waged workplace. In the reorganization, which involved a reallocation of administrative positions, twelve men were chosen to occupy twelve new positions, triggering a conflict.

At the beginning of this conflict, in the fall of 1974, four employees at the psychiatric hospital, including Hirschmann, were already interested in the Wages for Housework proposal. Two more women joined the group soon after. Rather than demanding that women be chosen instead of men to occupy

Figure 5.1   Joan Ennis of the New York Wages for Housework Committee, at the time of the struggle at the Maimonides Community Mental Health Center in Brooklyn in 1976. Photo: Angelo Pacifici, *Soho Weekly News*, January 15, 1976, p. 11.

these new administrative positions, they decided to sit with their colleagues and review all the jobs occupied by women in this workplace in light of the Wages for Housework perspective. They made analogies between the tasks that women were performing in families and the positions that they occupied at the hospital. "We realized that much of the work we do at the Center is unwaged, connected to our feminine role, and that we are treated as housewives on the job," Hirschmann wrote. "The Mental Health Center profits from this extended family situation by extracting more surplus labor from us women by not paying us for this work," she continued.[4]

The situation extended to all of the jobs filled by women, notwithstanding the hierarchy. This analysis was presented to the personnel numerous times in a series of meetings; after many discussions (including a study day, paid for by the employer, on sexism at the centre), a list of demands was agreed upon to take to the director. Finally, Hirschmann recounted, "management came up with revised job descriptions ... and one for clerical work was five pages long. It included things like making the doctor's lunch, which were blatantly sex-related."[5]

The struggle made it possible to verify the relevance of the Wages for Housework perspective applied outside the home, in the job market. It also revealed a particular focus: the tactic of the autonomous struggle in the workplace. It was, in effect, a struggle by women on the margin of the local union and its classic claims for women:

The Wages for Housework perspective ... is a perspective that makes links where none seemed possible. For example, if we had taken the route of only fighting for a reopening of those 12 positions so that women could take those jobs, we would have involved very few women. Most women cannot, and will not, ever be able to apply for those positions. However, when we begin to talk about our work, and how much we do that is unwaged, and how our femininity is connected to that, we can begin to make alliances. Secretaries could talk about their problems and so could professional social workers and psychologists. There was the beginning of a sense of unity where before there was mistrust, jealousy and silence. We talked about the different privileges afforded us by the institution which divides us – e.g. "professionals" get four weeks vacation and "non-professionals" two to three weeks. We listened to all these differences and together made demands that would benefit all women.[6]

This struggle in the workplace was notable because it prefigured the union struggles in different countries to address systemic discrimination in jobs and wages – what, in Quebec, was called the pay equity operation. Other countries used the concept of comparable worth.[7]

The Struggle of Female Workers in the Solari Factory (Udine, Italy)

The Solari factory struggle was one by women employees in a watch factory in northern Italy whose workforce was 50 percent female.[8] The factory was unionized, but the union had always ignored the specificity of women's work: the "double workday." In the spring of 1974, some of the women decided to organize a struggle around their health. They got together and called upon the Wages for Housework Committee in Padua for gynecological advice (they had learned through the newspapers that the committee had started a women's health centre). The meeting took place at the factory, after work. A social assistant working at the factory recounted,

> The comrades explained many things to us that have since been put into practice. For example, going to gynecology appointments in twos and threes, in order to have a minimum of power as individuals and thus a greater guarantee of the quality of the examination; asking that they address us formally rather than informally, in order to establish a more respectful and distanced relationship; requiring that they answer our questions by giving serious explanations and not evasive ones such as "You wouldn't understand." The comrades explained to us that the doctor was not a neutral figure, "above the fray," to whom we can entrust our bodies so that he will cure us like a magician. The doctor represents a class that has always served power and the system; we must therefore confront him as such. This destruction of the myth of the doctor was very useful to us after that.[9]

The workers began to talk to each other about their health problems – discussing and asking questions about them – without the intermediary of the union or doctors. They realized that they had conditions that had not been treated (vaginitis, cervicitis, vaginal discharge, inflammation, and other ailments). They decided that "the time had come to insist that they receive treatment." Yes to mammograms and Pap tests, but without taking two half-days off work for no pay. "The time for healthcare should be taken during work hours at the factory," they wrote. "Waiting for hours in a doctor's waiting room, going to INAM [the social security office], getting in line, being examined, getting treatment – it's work, not recreation: it's housework, it's time that we use to get our bodies back in shape – our bodies that others exploit every day in the home and at the factory."[10]

Time for healthcare therefore had to be taken during work hours at the factory, and female workers had to be paid for the time devoted to medical appointments. The women in the factory formed the Women's Health Commission, the goals of which were to solve the problem of payments for regular medical consultations, and to talk to female workers about shared problems and express these problems publicly.

Both the union and the employers put up resistance. The women were determined, however, and finally obtained official recognition for their commission and, through this struggle, fundamental gains: "Paid days for medical visits; extension of preventive medicine (gynecology) for all women in both factories; free contraception dispensed by the mutual insurance company with tolerance testing under gynecological supervision; extension of health measures to workers' wives, the houseworkers. They could that way exchange their houseworker role with their husband on Saturdays."[11]

The mobilization of female workers, organized essentially outside the factory union, subsequently spurred male workers to undertake their own mobilization, as they wondered why they, too, weren't being paid for the time they took for their medical appointments. The women concluded, "This time, our struggle gave political direction to the male workers too."[12]

This struggle by women factory workers is exemplary in that it was very concretely supported by a Wages for Housework committee. The Padua committee, called upon by women in the factory to provide advice on women's health, was an important element in the mobilization of female workers in terms not only of the health issue but also of housework: the long hours of waiting in the doctor's office, the appointment itself, the care provided – all of this was work time. "It is work. Domestic work."[13]

The Padua Wages for Housework Committee also helped publicize this struggle, notably through its journal, *Le operaie della casa*. Other IFC publications relayed the information throughout the network.

A Struggle by Nurses in England

In the spring and summer of 1974, nurses in England engaged in a struggle that was remarkable in many ways.[14] For the first time, their wage demands were combined with threats to take action, including work stoppages, as was common in industrial sectors of the economy. Action committees were set up in hospitals to represent different categories of nurses and sidestep the union and professional organizations. National demonstrations were organized, as were marches in several cities, with the support of other workers. A government commission was formed to study the situation; the report it tabled contained recommendations for higher salaries, differentiated by nursing category. But, as observers noted,

More important than the [final] report itself was the message which widespread action of nurses during their struggle announced: that nurses ... would no longer be kept in their place by the illusions of professionalism, which would prevent their challenging their low pay and the lousy conditions under which they work; that they would no longer submit to the blackmail, always used against service workers and especially women, which says that to fight in your own interest is to endanger someone else's.[15]

The Power of Women Collective in London, which had some members who were nurses, promoted this struggle, not only to publicize it but also to show the connection between their struggle and that of other women – "and other women began to see in the power that the nurses had exercised power for themselves also."[16] The Power of Women Collective analyzed the situation as follows: hospital work was paid housework. The female workers took care of very young children, very old people, and patients of all ages.[17] Their functions were fragmented, however, and different people did the work: some cooked,

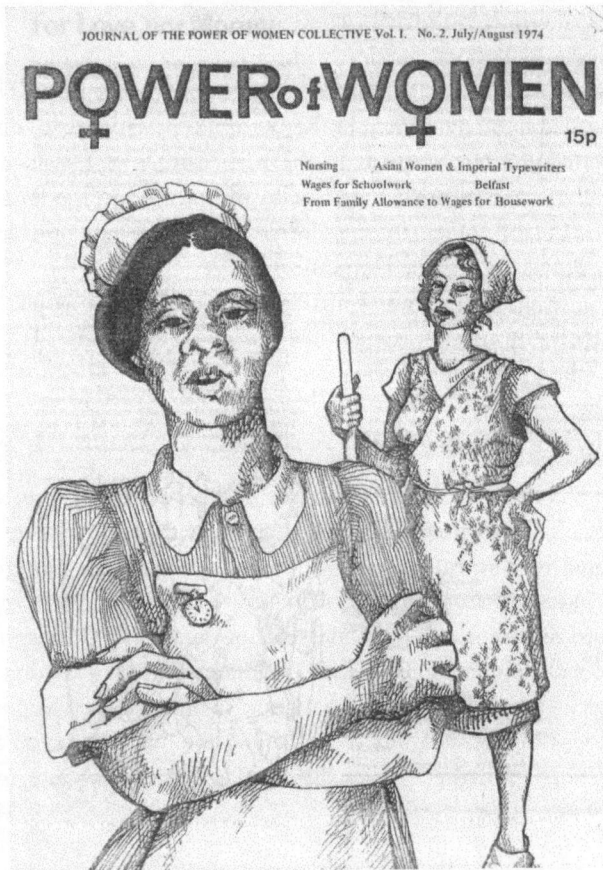

Figure 5.2 Power of Women (journal of the Power of Women Collective in London) 1, 2 (July–August 1974), published in conjunction with the nurses' struggle.

others cleaned, and still others made the patients comfortable. The nurses administered medications and treatments – something that houseworkers had always traditionally done. Hospital work was industrial housework, practised on the model of the factory, in which different functions were performed by different people, with distinct uniforms and positions that corresponded to specific wage scales.

The hierarchical division of hospital work was further strengthened by the myth of professionalism. Until recently, very few nurses saw themselves as workers. They were told that they were professionals, educated and specializing in scientific knowledge, like doctors. In a word, it was not work but a vocation, a sort of God's calling. In fact, in many countries, this work was performed by nuns.

In reality, the nurses' education stopped before the point where the doctor's authority might be at risk of being questioned, even though the nurse often had more experience and more and real knowledge about the state of the patients than the doctor did. One aspect of this hierarchy was the subordinate position of the nurse and the doctor's position of superiority and authority, all concealed by the fact that both were called "professionals."

Other hierarchies in hospitals were also examined, including those that existed within the nursing profession. For example, the jobs with the lowest wage levels corresponded to functions filled by immigrant women.

The nurses' struggle in the summer of 1974 was to throw the functioning of the hospital system into question. The nurses became less vulnerable to blackmail:

> They are undermining the conditioning that we have received as women and which has been reinforced by their conditioning as nurses. Women are always made to feel completely responsible for whatever happens to those in our charge, and guilty for considering our own needs. This is a direct result of our wageless work in the home ... When women's needs and others' needs appear to clash, women are made to feel selfish, ungrateful and uncaring if they consider themselves.[18]

The analysis summarized the link between the labour of workers in the services and that of women in the home:

> The nurse's job is to repair and reproduce, in the hospital, labour power that has been damaged. All service workers, in one way or another, do the same work: they produce not things but people, the labour power on which capital depends. The most crucial place where this work goes on, the foundation which all other service jobs are built around and assume, is the home ...

Teachers, caterers, nurses and other hospital workers are mainly women, who have gone out to do this work of reproduction for a wage. Their work is socialised, and directly supervised and controlled by capital, but it is essentially the same work in each case – a specialisation of an aspect of the work of the housewife.[19]

This organization of life under the capitalist system had always made the system look natural, as if it could not have been otherwise. The struggle of female workers in the services sector shows the contrary. Their demands and their refusal to continue to work in these conditions upset the status quo and subverted the "natural order of things."

The professions of teacher and nurse were those closest to the situation of women in the home: the teacher because she was responsible for developing the personality and the future of the child; the nurse because she was responsible for people's physical well-being. Houseworkers and mothers were held responsible for both of these things. This intimate link with others made them vulnerable to blackmail. Yet, "nurses have demonstrated that, despite the blackmail ... they can organise and assert their social power. In this they have shown what is possible too for the housewife." [20] They could also fight on their own terms and end this sort of intimidation. Nurses also opened the path to establishing a new kind of power for themselves and for all women – "the power we can have when we are all demanding money and refusing to work for love."[21]

That this power could be passed back and forth between waged and unwaged women was made possible by the fact that in reality they were the same people. Once at home, these waged women all became houseworkers. This power had the potential to unite them. Through their struggle, nurses were threatening the age-old role of women. It was, by extension, truly a threat to all invisible work done in families.

Demanding a wage for housework everywhere they worked required, however, a very broad level of organization, and one of a new type, "connecting a network of struggle through *a public, a massive and an international campaign*."[22] A Wages for Housework campaign could build this mass movement and benefit all women. The analysis ended with these words: "The cost of love is going up!"[23]

Tips on Trial: A Struggle by Waitresses in Canada

The struggle of restaurant waitresses in Toronto in 1977 was one in which the Toronto Wages for Housework Committee was very active. Some of the group's members were waitresses, and one of them, Ellen Agger, took the initiative of forming the Waitresses' Action Committee, which received support from a large number of stakeholders in Ontario as the mobilization went on.[24]

The spark that lit the fuse was the Government of Ontario's announcement, in March 1976, of a raise in the minimum wage to $2.65 per hour. At the same time, however, the government decided to change the pertinent regulation and introduce a new category of workers: those who served alcohol in establishments existing for this purpose. For these workers, the government established a lower wage of $2.50, under the pretext that they received tips. This was the government's response to the tourism industry, which was complaining about the high minimum wage in Ontario compared with the minimum wage in the United States. As this was a regulatory change rather than a legislative amendment, no public discussion or consultation process was planned.

Eighty percent of the people concerned, working for minimum wage in the tourism and restaurant industries, were women, and few of them were unionized. Often their family's only source of support and unskilled immigrants, they

...PETITION... PETITION... PETITION...

Money for Waitresses is money for all women!

The tourist industry claims to be in a crisis of declining profits. What are they proposing as a solution? That the government increase the difference between the standard minimum wage and that of workers earning tips in hotels and restaurants. They are suggesting 50¢ an hour less for us because they claim waitresses and waiters make "huge amounts" in tips and can well afford a cut in wages.

But who are they talking about? The majority (80%) of tipped workers in hotels and restaurants are women. Because we do the same kind of work for free in our homes, we are forced to accept bargain-basement wages when we get jobs outside. Most waitresses make only the minimum wage and many of us work part-time. As a result, we are forced to depend on tips to make ends meet.

The system of tipping makes us dependent on the goodwill of the individual customer. Like all other women, we resent being forced to hustle for our money, because often it amounts to a form of prostitution. We want it directly through higher wages. In fact, tipping subsidizes the industry and keeps everyone's wages low -- both waitresses and other employees who regularly receive a cut of the tips.

But we aren't going to give up our tips until we are assured of a decent wage in return. And we object to paying taxes on our tips as long as our wages are so low and benefits (such as unemployment insurance) are calculated on the wages alone and not on our tips.

As with the cuts in the family allowance and unemployment insurance, tightening up of welfare, and soaring prices, the government and industry are once again going after those with the least power -- women. The full-time housewife, the secretary, or the nurse of today is the waitress of yesterday or tomorrow. We are all feeling the

Figure 5.3 Petition by Waitresses' Action Committee, Wages for Housework Campaign, January 1977. (CWMA, box 625.4)

worked as waitresses, chambermaids, coatroom clerks, barmaids, and in other similar jobs. In reality, they performed in the labour market the same work that was performed free of charge in the home. They were thus the same type of workers: "The full-time housewife, the secretary, or the nurse of today is the waitress of yesterday or tomorrow."[25] The men in the restaurant and tourism industry were generally found in higher-end establishments, where they received better tips.

In December 1976, waitresses active in the Toronto Wages for Housework Committee formed the Waitresses' Action Committee. Joined by other waitresses and allies, they began their mobilization in January 1977. They demanded an end to all differentiated minimum-wage rates (the "tip differential"), an across-the-board increase, and a wage for all the hidden unpaid work that waitresses had to perform (setting tables, cleaning uniforms, and so on). They wrote a brief to present to the ministers of labour and of industry and trade. The brief was also sent to various groups to garner support, and more than thirty endorsed it. It also received the support of the Ontario Committee on the Status of Women and the Equal Pay Coalition.[26] Popular support came not just from waitresses but from entities ranging from groups in the women's movement and the community movement to legal clinics and employment centres.

Women from the Toronto Wages for Housework Committee provided crucial assistance in developing the waitresses' position and demands, and organizing the support campaign. The mobilization received extensive media coverage. The operation was funded by personal donations, appeals to endorsers and supporters, Ontario unions, and the general public.

One of the demands, supported by a petition, was a meeting with the minister of labour. Given the general outcry, a delegation was finally able to meet with him and the director of the Women's Bureau. A promise was made to start a public consultation on the question.

The various documents issued for this vast mobilization put the system of tips, based on subjective decisions by customers and often on the waitresses' sex appeal, and varying depending on the type of establishment and the region, on trial. In fact, this system was (and still is) a hidden subsidy to the industry, exerting downward pressure on wages. Even though they were arbitrary and not regulated by law, tips nevertheless had to be declared as income for tax purposes by those who received them.

The brief presented to the ministers of labour and tourism supported the claim about various hidden, unpaid aspects of waitresses' work.[27] These examples again foretold the content of pay equity operations that would be implemented more than a decade later in various types of companies, following which many workers would receive financial compensation.[28]

Conditions for getting and keeping the job

In the services sector, which included the restaurant sector, women were expected to perform a certain amount of sexual labour (to receive tips as a function of their charm, to parade before the manager before getting a job, or to be required to perform sexual favours and flirt to keep their job). Complaints made to the Ontario Human Rights Commission against managers of establishments provided proof of this.

Preparation for work

Physical appearance, especially for women employees, was of utmost importance in food and drink establishments. Hours had to be devoted to purchasing and maintaining clothing. Then there were standards of personal appearance to uphold (haircut, makeup, and so on), again requiring hours of unpaid work.

Set-up time

Part of the waitress's work consisted of setting tables and cleaning one or more sections of the restaurant. Very little time was officially allocated to this task in general, which meant that work hours had to be extended to perform it. This work received no concrete recognition on the paycheque. Therefore, it was free work, amounting to several hours at the end of the week that directly profited the employer.

Reimbursement of unpaid bills ("walkouts")

In general, waitresses were held responsible for the bills of customers who left without paying, which forced them to play a watchdog role and monitor the customers. The employer might require the waitress to reimburse it for the unpaid bill, even though the law forbade the employer from deducting such sums from her pay. If the waitress refused to reimburse said sum and was fired, she had no legal recourse against the employer.

Working as a cashier

Even though the waitresses were hired to serve food and drinks, they were often expected to also work as cashiers, thus saving the employer the obligation of paying another salary.

Kickbacks

One of the most common and most insidious practices used was the kickback. In certain establishments, the waitress was required to pay a percentage of her tips to the employer or to other staff members, or be fired. Here, the tip acted as a wage subsidy to other employees, thus enabling the owner to avoid increasing their salaries.

Breaks

Many establishments had small staffs, and there was therefore no time for waitresses to take the regulatory break set by law (a half-hour after five hours' work). As a consequence, they were rarely paid for their breaks. The result was another contribution of free work to the employer.

Serving minors and drunk people

The waitress was held legally responsible if she served alcohol to minors or to people who looked drunk, which put her in an untenable position: on the one hand, the boss pressured her to serve as many people as possible; on the other hand, she had to judge if she should serve them. Even though bouncers might be hired specifically to sort these things out, it was the waitress who was left to pay the bill in the end.

Finally, the Waitresses' Action Committee demanded an identical minimum wage level for everyone, without exception; the abolition of the special measure set out for waitresses and other employees receiving tips; payment for tasks done for free as part of waitresses' work; the prohibition of kickbacks; legislation protecting waitresses against employers who wanted to force them to pay the bills of "walkout" customers; and for the establishment alone to be held responsible for beverages served to minors and drunk people. The well-written, tightly reasoned document presented to the government was accompanied by testimonials by waitresses and statistics on wage discrepancies between men and women in other industries and services and those of waitresses, unionized and non-unionized, in large and small hotels and restaurants.

This mobilization, initiated by a subgroup of the Toronto Wages for Housework Committee, offers another example of the embodiment of the Wages for Housework perspective in a waged workplace in which women performed public reproductive work. The discourse formulated on this occasion shed light on these aspects of housework or reproductive work by women that was incorporated in an invisible or hidden way and was non-paid, generally profiting the employer. The conclusion that the initiator of the Waitresses' Action Committee drew from this struggle was unequivocal: "[Waitressing] is the work of serving and satisfying other people, only on a public instead of a private scale. That is why I call it housework. All women are taught to do this from the day we are born. In fact our very identities are tightly bound up in this work, whether we are secretaries, mothers, nurses, waitresses, or full-time housewives." Paying for housework or reproductive work, she concluded, was "to break down the connection between our role as women and the work we do."[29]

Support for "Sidewalk Workers"[30]

In a recent essay, Mariarosa Dalla Costa remembers the feminist ideological cleavage of the 1970s on the question of prostitution/sex work:

> In the feminist movement of the 1970s there were two positions on prostitution: one did not admit that such work could be pursued, the other argued that in any way, one had to recognize the self-determination of the woman who alone could judge which work she believed most acceptable among the few choices available. Above all, it was thought important to remove the debate from an area of a moral question and highlight the working aspect of prostitution. Since then *sexworkers* became the name to indicate prostitutes, the freedom of women's choice was reaffirmed, and the battle for civil rights of prostitutes was sustained.[31]

From the start, the Wages for Housework movement backed the second position: it supported the struggle conducted by the early sex workers' groups.[32]

It was, in fact, during the 1970s that prostitutes came out of the shadows to form groups and claim their rights as people and as workers. COYOTE (Call Off Your Old Tired Ethics), a San Francisco group initiated in 1973 by an ex-sex worker, Margo St. James, is recognized as the first structured sex workers' group. It was formed (on Mother's Day) to demand decriminalization of sex work and an end to police harassment. In France, 1975 was marked by occupations of churches (Saint-Nizier in Lyon and Saint-Bernard in Paris) by prostitutes denouncing police repression and corruption.[33] Other sex workers' groups then formed elsewhere: PUMA (Prostitutes Union of Massachusetts) in Boston in 1975, and BEAVER (Basic Education and Vital Equal Rights) in Toronto in 1977. These three groups (COYOTE, PUMA, and BEAVER), as we shall see below, were all supported on certain occasions by Wages for Housework groups during the IFC's existence.[34]

In January 1977, a vast operation of police repression and raids took place in the San Francisco area where street prostitution was practised. The following month, the Wages for Housework committees in San Francisco and Los Angeles organized, in coordination with COYOTE, a mobilization around a joint declaration to be presented to the Board of Supervisors of San Francisco. The declaration, endorsed by fifty organizations, demanded an end to harassment of street prostitutes, the abolition of all laws prohibiting prostitution, amnesty for all prostitutes, and expungement of their criminal records. Among the first groups to endorse the declaration were Black Women for Wages for Housework of Brooklyn and Wages Due Lesbians of Toronto.

In mid-April, the IFC international conference was held in Chicago.[35] Among the guests was Margo St. James, who received unanimous support for

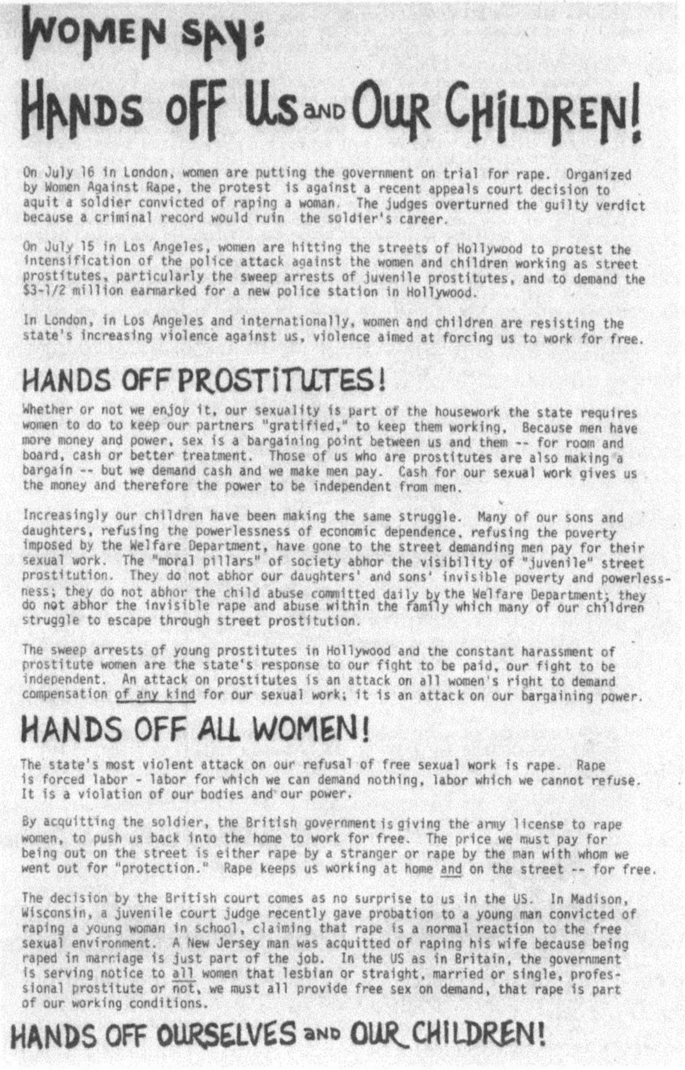

WOMEN SAY:
HANDS OFF US and OUR CHILDREN!

On July 16 in London, women are putting the government on trial for rape. Organized by Women Against Rape, the protest is against a recent appeals court decision to aquit a soldier convicted of raping a woman. The judges overturned the guilty verdict because a criminal record would ruin the soldier's career.

On July 15 in Los Angeles, women are hitting the streets of Hollywood to protest the intensification of the police attack against the women and children working as street prostitutes, particularly the sweep arrests of juvenile prostitutes, and to demand the $3-1/2 million earmarked for a new police station in Hollywood.

In London, in Los Angeles and internationally, women and children are resisting the state's increasing violence against us, violence aimed at forcing us to work for free.

HANDS OFF PROSTITUTES!

Whether or not we enjoy it, our sexuality is part of the housework the state requires women to do to keep our partners "gratified," to keep them working. Because men have more money and power, sex is a bargaining point between us and them -- for room and board, cash or better treatment. Those of us who are prostitutes are also making a bargain -- but we demand cash and we make men pay. Cash for our sexual work gives us the money and therefore the power to be independent from men.

Increasingly our children have been making the same struggle. Many of our sons and daughters, refusing the powerlessness of economic dependence, refusing the poverty imposed by the Welfare Department, have gone to the street demanding men pay for their sexual work. The "moral pillars" of society abhor the visibility of "juvenile" street prostitution. They do not abhor our daughters' and sons' invisible poverty and powerlessness; they do not abhor the child abuse committed daily by the Welfare Department; they do not abhor the invisible rape and abuse within the family which many of our children struggle to escape through street prostitution.

The sweep arrests of young prostitutes in Hollywood and the constant harassment of prostitute women are the state's response to our fight to be paid, our fight to be independent. An attack on prostitutes is an attack on all women's right to demand compensation of any kind for our sexual work; it is an attack on our bargaining power.

HANDS OFF ALL WOMEN!

The state's most violent attack on our refusal of free sexual work is rape. Rape is forced labor - labor for which we can demand nothing, labor which we cannot refuse. It is a violation of our bodies and our power.

By acquitting the soldier, the British government is giving the army license to rape women, to push us back into the home to work for free. The price we must pay for being out on the street is either rape by a stranger or rape by the man with whom we went out for "protection." Rape keeps us working at home and on the street -- for free.

The decision by the British court comes as no surprise to us in the US. In Madison, Wisconsin, a juvenile court judge recently gave probation to a young man convicted of raping a young woman in school, claiming that rape is a normal reaction to the free sexual environment. A New Jersey man was acquitted of raping his wife because being raped in marriage is just part of the job. In the US as in Britain, the government is serving notice to all women that lesbian or straight, married or single, professional prostitute or not, we must all provide free sex on demand, that rape is part of our working conditions.

HANDS OFF OURSELVES and OUR CHILDREN!

Figure 5.4 Leaflet produced by the Los Angeles Wages for Housework Committee, "Women Say: Hands Off ...," opposing harassment of prostitutes, among other things, 1977. (CWMA, box 624.27)

her struggle. She noted that COYOTE and the Wages for Housework groups had found common ground in the issue of women's economic and financial security. "Prostitutes and housewives unite, forming a surprising sisterhood!" ran the headline in the *Chicago Tribune*.[36]

In Canada, in the summer of 1977, the City of Toronto gave the police the green light for an operation of repression and a "sweep" of Yonge Street, a commercial street that was home to many entertainment venues. Massage parlours were targeted. Owners and customers were accused of running or being found in a bawdyhouse. The city wanted these establishments closed. Also targeted were sex shops and strip clubs. Between mid-July and early September, 224 charges were laid. In total, in 1977, 1,700 general "morality" charges were laid, many of them targeting presumed prostitutes.[37]

The Toronto Wages for Housework Committee compiled data on the arrests and raids, and supported the sex workers' demands. Judy Ramirez, the group's spokesperson, produced a feminist analysis of the situation.[38] The committee invited St. James to a series of events in the city between November 25 and December 1. It also supported and assisted with the formation of the first group defending sex workers' rights in Canada, BEAVER, in November of that year.[39]

HOUSEWIVES & HOOKERS COME TOGETHER

Housewives do it for love. Hookers do it for money. Right? Wrong. Between Nov. 25 and Dec. 1 housewives and hookers will be appearing together to start setting the record straight.

In our society, sexuality is a commodity all women are forced to "sell" in one way or another. Our poverty as women leaves us little choice. Hookers get hard cash for their sexual services while other women get a roof over their heads or a night out.

An act of exchange is involved in both cases, but neither housewives nor hookers are recognized as workers.

Neither has many rights under the law. A wife can be raped by her husband and she has no legal recourse whatsoever. Hookers are subject to harassment and arrest at the whim of police and politicians. Both groups of women are treated like second class citizens.

But housewives everywhere are demanding recognition of their work in

"Every little girl learns by the time she's five how to put the hustle on her Daddy for a new toy."
— Margo St. James, ex-hooker and founder of COYOTE (Call Off Your Old Tired Ethics)

the home and financial independence from men. And hookers are demanding an end to the hypocrisy which makes payment for their sexual (house)work a criminal activity.

Housewives and hookers are each other's natural allies. Especially now when women are paying the highest price for the mounting "economic crisis". Tight money is stretched by more free work in the home and the income of hookers is jeopardized by street crackdowns everywhere.

To help strengthen this alliance, the Wages for Housework Campaign has planned a series of events in Toronto featuring Margo St. James, ex-hooker and tireless campaigner for the decriminalization of prostitution.

''My grandmother once said of being a housewife, 'I'm a slave during the day and a whore at night.'"
— Judith Ramirez, spokeswoman for the Wages for Housework Campaign

HEAR MARGO ST. JAMES

Figure 5.5 Photographs of Margo St. James and Judy Ramirez, "Housewives & Hookers Come Together," *Wages for Housework Campaign Bulletin* 1, 4 (Summer 1977).

Why did Wages for Housework groups so spontaneously give their support to the prostitutes? What links were established between the situation of house-workers and that of prostitutes?

The police operations known as "street sweeps" were conducted above all, according to the Wages for Housework committees, to punish these women for the crime of trying to make a living for themselves and their children. Refusing to be poor was their crime.

Street prostitutes were hassled because "prostitution exposes our sexuality as work which should be paid."[40] And yet, it was no crime for the advertising industry and employers of women in certain jobs to use female sexual "attractions" to please customers and help with sales.

Quickly, members of Black Women for Wages for Housework saw their own situation reflected in the prostitutes' struggle. Fighting against police harassment on the street, assaults, prison, and fines, accused of being "unworthy mothers," the risk of having their children taken away, seeking money to feed their families – these were daily struggles for both black women and prostitutes:

> Prostitution is not a game. IT IS WORK ... Prostitution is work that Black women were forced to do on the plantations and that we are forced to do today ... We are forced to sell our sexual services on the streets, in hotels and massage parlors, or in our apartments – to take on the second job of prostitution – because we are not paid for the first job we all do as women, housework, the job of producing and taking care of everybody so that we all can work and make profits for the Man. Prostitution is one way that Black women are using increasingly to refuse our poverty and dependency on men which is brought about by not getting paid for our first job.[41]

Was there any black woman who could say that she was above prostitution? wondered Black Women for Wages for Housework. Due to racism, black women were reduced to being those with the least money of everyone, the fewest possibilities to find a job, the least access to school, and the worst housing, and they were the first to be killed or imprisoned; in short, black women were suspected of prostitution in every case. When a raid occurred, black women who unfortunately happened to be walking in the area could expect to be the first to be arrested. "It's always open season on Black women." The reason that they couldn't say no to all of this, they wrote, was their lack of money: "We don't have the money to be able to say NO, to be able to choose where and how we want to live, and whom we want to sleep with."

> By organizing themselves, by being public in their organizations whenever they can, prostitutes, like Black women, are saying by our actions that we have a story to tell, a story about the struggle we are making to be independent.

In their statement in Lyon, the French prostitutes said: "We are women like all women."[42]

Black Women for Wages for Housework spontaneously threw support behind the sex workers. "Money for prostitutes is money for Black women!" they said. This was also true for the English Collective of Prostitutes and Wages Due Lesbians in Toronto and London: "The attack which governments are organising against prostitute women everywhere in the world is an attack on every woman's right to determine whether, and on what terms, she will have sexual relations with men."[43] These two groups declared that lesbians, too, were harassed by everyone in a situation of authority for having committed the crime of having a sexual life that aligned with their own needs: "Any woman who steps out of line gets the same treatment."[44] They pointed out that many women working as prostitutes were also lesbians and had the same struggle against free sexual service upon command: "We urge all lesbian groups and individuals to support the struggle of prostitute women against these crackdowns."[45] "Women, lesbian or 'straight', prostitute or not, are everywhere houseworkers, the servants of the world. We are all entitled to money for this work, and entitled to obtain it in any way open to us as women."[46]

Ramirez was also of the view that the goal of the harassment and arrests of prostitutes was to bring them back to the right path, because they were becoming too visible and, especially, too numerous:

Politicians everywhere have tolerated "the world's oldest profession" as long as prostitutes remained isolated from other women. They have always been held up as the symbol of female degradation, precisely to keep the rest of us "coming across" for free. And not only in bed. For many of us it's a package deal which includes cooking, cleaning, shopping, and raising children. But all that is changing. Women have been demanding their wages in many ways, and "alarming" increases in the rate of prostitution have become common in large cities everywhere. So have struggles for welfare, daycare, unemployment insurance, family allowances, etc. And the politicians are worried.[47]

For the Wages for Housework groups, the prostitutes' struggle was a struggle for the right to economic survival. It was the refusal to be poor. For "*nothing* is more degrading than having no money," concluded Ramirez.[48]

Apart from the Toronto Wages for Housework Committee and Wages Due Lesbians, few feminist groups – perhaps none in Canada in 1977 – analyzed prostitution in this way. Most, in fact, analyzed it as being the worst degradation of women possible.[49]

It is thus obvious that the Wages for Housework perspective and its embodiment in action were innovative in several ways. First, an alliance between housewives and hookers defied and deconstructed two great age-old female archetypes: mother and whore, "good" women on the one hand, and "bad" women on the other.[50] As the feminist author and researcher Gail Pheterson would later observe, it was an inegalitarian social categorization, created by the patriarchy to control women's sexuality. It constructed the "whore stigma," which kept women from acting in solidarity.[51] Therefore, this "unnatural" alliance was a powerful symbolic transgression.

In addition, by also rallying racialized women – who had always been suspected of prostitution – and lesbians, classified as bad because they were fugitives from the family and "perverts," this alliance between housewives and sex workers broke down barriers between bad, good, and perverted women, whether they were "white" or "black." This was another powerful transgression, all of these women and their claims, each in her situation, embodying a threat to the reproduction of the family and to power structures based on the divisions among women.

STRUGGLES IN SOCIAL SERVICES AND COMMUNITIES

In the perspective of the Wages for Housework movement, the community – that is, the community sphere – was part of the "social factory," in which women's housework or reproductive work was done, in which the labour power of people was reproduced:[52]

> The community is where the wealth, in the form of consumption, is present. Houses, transport, supermarkets, hospitals, welfare offices, etc. All these are areas where we can organize our power, all these are moments of struggle to reappropriate what belongs to us. And all these are wages for housework struggle.
>
> Clearly women are the first protagonists of these struggles because we live and work primarily in the community and that's where we can best organize our power.[53]

Community facilities and community services were therefore also an area of reflection and struggle by Wages for Housework groups during the IFC's existence. Two examples seem particularly significant: one in Italy and the other in Canada.

Reflections on Community Facilities in Emilia, Italy

In 1974, the region of Emilia, in northern Italy, had a Communist government, and its social services were considered a symbol of success. "Women were leaders and protagonists in these struggles," noted the document written by

Lotta Femminista (Modena group) from which most of the information and quotations below were drawn.[54]

At the time, occupations of houses with the aim of obtaining decent apartments were held in numerous cities in the region. Other actions were aimed at construction of daycare centres and nursery schools, and female blue- and white-collar workers mobilized to get their bosses to bear part of the costs of these services. For Lotta Femminista in Modena, these struggles, which rallied mainly women, were in reality challenges to the "hidden, but no less crushing, exploitation that they suffer in the home" (18). They were struggles to "lighten the load of housework [and] attain a minimum of living space" (19). However, the group observed that "women are almost always left out of the management of such struggles" (20). Under the circumstances, they wondered, "Are these struggles worthwhile?" (19).

The analysis produced by Lotta Femminista first summarized the group's position on the issue of housework: as long as housework was done in exchange for their upkeep or in exchange for "moral recognition" (21) when they supported themselves, women would find themselves in a position of inequality in relation to men. This inferior position had repercussions for women when they entered the job market. "We are fed up with dependency ... We want to struggle on all fronts against the material roots of our dependence" (21).

This analysis led Lotta Femminista to observe, "Today, the existence of free housework limits the possibilities for expansion of social services concerning housework" (27). In fact, as long as women supplied this reproductive work for free, the public powers would be little inclined to socialize it. The tendency was, rather, to encourage women to work part time, to develop support mechanisms

Figure 5.6 "Down with the exploiters! The nuns are tired of being good; they want a wage!" *Le operaie della casa* 2–3 (September–December 1976): 18.

in the family (rather than to socialize a series of tasks), and to deinstitutional-
ize patients, old people, and disabled people and return them to families. All
of these observed trends demonstrated that as long as women supplied their
services in the home free of charge, social services and community facilities
would always be deficient.

Lotta Femminista also analyzed the type of community services set up by the
Italian Communist Party in Emilia, where there had been a great effort at creating
social infrastructure and social services. The authorities' primary objective was
for these new facilities to be women's main means of access to salaried work,
"a great step on the road to 'emancipation'" (30). Lotta Femminista saw it as a
partial solution: "This type of social service, as conceived and intended, does
not free women except for the purpose of working outside the home" (30). The
proof included the fact that schools and daycare centres were accessible only
during hours of waged work, the absence of any plan to socialize housework
tasks that might lighten the burden of women's work, and the deinstitutional-
ization of mentally ill people, which considerably expanded women's workload.

The group's detailed examination of the social services system in place in
Emilia brought them back to their initial questions: "What is the meaning of
women's struggle for social services? How can this struggle be linked with the
Wages for Housework demand?" (38). The particular situation in Emilia, which
was atypical in comparison to other regions and counted on greater social infrastructure, led Lotta Femminista to study complementary solutions to wages for
housework:

> Demanding money is an objective that many women (especially housework-
> ers, home-based workers, young women looking for work, and others) want
> to see as possible, credible. It is an immediate response to the dramatically
> felt need for money, *economic autonomy*. But many women already earn a wage
> (even if it is low) at the factory, in offices, in department stores, in [the]
> services [sector]; these women put on the agenda just as urgently and dra-
> matically *the need to free themselves from double work*, to fight it *now* to reduce
> the workday that lasts 14 hours or more; they require services that immedi-
> ately free them from at least one part of their housework. (38–39, emphasis
> in original)

In the view of Lotta Femminista, these were the two aspects of the Wages for
Housework demand: to have money for oneself and to reduce one's work time.
These two aspects

> have to be carried forward together and unified in the general perspective of
> the struggle against [free] housework ... We are not thinking of launching
> out of the blue a generalized women's struggle for wages. In England, it

would never have been possible to speak of a campaign for wages if women had not been mobilized en masse beforehand to defend family allowances. What we want to grasp, in women's autonomous movements, is moments of struggle and mobilization or situations of rupture that make it possible to lead conflicts that are specific, but limited, to the two aspects of the struggle for wages indicated above (that is, wages and reduction of work). (39)

Essentially, what Lotta Femminista was saying was that different links with the Wages for Housework question had to be discovered depending on the context and the conjuncture. The struggles to increase social services and improve community facilities, quantitatively and qualitatively, were relevant in this sense when they aimed to reduce women's workday and free them from housework.

Support for a Women's Shelter: Nellie's Women's Hostel in Toronto

Of the many struggles in community environments organized or supported by Wages for Housework groups, the one conducted to support Nellie's Women's Hostel, a women's shelter in Toronto, is exemplary. Supported by the Toronto Wages for Housework Committee, this struggle has the advantage, for analysis purposes, of having been well documented.[55]

Nellie's Women's Hostel was a short-term shelter for women in difficulty – in crisis, without money, homeless, victims of assault, or needing emergency support. Opened in Toronto in 1974 by a small group of women, with a low budget and a skeleton staff, it saw the number of women using its service grow from year to year.

In August 1976, in the context of draconian cuts to social services and facing the imminent possibility of the shelter having to turn women away for lack of space or even close its doors, the staff and the residents decided to occupy their locale. Their demand: guaranteed public funding in order to offer short- and long-term lodging to women in difficulty. Whereas there were 1,184 emergency beds for men in the city, there were only 77 for women.

Figure 5.7   Nellie's Women's Hostel's letterhead.

In the press release announcing the event, the occupiers noted that the case of Nellie's was typical: lack of funding was only "the tip of the iceberg of how the government is making its cutbacks on the backs of women."

> At Nellie's emergency hostel, the staff is basically doing housework for other women. We keep a house open where women can find food, shelter and a sympathetic ear ... But housework comes cheap ... We feel it with our low wages; we feel it with our long shifts; we feel it when we are exhausted at the end of a shift because the hostel is understaffed, but we can't afford to hire anyone else ... The separation between the staff and the residents is rapidly diminishing ... [By] organizing an occupation at Nellie's ... we want to make visible the appalling lack of accommodation for women.[56]

The occupiers asked members of the public to sign a petition, write to the newspapers to show their support, and to join the occupiers by bringing mattresses, bedding, food, kitchen items, toys, and money to fill urgent needs. The appeal to solidarity with the occupiers was heard.[57] Reinforcements joined the mobilization. Letters were published in the city's three dailies. Every afternoon of the first week of the two-week occupation, a "special program" lasting an hour and a half was organized by the Wages for Housework Committee onsite, composed of movies, comedies, and other entertainments, as well as discussions. Representatives of community services groups whose budgets were being cut joined the occupation.

At the end of a meeting of support and reflection on the funding for Nellie's, involving about thirty community groups, a statement, "In Supporting Nellie's, We Support Ourselves," was issued.[58] Addressed to three levels of government in Canada (municipal, provincial, federal), the statement was co-signed by fifty-three groups.

The statement affirmed that government cuts to family allowances and social assistance, and the freeze in funding for daycare centres, were in fact responsible for the rising number of requests for assistance in shelters. In this sense, the situation at Nellie's Women's Hostel reflected the lives of women and the crisis being experienced by certain community services directed by and for women. Yet, most of the services met basic needs such as housing, social assistance, daycare, legal aid, family planning, healthcare, and care for people with disabilities, and dealt with issues such as the status of Aboriginals and immigrants, rape, suicide prevention, and violence against women.

"No level of government presently accepts responsibility for funding these services," the statement emphasized, as dispensing them was "seen as mere 'women's work' ... the same one that works for nothing in the home." "It is high time," the statement concluded, that "the different levels of government re-order their priorities and begin recognizing the value of the services which 'women's work' provides."

The position paper was presented by a delegation of sixty women, along with children and a few men, to the mayor of Toronto and the premier of Ontario. The event was widely covered by the media, keeping the public's attention on the crisis that the shelter was going through. Finally, two and a half months later, in October 1976, the mobilization bore fruit. Among the immediate gains was that Nellie's Women's Hostel would now be recognized and funded as an emergency shelter (room and board). Politicians assured the staff that the shelter would never again be faced with having to close because of a lack of funds. The municipal administration also authorized a study on the need to formulate a long-term housing policy for women in difficulty.

The final report written by the shelter's staff noted, however, that all psychological interventions, counselling, referrals, and guidance – services intrinsic to emergency shelters – continued to be dispensed on an unfunded basis. "The solution to our situation ultimately has to be based on the struggle to recognize ALL women's work," the report noted.[59] The struggle had, in fact, demonstrated the point to which women's work was taken for granted, and the point to which governments thus saved money on the backs of women.

The final report also noted that at the top of the list of the many groups that provided support was the Wages for Housework Committee of Toronto. In a letter to Judy Ramirez, the manager of Nellie's thanked her personally for her deep commitment to the mobilization, which had decisively contributed to bringing the conflict to the public's attention and "making our struggle an enormous success."[60]

Also among the most active support groups in the mobilization and the occupation was Wages Due Lesbians, affiliated with the Toronto Wages for Housework Committee. This group recognized that the situation at Nellie's was an indication of a much broader crisis in the social services, and especially those dispensed by and for women. Many lesbians benefitted from the services, notably those who were without resources after having left untenable family situations. With such cuts in the services for women in difficulty, it would be even harder for them to leave this type of situation. The slogan of the mobilization applied to them as well: supporting Nellie's was to support lesbians. Wages Due Lesbians described how it participated in the struggle: "Lesbian women among the staff, residents, and supporters of Nellie's have helped build the occupation by writing letters to the newspapers and carrying our own placards in a large delegation to Queen's Park. We have spoken as lesbians on behalf of the struggle at Nellie's about how fed up we are with the cutbacks."[61]

Wages Due Lesbians and the Toronto Wages for Housework Committee were active in other struggles and community services in Toronto also. For example, they provided support for mobilizations around housing, participated in the publication of a guide on unemployment insurance for housewives, offered services to immigrant domestic workers, were involved in the struggle against rape, and set up a defence fund for lesbian mothers.

I have simply brushed the surface of the activism of the Toronto Wages for Housework Committee and Wages Due Lesbians. This is very probably true too for mobilizations by other Wages for Housework groups that belonged to the IFC. In these last two chapters, I have given only a glimpse at the struggles and mobilizations that embodied the Wages for Housework political perspective during the IFC's existence, that is, from 1972 to 1977, and for which I had access to documentation.

There were, however, other groups that put into action the Wages for Housework political perspective during the same period, and that acted on the periphery of the IFC. Among them were the Berlin group Lohn für Hausarbeit, briefly discussed in the next chapter, and Collectif L'Insoumise of Geneva, described in greater detail, who put forward the Wages for Housework demand in their own way. As the Collectif L'Insoumise put it, "There is not just one way to express our Wages for Housework demand."[62]

6
Mobilizations by Groups on the Periphery of the Network: Lohn für Hausarbeit in Berlin and Collectif L'Insoumise in Geneva

> Our main problem is that they make us not into dolls but into servants. Our struggle is directed not against allure or against all men, but against exploitation of our work, twenty-four hours a day.[1]

Most, if not all, second-wave feminist groups discussed Wages for Housework during the 1970s. Although many subscribed to the analysis presented in *The Power of Women and the Subversion of the Community*, a great majority of these groups were reluctant to mobilize to demand such a wage, and finally decided not to. The usual reason for this decision was the fear that a wage for housework would chain women to the home.

The francophone Quebec activists belonged to groups that ultimately decided not to take up concrete Wages for Housework activism. Some of their initiatives were examples of "sitting on the fence" positions that involved recognizing housework as work, on the one hand, but being opposed to its being paid, on the other.

PREAMBLE: INITIATIVES IN FRANCOPHONE QUEBEC

The high point of the North American tour taken by Mariarosa Dalla Costa and Selma James, who were aiming to launch the Wages for Housework perspective and demand in North America, was the Feminist Symposium held in Montreal in June 1973, at which attendees voted unanimously in favour of Wages for Housework.[2] As this resolution was adopted in Montreal, one might have expected Wages for Housework groups to form there. In reality, only one group, the Montreal Power of Women Collective, composed of English-speaking women activists, was created; not one, in francophone Quebec.[3] To my knowledge, a meeting and an interview, organized by the Centre des femmes de Montréal, were the only initiatives taken by francophone feminists with Dalla Costa and James during their North American tour in the spring of 1973.[4]

182 WAGES FOR HOUSEWORK

Even though no francophone feminist groups in Quebec threw themselves into a mobilization for Wages for Housework, awareness-raising initiatives were instigated. An exemplary case is Le Théâtre des cuisines.

Le Théâtre des cuisines began its adventure in 1974. A feminist theatre collective, it was intended "to perform political theatre with women, dealing with the specific exploitation of women," and "to reach out to the most exploited women, and also the most isolated women."[5] It was intended to perform in front of community groups; in neighbourhoods; on worksites; for women on strike, women's committees in unions, and parents' committees; and in schools.[6] After producing a play on abortion, the company addressed housework:

At first we were reluctant to do a show on a subject that wasn't attached to an existing struggle. (There was no organization in Quebec taking concrete action with regard to housework.) However, we think it's very important to

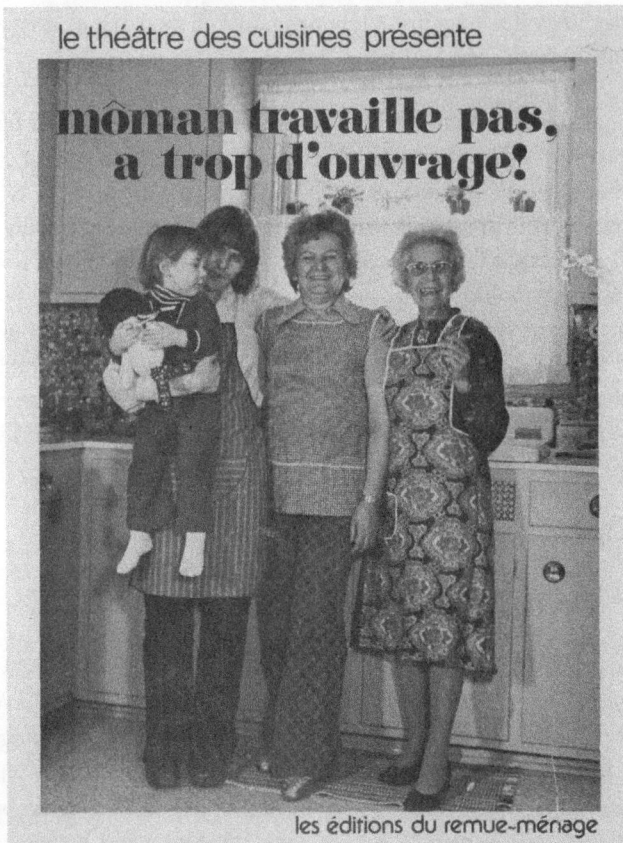

Figure 6.1 Cover page of *Môman travaille pas, a trop d'ouvrage* (Mama doesn't have a job, she's got too much work), by Le Théâtre des cuisines (Montreal: Éditions du remue-ménage, 1976).

talk about housework as the basis of exploitation of women. It seems to us that even if there is no organized struggle, that is not a reason to avoid the subject ... We want to talk about the role of housework in our society, the conditions under which it is done, and who profits. We also want to say to other women that, each in her kitchen, they do work that is indispensable for the community and should be acknowledged. We know that it is a vast undertaking, but we find the challenge very stimulating.[7]

The play premiered on March 8, 1975. By means of a small grant, it was performed in Montreal and some regions of Quebec. It raised a good deal of interest and heated discussion – so much so that a scene in which the house-workers demanded a wage for housework had to be changed. Because of certain negative reactions expressed during some performances, the authors withdrew the entire scene in which the wage demand was made and wrote a second version.[8] They justified the cut this way:

After a while, we found ourselves unable to assume leadership of this debate with the public. The idea that we were putting out there, that of a wage, had repercussions that we could no longer control. We therefore decided to change the scene so that our houseworkers no longer demand a wage at the end of the trial.

Still, proving that housework is work without talking about a wage for it is a very delicate thing. We know that ambiguity remains, but for the moment, we prefer to stick with what we are truly capable of defending. If ever we have new views on the subject, there may be a third version.[9]

This incident in Quebec feminist history reveals the vehemence of certain feminists' reactions to the very idea of wages for housework. It would probably still provoke very similar reactions.[10]

Moreover, the feminist current to which I belonged at that time, represented by Intergroupe (1975–76), was, with Le Théâtre des cuisines, the one that went the furthest on the Wages for Housework question. However, it was not intended to cross a certain threshold: the overall Wages for Housework *perspective* was accepted, but not the concrete *campaign* to claim it.

Intergroupe was an alliance of autonomous Montreal francophone women's groups that had emerged from the Front de libération des femmes (1969–71) and the Centre des femmes (1972–75). It was composed of the Comité de lutte pour l'avortement et la contraception libres et gratuits, the Centre de santé des femmes du quartier Plateau-Mont-Royal, Le Théâtre des cuisines, the Centre de documentation féministe, and Éditions du remue-ménage. A jointly written text marked the consensus that linked them on the Wages for Housework question, but also the limitations of that consensus: the manifesto

Figure 6.2   March 8: "Ménagères et travailleuses: Un même combat" (Houseworkers and waged women workers: Same struggle), poster by Lise Nantel.

La lutte des ménagères est la lutte de toute la classe ouvrière (The Houseworkers' Struggle Is the Struggle of the Working Class as a Whole), read in Montreal on March 8, 1976, during an International Women's Day celebration held by union, community, and feminist groups.[11] The manifesto described "the specific relation of exploitation that houseworkers maintain with capital" and specified that "we must always fight from the starting position of how we suffer capitalist exploitation – that is, starting from our relationship with capital." The exploitation in this case was that linked to housework.

One might quote here the Théâtre des cuisines manifesto regarding the second version of its play: it was awkward, not to mention ambiguous, to "prov[e] that housework is work without talking about a wage for it." In fact, the Intergroupe manifesto reflected the oppositions to the Wages for Housework strategy that reigned within the alliance, the goal of which was to develop "anti-capitalist and anti-patriarchal" thought. This "yes to the perspective, no to the wages campaign" cleavage was also, it must be remembered, a major obstacle not just in Quebec but elsewhere too.[12]

The Collectif L'Insoumise of Geneva demanded wages for housework, "moving in the wake of other groups in the network [the IFC], but taking quite a different path" – a "special" path, according to one ex-member of L'Insoumise. Something similar could be said for the Lohn für Hausarbeit group in Berlin (West Berlin, as it was at the time).

These groups, which identified with the Wages for Housework perspective but did not become formal members of the IFC, nevertheless stayed in contact with activists in the network's groups. Ties were formed mainly through correspondence, exchanges of documentary materials, reports on local and international situations, and mutual visits. These groups studied the IFC's documentary materials, translated them into their respective languages, and also produced their own documents.

LOHN FÜR HAUSARBEIT IN BERLIN[13]

In Germany, several groups and individuals advocated for and promoted wages for housework, notably in Munich (around Gisela Erler), Bremen (around Ute Brockhaus), Bielefeld (Claudia von Werlhof and Maria Mies), Göttingen (Hannelore Schröder), and Hamburg. However, these groups remained at a greater distance from the IFC than did the group in West Berlin and had a shorter lifespan.[14]

Circumstances of Formation

The Wages for Housework group in Berlin was created in 1975. *The Power of Women and the Subversion of Community* had been translated into German in 1973, and various Italian, English, and French texts by IFC groups, including the IFC's founding manifesto, were published in German the following year.[15]

Gisela Bock was behind the creation of the Berlin group. She had met Mariarosa Dalla Costa and the activists of Lotta Femminista in 1972 during one of her stays in Italy. She had also met Selma James and some of the activists in the London Power of Women group when they visited Germany to give talks around the same time. Then, during a one-year stay at Harvard University (where she was researching American worker and feminist movements) in 1974–75, she met Silvia Federici and American and Canadian activists (including Judy Ramirez) of the Wages for Housework groups.

The Berlin group, which was formed when Bock returned from the United States, had about twenty members. Several were active at the same time in lesbian groups, or with "prostitutes," or with Afro-German or Berlin Turkish women, or in the healthcare sector, or in the scholarly environment of feminist studies.[16] So, these women who lived in Berlin, some of whom were not German, who joined Lohn für Hausarbeit had diverse interests that they grafted to the Wages for Housework campaign in an attempt to integrate the multiple dimensions of the situation of women and of feminism.

Dissemination and Information Activities

The Berlin group, which was in close contact with the Bremen group, concentrated on publicity and dissemination activities: public interventions by group members and lectures throughout West Germany, including various talks by James. She went to Germany three times between 1975 and 1979, sometimes accompanied by Wilmette Brown of Black Women for Wages for Housework, who provided invaluable help with the formation of a similar group in Germany.[17] In addition, activists conducted interviews with journalists and

Figure 6.3 "An Alle Regierungen" (Notice to All Governments) by the Lohn für Hausarbeit (Wages for Housework) group of Berlin. (Silvia Federici Archives).

wrote newspaper and magazine articles. They also intervened in a houseworkers' union and with other women's groups interested in the Wages for Housework perspective.

The Berlin group's most active period, between late 1975 and late 1978, took two main forms. First, it had regular pieces in the wide-circulation radical feminist monthly *Courage* (1976–84, with a print run of approximately seventy thousand), thus disseminating to a large readership information explaining and promoting Wages for Housework. Three issues were devoted to this theme, along with other feminist subjects to which the group contributed (for example, on the situation of Roma women).

Second, on the occasion of the first (1976) and second (1977) Summer University for Women (Sommeruniversität für Frauen), the group organized panels on housework and on the Wages for Housework demand, launching major debates on the question, leading to the wide distribution of publications by authors who were members of the Berlin group.[18] The most widely read essay on the subject was (and still is) "Arbeit aus Liebe – Liebe as Arbeit: Zur Entstehung der Hausarbeit im Kapitalismus," written by Gisela Bock and Barbara Duden in 1976 (see sidebar).[19] Also notable were the presence and participation, at the Summer University for Women in 1977, of activists from Wages for Housework groups in Italy, the United States, and Great Britain.[20] This was an indication of the importance that the Berlin group placed on cooperation with the IFC.[21]

HOUSEWORK HAS A HISTORY[22]

One of the significant contributions by historians Gisela Bock and Barbara Duden of the Berlin Wages for Housework group to this perspective of thought was to have "historicized" housework – in other words, to have extracted it from the state of "nature" or "love" in which it was immersed in the mid-1970s, to buttress its historical dimension. In effect, as the second wave of feminism was beginning, this idea prevailed that housework was natural, that it did not have its own history, and that it therefore was not part of social history (similar to sexuality and childbirth).

In this essay, Bock and Duden present certain fundamental characteristics of the history of women's work seen from the angle of housework. They highlight its recent origin, which corresponds to the period of the emergence of capitalism, in the seventeenth and eighteenth centuries: "Everything which now constitutes housework seems to have changed during this time: what it is, who does it, how it is done; the attitude toward it, its socioeconomic significance, its relation to social and natural environment. Even the concept of housework and housewife does not seem to exist before this time, just as the modern concept of the family originated only with the development of the bourgeois family" (156).

▶

After the introduction, authored by Bock, is a section written by Duden, in which she studies different aspects of pre-capitalist society during the European *ancien régime:* the central place of women's work in the economy of the time, the absence of a mother's role, the social power of women and their resistances to the installation of capitalism, and, finally, their relationship with men in marriage. The third and fourth sections, written by Bock, are devoted to her study of the gradual establishment of housework in the United States (with parallels in Germany), as it is known today ("women's" work, "natural," "for love," and free) as a functional element in the development of capitalism starting in the late nineteenth century and up to the 1930s. Among other things, Bock analyzes the home economics movement, the mission of which was to professionalize housework. "Scientific management" (Taylorism) was to be adapted to the area of reproduction in the home. These profound changes in women's work, effected in just a few generations, had to be understood in the relationship between housework and capitalism, the underlying idea being to improve and guarantee productivity and the quality of the worker. The home therefore became "part of a great factory for the production of citizens," as a 1912 book on "home efficiency" had it (175). Talcott Parsons, the well-known American sociologist quoted by Bock, expressed himself similarly in 1955: "Families are 'factories' which produce human personalities" (175) – in other words, "social factories."

As Bock points out,

Modern housework, which comprises both the production (including the necessary sexuality) and reproduction (including consumption and immeasurable labors of love) of this "human machine" was a novelty, far removed from "feudal" or even "natural" relics. Housework was not eliminated by industrialization, but necessitated by it ... The modern family in its full-blown form was completed [in United States] in the early decades of this century as the organizational form for unwaged female housework, of housework as natural and therefore naturally unwaged woman's work. (177–79)

And the author goes on: "This transition from the early stage of capital accumulation ... to the reform capitalism of the 20th century ... was possible only at women's expense: namely through the creation, generalization and institutionalization of housework" (185), work that subjected them to the reproduction of labour power. These are just a few of the general thrusts of this essay, which had a huge impact in 1976, when it was presented for the first time at the lectern of the first Summer University for Women, held at the Berlin Free University.

"Arbeit aus Liebe – Liebe as Arbeit: Zur Entstehung der Hausarbeit im Kapitalismus" was a pioneering work that contributed a new dimension to the system of thought of the Wages for Housework current and to the field of women's history. A great deal of research subsequently underpinned the historical canvas painted in this essay.

The Berlin group closed its doors in 1979, a year that corresponded to a period of crisis for the majority of feminist groups in Berlin (as elsewhere). It was "the end of the first phase of the new feminism," according to Gisela Bock. And in Berlin, she added, there was "great geographic mobility among members. All had to find activist pursuits closer to their daily life and their job."[23]

The ending of commitment to the Berlin group, however, went beyond the question of having time to devote to it and the need to earn a living, Bock felt:

Organizational problems within the International Wages for Housework Campaign began to emerge. Conflicts, divisions, expulsions, and a process of centralization of leadership emerged over the months.[24] In addition, the Wages for Housework demand gradually lost much of its attraction to the feminist movement as a whole, as it had been rejected more and more by all of the left, Marxist, social-democrat, communist, and green movements. Due to this combination of factors, the Wages for Housework perspective and strategy seemed more and more like a utopia in German women activists' eyes.

With the dissolution of the Berlin group in 1979, the public Wages for Housework demand also disappeared in Germany. It would nevertheless resurface, according to Bock, no longer in an organized form and as a strategy and political practice, but as a theoretical tool for historical, cultural, sociological, and political analysis. "And from time to time," she concluded, "the demand would burst out again in various, and sometimes unexpected, forms, either in Western metropolises (even in Germany), or on a global scale, with respect to the infinite work, unpaid or poorly paid, performed mainly by women."[25]

L'INSOUMISE IN GENEVA

The Collectif L'Insoumise was born in Geneva in 1974.[26] Most of the fifteen women who were members, who called themselves Les Insoumises, came from the small groups that had formed the 1968 protest movement, which they began to critique and leave. The majority had gone to university; some came from middle-class families; others, from working-class families that had benefitted from early measures to democratize education. One of them had been one of the founders of the Mouvement de libération des femmes (MLF) in Geneva in 1971, and the others had "entered" soon after.

Circumstances of Formation

The creation of the Collectif L'Insoumise was actually a process that took place between 1972 and 1975, the latter date marking the year that the first issue of the group's eponymous journal, *L'Insoumise*, appeared. During this period, the group gradually constructed its point of view on Wages for Housework from readings and the personal experiences of each of its members. In the context of the MLF, some of them participated in editing two journals: *De fil en aiguille*, published in 1973, and *De mère en fille*, in 1974, the result of discussions of the Groupe de mères, an MLF subgroup.

In 1975, the UN-proclaimed International Women's Year, the Insoumises launched their own journal, *L'Insoumise*. It was published until 1978. They participated in MLF assemblies and actions, but at the same time they began to meet on their own, in order to "figure out how to think of the link between the class struggle and the feminist struggle."[27]

Mariarosa Dalla Costa and Selma James's book *Potere femminile e sovversione sociale* had made its way into the hands of the Insoumises through their links with Italian extra-parliamentary left-wing movements with a workerist tendency, to which Dalla Costa was close, as well as through links woven with Selma James and the Power of Women Collective in London. It was through these channels that they became aware of the book that "excited" them.

And so, contact was made with a progressive publisher in Geneva, François Grounauer, who published writings from protest movements, for the purpose of having the book in question translated into French and published.[28] The group that was to become the Collectif L'Insoumise immediately "adopted it as a bible." A meeting was soon organized in the Ticino canton; it was attended by feminists interested in Wages for Housework from the canton and from Zurich and by Dalla Costa, accompanied by several women from Padua's Lotta Femminista.[29]

It was thus in large part through Dalla Costa that the Collectif L'Insoumise was created. Its members (who did not all share a single ideological background) then formed ties with Lotta Femminista, read its publications, participated in meetings with its activists in Italy, and followed its activities with great interest. These were the circumstances under which the collective was founded.

> We were looking for a "Marxist" perspective for our feminist commitment, and we found it in the "Wages for Housework strategy" (which we always took care to explain as a strategy "against" free housework for women only, and sometimes signed our papers "Collectif Salaire contre le travail ménager" [Wages against Housework Collective]). It was also a way of attacking one of women's great taboos, that of having their own money. The discovery of this strategy gave us wings, and enabled us to become very active in the MLF, finding transverse paths to practise it, without "sectarianism" and avoiding the controversies that the demand aroused in the movement.

Figure 6.4 Issue 1 of the journal *Insoumises*, 1975, which later became *L'Insoumise*.

The Insoumises were activists integrated into the broader MLF movement in Geneva: "A number of us were among the initiators of some of the 'big' actions under the banner of the MLF, which was formed of a galaxy of small groups brought together in the general assembly, in concrete actions, and in management of the Centre-femmes." They often called the shots in the MLF, "for we were almost all full-time activists, very young, making a living with odd jobs, scholarships, unemployment allowances, and so on." The fact that some of them became mothers did not change their way of life: "On the contrary, we were able to use other 'taps,' such as welfare, to find money without having to turn to a double workday."

The group was composed of women with various activist interests: the Wages for Housework strategy first of all, but also women's health, childbirth, abortion,

Figure 6.5   Insoumise banner with a few Insoumises. Photo: Viviane Gonik, Geneva.

contraception, sexuality, lesbianism, repression, and more. All of these subjects were, however, addressed with the particular "Insoumise style," a "radical and impertinent" style, which unified the group in its reflections and actions. What differentiated the Insoumises from the MLF was

> the catch-all demand for "equality" that we were contesting. We designated "the family" as the site of exploitation par excellence. We were not interested in demands such as "encourage women's access to paid work," "sharing household chores with men," and so on. Our position was, women's financial independence, yes, but not at the price of the double workday. Sharing chores with men, yes, but first let us build social power as women in order to be capable of imposing this collectively. We refused to advocate the "guilt-inducing" path of individual negotiation of sharing of chores in the couple as the miracle solution, even if, in one way or another, we were personally confronted by it ourselves. The rest of the demands – that is, most of them – were common and shared by all.[30]

For the Insoumises, the Wages for Housework perspective represented "a way of 'avenging' our mothers' fate and returning dignity to the work of past generations, present and future mothers and grandmothers!"

> We no longer wanted to have to live, like most of them, in submission to patriarchal values and structures. But, unlike the feminism dominant in the 1970s (which demonized housework), we valued just as much the work that

all women provided at home as the development of behaviours and signs of refusal of this workload that was unrecognized, unpaid, and reserved for women (increases in number of divorces demanded by women, lowering of the birth rate, right to abortion, a stampede by women toward university studies, and so on).

What was the Insoumises' "fairly different path" taken to "practise" Wages for Housework? But first of all, what was their conception of a wage? An internal document, *La perspective du salaire ménager*, gave an explanation:

Through the Wages for Housework perspective, we see for the first time the fragmented life of women – with its apparently separate compartments – as a whole. For example, we want to have control over our bodies. But this control is the power to demand control of births that do not poison our bodies; to have children when we want them, independent of our dependence on a man and of our slavery in the home; to be capable of raising children without constant financial turmoil or household crises; to not be forced to stay confined to heterosexuality; to not be forced to be dragged into an assembly line. If we organize a daycare centre in our neighbourhood and if we ask the Commune to finance it, that is wages for housework. There is not just one way to express our Wages for Housework demand. In medicine, in social services – everywhere, we can organize in the Wages for Housework perspective.[31]

The Collectif L'Insoumise initiated many struggles in Geneva between 1974 and 1979. According to the Insoumises with whom I met, the group's life can be divided into two periods:

1. From 1975 to 1978, which was the most active period, characterized by multiple occupations.
2. Beginning in 1978–79, when the collective split into small groups. This was also the period during which the women from the MLF wanted to go beyond making demands and began creating alternative self-managed structures, offering assistance and information services for women, such as the Dispensaire des femmes (a dispensary for women), Viol-secours (a rape-crisis centre), and SOS Femmes battues (a centre for battered women). "Little by little, we lost the MLF dimension," said one of them. "And little by little no one availed herself of MLF anymore."

Landmark Struggles and Publications, 1975–79

The Collectif L'Insoumise stood out for its action – often direct action – but also for its reflective and information work. For example, the collective produced a journal, *L'Insoumise*, with ten issues published between 1975 and 1978. It also translated into French a number of texts by Italian, English, and American Wages for Housework groups, starting with the major anthology *Le foyer de l'insurrection*. Dalla Costa's *Le operaie della casa* was translated into French by one of the Insoumises but never published; it had limited circulation in a ready-to-print format. The collective also produced other publications more closely related to the group's occasional actions.

First, let's take a look at the collective's struggles. One of the methods emphasized was direct action:

> We did not throw ourselves into a Wages for Housework campaign, as they did in England and Italy. Nor did we do lobbying, as the English group did, for example, intending to influence structure, laws, and so on, but we found forms of expression such as, for example, the demand for two thousand francs for all mothers for three years. Nor did we go to see the unions in order to persuade them to include our demand within their action programs. We didn't want to make an alliance with them – rather, units of action. Instead, we were plugged in to direct action and alternative autonomous solutions. For example, when the struggle for free gynecological exams seemed already lost, a few women from the MLF, two of whom were members of L'Insoumise, set up a women's dispensary. Same thing for daycare centres. Rather than ask the state to create daycare centres, we preferred to create "wild" kindergartens. We wanted a "different" way to take charge of women's health and childcare. In fact, we positioned ourselves within a broader movement of creating alternative living and working structures.

The Collectif L'Insoumise had many fields of struggle and action, among them:

1. actions with respect to abortion, contraception, health, and maternity
2. actions with women waged workers (factory workers at Bulova and Lip, and nurses at the Geneva cantonal hospital)
3. actions against repression and conditions of detention for female prisoners
4. actions against rape, sexual harassment, and violence against women
5. occasional occupations of government offices (welfare and unemployment) and some public sites (such as the headquarters of the Christian Democratic Party or an abandoned bistro to make it into a women's centre)
6. "post-Insoumises" actions.

The splitting up of the collective gave rise to Vanille-Fraise (a lesbian group), Radio Pleine Lune, and Blé et Tchador. From the information available to me,

I have reconstructed the actions in which L'Insoumise participated or that it initiated.

Abortion, Contraception, and Self-Management of Health

In Switzerland at the time, abortion was illegal.[32] In reality, to obtain an abortion, one had to have the prior agreement of a gynecologist and another physician, who acted as an "expert" chosen by the state. Due to the nebulous nature of the law, however, each of Switzerland's twenty-five cantons did more or less what it wanted with regard to abortion. For instance, in five cantons, it was easy to get an abortion. Because Geneva was situated in one of these cantons, women came from France and Italy (where abortion was illegal) to have abortions. An abortion cost around one thousand Swiss francs.[33]

For the UN's declared International Women's Year, in 1975, the Collectif L'Insoumise took a bold initiative: it printed and distributed a coupon for an abortion signed by the UN secretary general (Figure 6.6). Then it participated in an action organized by women from various Swiss MLF groups to disrupt the Bern Parliament during the debate on abortion, throwing dirty diapers from the public gallery onto the parliamentarians' heads.

On October 2, 1975, members occupied the headquarters of the Christian Democratic Party, which had "blocked debates on abortion during the last session in the legislature" and "had voted for a new anti-abortion law." They

Figure 6.6 "Coupon for an abortion paid for by the UN as part of Women's Year. The Secretary General." Produced by the Collectif L'Insoumise.

used the occupation to publish a journal on the action, *Avortement: La lutte continue; Feuille de l'occupation*.[34] Not only did they use the party's presses and paper to print it and to send press releases to the media, they also used the party's phone lines to call women in the movement all over the world.

In fact, the abortion struggle was more global; it affected hospital practices, "contraception, against the experts and the vampire gynecologists."[35] For instance, on April 24, 1976, in Zurich, under the theme "Let's organize our collective refusal to pay for gynecological tests," they demonstrated against cuts in the health insurance fund *(caisses maladies)* that resulted in women having to pay for their own gynecological exams.[36] In 1978, they participated in the formation of an MLF subgroup, Attaque aux gynécologues (Attack on Gynecologists). At the same time, a list was compiled of gynecologists who agreed to perform abortions, under what conditions, the cost, and other information. The struggle was also expressed in actions with regard to contraception: putting the Pill on trial and refusing to be test subjects.[37] Other actions were aimed at humanizing and demedicalizing childbirth at the maternity ward of the cantonal hospital in Geneva, which finally gave rise, in 1978, to the creation of an autonomous women's dispensary.

From "Angry Mothers" to "Bad Mothers"

One of the most significant actions of the Collectif L'Insoumise addressed the experiences of the lot of mothers – refuting the idea, regularly spread about feminists in the 1970s, that they rejected or ignored the question of maternity. It is true that the Insoumises addressed "bad mothers" and "angry mothers." Who were these bad mothers?

> Bad mothers [are] those whom society and right-thinking people consider bad because they don't do exactly what the state, the family, the Church, and the cops want them to do. For their children, [they are] the best mothers in the world, as they are vibrant, full of life, and they don't have the smell of resignation and sacrifice; instead, they have the good scent of revolt and freedom![38]

On January 19, 1978, the Insoumises occupied the offices of the Caisse cantonale de chômage, the canton's unemployment bureau, in support of one of them – no doubt one of the "bad mothers" – who had just given birth and to whom the bureau was refusing to pay the planned allowance. Since "women were never unemployed," Les Insoumises demanded:

1. immediately, sixteen weeks of paid maternity leave for all women
2. a benefit – or a salary – of two thousand francs per month for all mothers.[39]

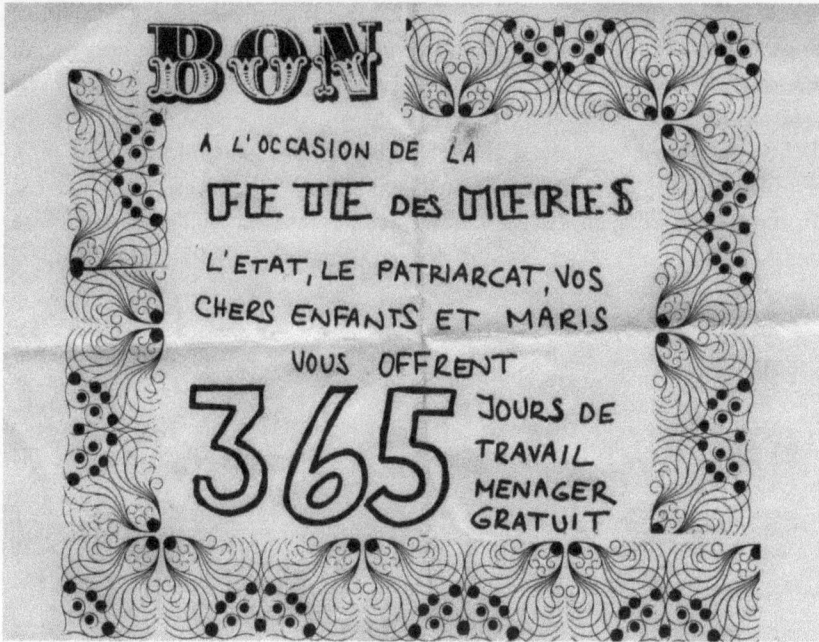

Figure 6.7   "Bon pour la Fête des mères" (coupon for Mother's Day), "L'État, le patriarcat, vos chers enfants et maris vous offrent 365 jours de travail ménager gratuit" (The state, the patriarchy, and your dear children and husbands offer you 365 days of free housework). Les Insoumises. Photo: Viviane Gonik, Geneva.

The battle was (partially) won on the spot: the "bad mother" would receive her allowance. The conclusion: "The occupiers of the bureau were able to judge the effectiveness of direct action."[40] The demand for two thousand francs per month for all mothers would then be taken to the public forum by the Collectif L'Insoumise: "Mothers, if you want the two thousand francs as quickly as possible, come to the meeting on March 15 at 8:30 p.m. at the Centre-femmes, 5 bd St-Georges." Why the demand for two thousand francs?

Two Thousand Francs per Month for Spaces of Freedom

It was mainly through the action-mobilizations undertaken by the mothers' offensive movement that this Swiss expression of the Wages for Housework perspective was known. The discussion about the request for two thousand francs per month for three years, and the eventual use that women might make of it, framed this expression.[41]

In contrast to the claim of opponents to Wages for Housework, the journal *L'Insoumise* saw the two thousand francs per month as a means of giving women more choice: "2000 Frs per month that drops as 'cash' into the pocket each month would enable us to envisage life a bit differently. It is not everything we want, but it is a step in the right direction." For instance, the authors noted, "We might choose to go and work outside a bit, but not too much, to have even more money ... We might also choose to transform our housework." Specifically, "When we choose to make a child, we choose, anyway, to do housework ... Transforming [it] is not only to rationalize it and to do less, it's also to change it qualitatively, to socialize it as we want (and not as the state would like to impose on us)."[42]

Figure 6.8   L'Insoumise 8 (February 1978): 7.

And *L'Insoumise* detected clues to this socialization of housework "the way we do things," paths that had already been taken by a growing number of women "without even receiving the 2000 Frs yet":

- "wild" daycare centres and schools
- living in communes, some of which were for women only

- cooperative gardens for better nutrition
- alternative medicine, the use of which was already being advocated at the Centre-femmes
- the humanization of birthing care (a group had already been formed around the Centre-femmes).

All of these were examples of spaces of freedom for the women who worked there – unfortunately for free, as they had to work outside to make ends meet. Thus, these were spaces of freedom, but also spaces of poverty. The Geneva collective wanted mothers to have two thousand francs a month to "be able to do all this as *we* intend it, as *we* decide it, *we alone* ... We are demanding money for this very specifically."[43]

This transformation of housework, of daily life, also had to allow women to do something else: "to practise art in all its forms, to go down into the street, to go up to Paris from time to time, to put out *L'Insoumise* more often, to look for angry mothers in public parks, and so on." In diametrical opposition to the fears of the Wages for Housework opponents, such a wage, far from chaining women to the home, would truly free them, for "we are bad mothers. *We loved life before we had children,* and although children are an inconceivable pleasure, a draconian commitment, and an unending job in our life, even if they take up an inordinate space and are an enormous weight, *they are not everything for us*" (our translation; emphasis in original). Indeed, "We dance, we think, we drink, we smoke, we write, we travel, we struggle, we insult, we occupy, we demonstrate, we play, we laugh ... We are bad mothers, and we want wages for that!"[44] As an "Insoumise proverb" had it, "Money doesn't make happiness, but it helps."[45]

From the Angry Mothers List to the Angry Mothers Mutual

During the "2000 francs" campaign, the Collectif L'Insoumise created two original tools. The first was the Angry Mothers List, intended for "all mothers who want ... to defend themselves together to claim their due":

This means that a maximum of women ensure direct solidarity for themselves and others – in other words, they are able to establish among themselves a mutual relationship of active assistance and support, without there being "those who assist" on one side and "those who are assisted" on the other. The ANGRY MOTHERS LIST enables us to contact each other quickly and to intervene together when there is a need, as soon as one woman asks ... Our first demand, on which we will base all our actions: 2000 FRANCS PER MONTH FOR ALL MOTHERS FOR THREE YEARS. And for when our children are older than three, and for those whose children are already older than three, we will soon have more demands![46]

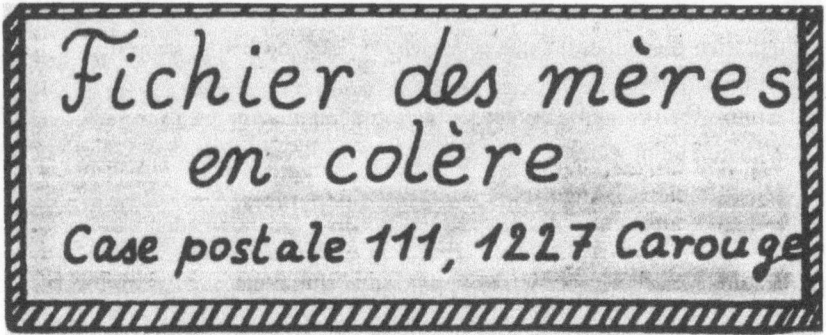

Figure 6.9   Fichier des mères en colère (Angry Mothers List)

Another tool was the Angry Mothers Mutual, the goal of which was "to become a strong, mothers' offensive movement":

> The top goal of Angry Mothers is to be less isolated, thus stronger, in confronting various "authorities" with which we have to deal: unemployment offices, welfare, employers, doctors, managers ... The Angry Mothers' Mutual would enable us to call on other women when we are in need or in difficulty ... or to conduct a public action to obtain what we want.[47]

On June 1, 1978, the newly created mutual conducted an "occupation" of BUCAS (the Bureau central d'aide sociale, or Central Welfare Office) to support a mother who had not received her allowance in two months: "We entered BUCAS at 10:00 a.m. with our children, their toys, and picnics; we left on the stroke of noon with what we wanted; from now on, mothers who go to BUCAS will be better treated."[48]

On May 12–13 of the following year, 1979, the Collectif L'Insoumise organized a Congrès des mauvaises mères (Congress of Bad Mothers), to "bring together, once and for all, the mothers living in Switzerland for discussions and immediate joint action. This congress will therefore be both a day of discussions and a day of actions of all sorts."[49]

The congress did indeed take place. A *Journal du Congrès des mauvaises mères* and an invitation leaflet were published. In addition, to make the congress accessible to women in German Switzerland, a German-language coupon was printed and distributed to interested women, a sort of false pass giving them the right to make the trip to Geneva by train free of charge. "And it worked! Women came to the congress by train without paying. This also was the 'wage spirit,'" said one of the organizers. And so, two hundred women, from all cantons, participated in the Congrès des mauvaises mères.

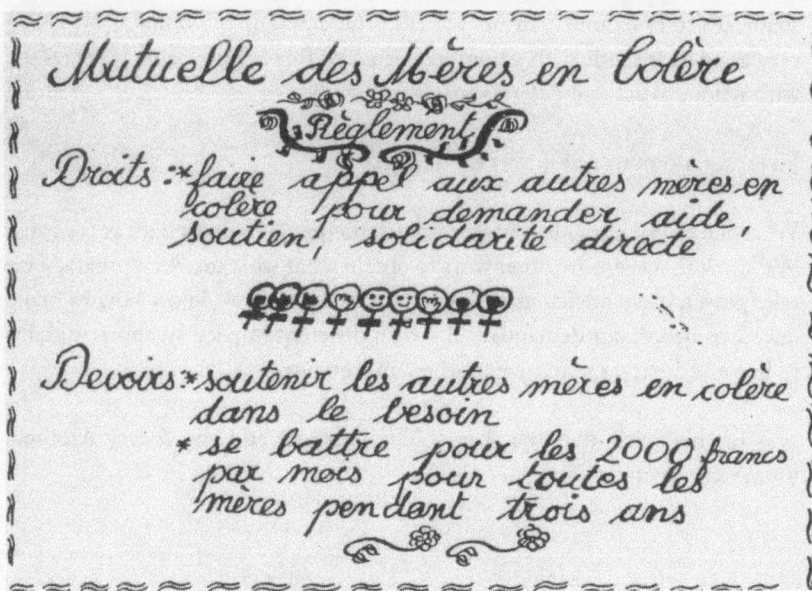

Figure 6.10 Angry Mothers' Mutual: Rights and Duties

The invitation leaflet described the types of mothers that the organizers were hoping to attract:

Those who aren't as they should be
Those who are trying to live as they like
Those who complain everywhere, at unemployment, at taxes, at the job
Those who shoplift
Those who go out at night
Those who would really like to but are too scared
Those who would like to take long trips
Those who don't live only for their kid
Those who detest Mother's Day
Those who are still obeying but it will change soon ...
Come to Geneva on May 12–13.[50]

In parallel with all this, the journal *L'Insoumise* offered "fact sheets," to explain to women and mothers how unemployment insurance and welfare worked, and above all how to gain access to them – for example, "How to obtain money when you are a mother."[51] There were no illusions in the conclusion:

The moral of these stories is that welfare, unemployment, social services are not there to help us. On the contrary, they are enemies on top of that. It is a sham, arbitrary regime ... In any case, the only safety, in our opinion, is to have very good girlfriends with whom to discuss all these things, and, if necessary, with whom to act and defend ourselves directly.[52]

Here, autonomous action was encouraged:

We'd like to say immediately that, for us, the parliamentary path is too long. We know that there are other ways to obtain what we want. As mothers, if we take power, if we maliciously defend our interests, if we know how to make ourselves heard, our demands will have a different impact. In short, we have to become a strong, offensive mothers' movement.[53]

It was in this spirit that the Angry Mothers List and the Angry Mothers Mutual were created.

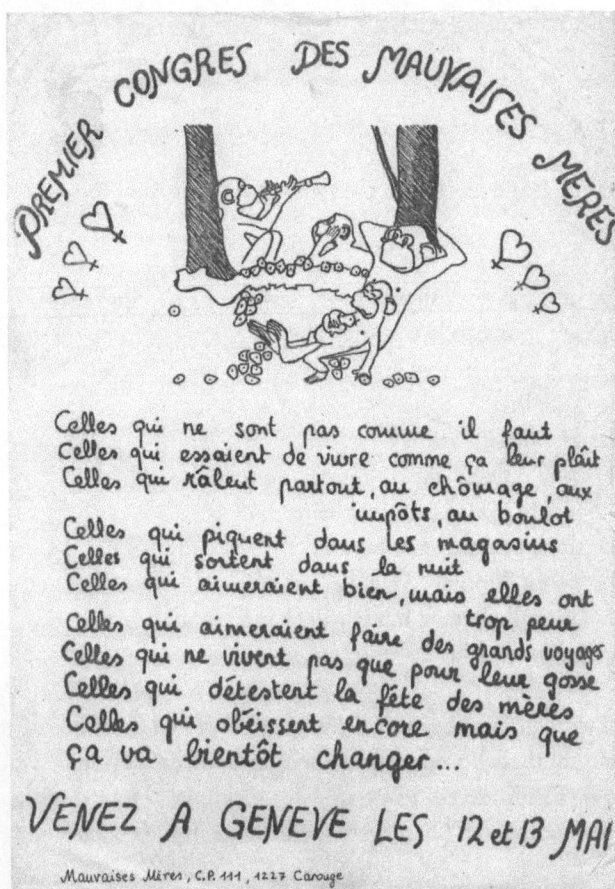

Figure 6.11 Poster for the Congrès des mauvaises mères. Les Insoumises.

Actions Targeting Waged Women Workers

The Collectif L'Insoumise also tried to engage with unionized women in labour conflicts. Three of these attempts are noteworthy: with the "women of Lip," the "women of Bulova," and "*insoumises* nurses."

Around 1975, a labour conflict was having a great impact in France. This was the strike at Lip, a watchmaking factory in Besançon. The long conflict spurred the women workers to action: they published a collection of testimonials, *Lip au féminin*, that raised great interest in the feminist world.[54] When it was published, the women of the Wages for Housework collective in Geneva had the idea of going, as they put it, to "contrast our political perspective with those women. We wanted to launch our political theory, which seemed so appropriate to us, to the women's collective in Lip to see how it would come out. And so, we went to see them." The meeting took place in September 1975 in Besançon. The content of the exchanges, in the form of an open letter to these women, was published first as a pamphlet, then in *Le foyer de l'insurrection*.[55]

The Insoumises then tried to approach the women working at the Bulova (another watchmaker) factory during an occupation there in 1976. The workforce was 75 percent women. This attempt, however, collided with the union establishment, run by men, which refused entry to the Insoumises who had come to meet the women workers. The group saw in this action by the union a sign of how little space and autonomy women workers were allowed in this struggle. They decided to devote an issue of their journal to these workers, raising questions on the need for the autonomy of women's struggle, and on the issue of housework and its remuneration.[56] Later, the Insoumises were finally able to meet with the women of Bulova, but in a recreation centre in Neuchâtel, where they had a discussion about the questions that they had raised in the journal.[57]

Today, the Insoumises recall that the actions they initiated among these unionized women were viewed with surprise, and even amusement. The striking women workers had first mobilized in their unions and wanted mainly to win their struggle to improve their working conditions and increase their salaries – "all things that the Insoumises were incapable of changing."[58] Therefore, the relationship went no further.

Finally, there was the "Infirmières insoumises" operation, a struggle by nurses against overwork, which began in summer 1977 on the seventh floor of the Geneva cantonal hospital: "Started due to the lack of personnel during the summer, the struggles on the seventh floor made it possible to address working conditions and power relations that reigned in the clinic."[59] The role of the Collectif L'Insoumise (which had at least three members who were nurses) in this struggle seems to have been to publish, in *L'Insoumise*, an account and analysis of the struggle, all leading to a sort of trial of the nursing practice.[60] The journal served as a vehicle for this analysis and also for their demand: "Three work days a week and 2500 francs per month."[61] The Collectif L'Insoumise did not intervene directly as a group.

Actions against Repression of and Violence toward Women

The suicide of a twenty-year-old woman who had spent three months detained in the Champ-Dollon prison in Geneva, on April 7, 1978, impelled thirty women at the Centre-femmes, including the Insoumises, and two mixed-sex prisoners' defence groups to rise up. Demonstrations in front of the prison gained the activists an opportunity to talk to the female prisoners about how they were being treated, the conditions under which they were being detained – including the use of confinement – and their demands. A hunger strike inside the prison supported the actions taking place outside. *L'Insoumise* reported on all these activities and gave a voice to the women prisoners.[62]

Figure 6.12 Support for the women prisoners. Photo: Viviane Gonik, Geneva.

These actions of solidarity with and support for women prisoners took place in a climate of repression that began to sweep through Europe in 1978 – especially in Germany and Italy, but also in France and Switzerland. Activists were arrested and political groups were under close surveillance; in short, a climate of suspicion reigned. It was the beginning of the end of "time to play." The great protest movement that had shaken societies in the West for a decade was running out of steam in Europe, and at the same time, power and repression were becoming organized.

It was also at this time that the Collectif L'Insoumise established a link between the repression that was stifling society and the repression that had always stifled women, in the latter case draining away all autonomy; women were scared of men and of the violence that they might perpetrate against them. Rape, harassment, and violence became new issues in the feminist struggle. Instead of prison terms for assaulters – prisons that they rejected – the Insoumises wanted to be compensated for the wrongs they had suffered:

> For us, damages and interest are also to be kept in mind. This is a path that may interest women, because we feel that our work and our bodies have a price: high, always too low, but there is one! And receiving 50 000 francs because I was raped gives me more strength than sending a guy to a prison (which I want to demolish).[63]

A group emerged from the MLF: Solidarité-Femmes en Détresse (Solidarity – Women in Distress). *L'Insoumise* published an appeal for financial support for the purpose of setting up a network of shelters for women who had been victims of violence.[64] They also wanted to find means of "collective self-defence" – that is, "how to use differently the strength that comes to us from being together in solidarity, in struggle." Actions were suggested in "fact sheets" (what to do after a rape or assault, what an anti-rape kit contains, and so on).[65]

In the December 1978 issue of *L'Insoumise*, it was announced that the collective "has decided to add to its many activities the provision of services at the Centre-femmes every Saturday morning." Taking care to specify that the Insoumises were "NOT A SOCIAL SERVICE BUT A SLIGHTLY 'BAD' GROUP FOR SOLIDARITY AMONG WOMEN, aiming to help each other to obtain what we need for our life to be a bit less oppressed," they added that they would "limit ourselves to a certain number of 'areas' in which we have a bit more experience," which were in fact those in which the Collectif L'Insoumise had been the most active:

- Stories about **money**, unemployment, welfare, etc.
- **Our bodies**, ourselves, our health
- **Motherhood** (single mothers or alone, right of filiation, etc.)
- **Repression** in the form of the police, prison, etc., and self-defence against this repression
- The entire question of **violence against women** (rape, harassment, etc.), which we are discussing at this time in order to be able to make our anger known, organize our collective self-defence, etc.[66]

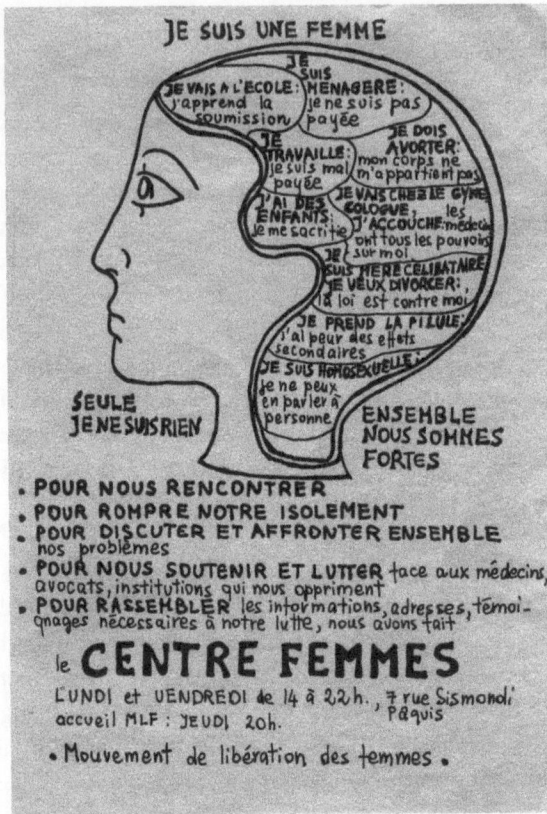

Figure 6.13 Woman's Brain. Detail of an MLF-Geneva
leaflet, 1974. Photo: Viviane Gonik.

This last field of concern would result in the publication in 1979 of *L'échappée belle*, a practical manual for struggle against the repression that was occurring at the time: a "practical and legal manual for self-defence: how to behave given the laws, the police, the judges."[67] Produced by the Insoumises "from their experiences of 'delinquency' and repression," the brochure was not signed, for security reasons.[68]

The Insoumises' Perspective on Wages for Housework

"We did not campaign directly for Wages for Housework, as they did in Italy, England, and Canada," the Insoumises told me, "but we found some expressions, such as, for example, the demand for two thousand francs per month for all mothers for three years." These "expressions" of the Wages for Housework perspective coloured the spirit in which each action was immersed, and also the very practice of the Collectif Insoumise as a group. "We 'practised' wages," said one Insoumise. "All of our actions were interpreted as a retaking of wages for housework that we should have had and didn't have. We took this wage where it wasn't given to us, and where we should have obtained it!" In their view, this is how the occupation of BUCAS and the cantonal unemployment bureau should be interpreted, as should the making of passes for free train rides during the organization of the Congrès des mauvaises mères, the occupation of Centre-femmes, and other events.[69]

The idea of "retaking" the wage that was due to them was linked, in their view, to the concept of social reappropriation, in the sense of reappropriating social wealth, popularized widely in Italy during the 1970s.[70] *L'Insoumise* therefore often highlighted the purse-snatchings perpetrated by women, as well as their testimonies. The Insoumises interpreted these actions as reappropriation of Wages for Housework: "If I steal, it is because I am a houseworker, because my work is not paid, because I depend, like many others, on my husband's low salary."[71]

Overall, this original expression of the Wages for Housework perspective did not go unquestioned. In an internal document, "Nous, collectif pour le salaire ménager," written 1977, the authors wrote:

But this practice of interpreting ambiguous or opaque events through the lens of Wages for Housework, these glasses perched on our noses, that will work for some time … I wanted to be able to practise these words, Wages for Housework, in a transparent way, and for everyone to understand right away what links us, what we think, what we do.
It will happen soon …[72]

If the Collectif L'Insoumise did not actually conduct a campaign as such for Wages for Housework, as was done elsewhere in the IFC network, it was partly because of local constraints – more precisely, the context of the city of Geneva, "a political space that was so limited and immobile":

It's true, in Geneva – unlike England and, especially, Italy – situations do not invite us to struggle directly for wages for housework. To find specific targets, specific levers of power, we have to look carefully through socialist motions, legislation concerning single mothers, and so on. On the other hand, anti-woman medical projects emerge much more easily and directly from the cantonal maternity hospital, constantly inviting us to advance in the struggle, to reply. In fact, the relative ease of information and mobilization with regard to motherhood is perhaps due, among other things, to our successive fights.[73]

And therefore, they preferred to demand, with the "bad mothers," two thousand francs a month for three years, and to support and encourage all the actions by women that appealed to them, whether it was collective struggles or individual gestures of rebellion (purse snatching, absenteeism), interpreting them as movements that went in the direction of wages for housework. Fifteen years later, delving into their memories, the Insoumises told me, "We went straight to the goal by creating alternatives. We lived as a community, we mobilized easily, we had wind in our sails, and we felt that we had the power to change our living conditions right away." And one Insoumise added,

At one point, I had a work problem when I was pregnant. I went to discuss it with my employer, the head of the ministry of health in Geneva, accompanied by friends. At one point, he said to me, "What do you want, in the end? Because I don't want to have the MLF standing under my window!" It was clear he was scared. And I got what I wanted – I no longer remember exactly what. That was how the deal was made. We felt the power of women.[74]

In the view of the Collectif L'Insoumise, "There is nothing in a woman's life that is not based on her condition of being unwaged in the home, and as a consequence, there is no place where women's struggle for money cannot be conducted. The Wages for Housework perspective covers the woman's workweek in its entirety, in the factory and in the kitchen." The Insoumises thus wanted to "practise" wages everywhere in these sites.[75]

In 2013, one of them looked back and summarized the Collectif L'Insoumise years:

For us, this "Insoumise and MLF" period was inscribed in a broader movement of politicization of daily life. We militated for ideas, while being engaged in changing our lives (rejection of marriage, refusal of exploitative waged work, living in a community of women; radical protest of society, of the sexual division of work, of male domination, of dominant sexuality, of

Figure 6.14 "Quel malheur! Je ne suis plus insérée dans la réalité sociale" (What bad luck! I'm no longer integrated with social reality). Les Insoumises.

the patriarchal and capitalist system) in the here and now. In the 1970s, we sincerely believed that revolution was possible![76]

Other Horizons

The Collectif L'Insoumise, the core group of which began to dissolve into smaller groups in 1979, gradually abandoned the Wages for Housework strategy, feeling that it was more and more difficult to apply, and too "confined in our Swiss reality of Northern women."[77] At a time when Swiss multinationals were casting long shadows all over the world, the Insoumises felt the need to develop a feminist point of view on everything, not just the situation of women but on global economic policy, international politics, underdevelopment, and more.

As early as 1976, some Insoumises had felt the need to extend their concerns beyond the "Swiss reality of Northern women." A major ecological disaster that occurred that year in a small town near Milan in northern Italy, Seveso, acted as a catalyst for raising awareness of the environmental question: the explosion of a reactor in a chemical products factory had allowed several tons of dioxin to escape in a toxic cloud that blanketed the surrounding area.[78] The vegetation was ravaged, hundreds of people had to be evacuated, and pregnant women were allowed to have abortions. The factory in question was owned by Givaudan, a Geneva company that was part of the Swiss multinational Hoffmann-La Roche.

An MLF group was formed in Geneva, the Groupe de travail Seveso, in which some Insoumises participated. Onsite investigations were conducted among women and female plant workers, and studies were compiled on the dangers of dioxin and its use in beauty products and medications. Hoffmann-La Roche and other Swiss multinationals were pilloried. An eighty-page document was made public: *Seveso est partout*.[79] The ecological disaster was seen as "a terrible assault on the bodies of women":

> We must think about controlling our bodies in a way that is more global now ... it is not just men and doctors who assault us, but also multinationals! What worse assault against women's bodies, against women's children, than that of Hoffman-La Roche in Seveso! ... Seveso is everywhere, but so are women. Write to us, come and discuss, let us organize all together.[80]

We should remember that in 1976, the ecology movement was in its infancy.

The initiatives that emerged from the Collectif L'Insoumise would also go in other directions. For example, the members of the group Blé et Tchador were interested in women in developing countries, women living under Islamic law, food products multinationals (Nestlé, a Swiss group), food speculation, hunger, agricultural policies, and similar issues. Radio Pleine Lune, "women's free radio," offered activists an opportunity to talk about all topics, expressing "radical" and feminist points of view on current events. Some Insoumises were also involved in the creation of the lesbian group Vanille-Fraise, which published the magazine *CLIT 007 (concentré lesbien irrésistiblement toxique)*.

The Insoumises thus took various paths related to the initial group. For instance, some of them later participated in developing international women's health networks, a local and international lesbian movement, and alternatives such as the Dispensaire des femmes and other structures for assistance and support to women. Others left with their families to live and be activists in Nicaragua. Only one continued to work in the housework domain, now in the context of a professional work – as one of the editors of the magazine *Ménage-toi* (ten issues published from 1985 to 1995) and other publications of the Syndicat des personnes actives au foyer à temps complet ou à temps partiel in Geneva. This wasn't about women demanding a wage for housework, but about evaluating its economic value and having the skills acquired through domestic and maternal work experience recognized.

Forty years after the Insoumise-MLF adventure began in Geneva, the Insoumises interviewed said that they were very aware that those years were for them, and for many other women, a foundational experience in many respects, and that it continued to guide them in their personal, activist, and professional lives. Despite this intense activity by the Insoumises, especially if one considers the relatively short period during which it took place, there are few remaining traces of this unique collective in feminist historiography.[81]

Conclusion

> "Once we have understood housework, we will understand the economy."
> — Claudia von Werlhof[1]

The Wages for Housework perspective was a completely original school of thought, and a toolbox for action, at the beginning of second-wave feminism. It was accused of being a simple demand for money, partial and reformist – even reactionary – that went counter to the objective of women's equality in society. But it was much more than that, and I hope that this book has dispelled some of the misconceptions.

As we have seen, among the groups in the International Feminist Collective (IFC), Wages for Housework was not conceived in terms of a political platform for demands, with strategies for negotiation or lobbying as such.[2] Rather, it had symbolic potential based on its capacity to unveil the extent of invisible private and public reproductive work on earth, the fact that this work was unpaid, and the profit that capitalist economies drew from it. In a word, it uncovered the hidden face of wage society.

The Wages for Housework campaign was pursuing a grand objective: to bring together people assigned to perform domestic work and housework – as it happened, women – in order to change their situation of dependency, reverse the relations of power, and redistribute the wealth that they produced. The vast majority of women who had waged jobs returned to being houseworkers once they got home, having worked during the day in specialized sectors associated with housework. It turned out that waged and unwaged women were, in reality, the same people. This was a potentially unifying force, and the strength of the Wages for Housework demand.

In this sense, the targets of the struggle became opportunities to politicize housework issues such as family allowances and welfare; abortion and women's health; sexuality; community facilities; women's shelters; and the situation of nurses, teachers, waitresses, lesbians, and "prostitutes." The demand was not always expressed in monetary terms. In different forms, it was aimed, too, at living conditions, which were also, in fact, houseworkers' working conditions: decent and affordable housing, free transportation, nearby services, green spaces, daycare centres accessible to women at home, and all services likely to reduce housework time. Overall, Wages for Housework remained more a general perspective on struggle than a formal demand.

The Wages for Housework political analysis made original theoretical and strategic contributions to early neo-feminism. Notable among these were the premises for an integrated vision of the different oppressions that divided the category "women" that could not be made uniform. Thanks in particular to the autonomous organization of each group, the strategy in fact involved building alliances beyond racial and ethnic barriers, beyond those erected by social class and age class, beyond divisions between "good" and "bad" women, between "beautiful" and "ugly," between lesbians and heterosexuals, between women at home and women working outside the home, between "whores, wives, and dykes." Through the embodiment of this thought in different struggles, Wages for Housework groups tried to act with a focus that today would be called intersectional, often performing unprecedented symbolic transgressions and ruptures of economic rules, both patriarchal and wage-related.

A HYPOTHESIS

Were these among the reasons for the hostile, often very emotional, reactions provoked by the Wages for Housework idea among so many feminists, beyond the arguments expressed?[3] The question is worth asking at least as a hypothesis, following a path explored in the early 1980s by anthropologist Louise Tassé. In a study on "the paradox of housework," she wrote that "objectifying" housework in this way – by demanding that it be paid just like any other work – referred to the symbolism of such work, "more precisely, to the transgression of ideologies on women's social role." In her view, "It is in the order of this transgression that feminist Wages for Housework struggles have been and are still being played out." She concluded, "It remains to conduct an analysis of the symbolism of housework as a political ethics of the family."[4]

Several transgressions performed by the Wages for Housework movement effectively buttress this hypothesis. First, there was the money taboo. Traditionally, it is known, women had a problematic relationship with money of their own, especially if it was demanded in return for services that were supposed to be free – such as those dispensed to the family, immediate or extended. Women's "labour of love," with its characteristic self-sacrifice and self-giving, became actual work that, like all work, deserved compensation in the form of cash. Feminine virtues had a price. This was the first taboo to lift. We only have to remember the discomfort caused at the time by the Wages for Housework movement logo, which featured the biological symbol for woman containing a fist holding a wad of dollars (or, depending on the country, of lire, Swiss francs, or deutschmarks).[5] Second, analyzing housework and reproductive work through the prism of work corresponded to changing not only the conditions of marriage as a contractual institution and the power relations underlying it but the wage system of capitalism itself: to demand wages for housework in effect disrupted all of the traditional measures of wages and work that were the foundation of this system.

Although many in the feminist movement defined these services as work, few committed themselves to the idea beyond denouncing the fact that they were free, preferring to pass directly to struggles involving waged work and obtaining daycare centres. Early neo-feminism was about escaping "the molasses pit of [our mothers'] kitchen," "escaping these kitchens of powerlessness, erasing them from our lives and our minds," showing that women were capable of detaching themselves from their traditional role – by adding a second job.[6] The path to emancipation promoted by most neo-feminists would thus be erected on the basis of a "repellent": fear of the houseworker.[7] Demanding a wage for what many perceived in this way could not help but raise the spectre of a fearful scarecrow in the garden of neo-feminism. And this spectre was, in fact, raised in the women's movement.

Analyzing housework and reproductive work through the prism of work and using union strategies disrupted the entire value system on which the age-old role of the houseworker was based. Demanding a wage was, first of all, to discover oneself as a worker. It was also to discover other possibilities, such as struggling against the conditions of this work, negotiating them, defining the duration and extent of the workday, and, as the case may be, refusing to work. Putting a price tag on this work would make it possible to negotiate the quantity and quality of services rendered and to be rendered. Demanding a wage meant not only negotiating, as an individual, one's personal sphere of freedom but also destroying the idea that doing housework was an integral part of the "nature" of women.

In short, analyzing and measuring housework in light of the notion of work had eminently subversive strategic implications, such as "counterplanning from the kitchen," which politicized the entire question of housework and reproductive work by challenging the conditions of marriage and wage society, as well as the power relations inherent to the wage relationship.[8] It meant attacking the system of domination of gender relations, class relations, and wage relations. This counterstrategy even opened the possibility of performing this work and receiving a wage to men, thus "degendering" – at least potentially – housework and domestic work. This is why the demand was for a wage "for housework," for any individual who performed it, and not a wage "for housewives," as so many people liked to claim in order to emphasize the "essentialism" that they felt the demand involved. Wages for Housework was in a position to destabilize the socio-sexual division of labour.

And then there was the question of sexuality (in this case, heterosexuality). Posing heterosexual sexuality as one of the many clauses in houseworkers' "work contract" – that is, marriage – went beyond taboo to pure scandal. When, in 1975, Wages Due Lesbians titled its "coming out" manifesto within the Wages for Housework movement *Fucking Is Work*, the walls of Jericho trembled ... Other ideas and sentences had a similar effect – for example, "Homosexuality and heterosexuality are both working conditions ... but homosexuality is workers' control over production, not the end of work."[9] In effect, for Wages Due Lesbians, lesbianism was an organizational form of women's struggle against work. Lesbianism and heterosexuality had never been studied through this prism up to then. The new insights made it possible to think of sexual relations in a different way. Similarly, Wages for Housework groups brought prostitution out of the moral sphere in order to highlight the "work" aspect of the activity. Even smiling was analyzed through the lens of work – as an implicit condition of employment required of women in most sectors. Although many aspects of women's situation were challenged in the 1970s, it was perhaps not permissible to go that far, and that quickly, in the questioning of the most intimate relationships.

The intersectional approach of certain Wages for Housework movement mobilizations was also one of the most disruptive and transgressive aspects of the perspective. Among these were the "counternatural" alliances built through Wages for Housework movement struggles, some of which I have discussed in this book – for instance, between "houseworkers and whores in solidarity," who broke the absolute separation between two great patriarchal feminine archetypes, "good" and "bad" women – archetypes that prevented them from working together. Such alliances, which rallied to the cause poor, racialized women (always suspected of "prostitution") and lesbians ("fugitives from the family"), also deconstructed and knocked down more barriers between "bad," "good," and "perverse" women, whether they were "white" or "black." The over-turning of these barriers also gave "bad mothers," those who did not live only for others, the courage to live as they wanted.

Many of the issues in Wages for Housework groups' mobilizations, and the documents explaining them, represented powerful and highly symbolic trans-gressions, a good number of which could be seen as constituting a threat to the family and impeding its reproduction. Might this intuition shed light on the opposition to the Wages for Housework strategy? It is true that relatively few activists at the time took a step beyond the simple demand, and the fears that it might provoke, to consider the full political perspective on which the Wages for Housework question was based. Had they understood this better, the fate of the Wages for Housework proposition may have been different. I would like to think so.

A VANTAGE POINT FOR UNDERSTANDING REPRODUCTION ON THE GLOBAL LEVEL

For theoreticians and activists of Wages for Housework groups, reproductive work constituted a vantage point from which the plural facets of women's lack of power over their personal life and in society as a whole could be understood and reconstructed; nevertheless, it was recognized that not all women, obviously, had the same kind of relationship with this work. It was also a position from which the resistance could be organized. To paraphrase the discourse of activists of the time, it involved organizing women's power, starting from their shared weakness: the lack of money, the fact that their work had been made invisible, that they therefore were not paid for all the work they accomplished, and that as a consequence they could not access the social wealth they contributed so greatly to creating. It involved returning dignity and power to women, however different the relations that each might maintain with this work, whether it was based on race, ethnicity, class, or "North-South" situation. And also, as Silvia Federici summarized, it was "to redefine in the public consciousness what this work is."[10]

In reality, Wages for Housework political thought was a feminist theory of reproduction, a theory for understanding reproduction on a global level and the central role that the vast majority of women and wageless people played in it. It was an innovative theory for understanding how the socio-economic system of capitalism was reproduced through this work; the place of wageless people and how they were divided among genders, sexualities, races, and classes; and the role of wageless people in wage society and how to resist that role.

This rereading of Wages for Housework theoretical works and how the current of thought was tested in action obviously are not intended to reopen the Wages for Housework debate in the terms of the 1970s, but to recognize the resources of the perspective, which were unique in the history of second-wave feminism. Also, and particularly, it offers a historical backdrop for many of today's debates, such as domestic and family work, care work, task sharing, family-job reconciliation, recognition of acquired knowledge and skills, sexuality as work, the international socio-sexual division of labour, the new stratifications and power relations among women, the intersectionality of struggles, the changing of dominant economic and environmental models, and more.

And there is another intention behind this book. Because the women's movement, since second-wave feminism, has not made social reproduction a true field of struggle, this book may offer an opportunity to reflect on the evolution of that question on the global scale and its current crisis, which I discussed briefly in the introduction. Notwithstanding an approach and a vocabulary that are not in common use today, the Wages for Housework perspective may nevertheless offer many paths from which tools for the present day might be drawn.[11]

Without impinging on the content of the interviews with the theoreticians whose intellectual trajectories are described in the afterword below – Mariarosa Dalla Costa and Silvia Federici, who address social reproduction in terms of broader parameters – one might sketch a portrait of the conjuncture that led to the version of the "crisis in domesticity" that arose in the late twentieth and early twenty-first centuries, which turned out to be one of the essential dynamics of globalization.[12] This evolving conjuncture, as we shall see, is not unrelated to the strategic choices of the women's movement with regard to work. The current crisis in reproduction may breathe new relevance into the texts of the Wages for Housework perspective.

THE CRISIS IN SOCIAL REPRODUCTION

The "crisis in reproduction" in the domestic and private sphere in the northern hemisphere arose from several factors, including the massive influx of women (including mothers of young children) into the labour market starting in the mid-twentieth century. Two conditions made this influx possible, according to Mariarosa Dalla Costa: first, women were having fewer children; second, they "called upon other women to perform free or underpaid domestic work."[13] Another demographic change accompanied the drop in the birth rate: the increase in life expectancy, which led to the ageing of populations, which in turn led to increased demand for retirement benefits and care for the elderly.

Particularly since the 1990s – to widely differing degrees, it goes without saying – under the influence of women's movements, Northern countries have instituted "job-family reconciliation" measures: daycare centres, parental leave, flexible work schedules, leave for dependent relatives, and more.[14] These measures, more easily adaptable to "stable" and formal jobs, do not come close to meeting needs, and the demand for domestic services and elder care has increased everywhere. The use of foreign (female) labour followed these developments.

According to economist Lourdes Beneria, this social policy model is more easily applicable north of the equator, where inexpensive domestic services were more accessible, as women would work for little money and under precarious conditions. It is more difficult to apply in the South, however, where the informal economy is more significant and underwent accelerated intensification with neo-liberal and globalization policies, particularly structural adjustment programs. Privatization programs, national budget cuts, and a reduction in the state's field of intervention have accompanied these changes, encouraging "investment" in various forms of exploitation and precarious, informal, unprotected jobs.

In certain countries, such as those in Latin America, the informal economy involves about half of the population (with a peak of 65 percent in Bolivia).[15] It was in this sector that "nomadic" workers were found. Job-family reconciliation policies, designed for formal jobs, were difficult to apply in economies in which the informal sector was so big.

The solution to the crisis in reproduction and care services in the North is recourse to foreign female labour. The women from the South who respond to the call, in their turn, have to suffer the repercussions within their own family organization and their care needs. Some studies shed light on the effects of such migrations on children and the trauma caused by "desertification of care providers in the third world."[16] After suffering a brain drain, poor countries are now suffering a "care drain": "migration leads to a transfer of a migrant's care capital from South to North."[17] And so, a new figure has made her entrance: the caregiver, the immigrant woman who dispenses care. We speak of "global chains of care." This gigantic "gift" with regard to work, as Silvia Federici rightly calls it, hiding behind emigration "is never considered in the computation of the 'Third World' debt."[18]

THE VICIOUS CIRCLE OF PRIVATE SOLUTIONS AND THE NEW POWER RELATIONS AMONG WOMEN

The new neo-liberal capitalist order, writes Lourdes Beneria, encourages us to "privatize the survival of individuals and families by reducing the effort devoted to social protection and by deuniversalizing it. This is true not only in the North but also in the South, even though the specific forms and circumstances differ widely."[19] Recourse to female immigration therefore contributes to the "privatization of social reproduction," in compliance with the framework of global neo-liberal capitalism.

However, this recourse is available only to people who can afford such services, whereas others are left "without a solution to regulate the tensions linked to time management ... contributing to the vicious circle in which private solutions might delay common efforts to implement public policies."[20] Indeed, most children left behind by migrant mothers are entrusted to other women who, if they work outside the home, must in their turn find another resource, usually another woman, more available – and generally poorer – to take care of the first woman's children. The use of female immigrant labour also means that, on "the international level, a class and 'race' dichotomy is being configured in the context of domestic and care work," as its beneficiaries profit from it "without assuming the reproduction costs involved in it."[21] And the vicious circle of reproductive work is thus closed and continues to turn endlessly, leaving in its wake a "new division of reproductive work in the world," new stratifications among women, and power relations among these strata.[22]

The women's movement in the North, which, in terms of its focus on work, had concentrated essentially on the waged relationship, facilitation of "reconciliation" between job and family, and the (private) sharing of tasks, was caught unprepared for this crisis in reproduction. In their analysis of the demands of the World March of Women, Elsa Galerand and Danièle Kergoat wrote,

The World March of Women (WMW) demand system may serve as an example that illustrates this difficulty ... Other than the limited space given to the question of work and work organization in the WMW platform for common struggle (and, more broadly, in the movement of opposition to liberal globalization, which is in itself questionable), it appears that the few demands with respect to work have to do with jobs (access to jobs and training, equality rights, parity, or pay equity), while the question of domestic work is still neglected. The denunciation of its being made invisible, of its not being shared, and the overwork that it represents for women runs through WMW discourses. The activists call for sharing of domestic work, but this demand is so symbolic in nature that no concrete provision is envisaged to transition from the principle of a redefinition of the relationship of men and women with domestic work to the reality of that redefinition.[23]

Observing that there was a "failed articulation" between domestic and waged work, Galerand questioned strategies for struggle "that circumvent the problem of domestic work." These strategies, she felt, "end up delaying the search for collective solutions to the profit of the white, middle-class, and well-off classes that can externalize [domestic work]," exacerbating the contradictions among women. These strategies therefore weakened "the struggle on all fronts, as they missed the target of the sexual division of labour, but also that of the social relations of exploitation of race and class formed among women in the domestic sector in particular."[24]

THE CIRCUMVENTION OF REPRODUCTIVE WORK AND ITS PERVERSE EFFECTS

In short, the strategic choice by the women's movement to circumvent the question of domestic work and social reproduction by not making it a true field of struggle would have effects that were, at the very least, embarrassing. These effects would include leaving the way clear to privatization of social reproduction, thus delaying the search for collective solutions; benefiting white Northern classes, while leaving to the employed workforce the task of assuming its own reproduction costs in its own households; bringing about a new stratification among women and power relations – notably of race and class – among them; and thus participating in something that proved to be new in the history of capitalism: a direct (not mediated by men) relationship of exploitation among women.[25] And finally, recourse to a female immigrant labour force would leave intact the dominant gender norms in hetero-gendered households.[26]

Galerand felt that these strategic choices by the women's movement would miss key targets in the feminist movement's struggles: the sexual division of labour and "the social relations of exploitation of race and class that are formed among women in the domesticity sector in particular." Sociologist Danièle Kergoat, however, asks us to "return domestic work to the centre of the reflection in our thoughts about emancipation."[27]

Although memory unfortunately seems to have failed here, is this not in fact the core issue developed in the early 1970s by the Wages for Housework movement? These observations are strangely similar to those that Wages for Housework theoreticians, notably Mariarosa Dalla Costa and Silvia Federici, made at that time.

In fact, Federici had already called the use of female labour from poor countries a "new colonial solution to the 'housework question'" that contributed to the new sexual and international division of labour.[28] This established, as Dalla Costa put it, "a subsequent stratification among women" and "a new division of reproductive labour in the world." In Federici's view, "This new colonialism must be a main target for feminist struggles, if women's liberation is to be really sought."[29]

Forty years ago, the Wages for Housework theoreticians and activists supplied, in both their documents and their mobilizations, tools for reflection and paths for action in this direction, as this book shows. They helped us to think about construction of a new world, seen from the vantage point of social reproduction – that invisible and submerged part of the economic iceberg on which capitalism and its inegalitarian system of social relations is built.[30] In this study, I want to bring out this current, reintegrate this vanished chapter into the history and ideas of the feminist movement, and offer a historical background for the feminist debates and reflections on the current crisis in social reproduction.

Some key theoreticians of the Wages for Housework movement have since pursued their reflection and considerably broadened the perspective. As we will see in the interviews that follow, Mariarosa Dalla Costa and Silvia Federici bring new insight to the original perspective.

Afterword

From Yesterday to Today: The Intellectual Journeys of Mariarosa Dalla Costa and Silvia Federici, from 1977 to 2013

In the interviews below, Mariarosa Dalla Costa and Silvia Federici offer a rigorous analysis of the crisis in reproduction on a global level, starting from their early theory of reproduction, formulated within the Wages for Housework movement. What both of these theoreticians are really constructing is a feminist critique of neo-liberal capitalist globalization. Here, each describes how her early perspective has broadened and evolved throughout her intellectual and activist journey since the 1970s – that is, since the International Feminist Collective came to an end. Both offer proof that the resources provided by the Wages for Housework perspective are relevant to an understanding and interpretation of present-day issues.

INTERVIEW WITH MARIAROSA DALLA COSTA[1]

Mariarosa Dalla Costa was born in Treviso, Italy, in 1943. She studied at the University of Padua, received her doctorate in law in 1967, and was a professor at the Istituto di Scienze Politiche e Sociali. She is the author of the founding document of the Wages for Housework perspective, "Donne e sovversione sociale," published in 1972 with an essay by Selma James, "Il posto della donna," as Potere femminile e sovversione sociale. *The book was translated into several languages, including into English as* The Power of Women and the Subversion of the Community.

Louise Toupin: *Potere femminile* had an international impact in the feminist world when it was published in 1972, first in Italian, then in English. In the years that followed, it was translated into several other languages, forcing feminists of all tendencies to situate themselves in relation to the analysis that it propounded. Before diving into the content of the book, we could first talk about the context of its production in Italy, and the ideological and political "soil" in which its ideas matured. That is, it would be interesting to spend a little time describing the intellectual and political conjuncture within which this book-manifesto was written.

First, I would like to know what influence the Italian workerist current, also called the "autonomy current," may have had on your thought. Then, what was the influence of the Italian and foreign feminist essays on housework that had begun to appear in 1969–70? Let's start with the workerist, or autonomy, current, an intellectual and political trend of the Italian extra-parliamentary left.

Some authors, such as Yann Moulier Boutang – the translator of Mario Tronti – who introduced the Italian workerist current into France, names you as one of "those who made a significant contribution" to the Italian workerist current. Another, Harry Cleaver, spoke of Selma James and you as being feminist theoreticians of "autonomist Marxism."[2] What do you think of this assessment, and how do you interpret it? And do you agree that *The Power of Women and the Subversion of the Community* matured in this intellectual soil?

Figure A.1   Mariarosa Dalla Costa. Photo: Dario De Bortoli.

Mariarosa Dalla Costa: My political formation began with workerism. I would not say with "autonomy," which is a definition formulated years later, when I was already active within the feminist movement, in the Wages for Housework movement. From the beginning, and throughout its life, that movement represented a reality that was completely independent of those male networks, including the ones labelled "autonomy." But I can understand why our discourses were later designated, as Harry Cleaver and then Nick Witheford did, as being "autonomous Marxism."[3] Indeed, starting from a Marxist matrix, we chose the point of view of autonomy of the class movement, of a class that we had redefined, and that included women's work of production and reproduction of labour power.

The origins of the discourse on class autonomy are found, however, in works by C.L.R. James and Raya Dunayevskaya, as well as in the group around the magazine *Socialisme ou barbarie* in France, whose most prominent representatives were Cornelius Castoriadis and Claude Lefort.[4] In fact, the significance of our work – mine and that of my friends in the Wages for Housework groups – is recognized as having been the discovery of the other pole of capitalist accumulation, the other path that it takes: production and reproduction of labour power. In other words, we discovered the home beside the factory. We discovered that the class was formed not only of waged workers but also of non-waged workers.

Today, taking this into account is fundamental to understanding the "capitalist command," which, from the world of production, is deployed in forms that are ever more "strangling" and lethal in the world of reproduction.[5] It is also fundamental to understanding the relationship between the formal and informal economy, the relationship between the monetary and non-monetary economy, and the relationship between the first world and the third world (to use a conventional shorthand). Also, to understanding the struggles that, arising from the world of global reproduction, tend to break this command, and to affirm other criteria in the relationship with production, with nature, and with life.

So, to answer your question: yes, *The Power of Women and the Subversion of the Community* matured in this workerist intellectual "soil." But I remember that there was some resistance, quite strong, from workerist intellectuals to broadening the concept of the working class to include, as we maintained in the early 1970s, houseworkers. Workerist theoreticians insisted that what we called production – that is, production and reproduction of labour power – belonged, rather, to the sphere of circulation, as Marx described in *Das Kapital*. When, later, they spoke of the "social worker" *(operaio sociale)*, they were alluding, rather, to different figures of workers in the context of the decentralization of production. They had recognized in the new political composition of class in the early 1970s the struggles of students and their demands for a wage for schoolwork, the technicians' struggle, and so on. But these intellectuals of the extra-parliamentary left seriously undervalued housework. I think their idea on this subject consisted of saying that women's problems would be solved with more and better-organized daycare centres. They believed more in solutions in terms of services. They always underestimated the real scope of reproduction work and the impact of the lack of money on women who were assigned to this work.

And I also believe that most theoreticians in this current, after reading *The Power of Women* and gaining a vague idea of the issue, never read the other documents that we in Wages for Housework groups produced afterward. And I think that, even today, they are still not aware of the existence of this intellectual output. The consequence is that they continue to ignore almost completely the question of reproductive work and the entire political debate about it advanced by feminists.

However, in recent years, as we have entered a new stage in our analysis, some of our most recent work – and the most important part of our past work – is now translated into English, Spanish, and Japanese, and it will soon be available in other languages. This enables us to continue to contribute, in the best way, we hope, to an international political debate that must address questions that are increasingly urgent and tragic.

LT: Let's talk now about the feminist readings that fed into *The Power of Women and the Subversion of Community.* For example, what notable essays from Western feminism on housework had begun to circulate in Italy at the beginning of the 1970s, and were you aware of them when you were writing *The Power of Women?* I'm thinking here, among others, of Margaret Benston's 1969 text, *The Political Economy of Women's Liberation;* Christine Delphy's text published in 1970 (under the pseudonym Christine Dupont), *L'ennemi principal;* and, in 1970–71, those by Betsy Warrior, *Housework: Slavery or Labour of Love* and Pat Mainardi, *The Politics of Housework.* In short, which feminist works had an impact on you at the time?

MDC: I didn't know about any of the foreign feminist works you mention. There had been Italian works on "women's condition" in general and on abortion. I think that the time was ripe, in Italy and abroad, for the issue to burst out, mainly because we were in a period of great social rebellion and struggles of all sorts. At the time I was completely absorbed by political activism and concentrating on Italian analyses linked to my political work. My feminist discourse was the result of the explosion of contradictions that I was experiencing in my political activity.

This activity began at four o'clock in the morning – I had to get up to distribute leaflets in front of large factories – and it continued in the evenings, and on Saturdays and Sundays. If I don't mention that this was my type of life, it would be difficult to understand why I didn't read, at the time, some of the books on the question of women that were beginning to be published. Also, I am Italian. My knowledge of English was very limited at the time; I later learned the language during my feminist activism by travelling through, among other places, North America. I knew French, but I didn't have particularly meaningful or frequent relations with France.

LT: Were you Marxist first and then feminist, or were you feminist first and then Marxist? Basically, I want to know whether Marxism made you into a feminist, or whether your life experience made you a feminist first who later discovered Marxism.

MDC: Fundamentally, I was pushed into activism and into discovering the "factory" by an ideal of justice. I wanted to understand where the evil in the world came from, the origin of the mechanism, in a sense the *omphalos*, of the social relations system.[6] And that is how I encountered the workerist version of Marxism.[7] In itself, Marxism was a great discovery that gave me, and continues to give me, essential tools for understanding the world.

Political activism was the other great experience of my life, because it provides thought with the coordinates for action. But, within this activism, I experienced, as did many other women in extra-parliamentary groups in the early 1970s, the contradiction of not feeling that my condition as a woman was represented or understood – neither by activism nor by this Marxist thought. Yet, that was what I was seeking.

My encounter with Selma James was fundamental in this respect. But our paths soon diverged due to a different conception of political action. To answer your question: yes, I was first Marxist, and then feminist; I have to add that my search for a different path from that which the society of the time expected of a young woman had obviously started long before.

LT: The Power of Women and the Subversion of Community contains three essays: yours, "Women and the Subversion of Community," written in early 1971; an essay by Selma James, "A Woman's Place," written in 1953; and an essay called "Maternity and Abortion" by the Paduan group Lotta Femminista; the introduction is written by James. Your essay "Women and the Subversion of Community," which was in circulation starting in June 1971, is historically linked to Lotta Femminista, though it preceded the group's formation.[8] In a way, it led to its birth. Can you share the circumstances under which you wrote this essay?

MDC: I had written a preliminary version of this text, copies of which were handed out for discussion to a group of female friends who were interested in feminism. It was signed "Movimento di Lotta femminile di Padova" (it was really an improvised name) and dated June 1971. This small group of friends recognized themselves in the analysis offered in the document. And soon after, the group became Lotta Femminista.

Later, I expanded this document and decided to publish it under the title *Potere femminile e sovversione sociale*. I thought it would be good to publish it, to ensure that it would be widely distributed. And that proved to be true. But I didn't have the time or sufficient mental calmness to take up in greater detail the series of questions that I would have liked to analyze better and develop because

I was already absorbed in a very intense activist life. And I must say that I still struggle with time, even today, and for reasons that are closely related to those of that period.

I dedicated my 1971 Christmas vacation to verifying *Potere femminile* with Selma, and to finalizing the book, which was aimed fundamentally at the movement and has become a classic in feminist curricula in the United States. I remember that Pia, feeling sorry for us, came over on the last day of the year with some spumante and panettone.[9] And it was also on a December 31, this time in 1995, that I put the final touches on a book analyzing the consequences of neo-liberalism and structural adjustment policies on the condition of peoples – and women in particular – in the new situation of economic globalization.[10]

LT: You said, in a speech at a colloquium in Montreal, that because of the particular Italian context in the early 1980s, feminism in Italy was certainly marked, more strongly than that in other countries, by the issue of work/refusal of work.[11] Was this because of the intellectual influence of the workerist current, which had made refusal of work one of its central themes of analysis?

MDC: The theme of refusal of work made it possible to act and to struggle from the perspective of a draconian reduction in the workday. This was the only approach that could open new prospects for women. It went counter to the perspective proposed by the institutional left, with its labour ideology that told women that adding another job to the work that they were already doing in the home was the only future path. We denounced this. To calculate women's work, one should have started with the work that they were already doing, housework, and, on that basis, one had to conceive of a major reduction in their workday. In parallel, their financial autonomy should start with economic recognition of their work in the home. It was the same thing for men if, as might happen, they were the ones who did this work, or part of it.

LT: When one reads *The Power of Women and the Subversion of Community*, it is surprising that the Wages for Housework strategy is not mentioned as such, except in passing, in a footnote.[12] Does this mean that the Wages for Housework strategy was clarified after the theory was published? And if so, when or on which occasion did it appear?

MDC: Yes. I think that our main wish was to open a new perspective of struggle on the condition of women. But the determination of a Wages for Housework demand required that we take a little more time. However, even though the demand for a wage appears in a later edition of *Potere femminile*, it was inscribed very quickly in our internal documents.

I think that some of the uncertainty with regard to this subject came because we were aware that, to a large extent, it would have been very difficult to obtain such a thing, which would truly have opened up an alternative to women's condition. The capitalist system was based on precisely the opposite – on opposition between waged workers and non-waged workers, mainly women as reproducers of labour power. This was very different from asking for a raise on an existing wage. On the one hand, we may have appeared unrealistic, but on the other hand, we knew that, like other struggling sectors of society, we truly wanted to create a different world, a different system, in which the subordination of one subject – in this case, a gendered subject – to another would become impossible. The Wages for Housework demand constituted, in this respect, the most radical claim we could make – a true lever of power for women because it could claim to subvert not only their condition but the condition of unwaged workers in general, as well as the condition of waged workers.

In fact, the waged work/unwaged work division represented the fundamental division within the working class in the broad sense, the basis for all other stratifications. In this sense, our demand constituted the pivot for the most powerful recomposition of class. And it wasn't by accident that, in reaction to such a recomposition, which was the expression of an international cycle of struggle representing the reunification of different sectors of working society, capital launched a political and economic counteroffensive. On the global level, this counteroffensive is still increasingly implacable. However, more and more subjects, from both the unwaged and the waged world, are emerging on the political scene and are capable of making their voices heard, such as Indigenous peoples – in Chiapas, for example.

LT: For you, the primary significance of the emergence of the women's movement was expression of women's massive revolt against their assignment to material and immaterial work of reproduction, but it was also the expression of a profound rupture in the social order, a rupture in the balance that you have called "society/factory dependence relationships" in Italy. What do you mean by that?

MDC: What was in play with the explosion of the feminist movement – and I mean by this everything that the feminist movement agreed on – was women's willingness to assert themselves as persons, as social individuals – to assert their own reproductive needs, as a function of themselves as women, and no longer only as a function of the satisfaction of others' needs. This had enormous implications for the area of sexuality, for how a woman organized her own life, for how she lived (alone? with other women? with a group of people? so, not necessarily with a man), for her procreative choices. In this last area, the women in Italy expressed the greatest possible refusal of work, also as a function of self-affirmation.

The meaning of emergence of the women's movement was to be found in the rupture of a purely functional relationship between reproduction and production, the rejection of modifications to the organization of reproduction induced solely as a function of changes in the world of production (for example, the fact that women would have to have more or fewer children as a function of the needs of production). The significance of this emergence was found in the assertion of women as autonomous social subjects as opposed to being, within the family, a simple appendage to economic programs. I developed this theme in "Reproduction and Emigration" by analyzing the state's attitude toward demographic policies and emigration.[13]

On the political level, it was a rupture from the preceding period: the assertion of women's autonomy meant struggling not only to support other subjects' struggles – in this case, those who were exploited within the factory – but to struggle in their own field of work, especially housework, which meant a broadening of the front of contestation, and therefore an even more powerful struggle.

LT: In *The Power of Women and the Subversion of the Community*, you write that in their struggle regarding conditions of reproduction and against men-women-children dependency, women did not ask simply the question of their own autonomy, but they opened also another possibility: that of strengthening the autonomy of others. Can you expand your thinking on this point?

MDC: I can add this to what I have already said: it was not by chance that almost all the leaflets of the early period of the feminist movement ended by mentioning women, children, and the elderly. Because women had suffered so much oppression and so much exploitation, they became, through actions by the feminist movement, the most sensitive interpreters of the cause of other oppressed subjects – and, above all, children and old people, who, in a situation of weakness, depended on their work, and therefore constituted a strong point for their demands. Historically, women often identified themselves with other oppressed subjects, helped them, and stood by their side in their struggles.

In this regard it is significant to observe that as soon as the feminist question arose in Italy in the early 1970s, the institutional discourse on the family was also transformed to take into account the rights of children as persons, and those of the elderly, the disabled, and the ill. I don't mean that the social and material situation in Italy was vastly improved. Indeed, it would be very difficult to support such an idea. But the social and political debate that we provoked opened, also on the institutional level, a new space for consideration of different oppressed subjects, and it stimulated practical initiatives that had not existed before.

LT: Let's talk about the theoretical innovations of *Potere femminile*. We could mention the new comprehension of the role played by the family in capitalist society (a centre of production and not just of consumption), of the position of women and of the work that they do in the family (producer and reproducer of labour power), and of women's power (if they do productive work, by refusing this work they may subvert society). Women thus are reintroduced into history as subjects – and revolutionary subjects. Another thing that was new was the Wages for Housework demand as a lever of power, to begin the "negotiation on reproduction." Do you agree with this summary of the theoretical innovations of *Potere femminile*? And when you look back, what do you think was the most important thing you said?

MDC: You bring up key points. Before mentioning others, I want to remind you that *Potere femminile*, like the other documents that we produced, was inscribed in a Marxian horizon of analysis – that is, these documents express a discourse from a class point of view, broadened in our own way. This means that our privileged object/subject was women who *reproduced* individuals as *holders of labour power* – that is, women who lived materially within a proletarian condition.

But we also emphasized, in numerous documents and articles, the particular precariousness of many women's class affiliation. Indeed, as the feminist movement developed, the movement constituted an anchor point, a key element in the construction of a new identity for women. Many of them had then left marriages that had guaranteed them a certain social standing. From one day to the next, they found themselves facing the question of economic survival and obliged to perform precarious work, as it was quite difficult to imagine that the husbands they had just left would support them financially. The struggle of women of the working class (as we had redefined it), because it was aiming for a radical change in the world, was decisive in the opening of new perspectives and life possibilities for all women.

There is another point in *Potere femminile* that I consider fundamental, particularly today, in the context of the new global economy. I hope you don't mind if I quote a few passages on the subject. Here's one:

Since Marx, it has been clear that capital rules and develops through the wage, that is, that the foundation of capitalist society was the wage laborer and his or her direct exploitation. What has been neither clear nor assumed by the organizations of the working class movement is that precisely through the wage has the exploitation of the non-wage laborer been organized. This exploitation has been even more effective because the lack of a wage hid it. That is, the wage commanded a larger amount of labor that appeared in factory bargaining. *Where women are concerned, their labor appears to be a personal service outside of capital.*

And here's another:

> The rule of capital through the wage compels every able[-]bodied person to function, under the law of division of labor, and to function in ways that are if not immediately, then ultimately profitable to the expansion and extension of the rule of capital.[14]

And so, we can say that capital, in the family, through the husband's wage, commands the wife's work in the home. But this relationship can be read elsewhere, as much in the relationship between the monetary and the non-monetary economy, between the new global economy and the subsistence economy, and in the new divisions of labour within production and reproduction. For example, through waged work that an emigrant worker finds in New York, capital also commands the agricultural work of the wife who, having remained in her village, continues to maintain that economic structure, which constitutes life insurance for the worker if he must or wants to return to the village.

It is important to keep all of this in mind in order to grasp, in the current global scenario, the cycles of struggle that tend to break this capitalist reign. This theme continues to be central in my work, such as, for example, "Capitalism and Reproduction," "L'indigeno che è in noi, la terra cui apparteniamo," and "Neo-liberismo, terra e questione alimentare," and in the books that I edited with my sister, Giovanna Franca, *Donne e politiche del debito* and *Donne, sviluppo e lavoro di riproduzione*.[15] This theme is also at the heart of Giovanna Franca's book *Un lavoro d'amore*, published in Italy in 1978: she analyzes, in particular, the function of physical violence by the man, who, as a waged worker, commands, controls, and maintains discipline over the woman's unwaged work.[16] This theme is also central to the writings of Silvia Federici.

LT: How do you interpret the enormous international impact on the feminist movement of *The Power of Women and the Subversion of the Community* in the 1970s, and how do you interpret the failure of the strategy that accompanied it?

MDC: In my view, the book had an enormous impact not only because the analysis hit the mark but also because it was felt that it came from a world that was spirited, activist, and gave direction for action. The book highlighted the idea of capital as social relations and class relations to be destroyed and not simply as something to improve, or as a quantity of wealth to distribute more fairly. This was the difference between revolutionary feminism and reformist feminism.

Those years were part of a cycle of struggles that had developed at the international level starting in the second half of the 1960s, aimed at breaking the bases and balances of capitalism, in both East and West, in both North and South. And Italy, more specifically, saw during the 1970s a massive mobilization of workers, students, unemployed people, technicians, and people from other key sectors of the work world.

The feminist movement emerged from this framework of struggle. Activists from different countries, sympathetic with our perspective, or who had espoused this perspective, decided to translate and use *Potere femminile*, as well as the rich group of analyses and documentation materials produced by our groups, composed of our journals, newsletters, leaflets, mimeographed texts, and booklets published and designed for activist use.[17]

From this heritage were formed not only activist women but also several generations of women who occupied positions at different levels in institutions and universities. They had mastered the discourses but, unfortunately, often erased the origins, the sources, and the real scope of this discourse and raised obstacles of many kinds to the possibility of the existence and dissemination of later steps in the evolution of this type of analysis.

Why have we not succeeded? Well, for the same reasons for which the other sectors in struggle were defeated. Because against so powerful a cycle of struggles, which caused a very important recomposition of class power, above all between waged and unwaged work, the capitalist system responded by decentralizing production, changing the conditions of production, causing much unemployment, destabilizing work, lowering salaries, and making draconian reductions in public expenditures destined for social purposes. And this is increasingly true today [here, Dalla Costa is talking about the mid-1990s], making the possibilities for life, in general, very uncertain.

The systematic application around the world of structural adjustment policies, in the name of managing the international debt crisis, provoked underdevelopment of reproduction on a planetary level. In many countries, the 1980s were a decade of popular uprisings and struggles for bread. In Italy, they were years of political repression and "normalization." The history of the feminist Wages for Housework movement and the works of its theoreticians were practically erased from the feminist scene and from feminine culture in general, and were ignored in university curricula. This was true not only for works written in the 1970s but also for works published in the early 1980s, which were fundamental to the later formulation of this discourse.[18]

In Italy, the response by the capitalist system was even harder in the 1990s, related to what was going on all over the world. As I analyzed it in two essays in those years ("Capitalismo e riproduzione" and "Sviluppo e riproduzione"[19]), in

Italy we saw phenomena such as suicides due to lack of work or due to refusal to accept the only job offered because the employer was a criminal organization, cases of people trying to sell their organs to make money, cases of mothers who abandoned their child immediately after birth, the fact that a large part of the population was in debt to moneylenders, and so on.

The Gulf War was a kind of shock for Italian society. People in Italy had to reconsider the idea of sending their sons to die in the war. So, they began again to reflect on the world at a social level, the effects of this economic system, and what could be done. A new political debate arose, on the basis of discussion about the possibility of constructing other production, consumption, and life relations, other relations with nature and with all living beings. These last themes, more particularly, although expressed by a minority in the movement's debate, went counter to an institutional discourse that, submitted to the constantly more constraining structural adjustment directives imposed by the International Monetary Fund, completely shut off the social question and the question of relations with nature, starting with relations with the land and with food.

The Chiapas rebellion and the movement that represented it – within which women played a fundamental role – as well as a number of struggles and movements around the world that aimed for a different kind of development, different above all because not capitalist, constituted one indication, one possible alliance. At the same time it was a huge social and political laboratory for experimenting with inventions and new practices of production, consumption, and living, for the unwaged and the waged, men and women, throughout the world.

LT: How would you describe the stages in the evolution of your thought? How was the Wages for Housework perspective transformed through changes in the Italian and international conjunctures, and, finally, how would you update the Wages for Housework demand today?

MDC: The first thing to say about the evolution of my thought is that it is not integrated into an absolutely linear life path – that is, without interruptions or obstacles. Not only did I travel the world with a woman's body – and that means biological deadlines and conditioning – but work, responsibilities, and difficulties typical of the gender to which I belong formed obstacles, at different times of my life, to the possibility of giving written expression to thoughts and problems that I was wondering about. These obstacles, however, constituted at the same time a terrain of inspiration and analysis. The very fact of having privileged an intellectual and activist life involved fairly heavy costs and renunciations of all sorts for me. But everything I did was certainly not done without paying the costs.

"Safeguarding Our Heritage"

MDC: In the late 1970s and during the 1980s, I was absorbed with the task of confronting the consequences of political repression: helping people, including myself, to safeguard our heritage – that is, to keep everything that we produced during our activism of the 1970s from simply being destroyed; confronting an internal political debate that saw the painful necessity of dissolving our network and closing our women's centres.[20]

In the late 1970s, an era was ending. Activism based on a maximum of activities, on the one hand, and the lack of money that each of us could put into it, on the other hand, had brought us to a breaking point. Unlike what exists now for different women's initiatives, there was no articulation of funding on the national and international levels.

Incidentally, I wonder what limits, risks, and ambiguities today's initiatives may encounter because of this. It seems that the same logic at work in other major questions, such as the aggravated hardship of peoples of the world on the one hand, and the burgeoning of initiatives funded for and around this hardship, on the other hand, is also at work in the women's question. Indeed, it is impossible to ignore the massive deterioration in women's condition in the world. The risk is to see the numbers of professionals in women's hardship growing ever larger and a female bureaucracy controlling the rebellion and the attempts to construct radical struggles against all of this – that is, against this type of development, in its new neo-liberal expressions: structural adjustment policies, wars, continual expropriation of peoples' means of production, all oriented toward a single goal: everything must become a commodity, especially a commodity for export.

Let's return to our period in the late 1970s. Our organization found itself needing to transition to a new stage, as it was becoming obvious that the state would not grant us wages for housework. However, we had won at other levels: affirmation of a female identity no longer defined solely as a function of marriage, family, and children; affirmation of a female sexuality no longer defined solely as a function of procreation; affirmation of women's rights with regard to healthcare structures, abortion, childbirth, and, more generally, the types of treatments offered in obstetrics and gynecology departments (although much remains to be done in this area in several hospitals); we had achieved changes in the family code, and in many other things.

As for the question of wages for housework and economic conditions in general, we had not only a negative response, but again, as was the case for the other movements, a repressive response. Confronting all of this absorbed much of my time and activity.

Women/Welfare State/Mode of Production

MDC: With regard to my intellectual production during the 1980s, most importantly I finished the book on the relationship between women and the state during the New Deal – that is, during the phase of construction of the welfare state in United States.[21] This book was intended to be a study of the birth of the blueprint of the women/welfare state/mode of production relationship, which was to form the dominant model in Western countries up to the 1970s. At the same time, in this study, the women's struggles that accompanied this model, alongside those of workers and unemployed people, were read as expression of the desire for autonomy.

In the United States, the 1930s were the testing ground for the modern family in a time of crisis: the woman houseworker was to administer the husband's salary (when he had one), but she also had to be available for work outside, above board or under the table, and at the same time she had to support the family in a context of high male unemployment, an insecure job market, and a new social security system.

If the 1930s marked the birth of the welfare state in the United States, the 1980s marked the beginning of its dismantlement. Whereas during the 1930s the idea was to adapt reproduction of labour power to production of goods within the framework of creating an overall productive and social plan, in the 1980s reproduction was left to the "free initiative" of individuals, and production of goods was gradually moved abroad in an international context of escalating war.

Despite the context having changed since the 1930s, the constraints on women continued to be the same during the 1980s, just as they are today, under conditions that are simply more difficult. How have women been able to continue, in this context, to build their autonomy? I have written articles on the subject, in which I concentrated on public expenditures or employment policies in Italy.[22] In other articles, I have continued to reflect on the feminist movement of the 1970s, the crucial questions that it posed, and the struggles that it led.[23] This type of reflection is sometimes present in other articles that I have mentioned, such as the articles on public expenditures or employment. All of these works were conceived under very difficult conditions. I was always concerned with recording at least a few reflections in the face of a firestorm of events that was going to bury our world – the feminism of great struggles – in the dust of repression and normalization.

Demystification of the Discourse on Family Strategies

MDC: Another important theme that runs through many of my writings is demystification of the discourse by which strategies would be offered to women to reconcile work in the family and work outside the home. Female academics who exalted the "double presence" of women during the 1990s did not explain how many of them had resolved the housework problem.[24]

On this subject, I think that there were not, and still are not, many possible family strategies. There are only two. And it is particularly true in a country such as Italy, characterized by a very deficient, very expensive services system. Either women go to work outside and give up having children, thus avoiding the most important and the most problematic part of housework – this way, they may be able to combine housework and work outside; or women who have children will work outside by receiving support in the form of free help (in fact, work) from other women, generally relatives, or by paying other women to do part of the housework. But, in this case, the money given to these women must not cancel out what they themselves earn. Because of this, the amount of money received by the woman who comes into the home when the first one leaves is very small.

Thus, the problem is not resolved and results in an extra stratification among women. And, as I wrote in essays in the early 1980s – in which I analyzed the restructuring of productive and reproductive work that took place in Italy through the new immigration flows – immigrant women, mainly Filipinas, gradually assumed a large part of the housework, particularly care of children, the elderly, the disabled, and the ill.[25]

LT: You have written that two fundamental encounters forged your intellectual development starting in the 1990s: that with Indigenous movements (the trigger of which was reading *I, Rigoberta Menchú*) and that with ecofeminists (particularly Vandana Shiva).[26] Would you say that these encounters with women from the southern hemisphere caused a shift in your intellectual and activist journey?

MDC: On the whole, there was a shift. By analyzing the condition of women and men in terms of wages and time, I discovered a framework that was simply going to deteriorate. But, up to a certain point, I also felt that struggles in the field of work time and wages were too limited, because they left to capital the initiative of defining the type of world and the type of life on earth.

Not only had we not won on the question of wages, but this struggle did not take account of the policies of production of death and misery that gradually castrated the reproductive powers of nature, of the land, and of the bodies of human beings in general. So, on the one hand, there was our struggle to obtain money and time for ourselves, which was a field we had to fight in; but, on the other hand, we also had to fight in a different field to not leave to the adversary all of the initiative for defining "which world" and "which life."

Above all, we had to consider the question of the land, which was constantly being increasingly privatized, expropriated, poisoned. This question involved, first, thinking about what, from our point of view, would be an acceptable agricultural solution for the inhabitants of the globe – a solution that would avoid having only poison available to buy to feed ourselves, and that would leave room for access to "fresh and healthy food," to quote the slogan of a movement that was spreading particularly in the 1990s in both the southern and northern hemispheres.[27]

This issue continued to explode, in Italy and in the rest of the world, as could be observed during demonstrations by farmers who occupied the roads with their animals and agricultural products in 1997, 1998, and 1999. It played a central role in my works, within a critique of neo-liberal structural adjustment policies – that is, of this type of development.[28] It even plays a central role in the attention that I pay to movements and initiatives by Indigenous peoples, and in the southern hemisphere in general, to construct other types of economies and lives. This is evidenced in my attention to the struggle in Chiapas since it began.

I would like to say in this regard that there was a significant difference between Marcos (leader of the Zapatista movement in Chiapas) and other political leaders that I greatly appreciated: he was particularly sensitive to the difficulties experienced by women, members of the Revolutionary Army, living under extremely precarious conditions in the mountains, difficulties with their bodies and, every month, having their menstrual periods. He recognized this, he talked about it, and he took account of these biological differences in the struggle.[29]

LT: You have spoken of the "lethal process" that increasingly characterizes capitalist development today. What do you mean by this term?

MDC: It is well known that the capitalist economy is founded and continues to develop on the production of misery and death, and on the uprooting and transferring of entire strata of populations. These processes function to weaken organization and resistance networks that populations have formed – that is, they weaken the reproductive powers of populations.

These processes were very obvious even early in the history of capital, during the period called primitive accumulation.[30] Today, populations continue to be uprooted and displaced because of major development projects by the World Bank (hydroelectric projects, in particular); or they occur as an effect of adjustment policies and variations in agricultural prices, forcing enormous contingents of people to emigrate.

On another level, there is also, in my opinion, a different type of policy for uprooting individuals, which is related to new reproductive technologies that tend to treat individuals more and more as laboratory products than as children of a biological mother and father in the context of their social relations. It is also a way of depriving individuals of the context of these relations, of their history, of their memory, which is also transmitted down the generations. It is to deprive individuals of their roots and their past. This is a policy of weakening individuals by weakening the construction of their identity, because the very ground on which it was first constructed has disintegrated.

Similarly, the policies of production of death and creation of misery are propagated in new configurations. Death and misery are increasingly conveyed through the continual production of morbidity and disabilities of all sorts, flowing from a neo-liberalization of science that, through repeated experimentations that no one has authorized and no one has been able to stop up to now, brings new risks of disease, known or unknown, to weigh on people's bodies.

The continual wars taking place also offer the most convenient opportunity to experiment with all of this on a large number of living-dying test subjects. What is at play is the interruption of human bodies' reproductive powers, as those of the bodies of other living beings – plants and animals – have already been interrupted, in such a way as to render human bodies ever more dependent on medical science or, in other words, on the laboratory-market. This is an overall plan for castration of the reproductive powers of nature, the bodies of all living beings.

I think that it is not by accident that, while I was considering, theoretically and practically, the struggles of populations against what I call the castration of the soil, which has occurred during the different stages from the green revolution to the arrival of new technologies, biotechnologies, and genetic manipulations of living beings, I met on my way, as have many women, the medical proposition of hysterectomy.

LT: In your intellectual path, you took on this issue of hysterectomy. What took you there?

MDC: The surgery was proposed to me, as it was to many other women, for no reason. I had the capacity and the possibility to verify the situation, and I refused it. But is this the case for many women? The confrontations that I had in this regard with other women and other doctors in order to verify the basis (or lack of basis) for the proposal opened my eyes to the practice: beyond the cases where it may prove necessary, it has become, in this century, a practice of mass castration of women in many advanced countries, and for reasons that certainly are not related to the well-being of women.

In fact, I discovered a shockingly frequent use of this surgery by doctors. I discovered all the negative consequences that are not usually mentioned when women are subjected to the operation, even though, in many cases, there are other, non-mutilating solutions that are not brought to their attention or offered as possible alternatives.

I saw the same aggressive, castrating policy that did harm to the reproductive powers of nature-land do harm here to the reproductive powers of the nature-body of women, each of whose organs is intimately linked to the entirety of the body. Only mechanistic, reductionist thinking would manage to isolate these powers, and isolate uterus and ovaries, setting aside the very complexity of the functions of these organs in relation to the body as a whole, and consider them simply superfluous after a certain age.

In my view, this hysterectomy problem arose as the third station, the third stage of the struggle, after those we had had to organize around childbirth and abortion, that punctuated the life path of women's bodies. I decided to put forth the question and open the debate in Italy. After working alone for a few months, I prepared my first long presentation, which I would make as an invited speaker to a national conference of gynecologists in Palermo, on December 7, 1997.[31] It was a very important event, in terms of a confrontation between the discourse of a feminist woman and the discourses of doctors. I then organized a colloquium with gynecologists, but also with magistrates, on this same theme in Padua in 1998; a large number of women were in attendance. I had invited magistrates, among other reasons, because I had come to the conclusion – and this was the thesis I presented in Padua, as I had in Palermo – that unjustified hysterecto-mies constituted an attack on the psychophysical integrity of the individual, a crime of very serious personal injury and, at the same time, a terrible form of violence perpetrated by medical science on women's bodies.[32]

Then, I also organized a very big conference on the question in Venice with the participation of doctors, human rights specialists, jurists, and numerous women. After that, I was invited to a number of medical congresses in Rome and Milan. But this mobilization mainly offered an opportunity to come into contact with French female gynecologists and to participate in their great struggle to maintain the specialty of medical gynecology alongside that of surgical gynecology, instead of having only the latter, as the new policies would have had it. Women's bodies have always had difficulty traversing this world, designed for men.

I remember a definition that we gave for "woman" during the 1970s. It went something like this: "A woman is a subject who, whatever she is doing, must interrupt herself if there is an emergency in the family." Once again, I found myself with the obligation of interrupting what I was doing: my research on the question of land. It was, however, not family in this case, but my own body, the body of a woman who had to fight another obstacle to be able to continue her life's journey.

LT: What have been your intellectual and activist concerns since 2000?

MDC: I have devoted these years to analyzing the discourses and struggles of the peasants' and fishers' movements under globalization. For the first few years, I concentrated on peasants' movements. I observed, in effect, that despite the bitter, long struggles conducted by different subjects, it is truly difficult to be able to imagine how an alternative to this type of development, another plan for social organization and production, could be constructed. The dominant model was reproduced continuously through expropriation of land, just as it had been in early capitalism, but in new forms – by appropriating and overturning nature's reproductive powers. This model of development is perpetuated through different types of expropriation, through which masses of people are expelled. The workers' condition is rebuilt on the planetary level and restratified on terms that approach slavery.

The overturning of mechanisms for spontaneous reproduction of life (by patents on seeds, for example), international debt, and structural adjustment programs are all components of a single strategy through which capital tends to create a food dictatorship involving maximum dependence by populations, and in which these populations find themselves in conditions of absolute blackmail. We have to start from this question: How can this dictatorship be broken? Otherwise, it would be as if all the activism, all the struggles in the world, would be reduced to building a house without a foundation.

The peasants' movement addressed the problem of how to build this foundation. The desire to regraft the relationship between human life and the land, the negation of which constitutes the very soul of capitalist development, means reversing the conditions of this development and laying the basis for building a different kind of development – different first and foremost because it would not involve an increase in hunger and death as a fundamental premise.

The peasants' movement laid the groundwork for opposing the hunger strategy: food was a common good; it involved the right of populations to have access to food sources – above all land, water, and biodiversity – and the fundamental freedom to choose what to eat and how to produce it; a democracy had to begin by being a food democracy; food sovereignty is a true source of food security. Many other themes were central to this movement: responsible agriculture is responsible to other peasants, to consumers, and to the land itself; the idea that food security could derive from the availability of hard currency that makes it possible to buy foodstuffs from multinationals must be rejected. From my point of view, it was important not to deal with these themes as if they concerned only the southern hemisphere. Different movements around the world, including in Italy, were moving in the same direction, and I analyzed what they had and didn't have in common, but on the whole they were converging.[33] In the meantime, a broad consumers' movement in the cities joined the peasants' movement so that this movement, in Italy for example, became more and more a rural-urban movement.[34]

At a certain stage of my research in this field, I presumed that if such social forces were at work with regard to the question of the land, similar forces must be at work on the question of the ocean, the rivers, the lakes, and the water that flows in the veins of the earth. And I found the fishers' movement, whose activities had begun in Kerala, India, in the 1970s, and had quickly gone global.

This encounter with the sea, with the ocean, like my encounter with the land, arose because this research corresponded to a need that I felt deep within me, the need to tie my life to that of nature.[35] It was above all a poetic encounter. It is not by chance that in the book that Monica Chilese and I wrote about the ocean, I devoted several verses to the sea.[36]

The fishers' movement against the gigantic fishery conducted on ships outfitted with high-technology equipment posed the question of responsible fishing, practised with a sense of limits and responsibilities with regard to other fishers, coastal populations, and the sea. The fishers' movement posed the central question of the need to safeguard the organic connection between the trade of fisher and maintenance of the ecosystem. It expressed the need to develop an eco-friendly, rather than a destructive, relationship with the ecosystem and asserted that the real possibility for abundance resided in defence of the spontaneous reproduction of sources and cycles of life.[37]

LT: What is the link between this research on the questions of land and sea and your previous research on the situation of women and their movement?

MDC: The question of the land and the sea, the question of food policies, on the one hand, and that of the movements for an alternative food system, on the other hand, enabled me to approach the question of reproduction and relaunch it at a higher level. The struggles around money and time were not enough to enable us to imagine a different future that did not immediately presume the growth of hunger in the world. The dominant food system produced not only hunger, however, but also disease. Food scandals emerged in recent years. Traditionally a source of joy, food gradually became a source of suspicion and fear. The task of providing food, one of the primordial tasks of women's reproductive work, was now, as if randomly, facing many new problems: not only was food becoming rare, in both the southern and northern hemispheres, but it was also becoming unhealthy. As a consequence, in a number of regions, women were leading movements to preserve the land and food.

Furthermore, women who had traditionally taken care of the bodies of others had learned, with the women's movement of the 1970s, to take care of their own bodies. With determination, they raised questions about their autonomy and the satisfaction of their own desires, instead of living simply as a function of the satisfaction of others' needs.

Women's struggle to reappropriate their bodies did not concern just reappropriation of the knowledge and power to decide on procreation and their sexuality. They also refused to be machines for reproducing labour power and intended to reappropriate their own bodies as creative and desiring bodies. In opposition to a life completely devoted to work, they wanted to find time for themselves. In opposition to a femininity consisting solely of availability to satisfy others' needs, they intended to regain the right to emotions.

But today, the right to emotions and sensations is at the heart of the peasant agriculture movement, because peasants refuse the ugliness that destruction of landscapes brings in its wake; they reject the sensory deprivation that the countryside generates, the abolition and standardization of flavours, and the destruction of knowledge. The right to creativity and beauty is very present in this movement, as is the right to food security. After this long industrial and urban winter, the bodies of women, and the bodies of others along with them, will be able to blossom again only with the blossoming of the land-body.[38]

At a certain point in my research, I decided to sort through all the materials I had, the materials for activist use and the more-theoretical materials that I had either gathered or produced during my lifetime, in order to deposit them as an archive to be available to future generations. Some materials go back to the 1970s, but others are more concerned with the present day. There are materials on paper, such as leaflets, brochures, songs, and plays, and there are old records, cassettes, and films that I transferred onto CD or DVD.

I spent a few years collecting and ordering all of it, and in September 2011, I gave the entire collection to the municipal library in Padua, having been assured that it would do archival work and make it accessible to the public as soon as possible, as I had already put it in good order. This archive, with its millions of pieces, is now accessible for consultation by young (and old) generations.[39]

INTERVIEW WITH SILVIA FEDERICI[1]

Silvia Federici was born in Parma, Italy, in 1942. She has lived in the United States since 1967, and in 1980 she earned a PhD in philosophy from the State University of New York at Buffalo. She is a professor emeritus of social sciences at Hofstra University in Hempstead, New York, and the author of key works substantiating the Wages for Housework perspective, including her seminal work Wages against Housework *(Bristol: Falling Wall Press, 1975).*

Louise Toupin: After all these years, and to give today's feminists an understanding of what the Wages for Housework project meant, could you share some lessons that can be drawn from the life of the International Feminist Collective (IFC)?

Silvia Federici: The IFC served to launch the International Wages for Housework Campaign. It was therefore a very strong political experiment that deeply affected the lives of the women who took part in it.

To understand the meaning of our participation in this political project, one has to be aware of the general climate of the time. It was a revolutionary period for many women. We were coming from the Movement – the student movement, the anti-war movement, the civil rights and anti-colonial movements. We were certain that we were part of a process of historic transformation. And, in addition, we were active in the feminist movement, which was promising to completely change our lives. The experiences of those years were unique experiences that are possible only during specific historical periods, times when the "bottom rises up" and all of society seems to be in complete upheaval.

As for the experience in the Wages for Housework campaign, its power resided in the fact that it gave us great comprehension of society and the mechanisms of exploitation, and at the same time it touched the most personal aspects of our lives, while enabling us to connect to all other women with a new sense of solidarity. It was a perspective that allowed us to encompass and also to step beyond the entire spectrum of women's experiences. I must add to this the feeling of power that came to us from having lived a collective life, a life in which women came first; for all of us, that was our primary interest.

And then there was the joy of seeing our skills and talents develop. We began to learn how to write texts and speak in public, write songs, make posters, analyze the newspapers day after day, and find our life interesting.

The lesson to be drawn? Learn to make a "sustainable revolution." The feminist movement upset the world, but it did not create the structures necessary

Figure A.2   Silvia Federici and Louise Toupin. Photo: Jacques Keable.

to support its revolution (I'm talking about the strategic question of reproduction, which was left behind). The new political generations of women, if they
want to complete our work, would do well not to forget that.

LT: But more precisely, what are the specific lessons to be drawn from the
experience of the IFC?

SF: The campaign showed the importance of having an international network
for an exchange of knowledge, materials, and struggle experiences, giving us the
capacity to cooperate on many levels, to communicate about our struggle with
a coherent vision, and, periodically, to evaluate the effectiveness of our work.

At the same time, this experience showed us the limits of any organization
that exists in the absence of a mass movement. One of the limits of the International Wages for Housework Campaign was the tendency to interpret the
leadership role in a way that was too rigid, centralized, and hierarchical. This
would not have been possible if it had been a mass movement, in which people
make decisions autonomously, without waiting for permission from leadership.

LT: How did the Wages for Housework perspective influence your activism and
your intellectual trajectory after 1977, after the IFC came to an end?

SF: The wage perspective made me understand that capitalism is a production
system that depends structurally on non-contractual and unpaid work, in all
its forms, and a system that devalues the reproduction of labour power. So,
capitalism must continually create classes of workers with no rights who have
the task of reproducing labour power at low cost. This is why capitalism, historically, was always essentially a structurally sexist and racist system. Sexism and
racism are not moral problems. They are ideological and practical systems that
serve to justify and conceal unwaged work regimes. Unpaid work is justified by
the use of psychological and mental characteristics.

That is why I say that capitalism cannot be reformed. The Wages for
Housework perspective showed me that there is an urgent need to build, from
our daily struggles, an alternative to the capitalist system. My interest in the
question of the commons springs from that.

The wage perspective also helped me understand the function of underdevelopment and the political significance, starting in the late 1970s, of the
restructuring of the world economy as a process of "primitive accumulation"
– that is, as an attack on the most fundamental means of our reproduction and
the value of labour power.[2] This comprehension was reinforced by my stay in
Nigeria in the mid-1980s, during which I saw the effects of globalization – in
the form of the debt crisis and structural adjustment policies – on the population's living conditions.

My stay in Nigeria opened a new political horizon for me because, for the first time, I was in a country in which the majority of the population was still living off the land, and the land was still owned by the community. I understood then that the Wages for Housework struggle was only one aspect of the struggle for valorization of the work of reproduction and the construction of an alternative to capitalism.

LT: Could you explain the link between the question of land and Wages for Housework?

SF: The link is that in many countries, women's struggle around reproduction begins with reappropriation of the land, the land being the first and most fundamental means of reproduction, in that when we talk about "the land," we are also talking about water, forests, agriculture, and food production.

At first, I thought that women's struggles for land were the equivalent, the counterpart, of Wages for Housework in industrialized countries. However, I observe that, even in Europe and North America, the struggle concerning the land has been reopened. In New York, new waves of immigrants from the Caribbean and Latin America (the new diaspora induced by globalization) provoked the development of a network of urban food-producing gardens, which brought together people from different countries to build a community and thus created elements of independence from the market. Even more important, the ecology, anti-globalization, and, especially, eco-feminist movements taught us that land, and not money, is the fundamental means of reproduction. If we don't have access to the land, we have nothing. We are very vulnerable to monetary manipulations and also to manipulations of food production. Of course, there is no question of turning ourselves into farm owners jealously guarding "their" land, but the question of land is fundamental to winning autonomy and also for regeneration of the planet.

In Nigeria, I learned from African women's struggles first against colonization, and then against "development," that loss of land has meant an enormous loss of power, especially for women. Access to land and the production of harvests – harvests that women could once use for their own reproduction and that of their children or to sell in the marketplace – were the basis of women's social power. Even today, this dispossession strengthens women's dependence on men.

Each new phase of "development," each new economic recovery program, inevitably involves privatization of the land, and women are the first victims.

LT: Talk about your activism after 1977, after your participation in the New York Wages for Housework Committee.

SF: After my involvement in the Wages for Housework campaign ended, I participated in different movements. First I formed, with other women, a group that produced the journal *Tap Dance,* in which we analyzed the economic and social dimensions of the neo-liberal project, especially Reaganism. In *Tap Dance,* we also protested against the plan to recruit women into the army, which was supported by liberal feminist organizations.

In the 1990s, I began to participate in the Midnight Notes Collective and contributed to producing several issues of its magazine (of the same name, *Midnight Notes*).[3] Being in the collective helped me to interpret the "debt crisis" in Nigeria and to understand that this "crisis" was the instrument of a new process of enclosure and primitive accumulation.

In Nigeria, I worked with the feminist organization WIN (Women in Nigeria), and I helped write one of the documents that WIN presented at the 1985 Nairobi Conference.[4] I also continued my historical and political research on development of capitalism that I had begun in the 1970s. Between 1977 and 1983, I had co-written a book with an Italian feminist, Leopoldina Fortunati, *The Great Caliban: Story of the Rebel Body in the First Phase of Capitalism* (published in Italian in 1984), in which we discuss the reorganization of repro-duction during the period of transition from feudalism to capitalism.[5] During this project, I found what would become one of my main research subjects: the witch hunt, the persecution that inaugurated the history of women in capitalist society in the fifteenth and sixteenth centuries – a persecution that was funda-mental to defining women's social position within the capitalist regime. It was to better understand the relationship between the witch hunt and the devel-opment of capitalism that I continued my research on the period of transition from feudalism to capitalism, starting from medieval social movements, which resulted in a new book: *Caliban and the Witch: Women, The Body and Primitive Accumulation,* published in 2004.[6]

In the 1990s, I also began to work a good deal on the question of education, partly in connection with my experience in Nigeria (having witnessed the World Bank's assault on public education in Africa), and partly because a cultural battle was taking place in the scholarly arena in the United States at the time: con-servative intellectuals and professors had launched a crusade against all books and essays criticizing the canons of "Western civilization." In 1995, I edited an anthology titled *Enduring Western Civilization: The Construction of the Concept of Western Civilization and Its "Others."*[7] My goal with this book was to show that there is no such thing as Western civilization, that this concept is a fiction, a fabrication of Cold War ideology.

My work in this field, however, has been the struggle against the globalization and commercialization of education. It was oriented mainly toward denouncing the dismantling of education in Africa and mobilizing organizational support by North American teachers and students to get involved in the struggle of

African teachers and students against structural adjustment. In this regard, some colleagues, mainly from Africa, and I founded an organization called the Committee for Academic Freedom in Africa (CAFA), in which academic freedom was interpreted as being the right to education. CAFA was formed in response to the attack conducted, in the name of "structural adjustment," against the education systems in Africa and in other "third world" countries in the 1980s and 1990s. Since then, we have seen the same type of development in Europe, and also in the United States, where the commercialization and corporatization of education is ongoing.

For thirteen years, I was one of the co-editors of the newsletter published by CAFA, which documented the struggles of students and teachers in Africa against budget cuts to education and the dismantlement of public education systems in most African countries. In 2003, three years after publication of *A Thousand Flowers: Social Struggles against Structural Adjustment in African Universities*, which I co-edited, CAFA and its newsletter ceased activity.[8]

Even though the CAFA newsletter wasn't widely distributed, it played a very important role, as CAFA was the only organization of this type outside Africa, and the newsletter was the only publication during those years that documented the growth of a pan-African student movement. Some of the documents published in the newsletter were reprinted in *A Thousand Flowers*.

For seven years, from 1995 to 2002, I was also engaged in a campaign against the death penalty. In 1995, some other radical philosophers and I formed the Radical Philosophy Association's Anti-Death Penalty Project, the goal of which was to mobilize students and professors in this cause. Mainly, I was trying to develop a feminist perspective on the death penalty, to convince feminists to become engaged in this struggle.

Here again, as it was for the question of war, there were two opposed feminist positions. The first, the liberal position, saw the state as the saviour-protector of women and supported cooperation between women and the police to make the neighbourhood "safer." The other position refused to treat social problems as criminal problems. It took into consideration the true sources of crimes and questioned the biased and unilateral way in which crime is defined in this society: for example, work-related accidents and deaths due to environmental contamination were never considered to be criminal acts.

LT: Do you think that Wages for Housework analyses are still relevant today? And how could they be updated?

SF: Yes, I think they're still relevant, for a number of reasons. To start with, it is clear that the first task to undertake in the struggle is to adopt programs that can bring people together, that can unite them and undermine the hierarchies built on the division of labour. This is where the strategic importance of the Wages for Housework strategy lay – and still lies – because domestic work, reproductive work, is a question that affects all women and can therefore constitute a field of political reunification among us.

Second, the Wages for Housework perspective is still relevant because the capitalist reorganization of labour that occurred in the 1980s and 1990s (Reaganism, Thatcherism, neo-liberalism, globalization) resulted in a direct attack on public resources devoted to reproduction (health, education, working conditions, and so on), an attack on the means of reproduction which produced a very large crisis in reproduction.

Third, the sphere of unpaid work, instead of shrinking, has considerably expanded in the last two decades. In effect, we have seen the reappearance of slave-like labour conditions, even in industrialized countries, with the proliferation of sweatshops; the change from welfare to workfare; the development in the United States of a mass incarceration regime within which prison labour is often appropriated; overexploitation and criminalization of undocumented immigrants; and deployment in the "third world" of food-for-wages programs.[9] More than ever, unpaid work and devaluation of labour power – which is the devaluation of our actual lives – are essential components of capitalist development. The Wages for Housework politics is therefore still current.

Today, however, the Wages for Housework perspective and struggle need a broader basis. It is not enough to demand just a paycheque; we must also demand other means of reproduction less subject to monetary manipulations: houses, health services, communal spaces, urban collective food-producing gardens where people may sow and harvest.

Everywhere, the struggle over reproduction is very openly also a struggle for reappropriation of the land, and also for the control of territory. All dimensions of the land question are fundamental. Earth, water, air, the ocean, as well as health and education, must be considered common goods, not subject to market logic.

LT: What do you think of the evolution of feminism today?

SF: There is not a single feminism; there are feminisms. With the intervention of the United Nations in feminist politics, we have seen an attempt to institutionalize the movement in order to defuse and neutralize its struggles and its subversive potential. We have also seen an attempt to redefine the feminist program to make it compatible with the neo-liberal program. Since 1975, starting with the UN conference on women in Mexico City, the United Nations has tried to delegitimize all feminism that is not compatible with the needs of international capital, in the same way as it tried to dominate the anti-colonial movement in the 1960s, by ensuring that decolonization was compatible with the needs of ex-colonial powers and the United States.

With its global conferences on women, the United Nations has created "global feminism," with a category of feminists who believe that they have the right to define what women want, what the feminist program is, what a legitimate claim is and isn't. At the same time, feminism has become internationalized. Its battlefield has shifted to the international stage. And today there exists a feminist movement, what in Latin America is called "popular feminism," which formed in response to liberalization of the world economy and has grown up outside of the institutional constraints of the United Nations, creating forms of reproduction outside of the market and the state. For me, that is real feminism. I think, for example, of women's movements in Chile, Argentina, and Peru, which, in the 1980s and 1990s, built forms of reproduction oriented toward self-subsistence and organized collectively.

However, institutional feminism has caused great damage, in my view, because it has neutralized the subversive potential of the feminist movement and created a state feminism that has served to confuse and disarm many women. For "global feminism," the problems are no longer, or not mainly, the policies that emerge from the global development of capitalism and their effects on women, but the fact that women pay a disproportionate price compared with men, because of the restructuring of the global economy.

LT: Can you expand on this last point?

SF: I mean to say that for "global feminism" (the feminists who follow the political program of the United Nations), the problem is not the capitalist development and recolonization that flow from restructuring of the global economy. Rather, the problem resides in the fact that the policies of the International Monetary Fund and the World Bank have imposed an "unequal burden" on women. It is presumed that if women and men were to suffer equally, the structural adjustment and globalization of the economy would be more acceptable. The main concerns covered by these policies are gender relations, considered mainly in the context of the family but outside of capitalist relations. I explained this in greater detail in an essay published in *Revolution at Point Zero*.[10]

LT: Has Western feminism played a role in this evolution or this political appropriation?

SF: Certainly. The European and American feminist movements have played a large role in it. But we should not speak of "Western" feminism as if it were something uniform and monolithic. It must be noted that when we talk about Western feminism, we are talking about liberal feminism, which is highly visible because it is the only feminism that the media and the institutional political system recognize. Because of the activity of liberal feminism, which is integrated into United Nations policy, all anti-capitalist struggles are now excluded from the official women's movement.

Global feminism boils down to a question of rights and a struggle for wage parity and equal working conditions. But we have been able to observe that integration into the organization of waged labour cannot constitute a factor in economic and political emancipation, even if it is an economic necessity.

As we have seen, the entry en masse of women into waged workplaces has given them more autonomy with regard to men but has changed working conditions little. For example, in most workplaces, there is no daycare. There is no reduction in work hours; on the contrary. It is recognized today that waged workplaces are still organized as if everyone who worked there had a woman at home. In the United States, there is no maternity leave; such leaves must be negotiated on an individual basis with each employer. This means that women must forget their gender to have waged work.

LT: What do you think of the struggle to include women's unpaid work in countries' national (satellite) accounts?

SF: It's a legitimate struggle, but with a very limited range. I am suspicious of the fact that the work would be "counted" rather than "paid." The question becomes, what does it count for? For purely moral recognition? Or is it a compensatory gesture that leaves everything unchanged? I am particularly suspicious since the UN agencies, and the UN itself, adopted this recommendation in the Beijing Platform for Action.[11]

The UN has never been opposed to structural adjustment policies imposed in Africa, Latin America, and Asia by the World Bank and the International Monetary Fund, and it didn't bat an eye when public pension systems and other social programs were dismantled all over the world. So how is it possible that the UN might seriously envisage compensation for reproductive work? I am tempted to make the following syllogism, however, based on historical and political evidence: if the UN supports such a recommendation, it's because it cannot have any serious meaning, for the UN is compromised in this new world order and with the liberalization/globalization programs founded on the suppression of all forms of social welfare – which has ravaged the life of women throughout the planet.

LT: What should we think of the fact that history has forgotten the Wages for Housework strategy and the groups that carried on the struggle?

SF: The situation seems to have changed. Today, feminists – and social movements in general – are showing a good deal of interest in Wages for Housework, and especially in the question of reproduction. In all the conferences of various social movements in which I've participated recently, there were workshops on Wages for Housework and on reproduction. Young women and men who, a few years ago, were paying no attention to the question of wages, are now writing dissertations on the subject. It is also interesting to observe that the underlying Wages for Housework theory – that housework is work, the work of producing and reproducing labour power, a socially necessary work – this theory is now widely acknowledged in the academic world, and also by the left and by most feminists, as it has become "common sense." At the same time, however, its political implications are still ignored, except for the recommendation that housework should be counted, which is very meagre satisfaction, in my view.

However, it is true that starting in the late 1970s, and in the years that followed, Wages for Housework was almost forgotten by most feminists. In the United States, one of the consequences of this historical forgetfulness was the incapacity of the feminist movement to defend welfare women from the stigmatization to which they were increasingly subjected. They began to be presented as social parasites, and they were stripped of the gains resulting from the struggles that their mothers and they themselves had led in the 1960s within the Welfare Movement.[12] If the feminist movement had struggled for a redefinition of housework and had placed it on the same level as other forms of work, it would have been less easy to stigmatize women on welfare (especially in the United States, where women receive allowances from the Aid for Dependent Children program) and to cut these programs.

The forgetting of the Wages for Housework political strategy is symptomatic of the oblivion into which the entire question of reproduction fell in the 1980s and 1990s in North America. Starting in the mid-1970s, most feminists in the United States abandoned reproduction as a field of struggle, concentrating all their efforts on the question of equality (the Equal Rights Amendment) and access to waged work. As a consequence, today, women in the United States don't benefit from a right that is recognized for women almost everywhere else – the right to a maternity allowance. As I said, in the United States, women must negotiate this in their workplaces. It is not a parental right recognized by the state.

This is another reason for the exhaustion of the radical potential of the women's movement. The fact that the women's movement abandoned reproduction as a field of struggle meant that it was not able to reproduce itself. Now, women work in two workplaces: in the home and outside the home. They don't have the time to mobilize. I think that is one of the reasons the feminist movement was not capable of surviving and opposing the crisis of the 1980s, when the rights of all workers and all our living conditions were attacked.

We see the result today: we have lost many social programs; we work harder than ever before, and continue to do most of the housework (even if middle-class women have been able to "free" themselves from housework by hiring other women as maids). Childcare and healthcare remain inaccessible, except at exorbitant costs that are prohibitive for most women; we have even become the "poor of the nation" (if the concept feminization of poverty has meaning); we work so hard that we don't even have time for family relations – not to mention political activity. This scenario is quite different from the one for which many of us, in the women's liberation movement, struggled in the 1970s!

But this won't have been the first time that the feminist movement has gone underground, if I can put it that way, and then resurfaced. The problems are still there. It becomes clearer and clearer to all women that accessing a second job does not lead to liberation, and that it is not a strategy for attaining this goal. Similarly, it is now obvious that having the right to vote also doesn't mean liberation, even though women struggled hard to obtain it in the early twentieth century.

As for forgetting the groups that led the Wages for Housework struggle, this situation, as I said, is changing. I should note that these groups were not the only ones to be marginalized. All feminist groups that defied the status quo suffered the same fate. I'm thinking, for example, of those that struggled against nuclear rearmament in the late 1970s.

All of these groups that challenged the established order were marginalized in part because of the absence of media coverage, or because of media distortion in the coverage of them. In particular, they were neutralized politically, notably through the funding of liberal groups and their publications, and also through the development of academic feminism, which holds the appropriate discourse on the movement. One day, perhaps, we will be able to better understand what initiatives were deployed by governments to provoke the dismantling of feminist groups that question social hierarchies and inequalities.

But I want to end on a positive note: we are now seeing a change among the younger generations of women. This has been clearly demonstrated by the Occupy movement, in which women have played a central role.

LT: What have been your intellectual and activist concerns since 2000? We could start with your interest in the witch hunt, which gave rise to a book on the subject in 2004, *Caliban and the Witch*, now translated into several languages.

SF: After I came back from Nigeria, I returned to the work that I had started on the question of the witch hunt, situating it in the broader context of the phase of "primitive accumulation" of capitalism.[13] As I explained in the introduction to *Caliban and the Witch*, this new research was greatly influenced by my comprehension of the effects of the restructuring of the world economy that I could observe first-hand in Nigeria.

The feeling that we were witnessing a new phase of primitive accumulation accompanied me all throughout the writing of *Caliban and the Witch*, to the point that my reading of the past was always filtered through the experience of globalization. I think that is one of the reasons that the book has been so successful and has been published in so many languages – Spanish, German, Greek, Turkish, and French. Now, it is in the process of being translated into Italian, Serbian, Slovenian, Polish, and Japanese. I really didn't expect it! But I am convinced that it is because it provides a historical analysis and a theoretical framework that also sheds light on the present and, more importantly, enable us to identify the deep forces and mechanisms that structure the expansion of capitalist development and are required by the expansion of capitalist relations.

When I began to work on this book, I had no idea that a new wave of witch hunts was unfolding in several parts of Africa and in India, Nepal, and Papua New Guinea, clearly rooted in the changes activated by the process of economic liberalization. Confronted with these new persecutions, I realized the significance of the work that I did on the transition from feudalism to capitalism. This work gave me a framework, enabling me to interpret these new witch hunts and see their continuity with the surge of violence against women that globalization has produced. More specifically, I could see, once again, that the witch hunting is directly related to the extinction of communal systems of land tenure and the attack against subsistence economies, starting with subsistence farming, which is done mostly by women and, for millions across the world, is a source of sustenance and autonomy.

However, it has become a target of international financial institutions – like the World Bank, which promotes the idea that agricultural relations should be commercialized and that only money is truly productive of wealth. I have written several articles on the subject, including "Witch-Hunting, Globalisation, and Feminist Solidarity in Africa Today."[14]

Documenting and analyzing these new persecutions and the attempts that are being made to destroy all subsistence forms of production, for example through the promotion of microcredit, has been one of my main concerns in recent years. My work has gone in several directions. On one side, I've continued my analysis of the restructuring of the global economy and, in particular, the restructuring of the reproduction of labour power within it, its impact on the conditions of women, and women's resistance to it. My new book, *Revolution at Point Zero*, collects several articles that I wrote on this subject.[15]

I have also been very interested in documenting the efforts that people, women above all, are making in many parts of the world to create communal forms of existence and communal forms of production, both as a form of survival in the devastation produced in their community by capitalist development and as a way of reconstructing the social fabric lacerated by economic displacements, political repression, and privatization. All over the world, women are in the forefront not only defending the last remaining commons but also creating new ones. This has not been only theoretical work. Since the 1990s, as part of the anti-globalization movement in which I have been involved, I have been working with a broad network of people who are exploring, practically as well as theoretically, what today is the "politics of the commons" and how we can contribute to it.

Presently I have formally retired from teaching, but I still teach in many ways, through workshops I conduct on different subjects. I write. I have recently been doing a lot of travelling, doing book tours, and I am involved with an international network of women working in various ways around the question of social reproduction. My approach to it has broadened quite a bit since the time of Wages for Housework. However, I am still convinced that this perspective was a powerful strategy, and I have never reneged on my views on the subject.

Acknowledgments

As no studies existed on the International Feminist Collective and the Wages for Housework movement when I began this research, it was in large part through oral and written interviews with activists from the period concerned that I was able to get things rolling and bring the project to completion. I extend my warm thanks to everyone who supported and assisted me in one way or another during my long crossing of the desert from 1994 to 2013. Among those who made essential contributions to the achievement of this undertaking, I would like to thank some people in particular.

Silvia Federici acted as a resource person and inspiration during the final stage of synthesis of this research. Indeed, she was the one who urged me to return to this research in 2012, after I had put it aside for almost twelve years. Silvia was also present in 1996 for the reconstruction of the history of American Wages for Housework groups. I am grateful to her for her ongoing presence, her support, and her singular affability and availability.

Also at the top of the list is Mariarosa Dalla Costa, whom I thank from the bottom of my heart; I met her first, and she believed in my project from the very beginning. With her help, I was able to track down and meet with other Wages for Housework activists in Europe and the United States. Mariarosa is the very memory of the movement; she worked to safeguard its works despite unrest in Italy from 1978 through the 1980s, as well as during the phase of oblivion into which the movement and its theoreticians fell thereafter. A reconstruction of the history of the International Feminist Collective simply would not have been possible without her valuable archives and her advice, and she has my undying gratitude. Finally, I am appreciative of the efforts she made to complete the interview that appears in the Afterword.

In Padua, Mariarosa introduced me to other Wages for Housework activists and theoreticians, including Giovanna Franca Dalla Costa and Leopoldina (Polda) Fortunati. I would like to thank them for their kind reception, their availability, and their archives put at my disposal.

My warm thanks go also to historian Gisela Bock, first, for her letter of support for my post-doctoral research project on the history of the International Feminist Collective, presented at the European University Institute in Florence in 1994. It was the initial acceptance of this project that allowed my research to get underway. By the way, I am also grateful to historian Olwen Hufton, co-director of the theme for the institute's European Forum that year, for accepting and supporting my work-study project. And I have to thank Gisela Bock again; she was the key person of the Berlin Wages for Housework group,

Lohn für Hausarbeit, through which I was able to reconstruct some aspects of the Berlin group's existence.

I would like to express my gratitude to the three dynamic Insoumises, Viviane Luisier, Alda De Giorgi, and Suzanne Lerch, who opened their doors, their archives, and their memories to me in the fall of 1994, in order to reconstruct the history of L'Insoumise, a unique group in the activist universe of Geneva. In 2013, De Giorgi and her colleagues of that time reviewed the information gathered in 1994 and updated it. I would also like to thank Simona Isler, at the time a doctoral student in history at the University of Bern, who translated parts of her master's thesis that concern some elements of the Zurich Wages for Housework group for me.

A very special thanks goes to my old and dear friend Nicole Lacelle, who, in the mid-1970s, introduced the Wages for Housework perspective to our fran-cophone feminist group in Montreal and helped us to anticipate its richness. Thanks, Nicole, for that, and for many other things: giving me access to your personal archives; reading and commenting on an early version of my research; and organizing a Skype call with Ellen Woodsworth, who was a Wages for Housework and Wages Due Lesbians activist during those years and now lives in Vancouver. And a heartfelt thank-you to Ellen for sharing with me the joys and pains of her activism of that era.

Acknowledgment is also due to many other people who, at one point or another over the years, have assisted or done favours for me. Les Insoumises graciously put me up in Geneva. Dario De Bortoli lent me his residence in Padua and Suzanne Demczuk did the same in Paris (thanks, Irene, for putting me in touch with Suzanne!). Sharing their memories with me were Marie-Christine Gaffory, as an "orphan" Wages for Housework activist in Paris; and Véronique O'Leary and Martine Éloy, as activists at the Centre des femmes de Montréal who hosted Mariarosa Dalla Costa and Selma James when they came through Montreal during their North American tour in the spring of 1973. Finally, my thanks to Jacques Keable, who shares my life, for having read an early rough draft of this research and making very useful suggestions to ensure better coherence.

I cannot forget the archivists. In the early 1990s, an activist from the defunct Toronto Wages for Housework Committee, Francie Wyland, donated the group's archives to the Canadian Women's Movement Archives, situated in the Morisset Library at the University of Ottawa. This archival collection also contains numerous documents on the Wages for Housework network of groups. Wyland's concern with leaving a historical record of the Wages for Housework movement to future generations must be applauded. Without the wealth of documents contained in this collection, it would have been very difficult for me to complete this research.

My great thanks to the archivists of the Canadian Women's Movement Archives at the University of Ottawa, Lucie Desjardins and Véronique Paris, for their diligent assistance during the summer of 2013. My thanks go also to archivists Christine Benfill, Andrea Trudel, and Pauline Cadieux Villeneuve, who allowed me to consult the Wages for Housework collection onsite in 1996, when it was partially inventoried.

I would like to express my gratitude to the organizations that provided financial support to me. First is the Government of Canada's Social Sciences and Humanities Research Council, which awarded me a post-doctoral grant in 1994–96 that allowed me to travel to Europe to reconstruct the history of the European network of Wages for Housework groups. I am also very grateful to the Comité paritaire syndical-patronal sur le perfectionnement des chargés de cours of the Université du Québec à Montréal, which awarded me a grant for the 2012–13 academic year. Without this grant – which allowed me a period of peace and quiet during which I was finally able to concentrate and devote myself full time to synthesizing all of my data – this research would have been consigned to limbo. As a corollary, I would like to thank all the lecturers who fought for and won this very interesting clause in our contract, which remains one of the very few ways to support lecturers' research activities.

For the original French edition, thanks go to Les Éditions du remue-ménage and the unmatched professionalism of its team: Valérie Lefebvre-Faucher, Anne Migner-Laurin, and Rachel Bédard. Thanks to Rachel for being so solidly and tenaciously at the helm of feminist publishing in Quebec for almost forty years now!

I am even more indebted to Les Éditions du remue-ménage because the creation of this feminist publishing house in 1975–76 was, in a way, the very inspiration for this book. I was a member of the founding team, within which debates over the ideas of the Wages for Housework movement first made me aware of this current of thought. It was also there that the seed of translating and publishing the movement's documents was germinated. My gratitude goes to my friends from that early team, the fertile soil from which this book sprang.

Last but not least, my thanks goes to Darcy Cullen, acquisitions editor at UBC Press, for the kind reception offered to my book; to Ann Macklem, production editor, and her team for their singular editing work; and to Käthe Roth, who crafted an impeccable translation, and with whom I had a pleasant and profitable dialogue through the process.

Special thanks to David Shulman, commissioning editor at Pluto Press, who proposed the idea of a co-edition with UBC Press and acted as a catalyst. Thanks also to Robert Webb, managing editor at Pluto; and to Pluto's dynamic team for their work on this book, which will ensure a wider circulation to the Wages for Housework history.

Finally, the usual disclaimer: all omissions and errors of fact or interpretation that may have slipped into this book are my responsibility alone and in no way involve the people cited herein.

Notes

Introduction: A Political and Personal History

1. Montreal Power of Women Collective, *To All Wages for Housework Groups Present at the February Conference in Montreal, 1975* (CWMA, Box 624.8, p. 1, Roneo).
2. Ironic reference to the *desaparecidos* of Argentina, the people who were "disappeared" for political reasons by the military junta in power from 1977 to 1983. Personal interview with the author, Padua, November 2, 1994.
3. This essay was included in Mariarosa Dalla Costa and Selma James, *The Power of Women and the Subversion of the Community* (Bristol: Falling Wall Press, 1972), 19–54.
4. I exclude here groups that, during the same period, were demanding wages "for housewives," such as the Bérets blancs sect that was active in Quebec and demanding such a salary to impede the creation of public daycare centres. The Wages for Housework movement had a completely different perspective: it was demanding pay for housework, whoever – man or woman – was doing it, and it was setting out not to impede the creation of daycare centres but to make them accessible also to the children of women working in the home.
5. On this subject, see Danièle Kergoat, "La division du travail entre les sexes," in *Se battre, disent-elles ...* (Paris: La Dispute, 2012), 203. Silvia Federici, one of the main theoreticians of the Wages for Housework movement, believes that this may not be so true today. During her lecture tours in Europe in 2012 and 2013, the interest shown by students and activists in the analyses made by the Wages for Housework movement made her think that there is renewed interest in it. In my interview with her, reproduced in the afterword to this book, she returns to this question.
6. Collectif L'Insoumise, *Le foyer de l'insurrection: Textes sur le salaire pour le travail ménager* (Geneva: Collectif L'Insoumise, 1977), 109n1 (our translation).
7. With regard to Quebec, I note in this respect the universal daycare services and parental leave encouraging fathers' participation. See Diane-Gabrielle Tremblay, "Vers la conciliation emploi-famille au Québec: des politiques pour les enfants et/ou les mères?" *Informations sociales* 160 (2010): 106–13.
8. General Social Survey, 2010, drawn from Statistics Canada (2011), *Women in Canada: A Gender-Based Statistical Report*, cited in Carole Vincent, "Why Do Women Earn Less Than Men? A Synthesis of Findings from Canadian Microdata," *Canadian Research Data Centre Network Synthesis Series* (September 2013), 14, http://www.rdc-cdr.ca/sites/default/files/carole_vincent_synthesis_final_2.pdf. See also, for the OECD countries, Miranda Veerle, "Cooking, Caring and Volunteering: Unpaid Work around the World" (OECD Social, Employment and Migration Working Papers 116, OECD Publishing, http://dx.doi.org/10.1787/5kghrjm8s142-en).
9. General Social Survey, 2010, 16.
10. Annabelle Seery, "Travail de reproduction sociale, travail rémunéré et mouvement des femmes: constats, perceptions et propositions des jeunes féministes québécoises" (master's thesis, Université du Québec à Montréal, 2012), 69; "Famille et travail: Constats et propositions des jeunes féministes au Québec," *Enfances Familles*

Générations 21 (2012): 216–36. See also Annie Cloutier, "Mères au foyer de divers horizons culturels dans le Québec des années 2000: Représentations en matière de choix, d'autonomie et de bien-être" (master's thesis, Université Laval, 2011).

11. Seery, "Travail de reproduction sociale," 70 (our translation).

12. See the "Dossier Mères au foyer 2.0" from *Gazette des femmes*, newsletter, June 4, 2012, webzine of the Conseil du statut de la femme (Québec), https://www.gazettedesfemmes.ca/dossiers/meres-au-foyer-2-0/.

13. "Canada will admit 17,500 permanent residents through the Live-in Caregiver Program in 2014 – almost double the number [in 2013].This represents the highest number of LCP admissions in a single year since the program began in 1993." Government of Canada, "Live-In Caregiver Admissions to Reach an All-Time High in 2014," news release, October 29, 2013, http://s3.amazonaws.com/migrants_heroku_production/datas/1141/News_Release_—_Live-in_caregiver_admissions_to_reach_an_all-time_high_in_2014_original.pdf?1383068201.

14. See Lourdes Beneria, "Travail rémunéré, non rémunéré et mondialisation de la reproduction," in Jules Falquet et al., *Le sexe de la mondialisation: Genre, classe, race et nouvelle division du travail* (Paris: Presses de la Fondation nationale de science politique, 2010), 71–84.

15. See Barbara Ehrenreich and Arlie Russell Hochschild, eds., *Global Woman: Nannies, Maids, and Sex Workers in the New Economy* (New York: Henry Holt, 2004). See also Arlie Russell Hochschild, "Love and Gold," in *Global Woman*, 15–30. For a critique of the "care drain" concept, see Speranta Dumitru, "From 'Brain Drain' to 'Care Drain': Women's Labor Migration and Methodological Sexism," *Women's Studies International Forum* 47 (November-December 2014): 203–12, http://www.sciencedirect.com/science/article/pii/S0277539514001058.

16. Danièle Kergoat, "Division sexuelle du travail et rapports sociaux de sexe," in Helena Hirata et al., *Dictionnaire critique du féminisme* (Paris: PUF: 2000), 43–44 (our translation).

17. Silvia Federici, "Reproduction and Feminist Struggle in the New International Division of Labor," in *Women, Development and Labor of Reproduction: Struggles and Movements*, ed. Mariarosa Dalla Costa and Giovanna F. Dalla Costa (Trenton, NJ, and Asmara, Eritrea: Africa World Press, 1999), 62.

18. "In Canada, women do up to 80 percent of the unpaid caregiving. Many caregivers may be elderly and needing care themselves."Canadian Women's Health Network, "Self-Care for the Caregiver," http://www.cwhn.ca/en/node/40811.

19. Nancy Guberman, quoted in Marie Lachance, "Réinventer la famille," *Gazette des femmes*, "Mères au foyer 2.0" portfolio (June 4, 2012), http://www.gazettedesfemmes.ca/6085/reinventer-la-famille (our translation).

20. Théâtre des cuisines, *Môman travaille pas, a trop d'ouvrage* (Montreal: Remue-ménage, 1976).

21. On this subject, see the introduction to Chapter 6.

22. The introduction to the anthology *Québécoises Deboutte!*, co-edited by Véronique O'Leary and me, bears witness to this frustration. See *Québécoises Deboutte!*, ed. Véronique O'Leary and Louise Toupin, vol. 1, *Une anthologie de textes du Front de libération des femmes (1969-1971) et du Centre des femmes (1972-1975)* (Montreal: Remue-ménage, 1982), 18. Thereafter, my frustration only grew, throughout the 1990s and after, as I watched the gradual constriction of the issue of reproductive work in feminist sociology studies, and its reduction to "management of the double task." This article expresses that frustration: Louise Toupin, "Le féminisme et la question des 'mères travailleuses': Retour sur le tournant des années 1970," *Lien social et Politiques* 36 (Fall 1996): 69–75. See also, for a more recent expression

of the same frustration, this article in the anniversary issue of *La Vie en rose*: Louise Toupin, "L'épouvantail dans le jardin," *La Vie en rose*, special anniversary issue (Montreal: Remue-ménage, 2005), 70–71, http://bv.cdeacf.ca/CF_PDF/LVR/2005/126585.pdf.

23. Dalla Costa and James, *The Power of Women*; Selma James, *Sex, Race and Class* (Bristol: Falling Wall Press/Race Today Publications, 1975); Silvia Federici, *Wages against Housework* (London and Bristol: Power of Women Collective and Falling Wall Press, 1975); Collectif L'Insoumise, *Le foyer de l'insurrection*.

24. Chapter 2 discusses the theoretical contribution of Black Women for Wages for Housework.

25. See note 29 on the contribution of the group Housewives in Dialogue on this subject.

26. On this group, see Chapter 6.

27. There was, however, a short-lived (1978–79) journal there, *Jamais contentes*, which espoused the wages-for-housework demand.

28. It was impossible at that time to set a meeting with James, who still leads, in London, the International Wages for Housework Campaign and its components. Aside from the publications from Falling Wall Press in Bristol (which published and translated from Italian to English a certain number of publications by Wages for Housework groups), the documents on the English groups that I consulted come from my personal archives or the Canadian Women's Movement Archives, conserved at the University of Ottawa. Many of these documents are from the period 1972–77. Because of this, this research has obvious gaps with regard to the history of Wages for Housework groups in England and their influence on the network.

29. For example, the International Wages for Housework Campaign and its various components, for which the international coordination body in London, England, still exists, with Selma James as spokesperson (see www.globalwomenstrike.net/whoweare). Among its many activities, this nucleus of groups conducts a series of campaigns in several countries around the question of recognition of social reproduction. One of the campaigns, known as the International Women Count Network, was very active during UN conferences on women, particularly the ones in Nairobi in 1985 and Beijing in 1995. It is to this campaign that we owe the inclusion, in the closing reports, of paragraphs concerning evaluation of unpaid work in the satellite accounts of the GDP of various countries. This group was also active at the Non-Governmental Organization Forum at the Mid-Decade World Conference of the United Nations Decade for Women in Copenhagen in 1980. See Suzie Fleming, *Housework for Sale* (London: Housewives in Dialogue, Centrepiece 3, 1986), 3. See also Fahnbulleh, *The UN Decade for Women: An Offer We Couldn't Refuse* (London: Housewives in Dialogue, Centrepiece 6, 1987), which describes the ten years of struggle to have the United Nations take unpaid women's work into account. What the International Wages for Housework Campaign has become today is very different from the initial network. In this book, I discuss, more modestly, the initial network, known as the International Feminist Collective from 1972 to 1977.

30. That is, in the mid-1990s, at the time when I conducted interviews with some of them.

31. In fact, this period, which got underway in feminism in the late 1970s, was marked by the creation of groups with specific interests, especially in the area of social services; these took over from the general-interest groups that preceded them.

32. Nicole Lacelle, well known in Quebec as a feminist sociologist, educator, and facilitator, was extremely important in raising the profile of the Wages for Housework perspective in francophone Quebec. Among other things, she translated into French and analyzed the main texts in the Wages for Housework current in an article published in the special section of the feminist magazine *La Vie en rose:* "Gagner son ciel ou gagner sa vie? Le salaire au travail ménager," *La Vie en rose* (March-May 1981): 13–25.

As mentioned above, the basic materials for this research (documentation and interviews) were assembled during the period covered by my postdoctoral grant, between 1994 and 1996. Interviews with Mariarosa Dalla Costa, Gisela Bock, and Silvia Federici were continued in writing until 2000. I then returned to this material in the summer of 2012, making updates as required, notably by revisiting the Canadian Women's Movement Archives and contacting most of the people interviewed during the 1990s.

Chapter 1: 1972: Wages for Housework in the Universe of Feminism

1. The term "neo-feminism" was invented to distinguish this new type of feminism, which appeared in the early 1970s, from the feminist movement that preceded it, and to indicate that this was not the birth of feminism, as might have been believed at the time, but a resurgence or a new phase in feminism. Neo-feminism is often called second-wave feminism, the first wave having been the movement that extended over a century in the world before the 1960s and involved struggles to obtain women's rights to legal, political, and social citizenship.

2. The ban on sitting on juries was lifted in June 1971, provoked by a shock action (the storming of jury benches) by seven activists of the Front de libération des femmes du Québec in March 1971 – an act that got them thrown in jail. See, on this subject, Marjolaine Péloquin, *En prison pour la cause des femmes: La conquête du banc des jurés* (Montreal: Remue-ménage, 2007). For an idea of how lesbians lived in a state of illegality during the 1950s and 1960s, see Line Chamberland, *Mémoires lesbiennes: Le lesbianisme à Montréal entre 1950 et 1972* (Montreal: Remue-ménage, 1996). See also part 1 of Irène Demczuk and Frank W. Remiggi, eds., *Sortir de l'ombre: Histoires des communautés lesbienne et gaie de Montréal* (Montreal: VLB éditeur, 1998).

3. On the history of abortion in Quebec, see Louise Desmarais, *La bataille de l'avortement: Chronique québécoise, 1970–2010* (Montreal: Remue-ménage, 2016).

4. "From 1869 to 1972, the Criminal Code essentially made it an offence ('vagrancy') for a prostitute to be in a public place for the purpose of prostitution. Section 175(1)(c) deemed every woman being a vagrant who 'being a common prostitute or nightwalker is found in a public place and does not, when required, give a good account of herself,'" Canadian Advisory Council on the Status of Women, *Prostitution in Canada* (Ottawa: Department of Justice, 1984), 19.

5. See, on this subject, the brief that Mary Two-Axe Earley, a Mohawk woman from the Kahnawake reserve in Quebec, and initiator of the first claims by Indigenous women, presented in 1968 to the Royal Commission on the Status of Women in Canada, in Micheline Dumont and Louise Toupin, *La pensée féministe au Québec: Anthologie (1900–1985)* (Montreal: Remue-ménage, 2003), 347–50.

6. In comparison, the female labour force participation rate in Canada is now more than 75 percent. See Statistics Canada (2011), *Women in Canada: A Gender-Based Statistical Report*, cited in Carole Vincent, *Why Do Women Earn Less Than Men? A*

Synthesis of Findings from Canadian Microdata (Canadian Research Data Centre Network, n.d. [2013]), https://crdcn.org/why-do-women-earn-less-men-a-synthesis-findings-canadian-microdata.

7. The figure for Italy comes from Silvia Federici and Leopoldina Fortunati, "High Tide: Women in Motion" (1982; article rejected by *Feminist Review*; Archives Leopoldina Fortunati). The article contains a table from the OECD on the percentage of participation of women in the job-active population in five European countries between 1963 and 1974. It was observed that the Italian women's labour force participation rate had dropped during this decade, bucking the trend in other European countries. The figure on immigrant women comes from Commission de l'emploi et de l'immigration, *Trois ans de vie au Canada* (1974), cited in Irène Fournaris, Beatrix Herrera, and Maria-Luisa Iturra, "La meilleure façon d'être exploitée: Les travailleuses immigrantes," *Agenda des femmes 1980* (Montreal: Remue-ménage, 1980), page for the month of July.

8. Florence Bird et al., *Report of the Royal Commission on the Status of Women in Canada* (Ottawa: Information Canada, 1970), 34, para. 73.

9. Ibid., 37, para. 92.

10. Carmelle Benoît et al., *Analyse socio-économique de la ménagère québécoise*, mimeo (Montreal: Centre de recherche sur la femme, June 1972).

11. Report of the National Council of Welfare (Ottawa, June 1972), 20, quoted in Marcelle Dolment and Marcel Barthe, *La femme au Québec* (Montreal: Les Presses Libres, 1973), 138–41.

12. Ibid., 125–38. In 1972, Dolment started Réseau d'action et d'information pour les femmes (RAIF), a group with chapters in several Quebec cities. For a number of years starting in 1973, RAIF published a newsletter composed mainly of annotated newspaper clippings on current events and RAIF's positions.

13. Jocelyne Lamoureux, Michèle Gélinas, and Katy Tari, *Femmes en mouvement: Trajectoires de l'Association féminine d'éducation et d'action sociale, 1966-1991* (Montreal: Boréal, 1993), 70 (our translation).

14. Here I quote Véronique O'Leary and Louise Toupin, "Nous sommes le produit d'un contexte," in *Québécoises Deboutte!* vol. 1, *Une anthologie de textes du Front de libération des femmes (1969-1971) et du Centre des femmes (1972-1975)* (Montreal: Remue-ménage, 1982), 49 (our translation).

15. At the time, the word "autonomous" connoted organizational autonomy (not mixed male-female), as well as autonomy with regard to political parties, groups on the left, and traditional women's groups; autonomy of thought and of struggle; autonomy of the woman-subject in society in general.

16. I am speaking here only about the three trends *discernible* to activists at the turn of the 1970s, when neo-feminism emerged – that is, *before* feminism exploded and was funnelled into numerous currents; thus, before the critiques were formulated about white feminism by African American feminists, Chicanas, women from the South, lesbians, and others whose voices were clearly heard as the 1970s went on. Among these early critiques, see, for example, Cherrie Moraga and Gloria Anzaldua, eds., *This Bridge Called My Back: Writings by Radical Women of Color* (New York: Kitchen Table, 1980). Note that activists did not all claim one or another of these trends. I borrow this typology of the three trends, sketched out in the early 1970s, notably from Shulamith Firestone, *The Dialectic of Sex* (New York: William Morrow, 1970), and Centre des femmes de Montréal, in its journal *Québécoises Deboutte!* (March 1973): 2–3 (republished in Véronique O'Leary and

Louise Toupin, eds., *Québécoises Deboutte!* vol. 2, *Collection complète des journaux* (Montreal: Remue-ménage, 1983), 94–96).

17. On the intellectual sources of early Quebec francophone neo-feminism, see Véronique O'Leary and Louise Toupin, "Nous sommes le produit d'un contexte," in *Québécoises Deboutte!*, vol. 1, *Une anthologie de textes du Front de libération des femmes (1969-1971) et du Centre des femmes (1972-1975)* (Montreal: Remue-ménage, 1982), 21–50. See also Péloquin, *En prison*, especially chap. 1. Noteworthy too is the remarkable book by historian Sean Mills, *The Empire Within: Postcolonial Thought and Political Activism in Sixties Montreal* (Montreal and Kingston: McGill-Queen's University Press, 2010). Mills situates the development of contestation in Montreal during these years in relation to the essential role played by decolonization of the third world. In Chapter 5 of "Québécoises Deboutte!," Mills uses new archival sources to analyze the beginnings of neo-feminism in Montreal.

18. On its validity today, see Olivier Filleule and Patricia Roux, eds., *Le sexe du militantisme* (Paris: Presses de Sciences po, 2009). See also, on the position of female students active in the Quebec "Printemps érable" movement, Léa Clermont-Dion, "Femmes de grève," *Gazette des femmes*, August 20, 2012, www. gazettedesfemmes.ca/6237/femmes-de-greve/. See also Marie-Ève Surprenant and Mylène Bigaouette, eds., *Les femmes changent la lutte: Au cœur du printemps québécois* (Montreal: Remue-ménage, 2013). On its validity in earlier times, see, for example, for France, Marie-Claire Boons et al., *C'est terrible quand on y pense* (Paris: Galilée, 1983). For Quebec, see Lucille Beaudry, "Les groupes d'extrême-gauche au Québec et la question des femmes: de l'opposition à la conciliation," *Bulletin d'histoire politique* 13, 1 (2004): 57–64.

19. This in no way means that those who remained in the mixed-sex groups let themselves be exploited. At the turn of the 1970s, feminism began to penetrate all progressive organizations, unions, professions, and political parties, and this phenomenon was due above all to the women present in these groups.

20. For the evolution of the radical current in Quebec during these years, see "Le féminisme comme pensée autonome," in Dumont and Toupin, eds., *La pensée féministe*, 459–62.

21. Feminist studies were inaugurated in American universities in the late 1960s. In 1969, in Montreal, Marlene Dixon, a well-known figure in American feminism, taught a very popular course on sociology of the female condition at McGill University. On the francophone side, a multidisciplinary course on the condition of women inaugurated in 1972 at the Université du Québec à Montréal became just as popular (credited to students but taught on a voluntary basis).

22. As evidenced by the title of a special issue of a magazine in 1970: "Libération des femmes: A zéro" (Women's liberation: Year zero), *Partisans* 54–55 (July–October 1970).

23. Friedrich Engels, *The Origin of the Family, Private Property and the State*, trans. Alick West (New York: International Publishers, 1942 [first published 1884]); August Bebel, *Woman in the Past, Present, and Future*, trans. H.B. Adams Walther (New York: AMS Press, 1976 [first published 1883]).

24. To mention just some of the works published between 1968 and 1972 that later became classics on the issue: Margaret Benston, "The Political Economy of Women's Liberation," *Monthly Review* 21, 4 (September 1969): 13–27, reproduced in *From Feminism to Liberation*, ed. Edith Hoschino Altback (Cambridge, MA:

Schenkman, 1980), 231–42; Pat Mainardi (1970), "The Politics of Housework," in *Sisterhood Is Powerful*, ed. Robin Morgan (New York: Vintage Books, 1970 [first published 1968]), 447–54; Isabel Larguia, "Contre le travail invisible," *Partisans* 54–55 (1970) [first published 1969]: 206–20; Peggy Morton, "A Woman's Work Is Never Done," *Leviathan* 2, 1 (1970): 32–37; Christine Dupont (pseudonym for Christine Delphy), "L'ennemi principal," *Partisans* 54–55 (1970): 157–72; Mariarosa Dalla Costa, "Donne e sovversione sociale" (1971), English translation in Dalla Costa and James, *The Power of Women*, 19–54; Betsy Warrior, "Housework: Slavery or Labor of Love," in Anne Koedt et al., *Radical Feminism* (New York: Quadrangle, 1973 [first published 1971]), 208–12. For Quebec, see Benoît et al., *Analyse socio-économique*.

25. Engels, *Origin of the Family*. The other such thinker, of course, was Simone de Beauvoir. Women's history would later teach us that Engels was far from the only one to have written on the subject and that first-wave feminists had written about it. One thinks of Käthe Schirmacher, "Le travail domestique des femmes: Son évaluation économique et sociale," *Revue d'économie politique* 18 (1904): 353–79, and Eleanor Rathbone, *The Disinherited Family* (Bristol: Falling Wall Press, 1986 [first published 1924]), to mention just two.

26. For a recent analysis of Luxemburg's thought, see Diane Lamoureux, *Paroles rebelles: Autour de Rosa Luxemburg, Hannah Arendt et Françoise Collin* (Montreal: Remue-ménage, 2010), 23–79.

27. Clara Zetkin, *Batailles pour les femmes* (Paris: Éditions sociales, 1980); Alexandra Kollontai, *Conférences sur la libération des femmes* (Paris: La Brèche, 1978), *Marxisme et révolution sexuelle* (Paris: Maspéro, 1973), and *Selected Writings of Alexandra Kollontai*, trans. Alix Holt (New York: W.W. Norton, 1977). On Kollontai, see also Christine Fauré, "L'utopie de la Femme Nouvelle dans l'œuvre d'Alexandra Kollontaï," in Marie-Claire Pasquier et al., *Stratégies de femmes* (Paris: Tierce, 1984), 481–88.

28. The condemnation by the left of feminism as being essentially bourgeois was far from being an invention of the 1970s, having its roots in early-twentieth-century socialist discourses. See Françoise Picq, "Le 'féminisme bourgeois': Une théorie élaborée par les femmes socialistes avant la guerre de 14," in Pasquier et al., *Stratégies de femmes*, 391–406.

29. A short history of this "cold war" between Marxist-Leninist groups and feminist groups in Quebec is recounted in O'Leary and Toupin, *Québécoises Deboutte!* vol. 1, 34–39.

30. Benston, "Political Economy," 231–42.

31. Christine Dupont (Delphy), "L'ennemi principal," *Partisans* 54–55 (July–October 1970): 157–72; translated as Christine Delphy, "The Main Enemy," *Feminist Issues* (Summer 1980): 23–40. Dalla Costa's text was circulated in manuscript form in 1971, then was published with the essay by Selma James, "Il posto delle donna," in March 1972, under the general title *Potere femminile e sovversione sociale* (Marsilio, 1972). Both texts were then published in English in October of that year, as *The Power of Women and the Subversion of the Community* (Falling Wall Press). This book was translated into French and German in 1973, into Spanish in 1975, and into Japanese in 1980.

32. The quotation is from Delphy, "The Main Enemy," 25. In an interview that she gave me in 1996, Mariarosa Dalla Costa confirmed this information.

33. Benston, "Political Economy," 231.

34. Ibid., 234, 238.

35. Ibid., 240, emphasis in original.

36. Ibid., 238.

37. See Ellen Malos, "Introduction," in *The Politics of Housework*, ed. Ellen Malos (Cheltenham: New Clarion Press (1995) [first published 1980]), 5. See also "Women in Science and Technology: The Legacy of Margaret Benston," special issue of *Canadian Woman Studies/Les Cahiers de la femme* 13, 2 (Winter 1993).

38. Delphy, "Main Enemy," 25.

39. Ibid., 32.

40. Ibid. She notes in this regard that the wages earned by women outside of the family long belonged to the husband.

41. Ibid., 35.

42. Ibid., 33.

43. Ibid., 39.

44. It would later (in 1980) be translated into English.

45. She later developed this line of thought: Christine Delphy, *L'ennemi principal, 1- L'économie politique du patriarcat* (Paris: Syllepse, 1998), and *2- Penser le genre* (Paris: Syllepse, 2001). See also Colette Guillaumin, *Sexe, race et pratique du pouvoir: L'idée de Nature* (Paris: Côté-femmes, 1992); Nicole-Claude Mathieu, *L'anatomie politique: Catégorisations et idéologies du sexe* (Paris: Côté-femmes, 1991); Paola Tabet, *La construction sociale de l'inégalité des sexes: Des outils et des corps* (Paris: L'Harmattan, 1998), and *La grande arnaque: Sexualité des femmes et échanges économico-sexuels* (Paris: L'Harmattan, 2004). The journals *Questions féministes* (1977–80), then *Nouvelles Questions féministes* (after 1981) disseminated, and still disseminate, this current of thought. In Quebec, Nicole Laurin and Danielle Juteau, in particular, developed this perspective in "L'évolution des formes de l'appropriation des femmes: des religieuses aux 'mères porteuses,'" *Canadian Review of Sociology and Anthropology/La Revue canadienne de sociologie et d'anthropologie* 25, 2 (May 1988): 183–207.

46. Delphy's theory raised much criticism from classic Marxists, notably during the domestic labour debate, which I discuss briefly below in this chapter. Here I will mention only the exchange between Delphy and Michèle Barrett and Mary McIntosh: Michèle Barrett and Mary McIntosh, "Christine Delphy: Toward a Materialist Feminism," *Feminist Review* 1 (1979): 95–106; Christine Delphy, "A Materialist Feminism Is Possible," *Feminist Review* 4 (1980): 75–105. Regarding criticism of Delphy's essay, see also Maxine Molyneux, "Beyond the Domestic Labour Debate," *New Left Review* 116 (July–August 1979): 3–27, and the synthesis by Lise Vogel, "Domestic Labour Debate," *Historical Materialism* 16 (2008): 237–43.

47. Danielle Chabaud-Rychter, Dominique Fougeyrollas-Schwebel, and Françoise Sonthonnax, *Espace et temps du travail domestique* (Paris: Librairie des Méridiens, 1985), 131 (our translation).

48. Danièle Kergoat, "À propos des rapports sociaux de sexe," in *Se battre, disent-elles ...* (Paris: La Dispute, 2012 [first published 1992]), 108 (our translation).

49. Danièle Kergoat, "Division sexuelle du travail et rapports sociaux de sexe," in Helena Hirata et al., *Dictionnaire critique du féminisme* (Paris: PUF, 2000), 42 (our translation).

50. Chabaud-Rychter et al., *Espace et temps*, 131 (our translation).

51. This formulation is inspired by Jan Windebank's with regard to what differentiates socialist and radical feminists in their respective interpretations of domestic

work. Jan Windebank, "Comment expliquer le rapport des femmes au foyer et à la famille: Les débats français autour du travail domestique," *Nouvelles Questions féministes* 15, 1 (1994): 19.

52. The quotations below are drawn from the English edition, published in 1972 by Falling Wall Press.

53. Maria Mies, *Patriarchy and Accumulation on a World Scale: Women in the International Division of Labor* (New York: Zed Books, 1986), 32.

54. As we shall see below in this chapter, the current of revisited Marxism that she stemmed from is operaist Marxism, which is an Italian specificity. See also the interview with Mariarosa Dalla Costa in the Afterword.

55. Although it did appear in a document dated July 1971 issued by the group Movimento di Lotta Femminile (later Lotta Femminista) titled *Manifesto programmatico per la lotta della casalinga nel quartiere* (later translated as "Programmatic Manifesto for the Struggle of Housewives in the Neighborhood," *Socialist Revolution* 9 [May-June 1972]: 85–90). One must conclude from this that the strategy was under debate in the early feminist movement in Italy.

56. In these early writings theorizing housework, including those analyzed here, the word "gender" was not yet being used to characterize patriarchal exploitation. To illustrate this oppression, the term "caste" was used. Common use of the word "gender" was to arise in the following years, in particular following the publication of Ann Oakley's book *Sex, Gender, and Society* (New York: Harper & Row, 1972). French feminist sociologists used the concept of *rapports sociaux de sexe* (social sexual relations), and then, starting in 2000, *genre* (gender).

57. For an overview of these debates in Quebec, see the sidebar in the introduction to this book, in which I discuss the main objections to Wages for Housework. See also the position of some twenty groups (including political parties) on the issue in the special section of the magazine *La Vie en rose*, "Gagner son ciel ou gagner sa vie? Le salaire au travail ménager" (March-May 1981): 13–19, and in Louise Vandelac et al., *Du travail et de l'amour: Les dessous de la production domestique* (Montreal: Saint-Martin, 1985).

58. One example of this Marxist exegesis was the question of whether housework or domestic work created plus-value or whether one could apply the Marxist theory of value to the value of housework, or whether housework could be called "socially productive" or not, and so on. The "save Marx" criticism was formulated by Maria Mies. See Mies, *Patriarchy and Accumulation*, 33. See also the excellent compilation of the Domestic Labour Debate: Eva Kaluzynska, "Wiping the Floor with Theory: A Survey of Writings on Housework," *Feminist Review* 6 (1980): 27–49. See also Malos, *Politics of Housework*; Lise Vogel, "Domestic Labour Debate," *Historical Materialism* 16 (2008): 237–43.

59. Vandelac et al., *Du travail et de l'amour*.

60. For a Wages for Housework groups example, see, among others, Suzie Fleming, "All Women Are Housewives," *The Activist* 15, 1–2 (1975): 27–33. For an IFC example, see Mariarosa Dalla Costa, "Premisse," in *Le operaie della casa: A cura del Collettivo internazionale femminista* (Venice: Marsilio, 1975).

61. Wendy Edmond and Suzie Fleming, "If Women Were Paid for All They Do," in *All Work and No Pay: Women, Housework, and the Wages Due*, ed. Wendy Edmond and Suzie Fleming (London/Bristol: Power of Women Collective/Falling Wall Press, 1975), 9.

62. Gisela Bock and Barbara Duden, "Labor of Love – Love as Labor: On the Genesis of Housework in Capitalism," in *From Feminism to Liberation*, ed. Edith Hoshino

Altbach (Cambridge, MA: Schenkman, 1980), 153–92. This essay is composed of
excerpts of a text initially published in German in 1977. For the history of the text,
its content, and the group Lohn für Hausarbeit, see Chapter 6.

63. Dolores Hayden, *The Grand Domestic Revolution: A History of Feminist Designs for
American Homes, Neighborhoods, and Cities* (Cambridge, MA: MIT Press, 1982).

64. Ibid., 8.

65. Gisela Bock, "Pauvreté féminine, droits des mères et États-providence," in *Histoire
des femmes en Occident*, vol. 5, *Le XXe siècle*, ed. Georges Duby and Michelle Perrot
(vol. ed. Françoise Thébaud) (Paris: Plon, 1992) 381–409. In this essay, Bock
summarizes works on the subject by twenty European historians at the European
University Institute in Florence whose contributions were published in Gisela
Bock and Pat Thane, eds., *Maternity and Gender Policies: Women and the Rise of the
European Welfare States, 1880s–1950s* (London and New York: Routledge, 1991).
See also Bock's remarkable historical essay, *Women and European History* (Oxford:
Blackwell, 2002).

66. Among them, some openly asked for a wage for childcare activity. Here is a short
list, compiled from various readings. In France, Hubertine Auclert in 1879, Léonie
Rouzade in 1896, Marguerite Durand, Nelly Roussel, and Alexandra David-Néel
in 1906. Katti Anker Møller in Norway in 1915, Ellen Key in Sweden in 1909,
Käthe Schirmacher in Germany in 1904, Eleanor Rathbone in 1917, and Virginia
Woolf in 1938 in England, and in the United States, Katherine Anthony in 1915,
Melusina Fay Peirce starting in 1868, and Crystal Eastman in 1920 – to name just
a few.

67. Falling Wall Press, which was to translate and publish the main documents of
the IFC, republished Rathbone's book with an introductory essay on her life and
struggle. Eleanor Rathbone, *The Disinherited Family: With an Introductory Essay
by Suzie Fleming* (Bristol: Falling Wall Press, 1986). For another biography of
Rathbone, see Johanna Alberti, *Eleanor Rathbone* (London: Sage, Women of
Ideas, 1996).

68. Although, over the years, she had to attenuate her discourse on family allowances
as a means of ensuring financial independence for women, replacing it with
family allowances for children, her early discourse aimed first for the recognition
and compensation for services rendered by women in families. See, notably, the
revealing title of this article: Eleanor Rathbone, "The Remuneration of Women's
Services," *Economic Journal* 27 (March 1917): 55–60.

69. In Quebec, feminists also had to fight to avoid having family allowances paid
to fathers. See Denyse Côté, "Le versement des allocations familiales aux mères
québécoises," in *Thérèse Casgrain: Une femme tenace et engagée, Actes de colloque*, ed.
Anita Caron and Lorraine Archambault (Sainte-Foy: Presses de l'Université du
Québec, 1993), 221–37.

70. I return to the fight for family allowances in Chapter 4.

71. For debates raised by the claim for family allowances and the "endowment of
motherhood" in England during the interwar period, see Johanna Alberti, *Beyond
Suffrage: Feminists in War and Peace, 1914–1928* (New York: St. Martin's Press,
1989), 164–90; Rosalind Delmar, "Afterword," in Vera Brittain, *Testament of
Friendship: The Story of Winifred Holtby* (London: Virago, 1980 [first published
1940]), 443–53; Suzie Fleming, "Introduction: Eleanor Rathbone: Spokeswoman
for a Movement," in Eleanor Rathbone, *The Disinherited Family with an Introductory
Essay by Suzie Fleming* (Bristol: Falling Wall Press, 1986 [first published 1924]),

50–55; Gisela Bock, "Pauvreté féminine, droits des mères et États-providence," in Duby and Perrot, *Histoire des femmes en Occident*, vol. 5, 381–409.

72. Winifred Holtby, *Women and a Changing Civilization* (New York: Longmans, Green, 1935), 94–95. The Soviet Union was for many years a reference for progressives in terms of collectivization and socialization of domestic tasks.

73. Regarding the 1970s, see the sidebar on this subject in the introduction to this book. Regarding the late 1990s, for one example, see the debate raised in Quebec in 1997–98 by the reform of the income security program, which planned the abolition of the unavailability allowance for mothers of preschool age and the obligatory integration of these mothers into employment paths. See Francine Descarries and Christine Corbeil, "Regards sur le discours féministe québécois," *Le Devoir*, August 8, 1997: A-9, and "Comment amenuiser l'ostracisme social des femmes," *Le Devoir*, August 9–10. See also the response to their articles: Lucie Bélanger, Huguette Labrecque-Marcoux, Jocelyne Lamoureux, and Louise Toupin, "La reconnaissance monétaire du travail familial," *Relations* (April 1998): 84–88.

Chapter 2: A Wage as a Lever of Power

1. Toronto Wages for Housework Collective, "Editorial," *Wages for Housework Campaign Bulletin* 1, 1 (July 1976): 3.

2. Mariarosa Dalla Costa, *Le operaie della casa* (Venice and Padua: Marsilio, 1975), 72 (our translation).

3. The relationship between women and domestic and reproductive work is obviously not universal; in fact, these relationships differ by race, ethnicity, and class, according to researcher Evelyn Nakano Glenn, who observes, "What is consistent across forms, whether commodified or not, is that reproductive labor is constructed as 'female,'" with racialized and ethnicized women in this construct "assigned a distinct place in the organization of reproductive labor." Evelyn Nakano Glenn, "From Servitude to Social Work: Historical Continuities in the Racial Division of Paid Labor," *Signs* 18, 1 (Autumn 1992): 6. Black Women for Wages for Housework groups were to highlight and explore in depth this differentiated relationship between women and domestic work, as I describe below in this chapter. In addition, Nicole Cox and Silvia Federici discussed the variability of conditions for domestic work: "The conditions of our work vary from country to country. In some countries we are forced into an intensive production of children, in others we are told not to reproduce, particularly if we are black, or on welfare, or tend to reproduce 'troublemakers.' In some countries we produce unskilled labour for the fields, in others we produce skilled workers and technicians. But in every country our wageless slavery and the primary function we perform for capital are the same." Silvia Federici and Nicole Cox, "Counterplanning from the Kitchen," in *From Feminism to Liberation*, ed. Edith Hoshino Altbach (Cambridge, MA: Schenkman, 1980 [text first published 1975]), 275.

4. "Rencontre avec deux féministes marxistes," *Québécoises Deboutte!* 1, 6 (June 1973): 37. Reproduced in Véronique O'Leary and Louise Toupin, eds., *Québécoises Deboutte!* vol. 2, *Collection complète* (Montreal: Remue-ménage, 1983), 201 (our translation).

5. Personal interview with the author, Brooklyn, March 16, 1996 (our translation).

6. Silvia Federici, *Wages against Housework* (London and Bristol: Power of Women Collective and Falling Wall Press, 1975), 1–2.

7. Workerism (*Operaismo*) was a critical current of Italian Communism of the 1960s. On the historical roots of this current, see the interview with Mariarosa Dalla Costa in the Afterword. See also Harry Cleaver, *Reading Capital Politically* (Austin: University of Texas Press, 1979), 45–62. For a synthesis of the main notions of workerism, see Harry Cleaver, "Autonomist Marxism," syllabus for a course given at the University of Texas, http://www.oocities. org/immateriallabour/cleaver-autonomist-marxism.html. See also Massimo De Angelis, "Interview with Harry Cleaver," 1993, https//webspace.utexas.edu/hcleaver/ www/cleaverinterview. html; published first in Italian, "Intervista a Harry Cleaver a cura di Massimo De Angelis," *Vis a vis: Quaderni per l'autonomia di classe* 1 (Autumn 1993): 79–100. Finally, see Mario Tronti, "Social Capital," *Telos* 17 (Fall 1973): 98–121.

8. Federici and Cox, "Counterplanning from the Kitchen," 277.

9. Ibid., 278.

10. Selma James, "Introduction," in Dalla Costa and James, *The Power of Women*, 7, emphasis in original.

11. Modern Times Collective, "The Social Factory," *The Activist* 15, 1–2 (1975): 38. This essay was written in the spring of 1974 by several members of the collective, which was a political group active in Cleveland. Two of its members (Beth Ingber and Sydney Ross) later formed the Los Angeles Wages for Housework Committee.

12. The concepts of social factory and refusal of work, as well as the strategic nature of wage struggles, come from the Italian workerist movement (see note 7). Importantly, the Wages for Housework movement evolved completely outside the orbit of this current (and often in opposition to it). On this subject, Silvia Federici wrote, "It was *through* but also *against* the categories articulated by these movements that our analysis of the 'women's question' turned into an analysis of housework as the crucial factor in the definition of the exploitation of women in capitalism." Silvia Federici, *Revolution at Point Zero: Housework, Reproduction, and Feminist Struggle* (Oakland, CA: PM Press; Brooklyn: Common Notions and Autonomedia, 2012), 6, emphasis in original.

13. Statement issued at the end of the first IFC international conference, organized by the New York Wages for Housework group in October 1974, which I discuss in the next chapter: *Wages for Housework Is a Feminist Perspective*, mimeo (Silvia Federici Archives).

14. Dalla Costa, *Le operaie della casa*, 17 (our translation from the unpublished French translation by Viviane Luisier, *Les ouvrières de la maison* (Geneva: Collectif L'Insoumise, n.d. mineographed) (Archives Louise Toupin). The page numbers given here and in subsequent notes refer to the original Italian text.

15. Mariarosa Dalla Costa, "Women and the Subversion of the Community," in Dalla Costa and James, *The Power of Women*, 28, emphasis in original.

16. This manifesto is reproduced in *Power of Women* 1, 1 (March-April 1974): 14. This journal was published by the London Wages for Housework group Power of Women. See Chapter 3.

17. See, below in this chapter, Selma James's analyses in "Wageless of the World," in *All Work and No Pay: Women, Housework, and the Wages Due*, ed. Wendy Edmond and Suzie Fleming (London/Bristol: Power of Women Collective/Falling Wall Press, 1975), 25–34; *Sex, Race and Class* (Bristol: Falling Wall Press/Race Today Publications, 1975).

18. Mariarosa Dalla Costa (1972), "Préface à l'édition italienne," in Mariarosa Dalla Costa and Selma James, *Le pouvoir des femmes et la subversion sociale* (Geneva: Librairie Adversaire, 1973), 9, emphasis in original (our translation).

19. See Federici and Cox, "Counterplanning from the Kitchen." Now reprinted in Federici, *Revolution at Point Zero*, 28–40.

20. To provide the definition discussed here, summarized from the formulation by Wages for Housework theoreticians, I use the proceedings of the launch day for the Wages for Housework campaign in Italy, on March 8–10, 1974, in which this definition is explained. These proceedings are found in Comitato Triveneto per il Salario al Lavoro Domestico, "8, 9, 10 marzo '74. Un lungo weed-end di lotta," in *8 marzo 1974: A cura del Collettivo internazionale femminista* (Venice and Padua: Marsilio, 1975), 25–41. An English-language translation was published: "A Long Week-End of Struggle," *Women in Struggle* 3, "Italy Now" (Canadian Women's Movement Archives [CWMA], box 115). Unless otherwise indicated, the quotations in this subsection and in the next are drawn from this text.

21. This aspect is explored in greater detail later, notably in Chapter 5, which concerns mobilizations of Wages for Housework groups in the public sphere. Among these mobilizations was the support that some of these groups offered to the sex workers' groups that began to form in the United States and Canada. Such support provided an opportunity to reinforce an analysis of prostitution as sex work, and of links between houseworkers and sex workers.

22. The documentary basis for this section is M. Dalla Costa, *Le operaie della casa*, 17–54. Unless otherwise indicated, the quotations come from this book and are our translation from the French translation. See note 14.

23. The Toronto group Wages Due Lesbians said this about money: "Money is how power is measured within capitalism. Our wagelessness, then, is both a measure and the cause of our powerlessness." Wages Due Collective, Toronto, "Why Lesbians Want Wages for Housework," mimeo (1975), 7 (Archives Nicole Lacelle).

24. In *Le operaie della casa*, 19n1, Dalla Costa notes that the expression "work outside" is inaccurate. "We use the term 'work outside' in its most common sense of work outside the home. But we need to mention how inaccurate this terminology is. Indeed, housework is not done only inside the home but also, to a great extent, outside the home. We can think, for example, of tasks such as grocery shopping, taking the children to school, getting papers at city hall, visiting relatives in the hospital, and so on. Housework is also done inside the home, while working outside the home. Similarly, prostitution work is done in large part in the home."

25. One Wages for Housework slogan was "We are always cheap labour outside the home/Because we are slave labour in the home." *Wages for Housework International Network Newsletter* (1975): 4 (CWMA, box 624.28).

26. The documentary source for this section is Federici, *Wages against Housework*. Unless otherwise indicated, all quotations are from this source.

27. Federici and Cox, "Counterplanning from the Kitchen," 278.

28. The phrase "Nothing can be more effective than to show that our female virtues have a calculable money value" foretold exactly what the "pay equity" operation a few years later would consist of in various countries.

29. It is worth remembering that the institution of marriage in the Catholic Church could not be dissolved except "due to mental illness of one of the two spouses [or] the incapacity to perform the conjugal act (unconsummated marriage)." In these cases, and after meticulous inquiry, the marriage might be declared null. Henri Tincq, *Les catholiques* (Paris: Hachette Littérature, 2008), 278 (our translation). For the Church, reproductive sexuality was well and truly a clause in the marriage contract.

30. M. Dalla Costa, *Le operaie della casa*, 51 (our translation).

31. Silvia Federici, "Why Sexuality Is Work," in Federici, *Revolution at Point Zero*, 24. This was a presentation made to the fourth conference of the IFC in Toronto in October 1975. For more about the IFC, see the next chapter.

32. Silvia Federici untitled mimeo (1974), starting with "Capitalism uses people ..." (Silvia Federici Archives), 1.

33. Dalla Costa, "Women and the Subversion of the Community," 30.

34. The analyses of Giovanna Franca Dalla Costa, expressed notably in *Un lavoro d'amore*, are worth noting here, and I discuss them below in this chapter.

35. To my knowledge there were Wages Due Lesbians groups in Toronto, Brooklyn, Philadelphia, London, Winnipeg, Balgonie (Saskatchewan), and San Francisco. The most active groups during the period under study were those in Toronto and London.

36. This conference is discussed in detail in the next chapter.

37. I concentrate on the following documents:

    • Wages Due Collective, Toronto, "Lesbians and Straights," in Edmond and Fleming, *All Work and No Pay*, 21–25. The text was published in various versions and under various titles, including "Fucking Is Work," *The Activist* 15, 1–2 (Spring 1975): 25–26.
    • Lesbian Women, Power of Women, London, "Lesbian Women: Love and Power," in Edmond and Fleming, *All Work and No Pay*, 46–48. Initially published as "Lesbianism and Wages for Housework," *Power of Women* 1, 4 (Summer 1975): 11.
    • Ruth Hall, "Lesbianisme et pouvoir," in Collectif L'Insoumise, *Le foyer de l'insurrection*, 109–17.
    • Ellen Woodsworth, "Lesbians Want Wages for Housework Too," in *Women Speak Out: May Day Rally Toronto*, ed. Wages for Housework (Toronto: Amazon Press, 1975), 22–24.
    • Wages Due Collective, Toronto, *Why Lesbians Want Wages for Housework*, mimeo, 1975 (Archives Nicole Lacelle).

    The Toronto feminist periodical *The Body Politic* published numerous pieces by Wages Due Lesbians. See Becki L. Ross, *The House That Jill Built: A Lesbian Nation in Formation* (Toronto: University of Toronto Press, 1995), 258n44.

38. Wages Due Collective, Toronto, "Lesbians and Straights," 21.

39. Ibid., emphasis in original.

40. Ibid., 21–22.

41. Woodsworth, "Lesbians Want Wages," 23.

42. The title of this subsection is the title of the document discussed below in this chapter, Wages Due Collective, *Why Lesbians Want Wages for Housework*.

43. Ibid., 3–4.

44. Ibid., 5.

45. Introduction by Collectif L'Insoumise to Ruth Hall, "Lesbianisme et pouvoir," in *Le foyer de l'insurrection: Textes sur le salaire pour le travail ménager* (Geneva: Collectif L'Insoumise, 1977), 92 (our translation).

46. On the currents of thought in the mid-1970s, see, for Canada, Ross, *House That Jill Built*; for Quebec, Andrea Hildebran (1998), "Genèse d'une communauté lesbienne: Un récit des années 1970," in *Sortir de l'ombre: Histoires des communautés lesbienne et gaie de Montréal*, ed. Irène Demczuk and Frank W. Remiggi (Montreal: VLB éditeur, 1998), 207–33.

47. My overview of the content of Brown's essay that follows was presented at the international meeting organized by the Toronto Wages Due Lesbians group and held in Toronto in July 1976, as we shall see in the following chapter on the IFC. Wilmette Brown, *The Autonomy of Black Lesbian Women*, Toronto, July 24, 1976, mimeo. This text was in the CWMA when I consulted it in 1996. It was classified under "WFH Toronto, Public Events." Since then, the CWMA has conducted a detailed inventorying of the collection titled "Wages for Housework: Wages Due Lesbians and Lesbian Mothers' Defence Fund" (X-10-8). In 2013, when I wanted to verify all the references that I had drawn in 1996 and their new classifications, I was unable to find this text (which, fortunately, I had photocopied at the time). It is therefore now part of my personal archive. Unless otherwise indicated, the quotations in this section come from this text.

    Regarding the United States, Barbara Smith situates this text in the Black feminist criticism's tradition of thought. See Barbara Smith, "Toward a Black Feminist Criticism," *The Radical Teacher* 7 (March 1978): 20–27. Reprinted in Gloria Hull, Patricia Bell-Scott, and Barbara Smith, eds., *But Some of Us Are Brave: All the Women Are White, All the Blacks Are Men* (Old Westbury, NY: Feminist Press, 1982).

48. The terms *black* and *white* are used here as they appear in the quotations.

49. This essay by Brown, written in 1976, preceded the "Black Feminist Statement" written in 1977 by the Combahee River Collective, a leading text of African American feminist thought, which expressed this intersectional perspective of the overlapping of different systems of oppression. It is included, among other places, in Barbara Smith, ed., *Home Girl: A Black Feminist Anthology* (New York: Kitchen Table, Women of Color Press, 1983), 272–82.

50. On the distinctive relationship between African American Women and domestic work, documented by Black Women for Wages for Housework, see also *SAFIRE* 1, 1 (Autumn 1977). This was the newsletter of Black Women for Wages for Housework (USA) (Silvia Federici Archives). See also Black Women for Wages for Housework, *Money for Prostitutes Is Money for Black Women*, mimeo, 1977 (CWMA, box 624.12), as well as Margaret Prescod, *Black Women: Bringing It All Back Home* (Bristol: Falling Wall Press, 1980).

51. Mariarosa Dalla Costa, "Quartiere, scuola e fabbrica dal punto di vista della donna," *L'Offensiva: Quaderni di Lotta Femminista* 1 (1972): 27, 29. I return to this essay at the beginning of the next chapter.

52. This subsection is based on Maria Pia Turri, "L'école du point de vue des femmes," in *L'Italie au féminisme*, ed. Louise Vandelac (Paris: Tierce, 1978), 173–81. Unless otherwise indicated, all quotations are from this essay and are our translation.

53. Among the seventeen proposals, I mention only the following: "Let us support our interests as double workers in the school, let us address the question of domestic work"; "Let us require that the hours spent in school as mothers be reimbursed to us by the state"; "Let us require our full wage for each absence, whether it is due to children's illness (without age limit) or for family reasons (without limit on number of days)"; "Let us impose our right to leave from work for possible abortions, rapes, and all family violence, and so on"; "Let us refuse to use sexist textbooks starting with those that hide or mystify the work of women and housework"; "Let us immediately organize a 'Feminist Rescue' enabling all women to refer ... to different instruments of feminist organization to confront repression (threats, extortion, firings, and so on)" (our translation). See Turri, "L'école," 180, for the other proposals.

54. Laura Morato and Carla Fabbri (with contribution by Mariarosa Dalla Costa), "Rôle du mouvement pour le salaire au travail ménager dans le mouvement féministe italien," in *L'Italie au féminisme*, ed. Vandelac, 148 (our translation).

55. Giovanna Franca Dalla Costa, *Un lavoro d'amore: La violenza fisica componente essenziale del "trattamento" maschile nei confronti delle donne* (Rome: Edizioni delle donne, 1978). G.F. Dalla Costa was also a member of the Padua Wages for Housework group at the time of the IFC. The book was later translated into English as *The Work of Love: Unpaid Housework, Poverty and Sexual Violence at the Dawn of the 21st Century* (Brooklyn: Autonomedia, 2008). Unless otherwise specified, the quotations in this section come from the English-language version of this book.

56. The exact sentence by St. Augustine of Hippo is "The measure of love is to love without measure" ("La misura dell'amore è amare senza misura"). Quoted in G.F. Dalla Costa, *The Work of Love*, translator's note, 53.

57. Since this book was written (1977), changes have taken place, especially under the impetus of the women's movement. For example, in 1983, Canada recognized conjugal rape as a crime, under the Criminal Code of Canada. Conjugal violence and incest, though they still take place very often, are now more and more often reported by victims and charged criminally.

58. Concerning the contribution of Wages for Housework theoreticians to the analysis of prostitution, I must mention the pioneering essay by Maria Pia Turri, "La mogli di tutti," *Il Personale è politico: Quaderni di Lotta Femminista* 2 (1973): 51–62. See also the important essay written by Leopoldina Fortunati, *L'Arcano delle Reproduzione: Casalinghe, Prostitute, Operai e Capitale* (Venice: Marsilio, 1981). It was translated into English as *The Arcane of Reproduction: Housework, Prostitution, Labor and Capital*, trans. Hilary Creek (Brooklyn: Autonomedia, 1995).

59. The text of the resolution is in Chapter 3, in the section on international organizational perspectives, subsection "International Platforms."

60. See the next chapter on the organizational strategy of the IFC.

61. Selma James, *Sex, Race and Class* (Bristol: Housewives in Dialogue, 1986 [first published 1975 by Falling Wall Press]), 6, emphasis in original. See www.libcom. org/library/sex-race-classjames-selma. It was republished in 2012 within an anthology of James's most important essays: *Sex, Race, and Class: The Perspective of Winning; A Selection of Writings, 1952–2011* (Oakland, CA: PM Press; Brooklyn: Common Notions).

62. James, *Sex, Race and Class*, 6, emphasis in original.

63. Claudia von Werlhof, "The Proletarian Is Dead: Long Live the Housewife?" in *German Feminism: Readings in Politics and Literature* (Albany: State University of New York Press, 1984), 254.

64. James, *Sex, Race and Class*, 7.

65. Ibid.

66. Ibid., 7–8.

67. Ibid., 8.

68. Ibid., 9–10.

69. The "perspective" quotation is from ibid., 10.

70. James, "Wageless of the World." This essay is the preface to the Latin American edition of *Power of Women and the Subversion of the Community*, reprinted in Edmond and Fleming, *All Work and No Pay*, 25–34.

71. Ibid., 26.

72. Ibid., 27, emphasis in original.

73. The quotation is from ibid., 29, emphasis in original.

74. Ibid., 31–32, emphasis in original.

75. As the IFC was in existence from 1972 to 1977 (the period covered in this book), I had to restrain myself in this chapter to the theoreticians who published works during this period. Unfortunately, this leaves aside those whose books were published afterward. We may think notably of Leopoldina Fortunati, who published an important essay in 1981 that is part of the corpus of theoretical works on Wages for Housework: Leopoldina Fortunati, *L'Arcano della Reproduzione: Casalinghe, Prostitute, Operai e Capitale* (Venice: Marsilio, 1981). Her book has been translated into English: *The Arcane of Reproduction: Housework, Prostitution, Labor and Capital*, trans. Hilary Creek (Brooklyn: Autonomedia, 1995).

Chapter 3: The International Feminist Collective, 1972–77

1. Collectif L'Insoumise, *Le foyer de l'insurrection: Textes sur le salaire pour le travail ménager* (Geneva: Collectif L'Insoumise, 1977), 109n1.

2. On Italian workerism (*operaismo*) see Chapter 2, note 7, and the interview with Mariarosa Dalla Costa in this book's afterword.

3. The manifesto was published in Italian and English in the form of a pamphlet. See the Power of Women Collective's journal, *Power of Women* 1, 1 (April 1974): 14. Quotations below are from this.

4. The original edition was published in Italy in March 1972 by Marsilio Editori and in English in October 1972 by Falling Wall Press. In 2012, Selma James published an anthology of her writings: *Sex, Race, and Class: The Perspective of Winning* (Oakland, CA: PM Press, 2012), in which Mariarosa Dalla Costa's name had been deleted as author of "Women and the Subversion of the Community." See the written contestation in the form of an open letter by Dalla Costa on this subject: www.indybay.org/newsitems/2012/04/26/18712188.php. As for "A Woman's Place," it was first published in the United States in 1953 under two pseudonyms (the McCarthy era required such protection measures): Marie Brant and Ellen Santori. We know that these pseudonyms were protecting James and Filomena Daddario, who had been asked to work together to write it (see Grace Lee Boggs, *Living for Change: An Autobiography* [Minneapolis: University of Minnesota Press, 1998], 62). When the essay was republished in 1972 in *Power of Women and the Subversion of the Community*, the author was listed as Selma James.

5. This document was included at the end of the French translation of *Power of Women and the Subversion of the Community*. See Mariarosa Dalla Costa and Selma James, *Le pouvoir des femmes et la subversion sociale* (Geneva: Librairie Adversaire, 1973), 135–48. On the question of abortion in Italy in 1971, see Lucia Chiavola Birnbaum, *Liberazione della donna: Feminism in Italy* (Middletown: Wesleyan University Press, 1986), 87.

6. Movimento di Lotta Femminile – Padova (July 1971), *Manifesto programmatico per la lotta della casalinga nel quartiere*, mimeo. See "Programmatic Manifesto for the Struggle of Housewives in the Neighborhood," *Socialist Revolution* 9 (May-June 1972): 85–90.

7. *Quaderni di Lotta Femminista* (Torino: Musolini), two issues of which appeared in December 1972 and October 1973 under the titles *L'Offensiva* and *Il Personale è politico*. These collections contained, aside from numerous intervention documents, theoretical texts on various aspects of the Wages for Housework perspective,

written by activists of the new network. They can be found in the Archivio di Lotta Femminista per il salario al lavoro domestico, Donazione Mariarosa Dalla Costa (Archives of Lotta Femminista for wages for housework, Gift of Mariarosa Dalla Costa) at the Biblioteca Civica, Centro Culturale Altinate/San Gaetano (biblioteca.civica@commune.padova.it). Some of these texts were later translated into English in other of the network's publications.

8. Her text appeared in a letter to the author (our translation).

9. On James's activist past before 1972, see Maud Ann Bracke, "Between the Transnational and the Local: Mapping the Trajectories and Contexts of the Wages for Housework Campaign in 1970s Italian Feminism," *Women's History Review* 22, 4 (2013): 627–28.

10. Lyn Gamble, "The Great Wages for Housework Debate: How It All Began," *The Leveller* (November 1976): 7. Gamble notes that the "D." in "S.D." was for "Deitch," Selma James's maiden name.

11. Selma James, *Women, the Unions and Work* (London: Notting Hill Women's Liberation Workshop Group, 1972). Republished as "Women, the Unions and Work, or What Is Not to Be Done," *Radical America* 7, 4–5 (July-October 1973): 51–72. The six demands appear on pages 67 to 71.

12. Selma James, "Foreword," in *Women, the Unions and Work, or What Is Not to Be Done* (Pittsburgh: Know, 1974), 1. This was the foreword to the American edition of the book.

13. See, among others, Gamble, "Great Wages for Housework Debate"; Ellen Malos, "Introduction," *The Politics of Housework*, ed. Ellen Malos (Cheltenham: New Clarion Press, 1995 [first published 1980]), 14; Elizabeth Wilson and Angela Weir, "A Reply to Selma James," in *Hidden Agendas: Theory, Politics, and Experience in the Women's Movement* (London and New York: Tavistock, 1986), 28. See also the July-October 1973 issue of *Radical America*, which published other reactions to the text in question, as well as Selma James, "The Perspective of Winning," reprinted in *Sex, Race, and Class: The Perspective of Winning; A Selection of Writings, 1952–2011* (Oakland, CA: PM Press, 2012 [text first appeared in 1973]), 76–85.

14. See Gamble, "Great Wages for Housework Debate." See also, with regard to the London conference, Sylvine Schmidt and Priscilla Allen, "In Defense of Feminism: A London Conference Report," *Wages for Housework Notebook* 2 (February 1973): 26–56, CWMA, box 115.

15. Wilson and Weir, "Reply to Selma James," 28; Malos, "Introduction," 14.

16. Suzie Fleming, "All Women Are Housewives," *The Activist* 15, 1–2 (1975): 27. On the campaign itself, see Chapter 4.

17. Gamble, "Great Wages for Housework Debate," 7.

18. Personal interview with Silvia Federici, Brooklyn, March 15, 1996 (our translation).

19. Silvia Federici, "Putting Feminism Back on Its Feet," in *The 60s without Apology*, ed. Sohnya Sayres et al. (Minneapolis: University of Minnesota Press/*Social Text*, 1984), 338.

20. She returned to her doctorate only in 1979, after she ended her involvement with the Wages for Housework movement. The degree was required for a university teaching job.

21. They wrote "Counterplanning from the Kitchen" together in 1975. Silvia Federici and Nicole Cox, "Counterplanning from the Kitchen," 271–86.

22. Personal interview with Silvia Federici, Brooklyn, March 15, 1996.

23. See *Québécoises Deboutte!* 1, 6 (June 1973): 29, reproduced in Véronique O'Leary and Louise Toupin, eds., *Québécoises Deboutte!* vol. 2, *Collection complète* (Montreal:

Remue-ménage, 1983), 190. The Centre des femmes was formed in Montreal in 1972. It took over from the Front de libération des femmes du Québec (1969–71), the first francophone Quebec autonomous neo-feminist group.

24. The interview with Dalla Costa and James was published as "Rencontre avec deux féministes marxistes." It is reprinted in O'Leary and Toupin, *Québécoises Deboutte!* vol. 2, *Collection complète*, 190–203.

25. Dalla Costa, who had come to Quebec because, among other things, she could speak French, returned to Italy for the start of a trial involving abortion in Padua on June 5, 1973. Lotta Femminista had decided to make it a political trial, to begin the mobilization concerning the legalization of abortion.

26. At the time in Montreal, it seemed unacceptable to all francophone activist groups, mixed or autonomous, to participate in events held in English only. This practice was inevitably interpreted as a colonial gesture, a sort of affront to francophones, who were the majority population of Quebec. Holding the symposium at McGill University, a bastion of Anglo-Saxon culture, was also not likely to encourage francophone women to attend the event.

27. On the complexity of relations between anglophone and francophone feminists in Montreal in the early years of neo-feminism at the turn of the 1970s, see O'Leary and Toupin, *Québécoises Deboutte!* vol. 1, 76–77; Marjolaine Péloquin, *En prison pour la cause des femmes: La conquête du banc des jurés* (Montreal: Remue-ménage, 2007), 257–61; Sean Mills, "Québécoises Deboutte!," chap. 5 in *The Empire Within* (Montreal and Kingston: McGill-Queen's University Press, 2010).

28. Letter from Neva Pandos, president of the Committee for the Feminist Symposium, to the Toronto Women's Caucus soliciting funds to hold the event, March 15, 1973 (CWMA, box 151).

29. See Mills, *The Empire Within*, 140. See also Judy Rebick, *Ten Thousand Roses: The Making of a Feminist Revolution* (Toronto: Penguin Canada, 2005), 9–10. In 1984, Cools became a Liberal senator; she left the Liberal Party in 2004 to join the Conservative Party. She is currently an independent senator. She was the first person "of colour" to sit in the Canadian Senate. See womynsherstory, blogspot.ca/2009/10/anne-cools.html.

30. Sir George Williams University is now known as Concordia University. For an account of these events, see Mills, *The Empire Within*, chap. 4. See also David Austin, *Fear of a Black Nation: Race, Sex, and Security in the Sixties Montreal* (Toronto: Between the Lines, 2013) and http://www.blackhistorycanada.ca/events.php?themeid=21&id=10.

31. Maria Tell, *Interim Report on the Montreal Conference, June 1–3, 1973*, 1 (CWMA, box 115).

32. *Proposed Budget for the Feminist Symposium Féministe*, Montreal, 1973 (CWMA, box 151). The symposium program listed the following organizations and companies as contributors: Government of Canada, Students' Executive Council of McGill, Birks Company Limited, Royal Bank of Canada, Montreal Trust, Steinberg's Limited, Reader's Digest, Hiram Walker & Sons, Greenberg's, Sealtest, Corporation of Professional Social Workers of Quebec (English Chapter), and six individuals (CWMA, box 151).

33. Tell, *Interim Report*, 6.

34. Ibid.

35. The "participating organizations" were Women's Information & Referral Centre, Women's Centre YWCA, Sororité, Women's Place, and Indoor Park. Official symposium program (CWMA, box 151).

. The quotation is from Tell, *Interim Report*, 1. Aside from the fact that the symposium took place entirely in English, a few other elements may explain the absence of francophones. According to the symposium report, it seems that the organizing committee at first wanted the event to be bilingual, and that is why the conference was called "Feminist Symposium féministe." The committee approached a group of francophone women but did not persist, it seems, with its contact. The committee realized the absurdity of addressing francophones when the event would be taking place at McGill University, the bastion of English culture in Montreal, and given that all the panellists were English speaking. Finally, only the title of the conference was bilingual, and the committee decided to ignore the Quebec situation – not without difficulty, however, as an incident that occurred during the organization of the conference demonstrates.

In short, the idea was to honour a woman during the opening session. It was Anne Cools's idea to pay tribute, according to the interim report, to a woman who had fought for justice, and whom no one had yet thought of honouring. On the list that Cools presented, one name sowed division within the organizing committee and "exposed the differences of political view on Quebec, on women ... a basic difference." That name was Rose Rose, the mother of two well-known imprisoned members of the Front de libération du Québec (sentenced for the death of the Quebec labour minister of the time). Rose's name had to be withdrawn, as some people threatened to withdraw from organization of the conference: "But the discussion did show the frightening lack of understanding and sympathy for the Quebec reality we were living in on the part of women who were satisfied to have the word 'feministe' on the programme" (Tell, *Interim Report*, 2). Among the seven Montreal women finally chosen to be honoured on the symposium program were two francophones: Simonne Chartrand (social movement activist later known as Simonne Monet-Chartrand) and Pauline Julien (singer).

36. It must be remembered that organizational links between anglophone and francophone feminists in Montreal had broken off in the early days of neo-feminism, specifically within the Front de libération des femmes, which did not make things any easier. See note 27. I would like to thank Martine Éloy for making this connection in an interview I had with her.

37. Tell, *Interim Report*, 1.

38. My account of the deliberations of the meeting was constructed from the minutes taken by Tell, *Interim Report*, and Margo, "Feminist Symposium: A New Direction for the Canadian Movement," *The Other Woman* 1, 6 (July–August 1973): 15.

39. Dixon was a well-known American feminist who had been a professor in the Department of Sociology at McGill University since 1969, where she gave courses on sociology of the female condition that were very popular. She was influential in the formation of the Montreal Women's Liberation Movement that same year.

40. Margo, "Feminist Symposium," 15.

41. "Countless feminists who were present told me directly that they come to the symposium because it was termed feminist, only to discover that it was not a feminist gathering, but a Marxist oriented one." Dionysia Zerbisias, "Panelists on Women's Symposium Charge Predominant Marxist Bias of Views," letter to the editor, *Montreal Gazette*, June 15, 1973, 8. See also Gerry Sparrow, "Marxist Feminists Display Power of a Vocal Minority," *Montreal Gazette*, June 15, 1973, 9.

42. On the companies and organizations that funded the symposium, see note 32.

43. Information on formation of the Wages for Housework groups in the United States comes from interviews with Silvia Federici in Brooklyn on March 15 and 16, 1996.
44. The first group was called "Group 1" or the "Book Group." In 1974 and 1975, there would thus be two Wages for Housework groups in Toronto. On the fate of Group 1 within the IFC, see the second section of this chapter, in which I discuss the debates raised at the Montreal conference in February 1975.
45. Judy Ramirez, born in New York, lived in Italy and moved to Canada in 1968. *Curriculum vitae.* Mimeo (CWMA, box 625.4). She was coordinator of the Toronto Wages for Housework group and, later, the founder and director of the Toronto Immigrant Women's Centre.
46. "Women outside of the cities, especially in Canada where distances are so great, are isolated from each other and from the movement. The Bookmobile will be an attempt to break down this isolation by providing access to feminist materials and ideas, and helping women to contact each other. We are a few hard-working women who are tired of big-city centralization of the women's movement." Text of the ad, reproduced in *The Other Woman* 2, 5 (June 1974).The text continued, "We are paying our own way, but we need help," and asked for "money for books, shelves, pamphlets, record, gasoline, paper and pens, etc."
47. For an account of the first summer of Cora, see "Cora the Traveling Bookmobile," *The Other Woman* 3, 2 (Autumn 1974): 14–15.
48. See Chapters 4 and 5 for discussion on these struggles. See the discussion on leadership in the second part of this chapter.
49. The origin of "Wages Due" as a slogan comes from a 1940s pottery moneybox shaped like a rolling pin that bears the inscription "If women were paid for all they do, there'd be a lot a wages due." See Gamble, "Great Wages for Housework Debate," 7.
50. For Argentina, see Jo Fisher, *Out of the Shadows: Women, Resistance and Politics in South America* (London: Latin American Bureau, 1993). The information on the groups in Mexico and Argentina comes from Silvia Federici, written interview, April 1996.
51. "Indirizzario per la campagna per il salario al lavoro domestico in Italia," in Collettivo internazionale femminista, ed., *Aborto di stato: Strage delle innocenti; A cura del Collettivo internazionale femminista* (Venice: Marsilio, 1976), 87–88. See also Mariarosa Dalla Costa, "Workerism, Feminism, and Some Efforts of the United Nations," *The Commoner*, 2013, http://www.commoner.org.uk/?p=145.
52. I return to the music group Gruppo musicale del Comitato in the second part of this chapter, in the subsection concerning the tools for mobilization.
53. On the history of this group, see Nina Lopez-Jones, "Workers: Introducing the English Collective of Prostitutes," in *Sex Work: Writings by Women in the Sex Industry*, ed. Frédérique Delacoste and Priscilla Alexander, 2nd ed. (San Francisco: Cleis Press, 1998), 271–78.
54. The groups mentioned here certainly do not form an exhaustive list.
55. Personal interview with Silvia Federici, Brooklyn, March 16, 1996.
56. Collectif L'Insoumise, *Le foyer de l'insurrection*, 109n1.
57. On worker internationales, see Annie Kriegel, *Les internationales ouvrières (1864-1943)* (Paris: Presses universitaires de France, "Que sais-je?" collection, 1964), no. 1129. On female and feminist internationals of the late nineteenth and early twentieth centuries, see Leila J. Rupp, *World of Women: The Making of an International Women's Movement* (Princeton, NJ: Princeton University Press,

1997), and Catherine Jacques, "Construire un réseau international: L'exemple du Conseil International des femmes (CIF)," in *Le siècle des féminismes*, ed. Éliane Gubin et al. (Paris: L'Atelier/Éditions ouvrières, 2004), 127–41.

58. I was unable to find traces of good amounts of funding in the documents consulted. During the period from 1972 to 1977, only a few aspects of the Wages for Housework campaign seem to have received state funding. One example is Cora the Bookmobile. (*Agenda-Toronto Conference Wages for Housework*, CWMA, box 624.6.)

59. I have seen only the first newsletter, and I don't know whether the others were published (CWMA, box 624.28). The CWMA also has two issues of the *Wages for Housework Notebook*, 1 and 2, and two issues of *Women in Struggle*, 1 and 2 (CWMA, box 115).

60. The internal documents dealing with organizational politics such as those of the IFC that I was able to find were Power of Women, *The Organisational Perspective of Wages for Housework* (London, mimeo. n.d.) (Silvia Federici Archives); Silvia Federici, *Notes on Organization* (New York Wages for Housework Collective, August 1975) (CWMA, box 624.22); and *Proposal of Principles and Forms of Organization Outline* (n.d.) (CWMA, box 624.1). I would like to thank Silvia Federici for summarizing the latter two documents for me, as numerous successive photocopying operations, made over the years from a poor-quality original print (a Gestetner), had made them almost illegible. See also Comitato Triveneto Wages for Housework Committee, "A Long Week-End of Struggle," *Women in Struggle* 3, "Italy Now" (1975) (CWMA, box 115).

61. At this time, the word "propaganda" was widely used by leftist groups in general. It was also used for the Wages for Housework campaign. Here, I have replaced this word (heavily connoted today and also obsolete) with "promotion," "information," and "distribution," which seem to me to reflect more accurately the orientation that was intended for the campaign.

62. The two albums were *Canti di Donne in Lotta* (1975) and *Amore e Potere: Il Canzoniere Femminista* (1977); readers may access the song "Noi donne" on YouTube, which will link to other songs by the group: http://www.youtube.com/watch?v=tBalLPqLazo. Several tunes may also be found on the website of Il Deposito: www.ildeposito.org/archivio/canti/canzonedistrada.

63. The brochure *Wages for Housework International Conference Song Book* (Toronto 1975), containing the lyrics to Boo Watson's songs, was distributed at the Toronto IFC conference in October 1975 (CWMA, box 115).

64. Théâtre des cuisines, *Môman travaille pas, a trop d'ouvrage* (Montreal: Remue-ménage, 1976). See Chapter 6.

65. Written interview with Silvia Federici, February 1996 (our translation).

66. On the Bookmobile, see the subsection "The Post-Symposium Period and the Formation of the Network" in this chapter.

67. Le Comitato Triveneto (Committee of the Three Venices) combined Wages for Housework groups from three regions of northern Italy: Venezia, Venezia Giulia, and Trentino–South Tyrol). The committee took over from the Lotta Femminista, which dissolved in 1973.

68. A report on these days was produced several months later: Comitato Triveneto per il Salario al Lavoro Domestico, "8, 9, 10 marzo '74. Un lungo week-end di lotta," in *8 marzo 1974: Giornta internazionale di lotta delle donne; A cura del Collettivo internazionale femminista* (Venice and Padua: Marsilio, 1975), 25–41. An English

translation, "A Long Week-End of Struggle," was published in *Women in Struggle* 3, "Italy Now" (CWMA, box 115).

69. The decision was made during one of the IFC international conferences, held in Montreal in February 1975. See the section on international conferences below.

70. See Toronto Wages for Housework Committee, "Introduction," in *Women Speak Out: May Day Rally Toronto*, ed. Wages for Housework (Toronto: Amazon Press, 1975), 2.

71. Judy Ramirez, "Opening Remarks," in Wages for Housework, *Women Speak Out*, 5.

72. The leaflet distributed by the Los Angeles group, "Sisters: Why March?" was reproduced in *Women Speak Out*, 38–39. See also "Sisters: Why March?" in *All Work and No Pay: Women, Housework, and the Wages Due*, ed. Wendy Edmond and Suzie Fleming (London/Bristol: Power of Women Collective/Falling Wall Press, 1975), 123–24.

73. In the "Opening Remarks" to Wages for Housework, *Women Speak Out*, 2, Judy Ramirez gives an idea of how the day was organized: "For the 15 of us in Toronto Wages for Housework Committee, it meant an incessant flow of activity. We rented a small office in the attic of a women's centre, and each of us contributed a minimum of one day's pay per month to meet expenses. By stealing time away from housework, paid work, and 'leisure' hours, we each worked as hard as our resources allowed, discovering all sorts of 'hidden' skills and talents."

74. "Two weeks before the rally, there was a full-page article on the first page of the 'Women's Section' in the *Toronto Star* (cir. 750,000) titled 'Should Housewives be Paid?' It presented the Committee's position and spoke about our rally and the international network. For the next three days, the telephone in our office rang constantly." "May Day in Toronto," *Wages for Housework International Network Newsletter*, 1975: 10 (CWMA, box 624.28).

75. Unfortunately, the video has not been found.

76. *Wages for Housework International Network Newsletter*, 1975: 10.

77. Toronto Wages for Housework Committee, "Introduction," 3.

78. See "Wages for Housework Demonstrations," *Power of Women* 1, 4 (Summer 1975): 10.

79. See "Bristol Leaflet: A Woman's Work Is Never Done," in Wages for Housework, *Women Speak Out*, 35.

80. Suzie Fleming, "Wages for Housework Demonstrations," *Power of Women* 1, 4 (Summer 1975): 10.

81. "1 magio femminista in Italia," *Le operaie della casa*, no. o bis (November 1975–February 1976): 5.

82. See Chapters 4 and 5.

83. Diana E.H. Russell and Nicole Van de Ven, eds., *Crimes against Women: Proceedings of the International Tribunal* (East Palo Alto: Frog in the Well, 1984 [first published 1976]), 199. The resolution was signed by the following groups: Comitato Triveneto per il Salario al Lavoro Domestico; Coordinamento Emiliano per il Salario al Lavoro Domestico; Wages for Housework Committee, Toronto, Canada; Wages for Housework Committee, New York, USA; Power of Women Wages for Housework Campaign, London, Great Britain. After verification, the Collectif L'Insoumise of Geneva does not seem to have participated in the tribunal (as the wording of the resolution seems to indicate). The testimonials of Wages for Housework groups are found on the following pages: Mestre, 87–88; Ferrara, 34–37; unspecified Italian Wages for Housework groups, 198–99; Canada (letter to the tribunal), 88; Wages Due Lesbians London, 43–45. I return to the

content of the testimonial by the Ferrara group in Chapter 4, in the section on "Denunciations of medical practices." The quote "almost unanimously" comes from Giovanna Franca Dalla Costa, *The Work of Love*, 118n13.

84. Federici, *Notes on Organization*, 7.

85. This section on international conferences is based on the documentation that I was able to gather on each one at the Canadian Women's Movement Archives and in the personal archives of various people. This documentation was very unequal in quantity from one conference to the next, and fragmentary in each case, as no full account has been found. I have therefore used conference agendas, exchanges of letters, and internal documents that discussed one or another of these conferences in passing to reconstruct certain debates that took place at the conferences. Under the circumstances, I engaged with what I was able to understand and what caught my interest, the latter being motivated by the pertinence of the issues raised and what we can take from them today, at least from my point of view. See CWMA, boxes 624.4, 624.6 to 624.10. For the New York conference, I consulted the personal archives of Silvia Federici. Women who attended these conferences and participated in the discussions may, of course, have different perspectives.

86. Toronto Wages for Housework Committee, "Wages for Housework: Questions and Answers," *The Activist* 15, 1–2 (1975): 23. Wages for Housework Group II-Toronto, *Herstory*, 1974 (written for the New York international conference, October 1974), mimeo (CWMA, box 115). This mixed-sex political group, New Tendency, was in the workerist trend ("Workers' Autonomy Perspective") in Ontario. For the workerist trend, see Chapter 2, note 7.

87. Wages for Housework Collective (Group 2), *Statement on Political Differences with Wages for Housework Group 1* (n.d., written after the New York conference of October 1974 and before the Montreal conference of February 1975) (CWMA, box 624.2).

88. Only the interpretation of Group 2 is described here. I was unable to find documents showing Group 1's interpretation of these disagreements.

89. Stephanie Storey, "Housework: The Question Here Is Wages ...," *Montreal Gazette*, February 18, 1975, 42.

90. Susan Wheeler, of the Montreal group, later said in a network letter, "Where else can [the debate on the wages] take place if not during our conferences? To insist ... that the only discussion we need to engage in during conferences is organizational is to ignore the fact that many, if not most of us, want something more." Susan Wheeler, "To Everyone in the Wages for Housework Network," letter dated July 1, 1975 (Silvia Federici Archives).

91. This is the aforementioned *Statement of Political Differences with Wages for Housework Group 1*. Group 1, meanwhile, had not produced such a document at the time, which many of the groups in the network regretted.

92. The Montreal group noted, "Divergent tendencies which were buried at the conference represent differences in emphasis – for example, differences in the extent to which one emphasizes the non-cash aspects of the struggle in propagandizing, as well as differences in the extent to which one sees the revolutionary impact of the perspective as flowing automatically from the cash demand. These are the different tendencies, which should be discussed at an international conference. They are tendencies which are inherent in the perspective itself." Montreal Power of Women Collective, *To All Wages for Housework Groups Present at the February Conference in Montreal 1975*, mimeo, April 1975, 3 (CWMA, box 624.8).

93. Letter from Silvia Federici to participants, written after the Montreal conference, May 17, 1975, beginning with "Dear Sisters" (Silvia Federici Archives).

94. According to Susan Wheeler of the Montreal Power of Women Collective, to the question "What is the nature of the network that we will build?" she answered, "We oppose the authoritarian direction the network is taking." Susan Wheeler, "To Everyone in the Wages for Housework Network," letter dated July 1, 1975 (Silvia Federici Archives).

95. Notably the one written by Ruth Hall, of the London Group, *Why We Expelled Toronto Wages for Housework Group 1: Notes on the First Day of the Montreal Conference, Feb, 1975*. Some of the texts in this debate can be found at the Canadian Women's Movement Archives (boxes 115, 624.2, and 624.8). It is from these texts, added to those from Nicole Lacelle's and Silvia Federici's personal archives, that I was able to reconstruct the content of the debates that took place at the Montreal conference. Once again, I note that people who were present at the debate (which I was not) might have a different version.

96. Toronto Wages for Housework Committee, *Statement RE: Montreal Power of Women Collective*, n.d. (probably September 1975), mimeo (CWMA, box 625.25). The Montreal group likely dissolved soon after.

97. Federici, *Notes on Organization*, 9.

98. Ibid.

99. Ellen Agger, "Toronto: The Toronto Wages for Housework Committee," *Wages for Housework International Network Newsletter*, mimeo, n.d. (probably summer 1975), 6 (CWMA, box 624.28). Other Wages Due Lesbians groups existed in the network; those in London and Toronto were, however, the most active during the period under study here.

100. Ruth Hall, "Lesbianisme et pouvoir," in Collectif L'Insoumise, *Le foyer de l'insurrection*, 109 (our translation). This is a translation into French by Collectif L'Insoumise of a mimeographed text, *Lesbianism and Power*, London, Power of Women Collective, 1975.

101. Ibid. (our translation). See the preceding chapter for the broad outline of the group's theoretical position.

102. According to the archival documents consulted concerning this conference, two texts on the subject seem to have been presented: Francie Wyland, *Lesbian Separatism VS Wages for Housework*, mimeo (1975), and Judy Quinlan, *Presentation on Autonomy from Toronto Conference* (1975) (CWMA, box 625.26). The question of separatism seems to have been a litigious point that I was not able to sort out.

103. Heather Stirling, "Conference Explores Lesbian Autonomy," *The Body Politic* (September 1976). Reprinted in *The Other Woman* 4, 5 (1976): 9. For contrasting reactions that Wages Due Lesbians raised among activists in the Toronto lesbian movement, see Becki L. Ross, *The House That Jill Built: A Lesbian Nation in Formation* (Toronto: University of Toronto Press, 1995), 54.

104. From the mimeographed statement, without apparent title, that began with the sentence "Wages for housework is the feminist perspective" (Silvia Federici Archives).

105. In reality, the "Network List as of October 1975," which constituted the list of invitees to the Toronto conference, contained the names of fifty-nine women who were members of the network's groups. To these members were added twenty "observers" to the conference. The Black Feminist Group and the Network Lesbians were identified as such. The latter group comprised six women, including two observers. "Network List as of October 1975," mimeo (CWMA, box 115).

The *Star* quotation is from "Women Plotting to Gain Wages for Housewives," *Toronto Star*, October 1818, 1975.

106. This was the case for African American sympathizers from the New York group and sympathizers from francophone Quebec.

107. Regarding the May Day rally, the "Street Events" subsection earlier in this chapter deals with this example of concerted action. Also Wages for Housework, *Women Speak Out: May Day Rally Toronto*.

108. *Wages for Housework International Conference Song Book, Words and Music by Boo Watson, Toronto '75* (Silvia Federici Archives). For lyrics to the song "The Housewive's Lament, see Figure 3.8.

109. Regarding the resources item: the various elements that were to be discussed give an indication of how meagre the funding resources were to support a large-scale activist movement such as the IFC: "Organizational claim to monies from speaking, media, sale of literature, etc.; state funding for certain aspects of the campaign, e.g. Toronto Bookmobile; generating funds within the Network e.g. how do individual groups support their various initiatives?; general fundraising outside the Network and the coverage of expenses for those who tour, etc." *Agenda-Toronto Conference Wages for Housework Network* (CWMA, box 624.6).

110. The program listed presentations by Wages Due Lesbians and Silvia Federici. Part of Federici's presentation, with the title "Why Sexuality Is Work," is reproduced in Silvia Federici, *Revolution at Point Zero: Housework, Reproduction, and Feminist Struggle* (Oakland, CA: PM Press; Brooklyn: Common Notions and Autonomedia, 2012), 23–27.

111. A document, *Division of Labour Around October Conference*, gives a list of tasks to be performed for the conference (let's not forget there was no Internet in 1975!) and the names of the persons assigned to each of them. Fourteen tasks are identified: "Meeting Place. Food. Billets. Typing. Communication with network (agenda and notice of conference, second mailing of details). Preparation of materials (maps, directions, eating places). Daycare. Making flyer for public meeting. Media. Conference organizer/manager. Chairpeople for workshops. Registration at conference. Book table at conference. Research, research, research ..."This last was probably a search for funding (CWMA, box 624.3).

112. Personal interview with Silvia Federici, Brooklyn, March 16, 1996 (our translation).

113. The proposed agenda for the conference indicated that it would be held on April 9, 10, and 11, 1977; however, press coverage indicates that the dates were April 15, 16, and 17.

114. This was evidenced in a press release signed "International Wages for Housework Campaign" appearing in the *Wages for Housework Campaign Bulletin* 3, 1 (Summer-Fall 1978): 1. A special newsletter published by the Power of Women group in London on Mother's Day of 1978, *Mother's Money*, was published under the auspices of the International Wages for Housework Campaign. The last page listed the "Main Campaign Addresses." These were Black Women for Wages for Housework in Brooklyn and England, the London Wages for Housework Committee, the Toronto Wages for Housework Committee, and Wages Due Lesbians in England, Canada, San Francisco, and Philadelphia. Also mentioned were the addresses of the Wages for Housework groups in other American cities: Boston, Chicago, Cleveland, Los Angeles, Philadelphia, and San Francisco. One would conclude from this that the network, now called the International Wages for Housework Campaign, was composed of these groups. *Mother's Money*, from which this list is drawn, is in the CWMA, box 624.18.

115. *Proposed Agenda: April 9, 10, and 11, 1977* (CWMA, box 624.9). This is the only trace of this conference that I was able to find, aside from the press coverage.

116. Peter Gorner, "Prostitutes and Housewives Unite, Forming a Surprising Sisterhood," *Chicago Tribune*, April 17, 1977. For details on the network's support for the sex workers' struggle, see Chapter 5.

117. Toronto Wages for Housework Committee, *To the Women in the Wages for Housework Network in England, Australia, New Zealand, New York, Boston, Cleveland, Oberlin, Philadelphia, Chicago, San Diego, San Francisco and Los Angeles*, April 1979 (CWMA, box 624.10).

Overview to Part 2

1. Mariarosa Dalla Costa, "Quartiere, scuola e fabbrica dal punto di vista della donna," *L'Offensiva: Quaderni di Lotta Feminista* 1 (Turin, Musolini, 1972), 27 and 29. English translation: "Community, School and Factory from the Woman's Point of View," mimeo, 6 and 9 (Archives Louise Toupin).

2. Ibid., 5–6.

3. Silvia Federici and Nicole Cox, "Counterplanning from the Kitchen," in *From Feminism to Liberation*, ed. Edith Hoshino Altbach (Cambridge, MA: Schenkman, 1980 [first published 1975]), 275.

4. Mireille Neptune Anglade, *L'autre moitié du développement: À propos du travail des femmes en Haïti* (Port-au-Prince and Montreal: Éditions des Alizés and ERCE, 1986), 15 (our translation). Neptune Anglade died in Port-au-Prince during the earthquake in Haiti on January 12, 2010.

5. Cox and Federici, "Counterplanning from the Kitchen," 282–83.

6. Lotta Feminista (Modena), "Émilie: services sociaux," in Collectif L'Insoumise, *Le foyer de l'insurrection: Textes sur le salaire pour le travail ménager* (Geneva: Collectif L'Insoumise, 1977 [text first appeared in 1974]), 21 (our translation).

7. A word on the terms used in this book in this regard. The term most often used by Wages for Housework activists – in English, French, Italian, and German – to qualify women's invisible work was "housework" (or *travail ménager*, *lavoro domestico*, or *hausarbeit*), which encompassed, as we have seen, much more than material tasks. I also will use the term "housework" when I describe the thoughts expressed by activists or analyze their thought. For purposes of analysis, and to distinguish and characterize the invisible work of women in and outside the home, I will use, at certain times, the terms "private reproductive work," when it is a question of women's invisible work at home and its conditions of practice, and "public reproductive work," when it is a question of women's invisible work outside the home – in the waged workplace or in the community. I borrow this analytic terminology from Evelyn Nakano Glenn, "From Servitude to Social Work: Historical Continuities in the Racial Division of Paid Reproduction of Labor," *Signs* 18, 1 (1992): 1–43.

8. The term "intersectionality" is now commonly used, especially in feminist studies, to signify that the oppression of women is situated at the intersection of different relations of oppression, such as gender, "race," social class, ethnic origin, sexualities, and religion.

9. This is the translation of the title of a song "Le Operaie del Marciapiede," taken from *Amore e Potere: Canzioniere Femminista*, May 1977, by the music group of the Wages for Housework Committee in Padua. See Figure 3.9.

Chapter 4: Mobilizations around Women's Invisible Work in the Home

1. See the section "Feminist Forebears of Wages for Housework" at the end of Chapter 1.
2. Suzie Fleming, "Family Allowance: The Women's Money," in *All Work and No Pay: Women, Housework, and the Wages Due*, ed. Wendy Edmond and Suzie Fleming (London/Bristol: Power of Women Collective/Falling Wall Press, 1975), 92. About the allowance amounts when the struggle began, Fleming wrote, "In 1972, Family Allowance stood at 90 p [CAD1.80] for the second child, £1 [CAD2.00] each for the third and subsequent children [per week]. These rates were relative to the cost of living much lower than the 1945 rates, and were also subject to tax." Suzie Fleming, "Eleanor Rathbone: Spokeswoman for a Movement," in Eleanor Rathbone, *The Disinherited Family* (Bristol: Falling Wall Press, 1986 [first published 1924]), 117–18n297.
3. See "Hands Off the Family Allowance," *Wages for Housework Campaign Bulletin* 1, 1 (July 1976): 1–3.
4. I will summarize the following texts:
   Texts by the English group:
   Fleming, "Family Allowance," 89–92; Suzie Fleming, *The Family Allowance under Attack* (Bristol: Falling Wall Press and the Power of Women Collective, 1973); Suzie Fleming, "All Women Are Housewives," *The Activist* 15, 2 (1975): 27–31; Selma James, "The Family Allowance Campaign: Tactic and Strategy," in *Women in Struggle* I (1975), 17–21 (mimeographed publication of the IFC) (CWMA, box 115).
   Texts by the Toronto groups:
   "Editorial: Why a Campaign for Wages for Housework?" *Wages for Housework Campaign Bulletin* 1, 1 (July 1976): 3; The Wages for Housework Campaign of Canada (1977), *In Defense of the Family Allowance: Hands Off the Family Allowance*, a brief presented to the Hon. Marc Lalonde, Minister of National Health and Welfare (CWMA, box 625.9); Wages Due Lesbians, *Lesbians Join the Family Allowance Protest 1976*, mimeo (CWMA, box 625.9); Wages Due Collective, Ellen Agger, *Speech Given on March 11th at the Coalition against Cutbacks Rally, University of Toronto 1976*, mimeo (CWMA, box 625.36).
5. Fleming, "Family Allowance," 90.
6. Fleming, *Family Allowance under Attack*, 2.
7. Fleming, "Family Allowance," 91.
8. Fleming, "All Women Are Housewives," 27.
9. Fleming, *Family Allowance under Attack*, 12.
10. James, "Family Allowance Campaign," 21.
11. The Wages for Housework Campaign of Canada (1977), *In Defense of the Family Allowance*, 11.
12. Ibid., 3.
13. Ibid., 11. To gauge the difference between the perspective of the Wages for Housework Committees and that of mainstream feminism in Canada, see Wendy McKeen, "The Wages for Housework Campaign: Its Contribution to Feminist Politics in the Area of Social Welfare in Canada," *Canadian Review of Social Policy/Revue canadienne de politique sociale* 33 (1994): 21–43; see, in particular, 32, 33. McKeen acknowledges, "Wages for Housework activists were ahead of their time in their understanding of the implications of the social welfare system for women ... Moreover, it made an important contribution to feminist politics in the field of social welfare policy" (36, 37).

14. "Address to March 11 Cut-Backs Rally by Ellen Agger," *Body Politic* (June 1976): 6.

15. Ibid.

16. Lucie Bélanger and Ginette Boyer, "Autonomie financière, reconnaissance économique du travail de maternage et crise de l'État-providence: la lutte de la Coalition des femmes pour les allocations familiales" (master's thesis, Université du Québec à Montréal, 1989), vii (our translation).

17. Wages for Housework groups in England and Canada were not the only ones, among the member groups of the IFC, to support family allowances as a foothold for promoting wages for housework. In September 1973 in Italy, during a government attempt to change family allowances paid to husbands, the national coordinating body, Lotta Femminista, produced a tool for struggle in the form of a four-page journal (a *volantone*), whose central pages were devoted to a denunciation: "Against family allowances, for Wages for Housework." See Lotta Femminista, "Contro gli assegni familiari, per il salario al lavoro domestico," *Lotta Femminista*, single issue (September 1973) (Mariarosa Dalla Costa Archives, deposited at the Padua municipal library; see biblioteca.civica@comune.padova.it).

18. "Out of Our Bathrobes and into the Streets!" *Wages for Housework Campaign Bulletin* 1, 1 (July 1976): 6.

19. Similarly, the Power of Women Collective in London supported the struggle of the "unsupported mothers" who organized in a group called Claimants' Union to demand their right to an independent income, whether or not they lived with a man. See Monica Sjoo, "Married to the State," in Edmond and Fleming, *All Work and No Pay*, 92–97.

20. The Coalition of Labor Union Women, working in the United States for pay equity in the workplace, was formed in 1974. See www.cluw.org.

21. With regard to the struggles of the Mother-Led Union, the following documents were consulted: Frances Gregory, "Mother-Led Union Demonstration," *Wages for Housework International Network Newsletter* (1975): 6–7 (CWMA, box 624.28); Frances Gregory, "Mother-Led Union," in Edmond and Fleming, *All Work and No Pay*, 97–99; Frances Gregory, "The Mother-Led Union," *Power of Women, The Journal of Power of Women Collective* 1, 4 (Summer 1975): 4.

22. Gregory, "Mother-Led Union," 98.

23. With regard to the Welfare Conference of the New York group, the following documents were consulted: *Wages for Housework and Welfare* (1976), conference invitation brochure (Silvia Federici Archives); "The Crisis in New York: Women Organize," *Wages for Housework Campaign Bulletin* 1, 1 (1976): 5; "The US: Organizing for Welfare," *Power of Women: Magazine of the International Wages for Housework Campaign* 5 (1976): 4; "Birth Announcement," *Power of Women: Magazine of the International Wages for Housework Campaign* 5 (1976): 5.

24. "Crisis in New York," 5.

25. The New York group, however, was almost the only one in the feminist movement at the time to think this, according to Silvia Federici, as the movement was instead mobilized by the organization of women in the workplace (written interview with the author, February 1996). In McKeen's view, this remark would also apply to the Canadian feminist movement: "Much Wages for Housework activism took place within the social welfare field – an area neglected at the time by other sectors of the women's movement ... Workforce participation was seen as the key to women's liberation; even with pay, housewifery did not fit the image of the emancipated women." See Wendy McKeen, "Wages for Housework Campaign,"

25, 28. For McKeen's analysis of the complex links between the Toronto Wages for Housework Committee and mainstream feminism, see 26–29.

26. "Crisis in New York," 5.

27. *Come to a Conference Sponsored by The New York Wages for Housework Committee, Saturday, April 24, 10 a.m – 6 p.m.*, conference invitation leaflet, emphasis in original (Silvia Federici Archives).

28. The conference report comes from "The US: Organizing for Welfare," *Power of Women* 5 (1976): 4.

29. "Birth Announcement," *Power of Women* 5 (1976): 5.

30. For more details, see Milwaukee County Welfare Rights Organization, *Welfare Mothers Speak Out* (New York: W.W. Norton, 1972).

31. Margaret Prescod, *Black Women: Bringing It All Back Home* (Bristol: Falling Wall Press, 1980). Margaret Prescod was one of the co-founders of Black Women for Wages for Housework.

32. On the concept of a space of resistance, see bell hooks, "Homeplace: A Site of Resistance," in *Yearning, Race, Gender, and Cultural Politics* (Toronto: Between the Lines, 1990), 41–49. See also Angela Davis, "The Black Women's Role in the Community of Slaves," *Massachusetts Review* 13, 1–2, "Woman: An Issue" (1972): 81–100, http://www.bowdoin.edu/news/events/archives/images/Community%20of%20Slaves.pdf.

33. This aspect is covered in greater detail in Chapter 2. See discussion of a text by Wilmette Brown.

34. Francine Saillant and Françoise Courville, "Des femmes: objets et sujets de l'institution médicale," in *Critique féministe des disciplines V*, ed. Roberta Mura, Groupe de recherche multidisciplinaire féministe, Les Cahiers de recherche du GREMF, Université Laval, 1994, 29 (our translation).

35. See, in Louise Vandelac, *L'Italie au féminisme* (Paris: Tierce, 1978), the essays in the chapters "Avortement: 'Mon utérus m'appartient c'est à moi de décider'" and "Notre santé et notre corps: Des sorcières aux féministes," 37–100. See also, for a more general view of the feminist struggles in Italy during this period, Lucia Chiavola Birnbaum, *Liberazione della donna: Feminism in Italy* (Middletown, CT: Wesleyan University Press, 1986), 79–231.

36. The sources used for the sections below are Lotta Femminista of Padua, "Maternité et avortement," in Mariarosa Dalla Costa and Selma James, *Le pouvoir des femmes et la subversion sociale* (Geneva: Librairie Adversaire, 1973 [text first appeared in 1971]), 135–46; Mariarosa Dalla Costa, *Le operaie della casa: A cura del Collettivo internazionale femminista* (Venice and Padua: Marsilio, 1975), Collettivo internazionale femminista, ed., *Aborto di stato: Strage delle innocenti; A cura del Collettivo internazionale femminista* (Venice: Marsilio, 1976); *Le operaie della casa* 1 (June–July 1976); Silvia Federici, "Introduction à l'édition italienne," in Collectif L'Insoumise, *Le foyer de l'insurrection* (French translation of the Italian edition of *Wages against Housework*) (Geneva: Collective L'Insoumise, 1977 [first published 1975]), 93–97; Gruppo Femminista per il Salario al Lavoro Domestico di Ferrara, *Dietro la normalità del parto: Lotta all'ospedale di Ferrara* (Venice: Marsilio, 1978); Laura Morato, Carla Fabbri, and Mariarosa Dalla Costa, "Rôle du mouvement pour le salaire au travail ménager dans le mouvement féministe italien," in Vandelac, *L'Italie au féminisme*, 143–50; Louise Vandelac, "Les médecins accusent une femme," in Vandelac, *L'Italie au féminisme*, 89–93; Witness 1: Italy, "Brutality Towards Women Giving Birth," in *Crimes against Women: Proceedings of the International Tribunal*, ed. Diana E.H. Russell and Nicole Van de Ven (East Palo

Alto: Frog in the Well, 1984 [first published 1976]), 34–36; New York Wages for Housework Committee, "Forced Sterilization," *Wages for Housework from the Government for All Women* (n.d.) (Silvia Federici Archives); Wages for Housework International newsletter (1975); "Deciding for Our Selves" (three leaflets), in Edmond and Fleming, *All Work and No Pay*, 120–22.

37. Collettivo internazionale femminista, *Aborto di stato*, 43.
38. *Le operaie della casa* 1 (June-July 1976): 4; "The Witches Are Returning," *Power of Women* 5 (1976): 16.
39. Federici, "Introduction à l'édition italienne," 96 (our translation).
40. Ibid., 96–97 (our translation).
41. Power of Women Collective, "To the Readers of the Power of Women Journal," *Wages for Housework International Network Newsletter*, 1975: 1, emphasis in original.
42. "Statement of The Power of Women Collective," *Power of Women* 1, 1 (March-April 1974): 16.
43. Lotta Femminista of Padua, "Maternité et avortement," 138 (our translation).
44. Ibid. (our translation).
45. New York Wages for Housework Committee "Forced Sterilization," *Wages for Housework from the Government for All Women*, n.d., 2 (Silvia Federici Archives); "Forced Sterilizations in Los Angeles & New York," *Power of Women* 1, 5 (1976): 6.
46. Morato, Fabbri, and Dalla Costa, "Rôle du mouvement," 146 (our translation).
47. The struggle is described in Gruppo Femminista per il Salario al Lavoro Domestico di Ferrara, *Dietro la normalità del parto*. For a description of part of this battle, see Vandelac, "Les médecins accusent une femme," 89–93.
48. Gruppo Femminista per il Salario al Lavoro Domestico di Ferrara, *Dietro la normalità del parto*, 89–93. See also Russell and Van de Ven, *Crimes against Women*, 34–36. On IFC groups' participation at the tribunal, see Chapter 3.
49. Russell and Van de Van, *Crimes against Women*, 36.
50. See, in Chapter 3, the section on the Toronto International Wages Due Lesbians Conference, July 24–25, 1976 ("What did organizational autonomy ... mean inside the network?")
51. Wages Due Lesbians, "Lesbians on the Move," *Wages for Housework Campaign Bulletin* 2, 1 (Fall 1977): 2, emphasis in original.
52. Francie Wyland, *Motherhood, Lesbianism, and Child Custody: The Case for Wages for Housework* (Toronto: Wage Due Lesbians, 1976) (CWMA, box 626.23).
53. Issues of *Grapevine* can be found at CWMA, box 626.28. This archive possesses a large amount of documentation produced by Wages Due Lesbians and Lesbian Mothers' Defence Fund. See the eponymous collection, X10-8, series II and III.
54. Becki L. Ross, *The House That Jill Built: A Lesbian Nation in Formation* (Toronto: University of Toronto Press, 1995), 54. Other texts by Wages Due Lesbians members on the subject are listed in Ross's book; see 258n48.

Chapter 5: Mobilizations around Women's Invisible Work outside the Home

1. This reflection comes to me from an exchange on the subject with Nicole Lacelle, to whom I express my gratitude.
2. This account is based mostly on the following documents: Jane Hirschmann, "Organizing on the Second Job," in *All Work and No Pay: Women, Housework, and the Wages Due*, ed. Wendy Edmond and Suzie Fleming (London/Bristol: Power

of Women Collective/Falling Wall Press, 1975), 106–15; "Maimonides: Against Women's Unpaid Work," *Power of Women* 1, 4 (Summer 1975): 12.

3. Quoted in Wendy Schuman, "Brooklyn Women Seek Wages for Housework," *New York Times,* January 11, 1976.

4. Hirschmann, "Organizing on the Second Job," 109.

5. Quoted in Schuman, "Brooklyn Women."

6. Hirschmann, "Organizing on the Second Job," 112.

7. On this subject, see Joan Acker, *Doing Comparable Worth: Gender, Class, and Pay Equity* (Philadelphia: Temple University Press, 1989); Heidi Hartmann, ed., *Comparable Worth: New Directions for Research* (Washington, DC: National Academy Press, 1985); Marie-Claire Dumas and Francine Mayer, eds., *Les femmes et l'équité salariale: Un pouvoir à gagner* (Montreal: Remue-ménage, 1989).

8. This account is based on the following documentation: Lotta Femminista de Modène, "La lutte des ouvrières de l'usine Solari à Udine," in Collectif L'Insoumise, *Le foyer de l'insurrection* (Geneva: Collective L'Insoumise, 1977 [text first appeared in 1975]), 15–17. See also Anna Gottardo, "Histoire d'une lutte de femmes en usine," in Vandelac, *L'Italie au féminisme,* 96–100; "All Our Time Is Working Time," *Power of Women* 1, 5 (1976): 11–13; "Tutto il nostro tempo di vita è sempre tempo di lavoro," *Le operaie della casa,* special issue, May 1, 1975: 11–12.

9. Gottardo, "Histoire," 97 (our translation).

10. Quoted in Lotta Femminista de Modène, "La lutte des ouvrières," 16, and Gottardo, "Histoire," 98 (our translation).

11. Gottardo, "Histoire," 99–100 (our translation).

12. Quoted in Lotta Femminista de Modène, "La lutte des ouvrières," 17 (our translation).

13. Gottardo, "Histoire," 98 (our translation).

14. This section is based on the following documentation: "This Is Nursing: Introduction to a Struggle," in Edmond and Fleming, *All Work and No Pay,* 61–63; Power of Women Collective (1974), "The Home in the Hospital," in Edmond and Fleming, *All Work and No Pay,* 69–88; Suzie Fleming, "All Women Are Housewives," *The Activist* 15, 1–2 (1975): 27–31.

15. "This Is Nursing," 63.

16. Fleming, "All Women Are Housewives," 28.

17. See Power of Women Collective, "The Home in the Hospital," in Edmond and Fleming, *All Work and No Pay,* 69–88.

18. Ibid., 73.

19. Ibid., 81–82.

20. Ibid., 84.

21. Ibid., 86.

22. Ibid., emphasis in original.

23. Ibid., 88.

24. The information on this mobilization comes from the following documents: Waitresses' Action Committee, *Brief on the Minimum Wage and a "Tip Differential" to Ontario Ministry of Labour, Ontario Ministry of Industry and Tourism,* mimeo, 1977; Waitresses' Action Committee, *Press Release ... Report: Meeting with the Ministry of Labour on the Minimum Wage,* June 29, 1977; also a petition by the Waitresses' Action Committee to support their *Brief on The Minimum Wage and a "Tip Differential,"* "Money for Waitresses Is Money for All Women!"(n.d.), and a letter of April 17, 1977, reporting on the result of this appeal and the support expressed. All of these documents are found in the CWMA, box 116

(Wages for Housework and Waitresses' Action Committee) and box 624.30. The petition "Money for Waitresses Is Money for All Women" is in box 625.4. Other documents consulted: Ellen Agger, "Smile Honey," in *Women Speak Out: May Day Rally Toronto*, ed. Wages for Housework (Toronto: Amazon Press, 1975), 25–27, and Ellen Agger, "Tipping the Wage Scale," *Wage for Housework Campaign Bulletin* 2, 1 (Fall 1977): 4.

25. "Money for Waitresses Is Money for All Women!" (petition).

26. The list of endorsing and supporting groups appears on page 2 of the letter of April 17, 1977, reporting on the result of the appeal of the Waitresses' Action Committee, and the support expressed (CWMA, box 116).

27. Waitresses' Action Committee, *Brief on the Minimum Wage*.

28. See note 7.

29. Ellen Agger, "Smile Honey," 25, 26, 27.

30. As mentioned, the expression "sidewalk workers" is the translation of an expression (*le operaie del marciapiede*) in a song by the Gruppo musicale del Comitato per il salario al lavoro domestico di Padova (Music Group of the Wages for Housework Committee of Padua). It is taken from the group's album, *Amore e Potere: Canzoniere Femminista*, released in May 1977. The lyrics were translated into French in Vandelac, *L'Italie au féminisme*, 164. See Figure 3.9. The song can be heard online at www.youtube.com/watch?v=mWLeWqsrmXY. Other songs from the group's albums can also be found on YouTube.

31. Mariarosa Dalla Costa, "Workerism, Feminism, and Some Efforts of The United Nations," *The Commoner* 15 (2012), www.commoner.org.uk/?p=145.

32. Among the early analyses of prostitution performed by the Wages for Housework movement, I must mention the one by Maria Pia Turri, of the Wages for Housework Committee of Padua, "La mogli di tutti," *Il Personale è politico: Quaderni di Lotta Femminista* 2 (1973): 51–60. See also the analysis by Giovanna Franca Dalla Costa in *Un lavoro d'amore: La violenza fisica componente essenziale del "trattamento" maschile nei confronti delle donne* (Rome: Edizioni delle donne, 1978), an overview of which appears in Chapter 2. Finally, I should mention a study that I could not include here, as it was released after the end of the IFC (in 1981): Leopoldina Fortunati, *The Arcane of Reproduction: Housework, Prostitution, Labor and Capital* (Brooklyn: Autonomedia, 1995).

33. See Lilian Mathieu, "Une mobilisation improbable: l'occupation de l'église Saint-Nizier par les prostituées lyonnaises," in *Luttes XXX: Inspirations du mouvement des travailleuses du sexe*, ed. Maria Nengeh Mensah, Claire Thiboutot, and Louise Toupin (Montreal: Remue-ménage, 2011 [text first published in 1999]), 72–80.

34. In 1975, the English Collective of Prostitutes was formed as an autonomous group within the Power of Women Collective in London (which became the International Wages for Housework Campaign). The first spokesperson was Selma James. The English Collective of Prostitutes was composed of women who did or did not have experience with sex work. All were equal members, and this caused problems, especially during its participation in the first World Whores Congress, held in Amsterdam in 1985. See Gail Pheterson, ed., *A Vindication of the Rights of Whores* (Seattle: Seal Press, 1989), 36–37. On the history of the group, see Nina Lopez-Jones, "Workers: Introducing the English Collective of Prostitutes," in *Sex Work: Writings by Women in the Sex Industry*, ed. Frédérique Delacoste and Priscilla Alexander, 2nd ed. (San Francisco: Cleis Press, 1998), 271–78.

The information that forms the basis for this section comes in large part from the CWMA, X10-1, series 1, box 116, "Wages for Housework and Prostitutes." Also boxes 624.27 and 625.17.

35. See Chapter 3.

36. Peter Gorner, "Prostitutes and Housewives Unite, Forming a Surprising Sisterhood," *Chicago Tribune*, April 17, 1977; Laura Green, "Prostitutes Win Allies in Economic Bid," *Chicago Sun-Times*, April 18, 1977. The event was widely covered by the Chicago press. (Press coverage is found in the CWMA records, boxes 625.17 and 116.)

37. *Fact Sheet on the Yonge St. Crackdown, Compiled by the Toronto Wages for Housework Committee, 30 November 1977* (CWMA, box 625.17). See also Deborah R. Brock, *Making Work, Making Trouble: Prostitution as a Social Problem* (Toronto: University of Toronto Press, 1998). In chap. 2 of the book, "Campaigns and Moral Panics," 25–43, Brock analyzes these events.

38. Judy Ramirez, "Hookers Fight Back," *Wages for Housework Campaign Bulletin* 2, 1 (Fall 1977): 1.

39. Ellen Agger, "Hookers Organize," *Wages for Housework Campaign Bulletin* 3, 1 (Summer-Fall 1978), 2. On BEAVER, see an article by its founder: Margaret Dwight-Spore, "Speaking Up for Our Sisters: Decriminalization of Prostitution," *Fireweed* 1, 1 (1978): 23–26. At the end of this essay, the address given for BEAVER is that of the Toronto Wages for Housework Committee, a sign of the tight ties between the two groups. Another document indicates that Ramirez participated in the public launch of BEAVER in November 1977 (International Wages for Housework Campaign, *Mothers' Money*, special bulletin, Mother's Day, Spring 1978: 6) (CWMA, box 624.19).

40. Wages for Housework San Francisco and Los Angeles Wages for Housework Committee, *An Attack against Prostitutes Is an Attack on All Women* (CWMA, box 116).

41. Black Women for Wages for Housework (1977), *Money for Prostitutes Is Money for Black Women*, emphasis in original (CWMA, box 116).

A Black Women for Wages for Housework activist from New York was invited by the Collectif des femmes prostituées in Paris to address a crowd gathered during a large gathering at the Salle de la Mutualité on June 16, 1976. Her speech of support for French prostitutes is reproduced in "The State Is the Biggest Pimp," *Power of Women* 5 (1976): 15.

42. Black Women for Wages for Housewives, *Money for Prostitutes Is Money for Black Women*, 4.

43. Wages Due Lesbians – London and Wages Due Lesbians – Toronto, *Supporting Statements by Wages Due Lesbians* (1977) (CWMA, box 116). See also English Collective of Prostitutes, *Supporting Statement by the English Collective of Prostitutes* (1977) (CWMA, box 625.17). On this group, see note 34.

44. Wages Due Lesbians Toronto, *Sex Is Never Free: Lesbians Support Statement for San Francisco (and All) Prostitutes*, 1977 (CWMA, box 116).

45. Ibid.

46. Wages Due Lesbians – London, *Supporting Statements*.

47. Judy Ramirez, "Hookers Fight Back," *Wages for Housework Campaign Bulletin* 2, 1 (Fall 1977): 1.

48. Ibid., emphasis in original.

49. Historically, however, the positions taken by feminists on prostitution in Canada were not as closely aligned as they are now. For a short historical overview of these

290   WAGES FOR HOUSEWORK

positions, particularly starting in the 1980s, see Louise Toupin, "Prostitution: Positions féministes d'hier et d'aujourd'hui," *Le Devoir*, March 31–April 1, 2012, B5, http://www.ledevoir.com/societe/actualites-en-societe/346393/prostitution-positions-feministes-d-hier-et-d-aujourd-hui.

50. See Wages for Housework, "Housewives & Hookers Come Together," *Wages for Housework Campaign Bulletin* 1, 4 (Summer 1977), 1.

51. Gail Pheterson, *The Prostitution Prism* (Amsterdam: Amsterdam University Press, 1996). See also her attempt to establish an "alliance between whores, wives, and dykes": Gail Pheterson, "Alliance between Women: Overcoming Internalized Oppression and Internalized Domination," *Signs: Journal of Women in Culture and Society* 12, 1 (Autumn 1986): 146–60. See Gail Pheterson, ed., *A Vindication of the Rights of Whores* (Seattle, WA: Seal Press, 1989).

52. On the notion of social factory, see the first section of Chapter 2.

53. Silvia Federici, *Wages for Housework and the Crisis*, mimeo, 1975, 7 (Silvia Federici Archives). This was the text of the opening speech at the Montreal conference of the IFC, February 21, 1975. See Chapter 3.

54. Lotta Femminista (Modena), "Émilie: services sociaux," in Collectif L'Insoumise, *Le foyer de l'insurrection*, 18–40 (text first appeared in 1974).

55. The basic documentation for this section comes from the Canadian Women's Movement Archives, Canadian Women's Movement Archives Collection, box 116, and Wages for Housework, Wages Due Lesbians and Lesbian Mothers' Defense Fund, X10-8, series 1, box 624.21. Also box 625.3.

56. "Why an Emergency Occupation at Nellie's?" n.d., mimeo (CWMA, box 624.21).

57. "Many Support Occupation of Women's Hostel: Women at Nellie's Fight for Survival," *Wages for Housework Campaign Bulletin* 1, 2 (Fall 1976): 4.

58. "In Supporting Nellie's, We Support Ourselves," n.d., mimeo (CWMA, box 624.21).

59. *Report on Nellie's Struggle, November 1976*, mimeo (CWMA, boxes 624.21 and 116).

60. Letter from Paula Fainstat to Judith Ramirez, October 27, 1976 (CWMA, box 625.3). Nellie's still exists today as a women's shelter; see http://ckc.toronto foundation.ca/org/nellies-womens-shelter-womens-hostels-inc.

61. Wages Due Lesbians, "Lesbians Struggle at Nellie's Women's Hostel," *Body Politic*, October 1976.

62. Anonymous, *La perspective du salaire ménager*, mimeo, n.d. (our translation) (Archives L'Insoumise).

Chapter 6: Mobilizations by Groups on the Periphery of the Network

1. Back cover of the play *Môman travaille pas, a trop d'ouvrage* by Théâtre des cuisines (Montreal: Remue-ménage, 1976) (our translation).

2. See Chapter 3.

3. In Chapter 3, I give some context that might explain the absence of francophone feminist groups at the Feminist Symposium held at McGill University on June 1–3, 1973. See the section on the North American tour of Mariarosa Dalla Costa and Selma James.

4. The interview was published as "Rencontre avec deux féministes marxistes." It was reprinted in the anthology that reproduced the journal of the Centre des femmes, *Québécoises Deboutte!* See Véronique O'Leary and Louise Toupin, eds., *Québécoises Deboutte!* vol. 2, *Collection complète* (Montreal: Remue-ménage, 1983), 190–203.

5. Théâtre des cuisines, "Manifeste du Théâtre des cuisines (1975)," in *Môman travaille pas*, 4–5 (our translation).

6. Théâtre des cuisines has gone through different stages in its forty years of existence and is still directed by one of its founders, Véronique O'Leary, from the Bas-Saint-Laurent region of Quebec. The company, unique in Quebec, enhances its approach of creative research in the spirit of its original tradition: art in and with the community; production of interdisciplinary collective creations, informed by the art of the mask and the clown; "and its capacity to divert our fear of the 'authorities'" adds O'Leary (our translation). The company very often performs before publics that have little access to theatre. Théâtre des cuisines also trains new generations of multidisciplinary artists and offers workshops in various urban and rural communities. For its history and current projects, see www.theatredescuisines.org.

7. Théâtre des cuisines, "Manifeste," 4 (our translation).

8. O'Leary remembers that certain feminists, during the discussions that followed the performances, actually began to cry when Wages for Housework was mentioned. (Phone conversation, May 5, 2013.)

9. Théâtre des cuisines, "Manifeste," 9 (our translation). The play was the inaugural publication of Éditions du remue-ménage, launched on March 8, 1976. Both versions of the play were in the book.

10. See a reminder of the content of this debate in Louise Toupin, "Salaire au travail ménager: L'épouvantail dans le jardin," *La Vie en rose*, special anniversary issue (Montreal: Remue-ménage, 2005): 70–71.

11. The manifesto was read by Sylvie Dupont, at the time a member of the Remue-ménage team. She was later on the team that founded the feminist magazine *La Vie en rose* in 1980 and co-editor-in-chief of the twenty-fifth anniversary issue of the magazine. See *La Vie en rose*, special issue (Montreal: Remue-ménage, 2005). The manifesto is reproduced in Véronique O'Leary and Louise Toupin, eds., *Québécoises Deboutte!* vol. 1, *Une anthologie de textes du Front de libération des femmes (1969-1971) et du Centre des femmes (1972-1975)* (Montreal: Remue-ménage, 1982), 208–12, and in Micheline Dumont and Louise Toupin, eds., *La pensée féministe au Québec: Anthologie, 1900-1985* (Montreal: Remue-ménage, 2003), 471–80. The introductions to the text in each anthology situate it in the context of the time.

12. Several other francophone Quebec feminist initiatives were undertaken with regard to raising awareness of the Wages for Housework movement perspective. In 1977, Éditions du remue-ménage began to distribute the anthology *Le foyer de l'insurrection* (Geneva: Collectif L'Insoumise, 1977), which contained essays from the Wages for Housework movement (translated into French by the Collectif L'Insoumise of Geneva). In addition, in March 1981, excerpts of the main texts on the Wages for Housework perspective (translated by Nicole Lacelle) were published in the feminist magazine *La Vie en rose*. See "Gagner son ciel ou gagner sa vie? Le salaire au travail ménager," special section, *La Vie en rose* (March–May 1981): 13–25.

In the early 1980s, debates on the issue were held in other forums – for example, in 1983, in the women's committee of the Confédération des syndicats nationaux, at the Association féminine d'éducation et d'action sociale, at the Conseil du statut de la femme (Forum des femmes sur l'économie), and in the women's team of the Regroupement pour le socialisme. See Martine D'Amours, "Une hypothèse de lutte qui a fait des petites," *Pour le socialisme* 4 (Spring 1984): 18.

13. Information on the Berlin group was provided to me by Gisela Bock during personal interviews conducted in Fiesole, Italy, on November 5, 1994, and in Montreal on September 1, 1995. These interviews were followed by written interviews in 1996 and 2013. Bock is an internationally known historian and professor emeritus at the Free University of Berlin. She has written numerous works on women's history, including *Women in European History* (Oxford: Blackwell, 2002) and *Geschlechtergeschichten der Neuzeit: Ideen, Politik, Praxis* [Histories of gender in the modern era: Ideas, politics, and practices] (Göttingen: Vandenhoeck & Ruprecht, 2014). The latter is a collection of some of her most significant essays.

14. In East Berlin, Wages for Housework was rejected.

15. For the German translation by Gisela Bock, see Mariarosa Dalla Costa and Selma James, *Die Macht der Frauen und der Umsturz der Gesellschaft* (Berlin: Merve, Verlag, 1973; 3rd ed., 1978), no. 36 of the series Internationale Marxistische Diskussion. Merve, founded 1970, was a neo-Marxist publishing house that translated and published books of the Italian New Left, including those by workerist theoreticians such as Toni Negri, Mario Tronti, and Sergio Bologna. For the various IFC texts, see Gisela Erler, ed., *Frauen in der Offensive: Lohn für die Hausarbeit oder; Auch Berufstätigkeit macht nicht frei*, preface by Gisela Erler, trans. Gisela Erler and Gina Gierth (Munich: Trikont, 1974). The book contained texts by the Power of Women Collective of London, Lotta Femminista of Italy – including the IFC manifesto of 1972 – and Brigitte Galtier of Paris. Most of the texts were translated from "L'Offensiva" and "Il Personale è Politico": *Quaderni di Lotta Femminista* 1 and 2 (Turin: Musolini, 1972 and 1973).

16. On this subject, Bock told me, "We were able to obtain a half-year university teaching position for Priscilla Allen of the Power of Women Collective in London; she was a specialist in English literary studies." Allen was the co-author of the *Wages for Housework Notebook*, one of the IFC publications. (For details on IFC publications, see the second part of Chapter 3.) Allen collaborated with the Berlin group's Wages for Housework campaign.

17. Brown wrote, among other works, *The Autonomy of Black Lesbian Women* (1976). See Chapter 2 for a synthesis of that essay.

18. The Sommeruniversität für Frauen, or Summer Universities for Women, consisted of courses, projects, and events organized outside of the regular cycle of the school year. The holding of such events in 1976 and 1977 at the Free University of Berlin constituted one of the most significant activities of the women's movement in Germany in those years. After several months of intensive preparations, the week of activities brought together almost two thousand people in 1976 and four thousand in 1977 to study and discuss the situation of women and to critique the traditional university. These events attracted women from Berlin and elsewhere, students, employees, unemployed women, university lecturers (except professors, as there were almost no women in those positions at the time) and non-academics; thus, an intersection between the non-academic women's movement and the very beginnings of a movement of university feminist studies. After 1977, there were other summer universities in Berlin, and in other university cities in Germany.

19. Gisela Bock and Barbara Duden, "Arbeit aus Liebe – Liebe as Arbeit: Zur Entstehung der Hausarbeit im Kapitalismus," in *Frauen und Wissenschaft: Beiträge zur Berliner Sommeruniversität für Frauen, Juli 1976* (Berlin: Courage Verlag, 1977), 118–99. Excerpts were translated into English as "Labor of Love – Love as Labor: On the Genesis of Housework in Capitalism," in *From Feminism to Liberation*, rev. ed., ed. Edith Hoshino Altbach (Cambridge, MA: Schenkman,

1980), 153–92. The complete essay was recently put online as part of a project on the women's liberation movement funded by the European Union: www.fragen. nu/atria/fragen/FFBI-3-921710-006.pdf#search=country:Germany.

20. For example, Ruth Hall (Wages Due Lesbians, England), Margaret Prescod-Roberts (Black Women for Wages for Housework), and Polda Fortunati (Italy); and, from the Berlin group, Barbara Duden, Mona Glökler, Pieke Biermann. See *Frauen als bezahlte und unbezahlte Arbeitskräfte. Beiträge zur 2. Berliner Sommeruniversität für Frauen*, October 1977 (Berlin: Dokumentationsgruppe der Sommeruniversität e.V., 1978), 169–218; also, the summary by Gisela Bock, "Lohn für Hausarbeit – Frauenkämpfe und feministische Strategie" (206–14), excerpts of which were published in an English-language version: Gisela Bock, "Wages for Housework as a Perspective of the Women's Movement," in *German Feminism: Readings in Politics and Literature*, ed. Edith Hoshino Altbach (Albany: New York State University Press, 1984 [first published 1979]), 246–50. In Altbach's book, Bock's essay was followed by a vehement attack against Wages for Housework by Alice Schwarzer, "A Salary for Housewives?" (251–53), which had first been published in 1977.

21. Voices from the IFC also made themselves heard in the feminist magazine *Courage* (March 15, 1977): 20–29: Selma James, on single mothers (lecture in Bremen); anonymous, on married mothers; Pieke Biermann, on single women; speech by Mary Brant given at the prostitutes' meeting in Paris in June 1976; anonymous, on lesbians for Wages for Housework; Cornelia Mansfeld, Arbeitgeber Staat; the international campaign. The same issue of *Courage* included Gisela Bock and Pieke Biermann, "Auch in Deutschland gibt es jetzt eine Kampagne um Lohn für Hausarbeit vom Staat für alle Frauen" (16–21). Also, in 1977, Pieke Biermann, *Das Herz der Familie: Materialien für eine internationale feministische Strategie* (Berlin: Selbstverlag); and Pieke Biermann, *Wir sind Frauen wie andere auch! Prostituierte und ihre Kämpfe* (Reinbek: Rowohlt, 1980).

22. Quotations in the sidebar are drawn from the English translation: "Labor of Love – Love as Labor: On the Genesis of Housework in Capitalism," in *From Feminism to Liberation*, rev. ed., ed. Edith Hoshino Altbach (Cambridge, MA: Schenkman, 1980), 153–92.

23. Bock herself was interested in the international dimension of women's history and historiography. She was a founding member of the International Federation for Research in Women's History (1987).

24. See the second part of Chapter 3 on the end of the IFC.

25. Personal interview by email, October 3, 2013 (our translation).

26. The material in this section is drawn in part from an interview I conducted with three activists from the Collectif L'Insoumise (Viviane Luisier, Alda De Giorgi, and Suzanne Lerch), in Geneva, November 23, 1994. The material was updated in July, August, and September, 2013 by me and Alda De Giorgi, in close collaboration with the Insoumises. I also consulted the following documents:

- Collectif L'Insoumise, *Le foyer de l'insurrection: Textes sur le salaire pour le travail ménager* (Geneva: Collectif L'Insoumise, 1977).
- Several issues of the journal *L'Insoumise*. See the bibliography.
- *De mères en filles* (1973), published in the context of the MLF, as the "Femmes mères et ménagères" collective.
- *Journal du Congrès des mauvaises mères*, May 1979.
- *Journal de l'occupation* (documenting the occupation of the Centre-femmes), May 1976.

- *Avortement: La lutte continue; Feuille de l'occupation,* occupation leaflet.
- *Nous, du collectif pour le salaire ménager* (1977), mimeo.
- Groupe de travail Seveso (Paulette, Joséphine, Lili-Marlène, Florette, Emma, Colette, Zoé), *Seveso est partout* (Geneva: Groupe de travail Seveso, 1976).
- *L'échappée belle: Femmes face aux lois, aux flics, aux juges: Manuel pratique* (1979).
- *La perspective du salaire ménager* (n.d.), mimeo.

Aside from *Le foyer de l'insurrection,* all of the documents come from the activists' personal archives. I extend my warmest thanks to them. The archives of the Collectif L'Insoumise are now held in the Archives contestataires and are inventoried in the Fonds MLF de Genève, www.archivesmlf.ch.

27. Unless specified otherwise, quotations in this subsection are drawn from a personal communication from Alda e Giorgi to the author, email July 18, 2013 (our translation).

28. The book, edited by Marie-Madeline Grounauer and François Grounauer, was published by Librairie Adversaire in 1973. This was the edition that circulated throughout the francophone world.

29. A German-language Swiss Wages for Housework group existed in Zurich, Lohn für Hausarbeit (Wages for Housework), which became Bezahlt uns die Hausarbeit (Pay Us for Housework), at the same time. The housework debate in German Switzerland was the subject of a master's thesis by Simona Isler, at the University of Bern: "Zwischen Arbeit und Befreiung: Zur Haus- und Familienarbeitsdebatte der Neuen Frauenbewegung in der Schweiz, 1968-1989," Historisches Institut der Universität Bern, 2011. Isler writes, among other things, that Selma James visited Europe a number of times during the 1970s. In 1977, she went to Zurich. According to a source mentioned in the thesis, James "was accompanied by a prostitute to emphasize that the provision of sexual services was part of domestic work" (Isler, "Zwischen Arbeit," 45, our translation). I am very grateful to Isler, who translated into French, upon my request, the sections of her thesis concerning the Zurich Wages for Housework group and the debate raised by this demand. This meeting of the Insoumises with women from the Zurich and Ticino groups made it possible to develop collaborations and exchanges. For example, in September 1975, the Zurich group and the Insoumises jointly published *Payez-nous le travail ménager,* a single issue of a journal published in French and German, edited by the Gruppe Bezahlt uns die Hausarbeit, Zurich, and the Groupe Salaire pour le travail ménager, Geneva (Collectif L'Insoumise). There were contributions from both groups, as well as the French-language translation of an essay by Silvia Federici, "Wages for Housework and the Crisis" (February 1975), titled "Crise et salaire pour le travail ménager." And in 1979, the women from Zurich and Ticino participated in the Congrès des mauvaises mères (Congress of Bad Mothers), organized in Geneva by the Insoumises; I describe the congress later in this chapter.

30. The Swiss Wages for Housework group in Zurich, Lohn für Hausarbeit, shared the same view and the same incredulity regarding the dominant feminist strategy of "sharing chores": "At this moment, [the new appeal to] sharing the housework is only a theoretical chimera. [Its] goal is to divert our attention and keep us from struggling today against our unpaid housework. Like all ideologies, [this one] has the goal of concealing our enemies' intention. They want to make us believe that all those who haven't succeeded in sharing the housework are incapable and it's their own fault." Quoted in Isler, "Zwischen Arbeit und Befreiung" (translated into French by Isler; our translation into English).

31. Anonymous, *La perspective du salaire ménager*, mimeo, n.d. (our translation) (Archives L'Insoumise).

32. Rina Nissin, "Switzerland," *The Other Woman*, special issue, March 8, 1976.

33. Today, a Swiss franc is worth more or less 0.90€.

34. *Avortement: La lutte continue; Feuille de l'occupation* (Archives L'Insoumise).

35. *L'Insoumise* 9 (May 1978): 13 (our translation).

36. "Organisons notre refus collectif de payer les contrôles gynécologiques," *L'Insoumise* 4 (1976): 4 (our translation).

37. "J'oubliais toujours de prendre la pilule," *L'Insoumise* 9 (1978): 22–25. The Collectif L'Insoumise produced a three-page information leaflet on problems posed by the use of contraceptives.

38. "Éditorial," *Journal du Congrès des mauvaises mères* (Geneva) (May 12–13, 1979): 1 (our translation).

39. "2000 Fr pour toutes les mères," *L'Insoumise* 8 (February 1978): 7 (our translation).

40. "Occupation de la caisse cantonale," *L'Insoumise* 8 (February 1978): 2.

41. I speak here of a "Swiss expression" of Wages for Housework in the sense that very few groups in the IFC, to my knowledge, had so precisely calculated the price of the wage demand.

42. "2000 francs par mois pour toutes les mères," *L'Insoumise* 9 (May 1978): 29 (our translation).

43. Ibid., 30, emphasis in the original (our translation).

44. "Mauvaises mères," *L'Insoumise* 10 (December 1978): 31 (our translation). Of course, these words were written before the lead weight of anti-smoking fundamentalism fell first upon North America and then upon Europe. It was a blessed time when smoking was within the range of earthly pleasures, especially because women had just gained access to this pleasure! (Note by the author, nostalgic ex-smoker, but not anti-smoking.)

45. "Réajuster notre balance ...," *L'Insoumise* 8 (February 1978): 13 (our translation).

46. "La morale de ces histoires," *L'Insoumise* 8 (February 1978): 14 (our translation; capitals in original).

47. "Chères amies mères!" *L'Insoumise* 9 (May 1978): 26 (our translation).

48. "1er juin 78: Occupation du BUCAS," *L'Insoumise* 10 (December 1978): 32 (our translation).

49. "Mauvaises mères," *L'Insoumise* 10 (December 1978): 31 (our translation).

50. Archives of the Insoumises (our translation).

51. "Fiche pratique 2: Comment obtenir des sous quand on est mère," *L'Insoumise* 9 (May 1978): 27 (our translation).

52. "La morale de ces histoires," *L'Insoumise* 8 (February 1978): 14 (our translation).

53. Ibid. (our translation).

54. [Collectif], *Lip au féminin* (Paris: Syros, 1977).

55. Collectif L'Insoumise (1975), "Discussion avec les femmes de LIP," in Collectif L'Insoumise, *Le foyer de l'insurrection*, 140–50.

56. See *L'Insoumise* 3 (April 1976).

57. Issue 4 of *L'Insoumise* published excerpts from a discussion with the women at Bulova: "Bulova: 'Je ne fais pas, je n'ai pas de politique. Simplement, je suis une femme, c'est comme ça, ça vient tout seul!'" *L'Insoumise* 4 (May 1976): 8–10.

58. Details provided by two Insoumises, email September 8, 2013 (our translation).

59. Infirmières insoumises, "Lutte au 7e étage," *L'Insoumise* 9 (May 1978): 19 (our translation).

60. "Infirmière: Ménagère institutionnalisée," *L'Insoumise* 9 (May 1978): 16–17.

61. Ibid., 17 (our translation).
62. "Champ-Dollon, 7 heures du soir"; "À bas Champ-Dollon"; "Lettres de détenues"; "Paroles de ..."; "Prison torture: L'Amtshaus de Berne," *L'Insoumise* 9 (May 1978): 5–12.
63. "Procès pour viol," *L'Insoumise* 10 (December 1978): 7 (our translation).
64. "Solidarité: Femmes en détresse," *L'Insoumise* 10 (December 1978): 12–13.
65. "Auto-défense collective des femmes"; "Fiche pratique après un viol ou une agression"; "Prévention du viol et des agressions"; "Trousse anti-viol," *L'Insoumise* 10 (December 1978): 14–21 (our translation).
66. "De l'insoumission permanente à la permanence de l'insoumise," *L'Insoumise* 10 (December 1978): 36 (our translation; capitals and emphasis in original).
67. *L'échappée belle: Femmes face aux lois, aux flics, aux juges; Manuel pratique,* 1979 (Archives L'Insoumise), 1 (our translation).
68. Ibid.
69. Personal interview conducted with three activists from the Collectif L'Insoumise – Viviane Luisier, Alda De Giorgi, and Suzanne Lerch – in Geneva, November 23, 1994 (our translation).
70. On occupation of houses, self-reduction of electricity, telephone, and transportation bills, and "political purchases," see Yann Collonges and P.G. Randal, *Les autoréductions: Grèves d'usagers et luttes de classes en France et en Italie (1972-1976)* (Paris: Christian Bourgois, 1976). See also Bruno Ramirez, "The Working Class Struggle against the Crisis: Self-Reduction of Prices in Italy," *Radical America* 10, 4 (1975): 27–34.
71. See Les Voleuses heureuses, "Au bonheur des Dames: Enquête sur le vol dans les grands magasins," *L'Insoumise* 8 (February 1978): 15–16 (our translation).
72. "Nous collectif pour le salaire ménager," mimeo, n.d. (our translation) (Archives L'Insoumise).
73. Ibid.
74. Personal interview with three Insoumises, Geneva November 23, 1994.
75. Ibid.
76. Personal communication from Alda De Giorgi to the author, email July 18, 2013 (our translation).
77. Personal communication from three Insoumises, email September 20, 2013 (our translation).
78. Dioxin is a very toxic substance that was used by the US Army in Vietnam. It is found in defoliants, weed killers, and many cosmetics.
79. Groupe de travail Seveso (Paulette, Joséphine, Lili-Marlène, Florette, Emma, Colette, Zoé), *Seveso est partout* (Geneva: Groupe de travail Seveso, 1976) (Archives L'Insoumise).
80. Ibid., 76 (our translation).
81. As for the Wages for Housework demand in German-speaking Switzerland, "it is not mentioned" in "the secondary literature on the new feminist movement," according to Simona Isler, who studied the feminist debate on housework and family work in German Switzerland. See Isler, "Zwischen Arbeit."

Conclusion

1. Claudia von Werlhof, "The Prolerarian Is Dead: Long Live the Housewife?" in *German Feminism: Readings in Politics and Literature,* ed. Edith Hoshino Altback et al. (Albany: New York State University Press, 1984), 254.

2. Wendy McKeen, who studied the activities of the Toronto Wages for Housework Committee beyond the period under study here, feels that "payment of wages for housework ... in fact became *the* objective of the Wages for Housework campaigners in Canada" (emphasis in original). See Wendy McKeen, "The Wages for Housework Campaign: Its Contribution to Feminist Politics in the Area of Social Welfare in Canada," *Canadian Review of Social Policy/Revue canadienne de politique sociale* 33 (1994): 24.
3. See, in the sidebar in the introduction, a list of the main objections made regarding the Wages for Housework strategy during the 1970s.
4. Louise Tassé, "Entre la mère et l'eau douce. Le paradoxe du travail ménager," *Conjoncture politique au Québec* 3 (Spring 1983): 72 (our translation).
5. You can see this logo on the cover of this book.
6. These quoted words are those that open the book edited by Louise Vandelac, *Du travail et de l'amour: Les dessous de la production domestique* (Montreal: Saint-Martin, 1985), 12 (our translation). The metaphor of molasses is taken from a notable Quebec neo-feminist literary work: Louky Bersianik, *L'Euguélionne* (Montreal: La Presse, 1976). Translated as *The Euguelion*, trans. Howard Scott (Montreal: Alter Ego, 1996).
7. I owe the use of the "repellent" image (in French *repoussoir*) as the basis upon which feminist demands were built to Alda De Giorgi, as expressed in her essay "Le travail domestique, une question centrale dans la vie des femmes en Suisse: Introduction," *Ménage-toi: Bulletin sur le travail domestique* 3 (June 1989): 8. De Giorgi was a member of the Collectif L'Insoumise. On this group, see Chapter 6.
8. Recall that the book that ushered in the Wages for Housework current was actually titled *Power of Women and the Subversion of the Community*. As well, one of the major essays of the Wages for Housework current was titled "Counterplanning from the Kitchen." Federici and Cox, "Counterplanning from the Kitchen," in *From Feminism to Liberation*, ed. Edith Hoshino Altbach (Cambridge, MA: Schenkman, 1980 [essay first published 1975]), 271–86.
9. Federici, *Wages against Housework*, 1.
10. Tessa Echeverria and Andrew Sernatinger, "The Making of Capitalist Patriarchy: Interview with Silvia Federici," *Black Sheep: A Socialist Podcast*, December 2013, https://blacksheeppodcast.org/?s=silvia+federici.
11. Roland Pfefferkorn studies the phenomenon of the sudden rejection of class discourse in most social analyses in the late 1970s: Roland Pfefferkorn, *Inégalités et rapports sociaux: Rapports de classes, rapports de sexes* (Paris: La Dispute, 2007). He notes that we are now seeing a "return to classes" in a number of studies, notably in World Social Forums – and, I would add, in the Occupy movement.
12. The current crisis does not much resemble the one experienced by the bourgeoisie in Western countries in the late nineteenth and early twentieth centuries, who were disconcerted when their domestic help deserted them as soon as other jobs opened up (war-related, or in factories, department stores, offices, and other places). For Canada, see Claudette Lacelle, *Les domestiques en milieu urbain canadien au XIXe siècle* (Ottawa: Environnement Canada-Parcs, ministère des Approvisionnements et Services Canada, 1987); translated as *Urban Domestic Servants in 19th-Century Canada* (Ottawa: National Historic Parks and Sites, Environment Canada – Parks, 1987). See also Catherine Charron, "La question du travail domestique au début du XXe siècle au Québec: Un enjeu à la Fédération nationale Saint-Jean-Baptiste, 1900-1927" (master's thesis, Université Laval, 2007). On the crisis as an essential dynamic of globalization, see "Conclusion," in *Le sexe de la mondialisation: Genre,*

classe, race et nouvelle division du travail, ed. Jules Falquet et al. (Paris: Presses de la Fondation nationale de science politique, 2010), 275–78. For an overview of the social reproduction crisis notion, see George Caffentzis, "On the Notion of a Crisis of Social Reproduction," in *Women, Development and Labor of Reproduction: Struggles and Movements,* eds. Mariarosa Dalla Costa and Giovanna F. Dalla Costa (Trenton, NJ/Asmara, Eritrea: Africa World Press, 1999), 153–87.

13. "That is, female work outside the home became possible only at the price of reduction in domestic work to its lowest terms, or by establishing a subsequent stratification among women. The contradiction in women's fate led to the creation of another contradiction, and thus remained unsolved. Not only was there no range of strategies to respond to this old problem, but the few strategies attempted were far from being innovative, in relation to the past." Mariarosa Dalla Costa, "La femme entre la famille et les politiques d'emploi en Italie," *Les Cahiers de l'APRE* 7 (April–May 1988): 123 (our translation).

14. These paragraphs on the evolution in the crisis of reproduction since the 1990s are inspired by Lourdes Beneria, "Travail rémunéré, non rémunéré et mondialisation de la reproduction," chap. 4 in Falquet et al., *Le sexe de la mondialisation,* particularly 71–79.

15. Ibid., 75.

16. Uma S. Devi, Lise Widding Isaksen, and Arlie R. Hochschild, "La crise mondiale du care: point de vue de la mère et de l'enfant," in Falquet et al., *Le sexe de la mondialisation,* 133 (our translation). See also Rhacel Salazar Parrenas, *Children of Global Migration: Transnational Families and Gendered Woes* (Palo Alto, CA: Stanford University Press, 2005). On the positive and negative impacts of these migrations on women and their "transnational households," see Laura Oso-Casas, "Migration, genre et foyers transnationaux," in *Femmes, genre, migrations et mondialisation: Un état des problématiques,* ed. Jules Falquet et al. (Paris: CEDREF, Université Paris Diderot-Paris 7, 2008), 125–46.

17. Devi, Isaksen, and Hochschild, "La crise mondiale du care," 129 (our translation). On the "care drain," see Barbara Ehrenreich and Arlie Russell Hochschild, eds., *Global Woman: Nannies, Maids and Sex Workers in the New Economy* (New York: Henry Holt, 2004). For a critique of the "care drain" concept, see Speranta Dumitru, "From 'Brain Drain' to 'Care Drain': Women's Labor Migration and Methodological Sexism," *Women's Studies International Forum* 47 (November–December 2014): 203–12, http://www.sciencedirect.com/science/article/pii/S0277539514001058.

18. Silvia Federici, "Reproduction and Feminist Struggle in the New International Division of Labor," in *Women, Development and Labor of Reproduction: Struggles and Movements,* ed. Mariarosa Dalla Costa and Giovanna F. Dalla Costa (Trenton, NJ, and Asmara, Eritrea: Africa World Press, 1999), 57. See also Mariarosa Dalla Costa, "Women's Autonomy and Remuneration of Care Work in the New Emergencies," *The Commoner* 15 (Winter 2012): 10, www.commoner.org.uk; Arlie Russell Hochschild, "Global Care Chain and Emotional Surplus Value," in *On the Edge: Living with Global Capitalism,* ed. Will Hutton and Anthony Giddens (London: Jonathan Cape, 2000), 130–46.

19. Beneria, "Travail rémunéré," 72 (our translation).

20. Ibid., 79 (our translation).

21. Laura Oso-Casas, "Migration, genre et foyers transnationaux," in Falquet et al., *Femmes, genre, migrations,* 132, 129.

22. The quotation is from Dalla Costa, "Women's Autonomy," 10.

23. Elsa Galerand and Danièle Kergoat, "Le potentiel subversif du rapport des femmes au travail," *Nouvelles Questions féministes* 27, 2 (2008): 78 (our translation).
24. Elsa Galerand, "Mouvements féministes et articulation des rapports sociaux: Entretien avec Elsa Galerand, sociologue," IRESMO (Institut de recherche, d'étude et de formation sur le syndicalisme et les mouvements sociaux), 2012, iresmo.jimdo.com/2012/06/14/mouvements-féministes-et-articulation-des-rapports-sociaux/ (our translation).
25. It is worth mentioning the context for this thesis by Danièle Kergoat: "Simultaneously with the increasing insecurity and poverty of a growing number of women ... we are seeing an increase in the economic, cultural, and social capital of a considerable proportion of women on the job market. We therefore see, for the first time in the history of capitalism, a stratum of women whose direct interests (not mediated, as before, by men: father, husband, lover, and so on) are specifically opposed to the interests of those affected by the generalization of part-time work, by very poorly paid service jobs that are not recognized socially, and, more generally, by insecurity." Danièle Kergoat, "Division sexuelle du travail et rapports sociaux de sexe," in *Dictionnaire critique du féminisme*, ed. Helena Hirata et al. (Paris: PUF, 2000), 43–44 (our translation).
26. Eleonore Kofman, "Genre, migrations, reproduction sociale et Welfare State," in Falquet et al., *Femmes, genre, migrations*, 106.
27. Danièle Kergoat, "Penser l'émancipation," in *Se battre, disent-elles ...* (Paris: La Dispute, 2012 [first published 1992]), 238 (our translation).
28. Federici, "Reproduction and Feminist Struggle," 62.
29. Ibid., p. 48.
30. The image of "economic iceberg" is drawn from J.K. Gibson-Graham, *The End of Capitalism (as We Knew It): A Feminist Critique of Political Economy* (Malden, MA, and Oxford, UK: Blackwell, 1996). See the image at http://www.communityeconomies.org/home/key-ideas.

Afterword: Interview with Mariarosa Dalla Costa

1. Excerpts of an interview with Mariarosa Dalla Costa conducted between 1996 and 1998, and completed in 2013. The initial interview, conceived during the first phase of preparation for writing this book, had to be abridged in its final phase. I hope that I have preserved its overall organic logic.
2. Yann Moulier, "Avertissement pour *Ouvriers et capital* de Mario Tronti," in Mario Tronti, *Ouvriers et capital* (Paris: Christian Bourgois, 1977), 13n7. This book is a classic of Italian workerism, and its author is one of the prominent thinkers of the current. His most recent book is *Nous, opéraistes. Le "roman de la formation" des années 1960 en Italie* (Paris and Lausanne: Éditions de l'Éclat and Éditions d'en bas, 2013). See also Harry Cleaver, *Reading Capital Politically* (Austin: Texas University Press, 1979).
3. Nick Witheford, "Cicli e circuiti di lotta nel capitalismo high-tech (I)," *Vis a vis* 4 (1996): 61, 64.
4. For an introduction to the thought of C.L.R. James, born in Trinidad and an important anti-colonial leader during the 1950s and 1960s, readers may consult a dossier prepared about him by *Radical America* (4, 4 [1970]), in which his writings are excerpted. See also Paul Buhle, ed., *C.L.R. James: His Life and Work* (London: Allison & Busby, 1986). On Raya Dunayevskaya, see her contribution to the women's question: *Women's Liberation and the Dialectics of Revolution: Reaching*

the Future (Detroit: Wayne State University Press, 1996) (first published 1985). *Socialisme ou Barbarie* was the name of a group and its eponymous journal that was published from March 1949 to 1965. The group's objectives and program are described in Cornelius Castoriadis, *La société bureaucratique 2: La révolution contre la bureaucratie* (Paris: UGE, 10/18, 1973), 395–417, a chapter titled "Conceptions et programme de Socialisme ou Barbarie."

5. *Comando capitalistico*, translated here as "capitalist command," is a fundamental concept of "autonomy" thought. The term appeared in Italy, among Marxist autonomists, to describe capitalist domination. It evokes the "commandment" itself, those who are "commanded," and who may resist, defy, and break this commandment. The term therefore involves not only the faculty of capital to command and dominate society, but also, and above all, the means implemented by workers in their struggles to subvert and break the ability of capital to command society. I am grateful to Harry Cleaver, expert in "autonomy" thought, for having shared with me the general lines of this definition.

6. *Omphalos* is a Greek word that may be translated as "the navel of the world."

7. For references to workerist Marxism, see Chapter 2, note 7.

8. See Chapter 3, "Circumstances under Which the IFC Was Formed."

9. Pia Turri, a primary-school teacher and Wages for Housework movement activist in Italy, was very active in these groups and wrote the first texts on the question of "prostitution" in the Wages for Housework perspective. See "Le mogli di tutti," in *Il Personale è politico: Quaderni di Lotta Femminista* 2 (Turin: Musolini, 1973): 51–62. She also made a major contribution on the question of the school in the Wages for Housework perspective. The section "Housework: Before, within, and around the School" in Chapter 2 outlines her thought.

10. This book, *Donne, sviluppo e lavoro di riproduzione*, was translated into English as *Women, Development and Labor of Reproduction: Struggles and Movements*, ed. Mariarosa Dalla Costa and Giovanna Franca Dalla Costa (Lawrenceville: Africa World Press, 1997).

11. The colloquium was held at the Université du Québec à Montréal on November 16–17, 1984. The proceedings were published by éditions VLB in 1986 as *L'Italie, le philosophe et le gendarme*, edited by Marie-Blanche Tahon and André Corten. Her presentation was later published as "Domestic Labour and the Feminist Movement in Italy since the 1970s," *International Sociology* 3, 1 (March 1988): 23–34.

12. See Maria Dalla Costa and Selma James, *Power of Women and the Subversion of the Community* (Bristol: Falling Water Press, 1975), 52n16.

13. See Mariarosa Dalla Costa, "Riproduzione e emigrazione," in *L'operaio multinazionale in Europa*, ed. Alessandro Serafini (Milan: Feltrinelli, 1974). This article was translated into English: "Reproduction and Emigration," *The Commoner* 15 (Winter 2012): 95–157, www.commoner.org.uk.

14. Dalla Costa and James, *Power of Women*, 25–26, emphasis in original.

15. Mariarosa Dalla Costa, "Capitalism and Reproduction," in *Open Marxism*, vol. 3: *Emancipating Marx*, ed. W. Bonefield, R. Gunn, J. Holloway, and K. Psycopedis (London: Pluto Press, 1995), 1–16, reprinted at www.commoner.org.uk, *The Commoner* 8 (2004); Mariarosa Dalla Costa, "L'indigeno che è in noi, la terra cui apparteniamo," *Vis a vis* 5 (1997): 73–100, translated into English: "The Native in Us, the Land We Belong To," *Common Sense* 23 (1998), reprinted at www. commoner.org.uk, *The Commoner* 6 (2003); Mariarosa Dalla Costa, "Neoliberismo, terra e questione alimentare," *Ecologia politica* 1 (1997): 84–91, translated into

English: "Some Notes on Neoliberalism, on Land and on the Food Question," *Canadian Woman Studies/Les cahiers de la femme* 17, 2 (Spring 1997): 28–31, also in *Women in a Globalizing World: Transforming Equality, Development, Diversity and Peace*, ed. Angela Miles (Toronto: Inanna Publication and Education, 2013): 189–94; *Donne e politiche del debito*, translated into English as Mariarosa Dalla Costa and Giovanna F. Dalla Costa, eds., *Paying the Price: Women and the Politics of International Economic Strategy* (London: Zed Books, 1995); *Donne, sviluppo e lavoro di riproduzione*, translated into English as Mariarosa Dalla Costa and Giovanna F. Dalla Costa, eds., *Women, Development and Labor of Reproduction: Struggles and Movements* (Trenton, NJ/Asmara, Eritrea: Africa World Press, 1999).

16. Giovanna Franca Dalla Costa, *Un lavoro d'amore. La violenza fisica componente essenziale del 'trattamento" maschile nei confronti delle donne* (Rome: edizioni delle donne, 1978). Translated into Japanese in 1991 and into English in 2008: Giovanna Franca Dalla Costa, *The Work of Love: Unpaid Housework, Poverty and Sexual Violence at the Dawn of the 21st Century*, trans. Enda Brophy (Brooklyn: Autonomedia, 2008). (For a summary, see Chapter 2 of this book.)

17. These materials were collected by Mariarosa Dalla Costa, who recently donated them to the Municipal Library of Padua. They are found in the following archive collections: Archivio di Lotta Femminista per il Salario al Lavoro Domestico, Donazione Mariarosa Dalla Costa (Archives de Lotta Femminista pour le salaire au travail domestique, Gift of Mariarosa Dalla Costa). Address: Biblioteca Civica, Centro Culturale Altinate/San Gaetano, Via Altinate 71, 35121 Padova. Tel.: 049 8204811. Fax: 049 820 4804. Email: biblioteca.civica@comune.padova.it.

18. For instance, Leopoldina Fortunati, *L'arcano delle riproduzione: Casalinghe, prostitute, operai e capitale* (Venice: Marsilio, 1981). Translated into English: *The Arcane of Reproduction: Housework, Prostitution, Labor and Capital*, trans. Hilary Creek (Brooklyn: Autonomedia, 1995). See also Silvia Federici and Leopoldina Fortunati, *Il Grande Calibano: Storia del corpo sociale ribelle nelle prima fase del capitale* (Milan: FrancoAngeli, 1984); Mariarosa Dalla Costa, *Famiglia, welfare e stato tra Progressismo e New Deal* (Milan: FrancoAngeli, 1983). English translation: *Family, Welfare, and the State: Between Progressivism and the New Deal*, trans. Rafaella Capanna (New York: Common Notions, 2015).

19. See English translation: Maria Dalla Costa, "Development and Reproduction," in *Women, Development and Labour of Reproduction: Struggles and Movements*, ed. Mariarosa Dalla Costa and Giovanna Franca Dalla Costa (Lawrenceville: Africa World Press, 1997), reprinted at www.commoner.org.uk, *The Commoner* 10 (2005). See also Dalla Costa, "Capitalism and Reproduction."

20. Following the assassination of Italian politician Aldo Moro in 1978 by the Red Brigades, Italy went through an unprecedented wave of repression, such that any activist activity was very strongly impeded for several years.

21. Mariarosa Dalla Costa, *Famiglia, welfare e stato tra progressismo e New Deal* (Milan: FrancoAngeli, 1983) (3rd ed., 1997). See also Mariarosa Dalla Costa, "Famiglia e welfare nel Dew Deal," *Economia e lavoro* 19, 3 (July–September 1985): 149–52. English translation: "Family and Welfare in the New Deal," in *Women and the Subversion of the Community: A Mariarosa Dalla Costa Reader* (Oakland, CA: PM Press, forthcoming).

22. See, notably, Mariarosa Dalla Costa, "Percorsi femminili e politica della riproduzione delle forza-lavoro negli anni '70," *La Critica sociologica* 61 (1982): 50–73; "Politiche del lavoro e livelli di reddito: E le donne?" *Sociologia del lavoro*

26–27 (1985–86): 155–70; "Fuori dal mulinello," in AAVV, *Crisi delle politiche e politiche nella crisi* (Naples, Libreria L'Ateneo, 1981), 93–104; "La femme entre la famille et les politiques de l'emploi en Italie," in *Les rapports sociaux de sexe: Problématiques, méthodologies, champs d'analyses. Actes de la table ronde internationale des 4-5 et 6 novembre 1987, Cahiers de l'APRE* [Paris], 7 (April–May 1988): 121–27.

23. Mariarosa Dalla Costa, "Domestic Labour in the Feminist Movement in Italy since the 1970s," *International Sociology* 3, 1 (March 1988): 23–34; "Emergenza femminista negli anni '70 e percorsi di rifiuto sottesi," in *La società italiana, crisi di un sistema*, ed. G. Guizzardi and S. Sterpi (Milan: FrancoAngeli, 1981): 363–75; "Percorsi femminili."

24. The term "double presence" used by Italian academics (*doppia presenza*) corresponds roughly to the notion of family-job reconciliation. For a critique of this notion, see Louise Toupin, "Le féminisme et la question des 'mères travailleuses': Retour sur le tournant des années 1970," *Lien social et Politiques* 36 (Autumn 1996): 69–75.

25. See Mariarosa Dalla Costa, "Emigrazione, immigrazione e composizione di classe in Italia negli anni '70," *Economia e lavoro* 4 (October-December 1981). This article was the complement to a previous article on, among other things, emigration: Mariarosa Dalla Costa, "Riproduzione e emigrazione," published in English in the electronic magazine *The Commoner* 15 (2012), www.commoner. org.uk.

26. Elisabeth Burgos, *I, Rigoberta Menchú: An Indian Woman in Guatemala*, ed. and intro. Elisabeth Burgos-Debray (New York and London: Verso, 1984); Vandana Shiva, *Staying Alive: Women, Ecology and Development* (London: Zed Books, 1989); Vandana Shiva and Maria Mies, *Ecofeminism* (London: Zed Books, 1993).

27. The organizations were Via Campesina and the Community Food Security Coalition. For other examples, see Dalla Costa, "L'indigeno che è in noi."

28. See, for example, Dalla Costa, "Capitalism and Reproduction"; "Development and Reproduction"; "Some Notes on Neoliberalism"; "L'indigeno che è in noi"; M. Dalla Costa and G. Dalla Costa, *Paying the Price: Women and the Politics of International Economic Strategy*.

29. Marcos talked expressly about menstruation in his book *Yo Marcos* (Mexico City: Editiones del Milenio, 1996).

30. For a definition of primitive accumulation, see "Interview with Silvia Federici" below, note 2.

31. Mariarosa Dalla Costa, "L'isterectomia: Un punto di vista di donna su risvolti storici e quesiti etici," presentation given to the congress organized by the Società Italiana di Ginecologia e Ostetricia in Palermo, December 7, 1997. See also Mariarosa Dalla Costa, ed., *Isterectomia: Il problema sociale di un abuso contro le donne*, 3rd ed. (Milan: FrancoAngeli, 2002) (1st ed., 1998). Translated into English: *Gynocide, Capitalist Patriarchy and the Medical Abuse of Women* (Brooklyn: Autonomedia, 2007).

32. "Personal injury," according to the Italian penal code at section 582 c.p. and "very serious" at section 583, paragraph 2, point 3.

33. Mariarosa Dalla Costa and Dario De Bortoli, "Per un'altra agricoltura e un'altra alimentazione in Italia," *Foedus* 11 (2005). English translation: "For Another Agriculture and Another Food Policy in Italy," *The Commoner* 10 (Spring-Summer 2005), www.commoner.org.uk.

34. Articles written by Mariarosa Dalla Costa on these themes were published in a Spanish-language book, *Dinero perlas y flores en la reproduccion feminista* (Madrid:

Akal, 2009). Some of these articles are available in an English translation in the online magazine *The Commoner*: "The Native in Us, the Land We Belong To," 6 (2002); "Capitalism and Reproduction," 8 (2005); "Development and Reproduction," 10 (2003); "Seven Good Reasons to Say Locality," 6 (2002); "Rerutalize the World," 12 (2007); "Two Baskets for Change," 12 (2007); "Food as Common and Community," 12 (2007); "Food Sovereignty, Peasants, and Women," 13 (2008); "So That Fish May Flop in Vegetable Gardens," 15 (2012). "Rustic and Ethical" was published in *Ephemera: Theory and Politics in Organization* 7, 1 (April 2007), 107–16, www.ephemerajournal.org. See also Dalla Costa, "Some Notes on Neoliberalism."

35. Mariarosa Dalla Costa, "La puerta del huerto y del jardin," *Noesis, Revista de Ciencias Sociales y Humanidades* (Universitad Autonoma de Ciudad Juarez) 15, 28 (July–December 2005): 79–100. English translation: "The Door to the Garden," in *Women and the Subversion of the Community: A Mariarosa Dalla Costa Reader* (Oakland, CA: PM Press, forthcoming).

36. Mariarosa Dalla Costa and Monica Chilese, *Nostra madre Oceano: Questioni e lotte del movimento dei pescatori* [Our mother the ocean: Questions and struggles of the fishermen's movement] (Rome: DeriveApprodi, 2005). English translation: *Our Mother Ocean, Enclosures, Commons and the Global Fishermen's Movement*, trans. Silvia Federici (New York: Common Notions, 2014).

37. On the relationship with the ecosystem, see Mariarosa Dalla Costa, "Fishermen and Women for Food Sovereignty," *The Commoner* 13 (2008), www.commoner.org.uk.

38. Mariarosa Dalla Costa, "La sostenibilidad de la reproduccion: De la luchas por la renta a la salvaguardia de la vida," in *Laboratorio feminista: Transformaciones del trabajo desde una perspectiva feminista; Produccion, reproduccion, deseo, consumo* (Madrid: Terradenadie Ediciones, 2006). Among the most recent articles by Mariarosa Dalla Costa on the situation of women are the following, published in the online magazine *The Commoner*: "To Whom Does the Body of This Woman Belong?" 13 (2009); "Women's Autonomy and Remuneration of Care Work in the New Emergencies," 13 (2009); "Workerism, Feminism and Some Efforts of the United Nations," 15 (Winter 2012), www.commoner.org.uk.

39. The archives have been available since May 2014. For information on accessing them, see note 17.

Afterword: Interview with Silvia Federici

1. This interview was started in 1996 and completed in 2013.

2. For Marx, primitive accumulation refers to the origin of capital and the formation of the proletariat in the initial phase of capitalism (sixteenth–seventeenth centuries). The formation of the proletariat took place through, among other things, expulsion of peasants from the land, violent appropriation of communal land and that reserved for community use, and its use for private and commercial purposes. Primitive accumulation thus refers notably to the expropriation of the populations that use these common spaces (the commons), to their being pushed into the cities, and to their consecutive proletarianization (the Enclosure movement in England in the sixteenth century). It corresponds to the transition from communal agriculture that had assured people the means of their reproduction to a system of private landownership, the precondition for the transition from feudalism to capitalism.

3. Midnight Notes was a collective, with members from several countries, that emerged from the anti-nuclear movement of the late 1970s. For almost thirty years, Midnight Notes produced an analysis of capitalist development that, like the Wages for Housework perspective, contested the centrality of waged work in the class struggle and capitalist accumulation (note by Silvia Federici). See www. zerowork.org.

4. This was the third UN conference on women; the first took place in Mexico City in 1975; the second, called "the mid-decade for women," in Copenhagen in 1980.

5. Silvia Federici and Leopoldina Fortunati, *Il Grande Calibano: Storia del corpo sociale ribelle nella prima fase del capitale* (Milan: FrancoAngeli, 1984). Leopoldina Fortunati was an activist of the Padua Wages for Housework group. She had pursued research in the field of technology in the Wages for Housework perspective, after publishing an important book in 1981 that was part of the intellectual heritage of the Wages for Housework perspective. It was *L'arcano della riproduzione: Casalinghe, prostitute, operai e capitale* (Venice: Marsilio, 1981), translated into English as *The Arcane of Reproduction: Housework, Prostitution, Labor and Capital* (Brooklyn: Autonomedia, 1995). I did not analyze this book because it was published after the period covered by my study, which corresponded to the existence of the IFC (1972–77). For an overview of Fortunati's intellectual journey, see https://en.wikipedia.org/wiki/Leopoldina_Fortunati.

6. Silvia Federici, *Caliban and the Witch: Women, the Body and Primitive Accumulation* (Brooklyn: Autonomedia, 2004).

7. Silvia Federici, ed., *Enduring Western Civilization: The Construction of the Concept of Western Civilization and Its "Others"* (Westport, CT: Praeger, 1995).

8. Silvia Federici et al., *A Thousand Flowers: Social Struggles against Structural Adjustment in African University* (Trenton, NJ: Africa World Press, 2000).

9. This is a program managed by USAID (United States Agency for International Development) and applied in many African and South American countries, consisting of paying workers not with wages in money, but with food.

10. See Silvia Federici, "Reproduction and Feminist Struggle in the New International Division of Labor," in *Revolution at Point Zero: Housework, Reproduction, and Feminist Struggle* (Oakland, CA: PM Press; Brooklyn: Common Notions and Autonomedia, 2012), 65–75.

11. This is the platform adopted by the UN conference on women held in Beijing in 1995.

12. See Milwaukee County Welfare Rights Organization, *Welfare Mothers Speak Out* (New York: W.W. Norton, 1972).

13. See note 2 above (this interview).

14. Silvia Federici, "Witch-Hunting, Globalisation, and Feminist Solidarity in Africa Today," *Journal of International Women's Studies* 10, 1 (2008): 21–35, http://vc.bridgew.edu/jiws/vol10/iss1/.

15. Federici, *Revolution at Point Zero.*

Selected Bibliography

ARCHIVES

Archives canadiennes du mouvement des femmes/Canadian Women's Movement Archives (CWMA) – University of Ottawa

- Fonds des archives canadiennes du mouvement des femmes/Canadian Women's Movement Archives Fund, X10-1
   Series I: Main Files, boxes 115 and 116
   Series II: Conferences, box 151
- Wages for Housework; Wages Due Lesbians and Lesbian Mothers' Defense Fund, X10-8
   Series I: Wages for Housework, boxes 624 and 625
   Series II: Wages Due Lesbians, boxes 62, 624, 625, 626, and 627

Centro di studi storici sul movimento di liberazione delle donna in Italia (CSSMLDI), Milan

   Faldone Toscana
   Faldone Sicilia
   Faldone Veneto
   Faldone Emilia Romagna

Personal Archives

   Gisela Bock
   Giovanna Franca Dalla Costa
   Mariarosa Dalla Costa
   Mariarosa Dalla Costa's archives are now housed at the Padua Municipal Library, in the collection "Archivio di Lotta Femminista per il salario al lavoro domestico. Donazione Mariarosa Dalla Costa" (Wages for Housework Archives of Lotta Femminista. Gift of Mariarosa Dalla Costa). Biblioteca Civica, Centro Culturale Altinate/San Gaetano, Via Altinate 71, 35121 Padova. Tel: 049 8204811. Email: biblioteca.civica@comune.padova.it.
   Silvia Federici
   Leopoldina Fortunati
   Les Insoumises
   The archives of the Collectif L'Insoumise are now housed in Geneva at the Archives contestataires, and inventoried in the Fonds MLF de Genève, www.archivesmlf.ch.
   Nicole Lacelle
   Louise Toupin

WAGES FOR HOUSEWORK GROUPS' JOURNALS

Wages for Housework Campaign Bulletin (Toronto)

   Vol. 1, 1 (July 1976)
   Vol. 1, 2 (Fall 1976)

Vol. 1, 3 (Spring 1977)
Vol. 1, 4 (Summer 1977)
Vol. 2, 1 (Fall 1977)
Vol. 3, 1 (Summer-Fall 1978)
Vol. 4, 1 (Summer-Fall 1979)
Vol. 4, 2 (Winter 1979)
Vol. 5, 1 (Spring 1981)

Power of Women Collective (London)

Vol. 1, 1 (March-April 1974)
Vol. 1, 2 (July-August 1974)
Vol. 1, 4 (Summer 1975)
No. 5, 1976

Le operaie della casa (Padua, Italy)

Single issue, May 1, 1975
No. o bis (November-December 1975/January-February 1976)
No. 1 (June-July 1976)
No. 2–3 (September-December 1976)
No. 4 (January-April 1977)

Bollettino del Comitato per il Salario al Lavoro Domestico di Trieste

Donne all'attaco, March 8, 1975
Donne all'attaco, supplement to "Le operaie della casa," November 1977

Coordinamento Emiliano per il Salario al Lavoro Domestico

Bollettino, single issue, 1976

Comitato Veneto per il Salario al Lavoro Domestico

Bollettino delle donne 1 (March 8–10, 1974)

Gruppo Femminista per il Salario al Lavoro domestico di Roma

1°Maggio, single issue, 1976/1978

Black Women for Wages for Housework (USA)

SAFIRE 1, 1 (Fall 1977)

Cleveland (Ohio) Wages for Housework Committee

Wages for Housework Newsletter 2 (January-February 1977)
Wages for Housework Newsletter 3 (March-April 1977)

Oberlin Wages for Housework Committee

The Activist 15, 1 (Summer 1975)

Los Angeles Wages for Housework Committee

Wages for Housework Newsletter 1, 3 (November 1976) (Spanish-language edition: *Sueldos por Quehaceres del Hogar: Carta de Noticias*)
Wages for Housework Newsletter, Spring 1977

Boston Wages for Housework Committee

Boston Wages for Housework Newsletter, Spring 1977

International Feminist Collective

Wages for Housework International Network Newsletter, 1975

L'Insoumise (Geneva)

No. 1, 1975
No. 3, April 1976
No. 4, May 1976
No. 8, February 1978
No. 9, May 1978
No. 10, December 1978

Journal du Congrès des Mauvaises mères

Geneva, May 12–13, 1979

Journal de l'occupation

"L'occupation du Centre-femme continue," Geneva, May 1976

Gruppe "Bezahlt uns die Hausarbeit," Zurich and Groupe "Salaire pour le travail ménager," Genève

Payez-nous le travail ménager, single issue, September 1975 (edition in French and German)

SONGS

Gruppo musicale del Comitato per il Salario al Lavoro Domestico di Padova (two records)

Canti di Donne in Lotta (1975)
Amore e Potere: Il Canzoniere Femminista (1977)

Boo Watson

Wages for Housework International Conference Song Book, Toronto 1975 (CWMA, box 115)

INTERVIEWS

Gisela Bock
Giovanna Franca Dalla Costa
Mariarosa Dalla Costa
Alda De Giorgi
Silvia Federici
Leopoldina Fortunati
Marie-Christine Gaffory
Nicole Lacelle
Suzanne Lerch
Viviane Luisier
Ellen Woodsworth

SELECTION OF TEXTS PUBLISHED BY MEMBERS OF WAGES FOR HOUSEWORK GROUPS (1972–77)

N.B. A complete bibliography of sources used (cited in the notes to this book) is available upon request from Éditions du remue-ménage (info@editions-rm.ca).

The Activist (Oberlin, Ohio) 15, 1–2 (Spring 1975). Contains a number of articles written by members of Wages for Housework groups in Canada, the United States, and England.

Agger, Ellen. "Address to March 11 Cut-backs Rally." *Body Politic.* June 1976, 6.

——. "Hookers Organize." *Wages for Housework Campaign Bulletin* 3, 1 (Summer-Fall 1978).

——. "Smile Honey." In *Women Speak Out: May Day Rally Toronto*, edited by Wages for Housework, 25–27. Toronto: Amazon Press, 1975.

——. Speech Given on March 11th at the Coalition against Cutbacks Rally, University of Toronto. Mimeograph. 1976. CWMA, box 625.36.

——. "Tipping the Wage Scale." *Wage for Housework Campaign Bulletin* 2, 1 (Fall 1977): 4.

Biermann, Pieke. *Das Herz der Familie: Materialien für eine internationale feministische Strategie no. 1.* Berlin: Selbstverlag, 1977.

——. *Wir sind Frauen wie andere auch! Prostituierte und ihre Kämpfe.* Reinbek: Rowohlt Verlag, 1980.

Black Women for Wages for Housework. *Money for Prostitutes Is Money for Black Women.* Mimeograph. January 25, 1977. CWMA, box 116.

Bock, Gisela. "Wages for Housework as a Perspective of the Women's Movement." In *German Feminism: Readings in Politics and Literature*, edited by Edith Hoshino Altbach, Jeannette Clausen, Dagmar Schultz, and Naomi Stephan, 246–50. Albany: State University of New York Press, 1984. Translation of "Lohn für Hausarbeit – Perspektive der Frauenbewegung," in *Keiner schiebt uns Weg*, edited by Lottemie Doormann, 137–45. Weinheim: Beltz, 1979.

Bock, Gisela, and Pieke Biermann. "Auch in Deutschland gibt es jetzt eine Kampagne um Lohn für Hausarbeit vom Staat für alle Frauen." *Courage* 2–3 (March 15, 1977): 16–21.

Bock, Gisela, and Barbara Duden. "Arbeit aus Liebe – Liebe as Arbeit: Zur Entstehung der Hausarbeit im Kapitalismus" [Labour of love – love as labour: On the genesis of housework in capitalism]. In *Frauen und Wissenschaft: Beiträge zur Berliner Sommer-universität für Frauen, Juli 1976* (Berlin: Courage Verlag, 1977), 118–99. Excerpts of this essay were translated into English and published in *From Feminism to Liberation*, rev. ed., edited by Edith Hoshino Altbach, 153–92. Cambridge, MA: Schenkman, 1980.

——. "Labor of Love – Love as Labor: On the Genesis of Housework in Capitalism." In *From Feminism to Liberation*, rev. ed., edited by Edith Hoshino Altbach, 153–92. Cambridge, MA: Schenkman, 1980.

Brown, Wilmette. *The Autonomy of Black Lesbian Women.* Mimeograph. July 24, 1976.

Collectif L'Insoumise. "Chères amies mères." *L'Insoumise* 9 (May 1978): 26.

——. "Infirmière: ménagère institutionnalisée." *L'Insoumise* 9 (May 1978): 16–17.

——. *Le foyer de l'insurrection: Textes sur le salaire pour le travail ménager.* Geneva: Collectif L'Insoumise, 1977. The main anthology of texts translated into French.

——. *Nous du Collectif pour le salaire ménager.* Mimeograph. 1977. Archives Les Insoumises.

——. "Mauvaises mères." *L'Insoumise* 10 (December 1978): 31.

——. "La morale de ces histoires," *L'Insoumise* 8 (February 1978): 14.

——. "La perspective du salaire pour le travail ménager." In *Le foyer de l'insurrection: Textes sur le salaire pour le travail ménager*, 7–11. Geneva: Collectif L'Insoumise, 1977.

——. "Organisons notre refus collectif de payer les contrôles gynécologiques." *L'Insoumise* 4 (1976): 4.

——. "Réajuster notre balance." *L'Insoumise* 8 (February 1978): 13.

——. "Solidarité: Femmes en détresse." *L'Insoumise* 10 (December 1978): 12–13.

——. "2000 Fr par mois pour toutes les mères." *L'Insoumise* 9 (May 1978): 29.

Collettivo internazionale femminista, ed. *Aborto di stato: Strage delle innocenti; A cura del Collettivo internazionale femminista*. Venice: Marsilio, 1976.

——. *8 marzo 1974, giornata internazionale di lotta delle donne*. Venice and Padua: Marsilio, 1975.

Collettivo per il salario contro il lavoro domestico-S.Dona': *Conquistiamo il potere di star bene: Le streghe son tornate*. Padua: CLEUP, February 1977.

Dalla Costa, Giovanna Franca. *Un lavoro d'amore: La violenza fisica componente essenziale del "trattamento" maschile nei confronti delle donne*. Rome: Edizioni delle donne, 1978. Translated into English: *The Work of Love: Unpaid Housework, Poverty and Sexual Violence at the Dawn of the 21st Century*. Brooklyn: Autonomedia, 2008.

Dalla Costa, Mariarosa. *Le operaie della casa*. Venice and Padua: Collettivo internazionale femminista and Marsilio, 1975.

——. "Quartiere, scuola e fabbrica dal punto di vista della donna." *L'Offensiva: Quaderni di Lotta Femminista* 1 (1972): 23–33.

——. "Reproduction and emigration." *The Commoner* 15 (Winter 2012): 95–157. First published 1974. www.commoner.org.uk.

——. "Women and the Subversion of the Community." In *The Power of Women and the Subversion of the Community*, edited by Mariarosa Dalla Costa and Selma James, 19–54. Bristol: Falling Wall Press, 1972. Translation of *Donne e sovversione sociale*.

——. *Women and the Subversion of the Community: A Mariarosa Dalla Costa Reader*. Oakland, CA, and Brooklyn: PM Press, forthcoming.

Dalla Costa, Mariarosa, and Leopoldina Fortunati. *Brutto Ciao: Direzioni di marcia delle donne negli ultimi 30 anni*. Rome: Edizioni delle donne, 1976.

Dalla Costa, Mariarosa, and Selma James. *Die Macht der Frauen und der Umsturz der Gesellschaft*. Berlin: Merve Verlag, 1973. Translation of *The Power of Women and the Subversion of the Community*.

——. *Le pouvoir des femmes et la subversion sociale*. Geneva: Librairie Adversaire, 1973.

——. *The Power of Women and the Subversion of the Community*. Bristol: Falling Wall Press, 1972.

Edmond, Wendy, and Suzie Fleming, eds. *All Work and No Pay: Women, Housework, and the Wages Due*. London/Bristol: Power of Women Collective/Falling Wall Press, 1975. One of the main English-language anthologies.

Federici, Silvia. "Crise et salaire pour le travail ménager." *Payez-nous le travail ménager*, September 1975: 21–29. Translation of "Wages for Housework and the Crisis" by the journal of the Zurich Wages for Housework group, Lohn für Hausarbeit, special edition produced in collaboration with Le Collectif L'Insoumise, Geneva.

——. "'Introduction à l'édition italienne,' by Silvia Federici, *Salaire contre le travail ménager*." In *Le foyer de l'insurrection: Textes sur le salaire pour le travail ménager*, edited by Collectif L'Insoumise, 93–97. Geneva: Collectif L'Insoumise, 1977 (first published 1975).

———. *Notes on Organisation*. New York Wages for Housework Committee, Mimeograph. April 1975. CWMA, box 624.22.

———. *Wages against Housework*. London/Bristol: Power of Women Collective/Falling Wall Press, 1975. Reprinted in Silvia Federici, *Revolution at Point Zero: Housework, Reproduction, and Feminist Struggle*, 15–22. Oakland, CA: PM Press; Brooklyn: Common Notions and Autonomedia, 2012.

———. "Why Sexuality Is Work." In Silvia Federici, *Revolution at Point Zero: Housework, Reproduction, and Feminist Struggle*, 23–27. Oakland, CA: PM Press; Brooklyn: Common Notions and Autonomedia, 2012 (first published 1975).

———. *Women and Welfare*, Mimeograph. January 1975. CWMA, box 115.

Federici, Silvia, and Arien Austin, eds. *Wages For Housework: The New York Wages For Housework Committee – History, Theory, Documents*. Brooklyn: Autonomedia, 2017.

Federici, Silvia, and Nicole Cox. *Counterplanning from the Kitchen*. Bristol: Falling Wall Press, 1975. Reprinted in Silvia Federici, *Revolution at Point Zero: Housework, Reproduction, and Feminist Struggle*, 28–40. Oakland, CA: PM Press; Brooklyn: Common Notions and Autonomedia, 2012.

Federici, Silvia, and Leopoldina Fortunati. *Il Grande Calibano: Storia del corpo sociale ribelle nelle prima fase del capitale*. Milan: FrancoAngeli, 1984.

Federici, Silvia, and Mariarosa Dalla Costa. *Crisis and Revolution*. Mimeograph. 1976. Silvia Federici Archives.

Federici, Silvia, and Rhona Rothman. *Our Mental Health Begins with the Struggle against Housework*. Mimeograph. Mimeograph. 1977. Silvia Federici Archives.

Fleming, Suzie. "All Women Are Housewives." *The Activist* 15, 1–2 (1975): 27–33.

———. "Family Allowance: The Women's Money." In *All Work and No Pay: Women, Housework, and the Wages Due*, edited by Wendy Edmond and Suzie Fleming, 89–92. London/Bristol: Power of Women Collective/Falling Wall Press, 1975 (text first appeared in 1973).

———. *The Family Allowance under Attack*. Bristol: Falling Wall Press and the Power of Women Collective, 1973.

Fortunati, Leopoldina. *L'arcano delle riproduzione: Casalinghe, prostitute, operai e capitale*. Venice: Marsilio, 1981. Translated into English: *The Arcane of Reproduction: Housework, Prostitution, Labor and Capital*. Translated by Hilary Creek. Brooklyn: Autonomedia, 1995.

Gaffory, Marie-Christine. "Le travail ménager." *Alternatives* 1 (June 1977): 34–39.

Gregory, Frances. "Mother-Led Union." In *All Work and No Pay: Women, Housework, and the Wages Due*, edited by Wendy Edmond and Suzie Fleming, 97–99. London/Bristol: Power of Women Collective/Falling Wall Press, 1975.

———. "The Mother-Led Union." *Power of Women: The Journal of Power of Women Collective* 1, 4 (Summer 1975): 4.

Groupe de travail Seveso. *Seveso est partout*. Geneva: Groupe de travail Seveso, 1976. Archives Les Insoumises.

Gruppo Femminista per il Salario al Lavoro Domestico di Ferrara. *Dietro la Normalità del parto: Lotta all'ospedale di Ferrara*. Venice: Marsilio, 1978.

Hall, Ruth. "Introduction: Women against Rape." In *No Turning Back: Writings from the Women's Liberation Movement, 1975–1980*, edited by Feminist Anthology Collective, 216–20. London: Women's Press, 1981 (text first published in 1976).

———. "Lesbianisme et pouvoir." In *Le foyer de l'insurrection: Textes sur le salaire pour le travail ménager*, edited by Collectif L'Insoumise, 109–17. Geneva: Collectif L'Insoumise, 1977 (text first appeared in 1975).

Hirschmann, Jane. "Organizing on the Second Job." In *All Work and No Pay: Women, Housework, and the Wages Due*, edited by Wendy Edmond and Suzie Fleming, 106–15. London/Bristol: Power of Women Collective/Falling Wall Press, 1975.

Intergroupe. "La lutte des ménagères est la lutte de toute la classe ouvrière." In *Québécoises Deboutte!* Vol. 1. *Une anthologie de textes du Front de libération des femmes (1969–1971) et du Centre des femmes (1972–1975)*, edited by Véronique O'Leary and Louise Toupin, 208–12. Montreal: Remue-ménage, 1982. Also in *La pensée féministe au Québec: Anthologie, 1900–1985*, edited by Micheline Dumont and Louise Toupin, 471–80. Montreal: Remue-ménage, 2003 (text first published in 1976).

International Feminist Collective. "International: The IFC Statement." *Power of Women* 1, 1 (March-April 1974): 14. First published 1972.

International Feminist Collective and Montreal Power of Women Collective. *Wages for Housework Notebooks* 1 (1975). CWMA, box 115.

International Feminist Collective and New York Wages for Housework Committee. *Wages for Housework Notebooks* 2 (1975). CWMA, box 115.

International Feminist Collective and Toronto Wages for Housework Collective. *Women in Struggle* 1 and 2 (1975). CWMA, box 115.

International Feminist Collective, Comitato Triveneto per il Salario al Lavoro Domestico, and New York Wages for Housework Committee. *Women in Struggle* 3, "Italy Now" (1976). CWMA, box 115.

International Wages for Housework Campaign. *Mothers' Money*. Special bulletin, Mother's Day, Spring 1978. CWMA, box 624.19.

James, Selma. "A Woman's Place." In *The Power of Women and the Subversion of the Community*, edited by Mariarosa Dalla Costa and Selma James, 55–77. Bristol: Falling Wall Press, 1972 (first published 1953).

——. "The Family Allowance Campaign: Tactic and Strategy." *Women in Struggle* 1 (1975): 17–21. CWMA, box 115. Text first appeared July 9, 1973.

——. "Introduction." In *The Power of Women and the Subversion of the Community*, edited by Mariarosa Dalla Costa and Selma James, 1–17. Bristol: Falling Wall Press, 1972.

——. *Sex, Race and Class*. Bristol: Falling Wall Press/Race Today Publications, 1975. http://www.libcom.org/library/ sex-race-class-james-selma.

——. *Sex, Race, and Class: The Perspective of Winning; A Selection of Writings, 1952–2011*. Oakland, CA: PM Press; Brooklyn: Common Notions, 2012.

——. "Wageless of the World." In *All Work and No Pay: Women, Housework, and the Wages Due*, edited by Wendy Edmond and Suzie Fleming, 25–34. London/Bristol: Power of Women Collective/Falling Wall Press, 1975.

——. *Women, the Unions and Work*. London: Notting Hill Women's Liberation Workshop Group, 1972.

——. "Women, the Unions and Work, or What Is Not to Be Done." *Radical America* 7, 4–5 (July-October 1973): 51–72.

La Vie en rose. Dossier "Gagner son ciel ou gagner sa vie? Le salaire au travail ménager." *La Vie en rose* (March-May 1981): 13–25. Translation by Nicole Lacelle of important Wages for Housework texts.

Le operaie della casa. "La lutte des ouvrières de l'usine Solari à Udine." In *Le foyer de l'insurrection: Textes sur le salaire pour le travail ménager*, edited by Collectif L'Insoumise, 15–17. Geneva: Collectif L'Insoumise, 1977. Translation of an article published in *Le operaie della casa* 1 (May 1975).

Lesbian Women, Power of Women – London. "Lesbian Women: Love and Power." In *All Work and No Pay: Women, Housework, and the Wages Due*, edited by Wendy

Edmond and Suzie Fleming, 46–48. London/Bristol: Power of Women Collective/
    Falling Wall Press, 1975.
Les voleuses heureuses. "Au Bonheur des Dames: Enquête sur le vol dans les grands
    magasins." *L'Insoumise* 8 (February 1978): 15–16.
Lohn für Hausarbeit. *Frauen in der Offensive: Lohn für die Hausarbeit oder; Auch Beruf-
    stätigkeit macht nicht frei.* Edited and with a preface by Gisela Erler. Munich: Trikont,
    1974. Translation by Gisela Erler and Gina Gierth of texts by the Power of Woman
    Collective of London and Lotta Femminista of Italy, including the 1972 IFC
    manifesto, and by Brigitte Galtier of Paris.
Los Angeles Wages for Housework Committee. *Nationwide Campaign: Put Housewives
    on Uncle Sam's Payroll.* Mimeograph. October 18, 1976. Silvia Federici Archives.
———. *Women's Declaration of Independence.* Mimeograph. May 21, 1976. (Declaration and
    petition in favour of Wages for Housework.) CWMA, box 624.27.
Lotta Femminista. *Contro gli assegni familiari, per il salario al lavoro domestico.* Special
    issue, September 1973. Volantone (pamphlet).
———. *Donne, referendum, divorzio. Vogliamo dedidera noi.* Mimeograph. March 1974.
    Mariarosa Dalla Costa Archives.
———. *Il Personale è politico: Quaderni di Lotta Femminista* 2. Turin: Musolini, 1973.
———. *L'Offensiva: Quaderni di Lotta Femminista* 1. Turin: Musolini, 1972.
———. *Processo per aborto.* Mimeograph. March 12, 1973. Mariarosa Dalla Costa Archives.
Lotta Femminista – Modena. *I servizi sociali e le donne in Emilia.* Mimeograph. Modena,
    1974.
Miles, Angela. "Economism and Feminism: Hidden in the Household; On the Domestic
    Labour Debate; A Comment." In *Feminist Marxism or Marxist Feminism: A Debate,*
    edited by Pat Armstrong, 39–50. Toronto: Garamond Press, 1985.
Modern Times Collective. "The Social Factory." *The Activist* 15, 1–2 (1975): 38–41.
Montreal Power of Women Collective. "To All Wages for Housework Groups Present
    at the February Conference in Montreal, 1975." Mimeograph. 1975. CWMA, box
    624.8.
Morato, Laura, and Carla Fabbri, with a contribution by Mariarosa Dalla Costa. "Rôle du
    mouvement pour le salaire au travail ménager dans le mouvement féministe italien."
    In *L'Italie au féminisme,* edited by Louise Vandelac, 143–50. Paris: Tierce, 1978.
Movimento di Lotta Femminista – Ferrara. *Basta Tacere! Testimonianze di donne: Parto,
    aborto, gravidanza, maternità.* Mimeograph. Ferrara, October 1974.
Movimento di Lotta Femminile – Padova. *Manifesto programmatico per la lotta delle
    casalinga nel quartiere.* Mimeograph. July 1971 (CSSMLDI). Translated into English:
    "Programmatic Manifesto for the Struggle of Housewives in the Neighborhood."
    Socialist Revolution 9, 2–3 (May-June 1972): 85–90.
Movimento di Lotta Femminile (Lotta Femminista) – Padova. "Maternità e aborto." In
    Potere femminile e sovversione sociale: Con "Il posto della donna" di Selma James, edited
    by Mariarosa Dalla Costa and Selma James, 103–11. Venice: Marsilio, 1972 (text first
    published in June 1971). French translation: "Maternité et avortement." In *Le pouvoir
    des femmes et la subversion sociale,* edited by Mariarosa Dalla Costa and Selma James,
    135–46. Geneva: Librairie Adversaire, 1973.
Nellie's Women's Hostel. "Why an Emergency Occupation at Nellie's?" Mimeograph.
    1976. CWMA, box 624.1.
———. "In Supporting Nellie's, We Support Ourselves." Mimeograph. 1976. CWMA,
    box 624.21.
———. "Report on Nellie's Struggle." Mimeograph. November 1976. CWMA, boxes
    624.21 and 116.

New York Wages for Housework Committee. "Forced Sterilization." *Wages for Housework from the Government for All Women.* Brochure, n.d. Silvia Federici Archives.

——. *A Woman's Home Is Not Her Castle.* Brochure, n.d. [on housing].

——. *Wages for Housework and Older Women.* Brochure, n.d.

——. *Wages for Housework Is a Feminist Perspective,* revised edition under the title *Theses on Wages for Housework.* Mimeograph. October 1974. Silvia Federici Archives.

New York Wages for Housework Committee. *Wages for Housework and Welfare.* Invitation brochure for the Women and Welfare conference, April 1976. Silvia Federici Archives.

——. *Come to a Conference Sponsored by the New York Wages for Housework Committee, Saturday, April 24, 10a.m. – 6p.m.* Invitation leaflet to the conference. 1976. Silvia Federici Archives.

Nissin, Rina. "Switzerland." *The Other Woman,* special edition, March 8, 1976.

Power of Women. "Immigration and Population Control." *Race Today,* July 1975.

Power of Women Collective (1974). "The Home and the Hospital." In *All Work and No Pay: Women, Housework, and the Wages Due,* edited by Wendy Edmond and Suzie Fleming, 69–88. London/Bristol: Power of Women Collective/Falling Wall Press, 1975.

——. "To the Readers of the Power of Women Journal." *Wages for Housework International Network Newsletter,* 1975: 1. CWMA, box 624.28.

Power of Women Collective. "The State Is the Biggest Pimp." *Power of Women* 5 (1976): 14–15.

Prescod, Margaret. *Black Women: Bringing It All Back Home.* Bristol: Falling Wall Press, 1980.

Ramirez, Judy. "Opening Remarks." In *Women Speak Out: May Day Rally Toronto,* edited by Wages for Housework, 5–9. Toronto: Amazon Press, 1975.

——. "Hookers Fight Back." *Wages for Housework Campaign Bulletin* 2, 1 (Fall 1977): 1.

——. "Women Lead Rent Fight." *Wages for Housework Campaign Bulletin* 1, 3 (Summer 1977).

Sjoo, Monica. "Married to the State." In *All Work and No Pay: Women, Housework, and the Wages Due,* edited by Wendy Edmond and Suzie Fleming, 92–97. London/Bristol: Power of Women Collective/Falling Wall Press, 1975.

Toronto Wages for Housework Campaign of Canada. *In Defense of the Family Allowance: Hands Off the Family Allowance; A Brief Presented to The Hon. Marc Lalonde, Minister of National Health and Welfare.* Mimeograph. 1977. CWMA, box 625.9.

Toronto Wages for Housework Committee. "The Crisis in New York: Women Organize." *Wages for Housework Campaign Bulletin* 1, 1 (1976): 5.

——. "Editorial: Why a Campaign for Wages for Housework?" *Wages for Housework Campaign Bulletin* 1, 1 (July 1976): 3.

——. Fact Sheet on the Yonge St. Crackdown, Compiled by the Toronto Wages for Housework Committee. Mimeograph. November 30, 1977. CWMA, box 625.17.

——. "Hands Off the Family Allowance." *Wages for Housework Campaign Bulletin* 1, 1 (July 1976): 1–3.

——. "Housewives & Hookers Come Together." *Wages for Housework Campaign Bulletin* 1, 4 (summer 1977).

——. "Many Support Occupation of Women's Hostel. Women at Nellie's Fight for Survival," *Wages for Housework Campaign Bulletin* 1, 2 (Fall 1976): 4.

——. "Mother-Led Union Demonstration." *Wages for Housework International Network Newsletter* (1975): 7. CWMA, box 624.28.

——. "Out of Our Bathrobes and into the Streets!" *Wages for Housework Campaign Bulletin* 1, 1 (July 1976): 6.

——. "Wages for Housework: Questions and Answers." *The Activist* 15, 1–2 (1975): 21–24.

——. *Women's Speak Out: May Day Rally Toronto.* Toronto: Amazon Press, 1975.

Turri, Maria Pia. "La mogli di tutti." *Il Personale è politico: Quaderni di Lotta Femminista* 2 (1973): 51–62.

——. "L'école du point de vue des femmes." In *L'Italie au féminisme*, edited by Louise Vandelac, 173–81. Paris: Tierce, 1978.

Vandelac, Louise, ed. *L'Italie au féminisme.* Paris: Tierce, 1978. Anthology of essays, some of them written by members of Italian Wages for Housework groups.

Wages Due Collective, Toronto. "Lesbians and Straights." In *All Work and No Pay: Women, Housework, and the Wages Due*, edited by Wendy Edmond and Suzie Fleming, 21–25. London/Bristol: Power of Women Collective/Falling Wall Press, 1975.

——. "Fucking Is Work." *The Activist* 15, 1–2 (1975): 25–26.

Wages Due Lesbians. *Lesbians Join the Family Allowance Protest.* Mimeograph. 1976. CWMA, box 629.9.

——. "Lesbians on the Move." *Wages for Housework Campaign Bulletin* 2, 1 (Fall 1977): 2.

Wages Due Lesbians London. *Supporting Statements by Wages Due Lesbians.* Mimeograph. 1977. CWMA, box 116.

Wages Due Lesbians Toronto. "Lesbians Struggle at Nellie's Women's Hostel." *Body Politic*, October 1976.

——. *Sex Is Never Free: Lesbians Support Statement for San Francisco (and All) Prostitutes.* Mimeograph. 1977. CWMA, box 116.

Wages for Housework International Network Newsletter. Mimeograph. 1975. CWMA, box 624.28.

Wages for Housework – San Francisco and Los Angeles Wages for Housework Committee. *Statement to the Board of Supervisors San Francisco.* Mimeograph. February 15, 1977. CWMA, box 116.

——. *An Attack Against Prostitutes Is an Attack on All Women.* Mimeograph. 1977. CWMA, box 116.

Waitresses' Action Committee. *Brief on the Minimum Wage and a "Tip Differential" to Ontario Ministry of Labour, Ontario Ministry of Industry and Tourism.* Mimeograph. 1977. CWMA, box 116.

——. "Money for Waitresses Is Money for All Women." Petition, Mimeograph. 1977. CWMA, box 625.4.

——. *Press Release ... Report: Meeting with the Ministry of Labour on the Minimum Wage.* Mimeograph. June 29, 1977. CWMA, box 116.

Wheeler, Susan. "Women and Political Economy: Wages for Housework." *Our Generation* 11, 1 (Fall 1975): 44–61.

Witness 1: Italy. "Brutality towards Women Giving Birth." In *Crimes against Women: Proceedings of the International Tribunal*, edited by Diana E.H. Russel and Nicole Van de Ven, 34–36. East Palo Alto, CA: Frog in the Well, 1984 (first published 1976).

Woodsworth, Ellen. "Lesbians Want Wages for Housework Too." In *Women Speak Out: May Day Rally Toronto*, edited by Wages for Housework, 22–24. Toronto: Amazon Press, 1975.

Wyland, Francie. *Motherhood, Lesbianism, and Child Custody: The Case for Wages for Housework.* Bristol: Falling Wall Press, 1977 (first published 1976).

Index